# TURNER'S HUMAN
# LANDSCAPE

*Europa and the Bull, c.*1845–8,
oil on canvas, 90.8 × 121 cm, The Taft Museum, Cincinnati, Ohio, USA.
(*See pages 292–4*).

# Turner's
# Human Landscape

## ERIC SHANES

HEINEMANN
LONDON

William Heinemann Ltd
Michelin House, 81 Fulham Road, London SW3 6RB
LONDON   MELBOURNE   AUCKLAND

First published 1990
© Eric Shanes 1990

ISBN 0-434-69502-5

A CIP data catalogue record for this book
is available from the British Library

Photoset by Rowland Phototypesetting Ltd
Bury St Edmunds, Suffolk
Produced by Mandarin Offset
Printed and bound in Hong Kong

In deeply loving memory of Oriel Glock

# Contents

# Abbreviations

B.J. refers to the numbering in M. Butlin & E. Joll, *The Paintings of J. M. W. Turner*, revised ed. 1984

R. refers to the numbering in W. G. Rawlinson, *The Engraved Work of J. M. W. Turner, R.A.*, 1908–13

T.B. refers to the numbering in A. J. Finberg, *A Complete Inventory of the Drawings of the Turner Bequest*, 1909. The revised inventory by A. Wilton, now in preparation, will include a concordance with Finberg's numbers

W. refers to the numbering of the catalogue of watercolours in A. Wilton, *The Life and Work of J. M. W. Turner*, 1979

Painting and Poetry flowing from the same fount mutually by vision, constantly comparing Poetic allusions by natural forms in one and applying forms found in Nature to the other, meandering into streams by application . . . that reflect and refract each others beauties with reciprocity of splendorous allusion.

*J. M. W. Turner*

To discover [Turner's] symbolism is an undertaking as delicate as it is risky. The Turner admired by the twentieth century is not the Turner admired – or spurned – by his own time, nor the Turner he admired himself.

*A. G. H. Bachrach*

It is a bit of sentiment, sir!

*J. M. W. Turner*

**1** *Borthwick Castle*, *c.*1818, watercolour on paper, 16 × 24.9 cm, Indianapolis Museum of Art.

# Introduction

THE title of this book is not a literary conceit. It describes exactly the imaginative foundation of many of Turner's landscapes. Rather than consider that 'he in effect super-imposed a public or literary meaning on a landscape of pure form and colour',[1] or that the human element of his scenes was 'added at the last',[2] we need to reverse our perspective in order to perceive that human motives and associations often provided Turner with the fundamental concept around which he organised his works.

This reversal can immediately be demonstrated. Turner drew the watercolour of *Borthwick Castle* (fig. 1) in or about 1818 as a design for engraving (fig. 2) in Sir Walter Scott's 'Provincial Antiquities and Picturesque Scenery of Scotland', a collection of historic descriptions and anecdotes which was issued in ten parts between 1819–26. In order to discuss the project with Scott and make studies for the illustrations Turner visited Scotland for two weeks in October 1818 and filled three sketchbooks with material as a result. It is from two sketches that he culled the topographical details of the watercolour[3], and one of them is reproduced here (fig. 3). It was made in what might be called Turner's blueprint manner, being an unemotional outline drawing bare of figures and any indications of light, colour and weather conditions. The fact that all the trees lean in different directions is worthy of note.

When he came to work up the final picture, however, Turner did not stop at merely recording one of his visual responses to the scene. Instead, he subordinated everything to the production of 'sentiment', that element of art he once defined as

> the application of interlectual feeling, forming the poetic, Historic or perceptions gained from nature and her works.[4]

A strong westerly wind blows leftwards across the scene, its intensity indicated by the degree to which a highlander's plaid is blown behind him as he leads two horses and a rider over the river Gore. The tremendous difficulty this man encounters in moving against the wind is amplified throughout the picture. A semi-circle that runs around the highlander's arms, head and plaid is taken up by tree boughs in the right foreground and by almost all the background trees. Like the man, they bend *into* the wind, not away, as one expects trees to do in near gale-force conditions. The semi-circles are repeated on a larger scale by an

11

implied line that runs up from the bottom left hand corner of the work. It touches the water splashed up by the highlander and the horses in the river, pivots around the woman and baby beyond him, moves up through the line of shadow on the foliage behind her, and continues along the edge of the hillside to the left. These semi-circles and ellipses increase the work's structural unity and greatly reinforce the viewer's awareness of the man's huge bending effort as he pulls the horses along. Equally, these reiterated curves contribute towards Turner's expression of 'sentiment', for their formal contrast to the straight lines of the castle reinforces our awareness of its immense vertical strength and stability as it resists the violent onslaught of the wind. Yet the castle is not alone in withstanding the force of the blast. In front of it stands a mother holding a baby dressed in swaddling (or, in the engraving, wrapped in a blanket). Although the woman is leaning slightly into the wind she also displays little difficulty in maintaining her stance. This curious similarity, and the way Turner isolates the woman in front of the castle, leads to the conclusion that he wished to create an association between her and the building. This is partly a visual association, since the sun is highlighting both the mother and castle, but more subtly it links parallel qualities of strength and stability. Turner may even be epitomising the larger theme of motherhood generally, for why else should the woman be standing comparatively effortlessly in this wind, or indeed why should anyone holding a baby be out in such inclement weather at all? Is it not unusual to see a mother, who would normally be anxious to protect her offspring, stand around exposing her child to hazardous weather conditions whilst she idly watches some men ford a river, even if she is related to them? We know from Turner's sketches that no gale was blowing when he visited the Vale of Chrichton to draw Borthwick Castle, nor did he draw such people there, so we may safely assume that he invented these figures, effects of light, weather and curving lines in the trees and elsewhere to create this sentiment.

As *Borthwick Castle* was a watercolour made to be later engraved in a topographical scheme accompanied by a literary letterpress, it is not surprising that the work contains a 'literary' meaning. And, indeed, it does seem to express something that derives specifically from the letterpress. As Scott tells us:

> Like many other baronial residences in Scotland Sir William de Borthwick built this magnificent pile upon the very verge of his own property. The usual reason for choosing such a situation was hinted by a northern Baron, to whom a friend objected this circumstance as a defect, at least an inconvenience: 'We'll *brizz yont*' (*Anglice,* press forward,) was the Baron's answer; which expressed the policy of the powerful in settling their residence upon the extremity of their domains, as giving pretext and opportunity for making acquisitions at the expense of their neighbours.[5]

It seems certain that when they met in 1818 Scott and Turner would have discussed how the artist might best illustrate some of the associations of the places to be depicted in his 'Provincial Antiquities' designs. Indeed, Scott may even have asked Turner to realise the

2 H. Le Keux after J. M. W. Turner, *Borthwick Castle*, engraving, 1819.

3 p. 75a of the *Scotch Antiquities* sketchbook, T.B. CLXVII,
Clore Gallery for the Turner Collection, London.

**4** J. Walker after J. M. W. Turner, *Elgin Cathedral, Morayshire*,
engraving, 1797.

'brizz yont' of Borthwick Castle in some way, so we need not be too surprised that the artist shows a highlander pressing forward into the wind, particularly since the world 'brizz' could equally have suggested the English word 'breeze' to him. But what is noteworthy here is that having realised one of the local associations of place Turner went on to make an associative statement about mankind.

Such an interpretation of *Borthwick Castle* as a metaphorical statement or signifier of something beyond the visible is admittedly somewhat speculative. So what evidence do we possess that Turner thought this way at all?

Turner was a taciturn man who usually went out of his way to avoid explaining his pictures. Clearly we cannot rely upon too much help from him. Nonetheless, although he left us scant evidence as to the covert meanings of his works, scant evidence is not necessarily insignificant evidence, and the evidence we do have is highly valuable in indicating Turner's characteristic thought processes. He even left evidence exactly as to why he did not make a habit of revealing his metaphorical meanings in words.

Our first example of Turner's use of metaphor concerns a picture of *Elgin Cathedral, Morayshire*, made for engraving in the 'Copper-Plate Magazine' in 1797 when the artist was twenty-two. The original watercolour (w. 99) is now untraced and it is represented here by the engraving copied from it (fig. 4). Turner based the picture on a sketch by the antiquary and amateur artist, James Moore, but he departed signally from the original in one significant detail:

**5** W. B. Cooke after J. M. W. Turner, *Battle Abbey, the spot where Harold fell*, engraving, 1819.

> In the original [sketch] . . . the windows in the nave were closed or built up, but in the drawing Turner made, he left them open. On being spoken to about this a few years since he said, 'They ought to have been open; how much better it is to see the light of day in God's house than darkness!'[6]

This story reveals how early in life Turner associated light with God and indicates his artistic awareness of the need to match light dramatically to the deeper content of a picture. This matching was called 'Decorum' in the aesthetic literature with which Turner was familiar, and we shall analyse it in some detail below.

Another example of the employment of light to enhance a work's content, and the associative use of staffage, can be seen in *Battle Abbey, the spot where Harold fell* (fig. 5). Here Turner devised a staffage, time of day and effects of light and weather perfectly suited to the *genius loci*, the unique spirit of place, working his picture up from a bare outline sketch devoid of such information.[7] The original watercolour dates from about 1815 but because it disappeared in 1908 it is represented here by the engraving made of it under Turner's supervision. The picture was created for a series of Sussex views and shows the view from

**6** J. Pye after J. M. W. Turner, *Wycliffe, near Rokeby*,
engraving, proof state, British Museum, London.

Senlac Hill where the Battle of Hastings was fought in 1066. The abbey was built by
William the Conquerer in thanksgiving for his victory and its altar is thought to have stood
on the spot where King Harold of England was killed by an arrow which purportedly
pierced his eye. The abbey church was demolished during the Reformation. In either 1822
or 1831, when Turner was in Edinburgh, he explained his pictorial reference to the death of
the king in his characteristic cockney accent:

> Thomson was examining the drawing with admiration when Turner called out 'Ah! I
> see you want to know why I have introoduced that 'are. It is a bit of sentiment, sir! For
> that's the spot where 'Arold 'arefoot fell, and you see I have made an 'ound a-chasing an
> 'are!'[8]

The creature and its immanent destruction are not the only visual metaphors in the picture. The leafage of the trees changes from verdant foliage on the right, to moderate leafage in the centre, to lightning-struck dead trees and timber lying on the ground on the left, a modulation that follows the direction taken by the animals.[9] The dead timber itself lends an air of morbidity to the landscape and, as Ruskin noted, the large tree on the left 'takes, where its boughs first separate, the shape of the head of an arrow'. This metaphor is reinforced by the branching of the dead timber lying on the ground beyond the hare, and between them the branches of the trees on the left display no less than fifteen V-shaped forks. Moreover, the decline of the day and the long sloping shadows both add a 'powerful impression of melancholy and sadness to the scene'.[10] The approaching storm introduces associations of the fury that will soon befall the hare, while the impending darkness to be brought by the storm suggests the darkness that will soon overcome it. Since Turner based his staffage on a verbal metaphor it is perhaps not surprising that he created visual metaphors throughout the picture. Ruskin added that 'this, which is mere fancy in itself, is imagination, as it supposes in the spectator an excited feeling dependent on the history of the spot'.[11]

A similar sense of decorum or matching of light effects to underlying content, and employment of fauna as a means of illuminating the human associations of place, is suggested by an anecdote relating to the picture of *Wycliffe, near Rokeby*. This was originally a watercolour (w. 568) made around 1816 for subsequent reproduction as a copper-plate engraving (fig. 6) in a topographical work on Yorkshire, the 'History of Richmondshire' by the Rev. Thomas Dunham Whitaker. It depicts the view of the river Tees looking towards Wycliffe Hall, the old Wyclif family home where the religious reformer John Wyclif (1330?–1384) was believed to have been born. Discussing this plate, its engraver John Pye

> remarked to Turner that 'the geese are large'. Turner replied, 'they are not geese, but overfed priests'. Turner told Pye that the light over Wycliffe's house indicated the symbolic light of the Reformation. Wycliffe's followers are driving away the geese-priests.[12]

A variant of this story sheds further light on the picture's meaning:

> Pye . . . stated that Turner, when 'touching' the Proof, introduced a burst of light (the rays seen above the Hall) which was not in the Drawing. On being asked his reason he replied: 'that is the place where Wickcliffe was born and the light of the Reformation'. 'Well,' said Pye, satisfied, 'but what do you mean by these large geese?' 'Oh, they are the old superstitions which the genius of the Reformation is driving away!'[13]

These versions[14] of the story elucidate the hidden meaning of the picture. Far from having 'made up that explanation of the geese on the spur of the moment'[15] or intending that 'the children are in fact shooing the geese away in order to take their eggs',[16] there is conclusive evidence that Turner intended deeper levels of meaning.

When the work was engraved in 1823 Turner added a long title and inscription to the plate but only three or four presentation proofs of this state were struck off[17] before Turner erased the inscription and changed the title. One of these (illustrated here) is in the British Museum and the others have not been traced. Turner may have suppressed the inscription for political reasons, since one part of it revealed his acquaintance and probable sympathy with radical politics and attitudes that could have proven highly dangerous to a Royal Academician.

Turner's longer title and inscription reads:

The Birthplace of John Wickliffe (*The Morning Star of Liberty*) near Rokeby, Yorkshire

In the fourteenth century he translated the scriptures into English and was persecuted for his opposition to the Clergy. A law was passed in the 2nd Year of Henry 5th by which whomsoever they were that should read the Scriptures in their Mother tongue (which was then called Wickleu's learning) they should forfeit land, Cattle, body, life and goods, for their heirs for ever and be condemned for heretics to God, enemies of the Crown and most errant traitors to the land —— In 1543, it was enacted that no women (except noblewomen and gentlewomen who might read to themselves alone, and not to others, for which indulgence they were indebted to the courtesy of Cranmer) nor Artificiers, 'prentices, journeymen, serving men, nor labourers were to read the Bible or new Testament in English to himself, or to any others privately or openly upon pain of one months imprisonment —— In 1804 a Society was established in London for the distribution of Bibles and to encourage the reading of it thro all classes of people it was translated by the Society into 126 different languages and dialects the expenditure of which for the Year 1818 amounted to £125,335. The Society issued 2,617,268 Bibles and Testaments in the course of 14 years —— On the Trial of Humphrey Boyle in May 1822 at the Old Bailey before Mr Common Serj[t.] Denman Women and Boys were ordered to quit the court while the defendent read extracts from the Bible.

A metaphorical description of John Wyclif, similar to the one Turner used in his title, was common in Protestant circles. It derived from Daniel Neal's *History of the Puritans*, published in 1732, wherein Wyclif was referred to as 'The morning star of the Reformation', possibly in allusion to Christ's name in Chapter 22, verse 16 of the Book of Revelation. Significantly Turner altered the ending of the phrase to make Wyclif 'The Morning Star of *Liberty*' and divided his inscription into four sections, each clearly demarcated by a line. In the opening sections Turner recounts the pre-Reformation struggles to translate the Bible into English and in the third section he contrasts those struggles with the widespread use of the English Bible in his own time. Turner's final section refers to what he evidently considered to be contemporary religious and political persecution, thus completing the historical cycle and demonstrating that little had changed over the years.

In this last section the artist describes the Old Bailey trial of Humphrey Boyle held on 24 May 1822. Upon refusing to disclose his identity Boyle was charged as 'a Man with Name Unknown' and he made great capital of this epithet. The charges accused him of sedition, disaffection, and of 'wickedly and profanely devising and intending to bring the Holy Scriptures and the Christian Religion into disbelief and contempt'.[18] (Boyle was a Deist whose belief in God was based upon reason and who rejected revelation and therefore the Bible.) Boyle was also charged with libelling 'our said Lord and King, and the Kingly Office, Royal Family, Nobility, Constitution, Government and Laws' and with impugning that they were all corrupt. In fact Humphrey Boyle's trial was one of several politically motivated trials of the 'shopmen' (i.e. shopkeepers) who had worked for a London bookseller, Richard Carlile, who was himself imprisoned for a total of nine years ostensibly on similar charges, but really for having had the effrontery (or courage) to publish the works of Thomas Paine, including *The Rights of Man* and *The Age of Reason*, books banned because they threatened the political and religious status-quo. In order to understand Turner's motives in citing the Boyle case, we have to know something of Richard Carlile.

G. M. Trevelyan has said of Carlile that he 'suffered and achieved more for the Liberty of the Press than any other Englishman of the Nineteenth century.'[19] He was born in Ashburton, Devonshire, in 1790 and died in 1843. In 1817 he printed and sold 25,000 copies of Southey's *Wat Tyler* (against Southey's wishes, since Southey had refuted his early republicanism) and the following year he published the works of Tom Paine from his bookshop, 'The Temple of Reason', off Fleet Street. In October–November 1819 he was tried for re-publishing *The Age of Reason* and sent to jail for three years and fined £1500. Carlile suffered further imprisonment for refusing to pay these fines. He published twelve of fourteen volumes of his paper *The Republican* between 1819 and 1826 in Dorchester gaol. His wife continued his publishing activities outside until she was sentenced to three years' imprisonment in 1821, at which point Carlile's sister took up the cause, until she too was imprisoned in 1822 for one year. Carlile reported her trial and it was from this report that Turner undoubtedly obtained the major part of the *Wycliffe* inscription.[20] Carlile's sister was then followed by a succession of shopmen, some 150 printers and vendors (including Boyle) who volunteered to print and sell the banned literature. Many of them were jailed in turn. As E. P. Thompson has stated, 'They came out of a culture', travelling to London from all over Britain in order to work for Carlile, and the majority of them were completely unknown to him.[21] Between them, Carlile and his shopmen served over 200 years in prison for their 'crimes'. Unless Turner moved in very radical circles he can only have obtained Humphrey Boyle's name from the *Report on the Trial of Humphrey Boyle* written by Richard Carlile, as the newspapers were unable to identify Boyle because of his refusal to give his name. The pamphlet which reported his trial was itself proscribed for repeating every last 'Blasphemous and seditious Libel' in the list of charges appertaining to the trial, as well as

Boyle's highly seditious refutations of them. As Carlile wittily ended his dedication of the *Report*, 'this report of the trial of Humphrey Boyle is inscribed as a striking specimen of the Utility of such trials . . . .' Evidently Turner read a number of these publications at the time.

Amongst the 'libels' with which Boyle was charged were ideas that certainly would have appealed to Turner, whilst on the charges of religious profanity Boyle tried to show that the Bible itself was profane. To achieve this he read various suitably 'disgusting' extracts from the Good Book. His reason for doing so was clear. Carlile and his shopmen were constantly being prosecuted not only directly by the government, but also indirectly on its behalf by two private organisations, the Constitutional Association for Opposing the Progress of Disloyal and Seditious Principles, and the Society for the Suppression of Vice. Boyle's prosecution had been instituted by the first of these groups, but in his defence (which was probably written from Dorchester Gaol by Richard Carlile), Boyle especially took the opportunity to attack the Society for the Suppression of Vice. By showing that the society hypocritically turned a blind eye to 'vice' described in the Bible he hoped to embarrass both sets of persecutors. Amongst the extracts he read aloud in court were descriptions of Lot's incestuous affairs with his daughters, Onan's seedy relations with his sister-in-law, and the roadside scene where Tamar plays the harlot with her father-in-law, Judah. During this recitation of unorthodox sexual practices in ancient Palestine one of the jurors protested 'we do not want to hear any of them' and the court was cleared of women and boys. Boyle confessed that he felt 'ashamed to read such obscenity but my situation compels me to it', although his quoting of what he termed 'the most infamous book I ever read' did his case little good for he was sentenced to eighteen months imprisonment soon afterwards.

Turner's reason for citing the trial in his inscription seems fairly clear. In his defence Boyle pointed out that during the founding of Christianity its converts were persecuted and that this persecution had continued down the ages, with different Christian sects being harassed in turn. He further stated that 'Avowed Deists are the next on the scale contending for toleration and the protection of the law and they will assuredly obtain it as I am standing here, in the height of my pride, to defend these principles. We are fast, and very fast progressing towards a superiority'. This plea for the tolerance of religious dissent and argument against the continuing persecution of spiritual belief, as well as perhaps a sympathy for Boyle's political stance, was almost certainly Turner's reason for citing his case. It also proves in passing that he meant to create a metaphorical level in the *Wycliffe, near Rokeby* engraving (if he had not already done so in the original watercolour) and that the answer he gave to Pye was true. For the inscribed print – probably just like the earlier versions – exists on three levels: as a lovely dawn river-scene; as an elaboration of the historic associations of the place; and, by linking together various metaphors, as an allegory

**7** *The Mew Stone at the Entrance of Plymouth Sound, c.*1814,
watercolour on paper, 15.6 × 23.7 cm, National Gallery of Ireland, Dublin.

of the birth of English religious and political liberty. The fundamental issues John Wyclif had fought for were clearly still relevant to the society in which Turner lived and worked.

Turner was not averse to the interpretation of his pictures by others. Indeed, his amenability to interpretation can be demonstrated by a story concerning his watercolour of *The Mew Stone at the Entrance of Plymouth Sound* (fig. 7). This large rock, named after the birds that inhabit it, was observed by Turner while on a tour of the West Country in 1813 and he made the watercolour for engraving in the 'Picturesque Views on the Southern Coast' series soon afterwards. Walter Thornbury tells us that

> In the . . . 'Mewstone' there were some strange clouds introduced, which had a demoniacal air about them; insomuch that Mr. Stokes [Turner's stockbroker and the owner of the drawing at the time] was struck by them, and asked Turner if he did not mean them for the demons and angels of the storm. Turner confessed the intention.[22]

We might justifiably suspect that Turner was merely proving himself agreeable to his patron in confessing 'the intention', were it not for the fact that the artist indeed showed demons and angels standing or flying in the sky in some of his later pictures. They appear in

**8** Solomon Hart, *Galileo, when imprisoned by the Inquisition
at Florence, visited by John Milton*, anonymous engraving
after the painting exhibited at the R.A. in 1847.

a watercolour vignette known as *The Evil Spirit* (T.B. CCLXXX–202, W. 1207), made around 1832 to illustrate Canto XII of Samuel Rogers's poem 'The Voyage of Columbus', where a winged figure looms above Columbus's flagship; in illustrations of 'Paradise Lost'[23] dating from 1834; and in a major painting exhibited at the R.A. in 1846, *The Angel Standing in the Sun* (B.J. 425). In *The Mew Stone* wisps of cirrus cloud immediately above the rock seem to resemble the curved wings that angels frequently sport. But here, because the rock has no celestial connections, it is doubtful that Turner invested the cirrus clouds or the sky with metaphorical significance. Most probably he agreed with Stokes because he found his remark suitably 'poetic', since 'demons' and 'angels' are creatures who very aptly personify extreme meteorological forces.

Nor was Turner averse to introducing symbolism into the works of others. Solomon Hart (1806–1881), a now-forgotten History painter, recalled in his *Reminiscences*:

At one of the varnishing days at the [1847 Royal Academy] Exhibition, I had a picture there[24] of *Galileo, when imprisoned by the Inquisition at Florence, visited by John Milton* [fig. 8]. I was setting my palette when [Clarkson] Stanfield invited my attention to an addition which Turner had made, with a view of increasing the interest, in the realisation of my theme. The head [of Galileo] in my picture was relieved from a light and bald back-ground and upon this Turner had, with a piece of chalk, sketched Galileo's solar system so ingeniously that it composed skilfully with the figure. Turner was upon the point of effacing his addition, but Stanfield, who was much interested, hastened to me, to persuade me to preserve the lines. He mixed up some paint and stood over me whilst I secured them with colour. All thought that Turner's suggestion had much improved my picture.[25]

It seems entirely characteristic that Turner did not fill a pictorial lacuna with a simple object of interest but that he used the opportunity to deepen the meaning of the painting, reminding us by his addition of Galileo's most renowned contribution to science. What is equally worthy of note, however, is that nobody seems to have found Turner's direct (as opposed to covert) metaphor surrealistic; after all, we do not normally witness people sitting beneath miniature globes that circulate and hover above their heads. Rather, the transference was considered quite inventive by the Academicians and their colleagues. The anecdote also usefully reveals how late in life Turner was devising extensions of pictorial meaning, just five years before his death.

These proven examples of Turner's use of visual metaphor will be augmented in the course of this book by others whose meaning is arrived at through circumstantial evidence. That the painter rarely explained himself should not surprise us, however. Images were Turner's forté and in any case he was a secretive man of whom his contemporary, David Roberts, remarked that

> . . . his life partook of the character of his works; it was mysterious and nothing seemed to please him so much as to try and puzzle you, or make you think so, for if he began to explain, or tell you anything, he was sure to break off in the middle, look very mysterious, nod, and wink his eyes, saying to himself 'Make that out if you can'.[26]

Once he even refused to explain the meaning of a picture, *War. The Exile and the Rock Limpet* (fig. 61), to Ruskin, his most impassioned advocate. The critic tells us that Turner

> . . . tried hard one day for a quarter of an hour to make me guess what he was doing in the picture of Napoleon, before it had been exhibited, giving me hint after hint in a rough way: but I could not guess, and he would not tell me.[27]

Yet one should not infer from these statements that Turner was verbally unable to explain his works. As his fluent explanations of the allusions contained in *Wycliffe, near Rokeby* or *Battle Abbey, the spot where Harold fell* show, he could easily elucidate his meanings. Not even the symbolic contents of many of the complex later paintings would have been difficult for him to explain, especially to somebody as sympathetic as Ruskin. Yet Turner seems to have realised that verbalisation would diminish the imaginative impact of his pictures. Clearly, through his exploration of how poetic and pictorial metaphors function he knew that a viewer receives an imaginative charge by making his own connections, and metaphorical enhancements would be completely lost if the artist enforced associations on our behalf.

**9** *Pope's Villa at Twickenham*, exhibited Turner's Gallery 1808, oil on canvas, 91.5 × 120.6 cm, Trustees of the Walter Morrison Picture Settlement, Sudeley Castle, Gloucs.

Fortunately evidence exists which proves that Turner was actively concerned to preserve the imaginative impact of his metaphors by making us work them out for ourselves. Far from being the product of verbal inability to explain what he meant, his reluctance to explain his pictures stemmed from conscious decision.

This emerges from his attitude towards the engraving of his painting *Pope's Villa at Twickenham* (fig. 9) which dates from 1808, when Turner exhibited it in his own gallery. The print (fig. 10) by John Pye, with the figures engraved by Charles Heath, was published in April 1811 by the antiquarian, John Britton. It was one of a series of plates in Britton's ambitious survey of 'The Fine Arts of the English School' which contained an extensive letterpress by Britton on each of the works included.

In the picture we look north-eastwards towards the famous home of the great poet,

24

Alexander Pope. The house had been demolished by Lady Howe in 1807 because, it was later thought, she 'was so much annoyed at the number of pilgrims who came to see the place that she razed it to the ground, cut down the trees, and endeavoured to obliterate all vestiges of its former distinguished occupant'.[28] (In reality she probably wanted a comfortable modern dwelling more able to accommodate her large family and busy social life).

Turner depicts the building in the course of demolition, but while it is likely that he did witness the dismantling of the house,[29] we cannot assume that his painting shows the demolition at the time he actually observed it. He might easily have witnessed the demolition on a morning in full summer, but such a timing would have ignored the need for dramatic decorum. Instead, as John Britton observed, Turner gives us the scene lit and timed to induce contending, suitably dramatic sensations of 'a pleasing sorrow, a pensive delight, a melancholy pleasure'. As Britton states in a passage that alerts us to the allusions in the work:

> Perfectly in unison with the declining sun, and the dilapidated Villa are the trees, plants and figures . . . the vegetable world displays the autumnal hues, or eve of nature, whilst the animals and human figures indicate the time of repose and calm meditation. Groups of sheep are reclining in their pasture; two fishermen are gently arranging their eel-pots; and on the left hand of the picture is introduced an interesting episode, consisting of a group of three figures, apparently labourers retiring from the ruined house, and animadverting on fragments of its decoration: attentive to whose 'rustic tale of lamentation' are a young man and woman; and in strict accordance with the subject, is a prostrate trunk of a willow tree.[30]

This is informative and responsive to the visual imagery, but why should the 'prostrate trunk of a willow tree' be 'in strict accordance with the subject'?

The depiction of a 'prostrate . . . willow tree' in fact embodies two allusions to Alexander Pope, one rooted in the past history of the villa, the other relating to its present sad predicament. Primarily it refers to a belief, widely shared in Turner's day but now completely forgotten, that it had been Alexander Pope who introduced the *Salix babylonica* or weeping willow into England. As was later written:

> It is believed that . . . Pope's willow was the eldest and first [such tree planted in this country] and the account given of its origin is that a present came from Spain to Lady Suffolk of Marble Hill, and that Pope was in the company whilst it was being unpacked. Amongst the contents he noticed some pieces of stick which appeared to have life in them and, fancying that they might produce some horticultural novelty, he planted them in his garden and thus his willow was produced . . . On [the death of Sir William Stanhope, a subsequent owner], the villa passed to the Right Hon. Welbore Ellis . . . [who] guarded with reverence every memorial and preserved the house, as far as possible, in its original condition; especially did he protect the far-famed weeping

willow which stood in front of the house . . . In spite of all the attention bestowed upon it, however, it perished and fell to the ground in the year 1801 . . . When it fell it was worked up by an eminent jeweller into trinkets and ornaments of all kinds, which had an extensive sale.[31]

In the original draft for the letterpress which he sent to Turner for his approval, Britton apparently stated that the trunk seen on the left was the very same 'Pope's willow'. This drew a protest from the painter. He replied that

making the willow tree the identical Pope's willow is rather strained – cannot you do it by allusion?[32]

Britton then amended his text to the form quoted above.

What we can detect here is Turner's concern to protect one of his visual allusions and not have it effaced through explanation in the letterpress. Evidently he felt that if it were suggested that the tree in the foreground was Pope's original willow this would both compromise its imaginative function and seem too obvious. By showing an unspecified dead willow tree lying in the foreground (with objects, including a picture, being considered by the labourers, one of whom points towards the villa, thus connecting the objects with the house) Turner was clearly hoping to create a comprehensible yet subtle set of associations. Knowledge of Pope's willow in his own time was so widespread that he could hope that his audience would recognise his allusion without it having to be spelt out (and if he had wanted to label the tree as Pope's own willow, he could easily have done so). An indirect reference to Pope's tree created a more forceful imaginative involvement with the image than might otherwise take place. However, that he did wish to help his audience *guess* the link, and that such an allusion was intended, may be inferred from his permitting Britton to draw attention to a particular species of tree at all. (This fact also proves that for Turner the words 'rather strained' meant 'too explicit' rather than 'unlikely'). Moreover, lest it be thought that Britton was reading in more than Turner had intended, and that the artist simply went along with him, Britton's insistence that the tree is in 'strict accordance with the subject' should also be noted, for presumably Turner approved of that emphasis. And it is of course the fact that 'in strict accordance with the subject' Turner gives us a *dead* tree which leads us to his other, and finally greater overall meaning in *Pope's Villa at Twickenham*: the dead willow is seen in front of the dying house of the dead poet amidst the dying daylight of the dying season of the year. Everything conspires to produce a single meaning in the work as Turner observes a sense of dramatic decorum, carefully selecting the appropriate objects, timing, light and season through which he can forge a dramatic unity that will entirely and most poetically be 'in strict accordance with the subject'.

In the very same year that the print of *Pope's Villa at Twickenham* was published, Turner indirectly made clear why he wanted Britton to downplay his visual allusion to Pope's

**10** John Pye and Charles Heath after J. M. W. Turner,
*Pope's Villa at Twickenham*, engraving, 1811.

willow. In a Royal Academy lecture given in 1811 Turner discussed the difficulty of pictorially realising poetic metaphors, pointing out that an imaginative stroke in words might be rendered redundant or even seem surrealistic if made visible. He was analysing a metaphor in line 83 of the poem 'Summer' in James Thomson's *The Seasons* where the poet describes the gradual intensification of blue in the sky after daybreak as 'The kindling azure'. Turner obviously appreciated the use of the word 'kindling' to describe this process but wondered how a painter could give it effect; if he somehow showed the sky in the act of 'kindling' he would create a visually absurd image. Turner first investigated this problem in the late 1790s, particularly in connection with a picture of *Norham Castle on the Tweed, Summer's morn* (fig. 22) which he exhibited at the R.A. in 1798. Below its title in the Exhibition catalogue he quoted the lines from Thomson's poem which include the metaphor of 'the kindling azure'. By presenting his picture in this way, and later in his lecture of 1811, the artist clarified his feeling that some metaphorical effects are better left to poetry, to be used in conjunction with painting, rather than being realised visually. (The way in which he reached this conclusion will be analysed in detail in Chapter One below). But there can be no doubt as to why he took that view. In 1811, after discussing the problems of realisation inherent to Thomson's 'kindling' metaphor, the painter went on to remind his audience of

Shakespeare's beautiful ballad that fancy, when established, dies.[33]

Turner is referring here to Bassanio's ballad, in Act III, Scene 2 of *The Merchant of Venice*:

> Tell me where is fancy bred,
> Or in the heart or in the head?
> How begot, how nourished?
>     Reply, reply

> It is engender'd in the eyes,
> With gazing fed: and fancy dies
> In the cradle where it lies.
>     Let us all ring fancy's knell.
>     I'll begin it – Ding, dong, bell.

In the context of the play Shakespeare uses the word 'fancy' to denote desire. Equally it may stand for 'imagination', of which the word is an antique form. For Turner, Shakespeare's ironic implication that fancy or imagination inevitably dies once it attains the object of its desire clearly had great bearing on the workings of the visual imagination. Through being 'established' or pictorially realised, the imaginative components of linguistic metaphors are effaced. Conversely, when rendered in words, the imaginative elements of a visual metaphor are made redundant. Surely this is why Turner prevented John Britton from spelling out his allusion in 1811. He wanted us to respond imaginatively to the dead tree he put before us, an impossibility had Britton explicated his stroke of fancy.

With *Pope's Villa at Twickenham*, then, we can judge exactly to what degree Turner preferred allusion to direct reference, and how other associative factors exist in the picture, elements like the time of day and year, and thus the choice of light. The careful searching out and imaginative participation that association and metaphor require explain why Turner found it uncongenial to spell out his meanings in words, preferring viewers to unearth them. This is surely why he 'nodded and winked' to David Roberts, saying 'make that out if you can', and why he worked so long and hard to make Ruskin *guess* rather than tell him the meaning of his picture. Ultimately a work of art has to exist independently of its creator, so it is imperative that its meaning communicate itself. Turner was evidently prepared to run the risk of not being understood rather than compromise the imaginative impact of his pictures by explaining them.

We can gain access to Turner's hidden meanings in two ways. First there are questions of anomaly and motive; Turner's ignoral of literal reality can alert us to the possibility of a metaphorical meaning, as when the mother unaccountably stands up to gale force winds without difficulty in *Borthwick Castle* (fig. 1), or the orbs circle around Galileo's head in Solomon Hart's picture (fig. 8). Such anomalies are useful and necessary. And with his usual perspicacity Ruskin understood their value as clues to meaning. In the midst of a complex discussion of the painting *Phryne going to the Public Baths as Venus – Demosthenes taunted*

**11** *Phryne going to the Public Baths as Venus – Demosthenes taunted by Æschines*, R.A. 1838, oil on canvas, 193 × 165 cm, Clore Gallery for the Turner Collection, London.

*by Æschines* (fig. 11, B.J. 373), first exhibited at the R.A. in 1838, he suggested that the two dogs playing with a circular reflective object in the foreground contribute a symbolic meaning, developing this view along these lines:

> Do not think two dogs playing with the crystal ball are meaningless. Dogs don't usually play with crystal balls. Turner intended you to notice them specially.[34]

Ruskin may have been wrong in stating that the circular object is a 'crystal ball' which, he went on to suggest, was intended to signify the world. More likely Turner intended the translucent globe to represent 'the bubble pleasure' which he pictorialised elsewhere in his work.[35] Yet Ruskin was not wide of the mark, for in either case the circular object is apposite to *Phryne going to the Public Baths as Venus – Demosthenes taunted by Æschines*. Given this title, Turner probably meant to show how a great orator like Demosthenes could be taunted by the purported son of a harlot and upstaged by the harlot herself. In this context a statement about the ephemeral nature of existence and pleasure is relevant. Phryne's representing of herself as Venus may signify by analogy that a preference for factitious beauty had replaced a comprehension of true beauty in the public eye. Turner had every cause to complain of this at the time.

But whether or not Ruskin was right about the meaning of the 'crystal-ball' or bubble, his thesis that the object played with by dogs is unusual and must therefore be a clue to further meaning is entirely correct. In the case of those pictures whose metaphorical meanings are analysed in this book, similar clues will be noted or become self-evident, and they will all help us to arrive at Turner's hidden meanings.

The other factor which enables us to arrive at Turner's underlying meanings is historical awareness. Nothing can better illustrate this than a work whose very subject has proved a source of puzzlement ever since it was first exhibited. Once again, only an understanding of the artist's social and historical background, an awareness of his interest in the history, sociology and culture of the places he painted, and the recognition that association held a vital importance for him, provide the keys to unlock his meaning.

The picture in point is *Juliet and her Nurse* (fig. 12), exhibited at the R.A. in 1836. Since Shakespeare's play gives us both a Juliet and her nurse we can safely assume that his Juliet is portrayed here. Yet at no point in the play does Shakespeare suggest that Juliet ever visits Venice, an inconsistency of Turner's painting that has always caused bemusement, bewilderment, or both. For instance, the Rev. John Eagles wrote a vituperative review of the painting upon its display in 1836 in which he said that the painting was so absurd 'we scarcely stop to ask why Juliet and her nurse should be at Venice'.[36] Recently an attempt was made to demonstrate[37] that we are not looking at Shakespeare's Juliet but at the 'Giulietta' mentioned in a short prose piece entitled 'Marcolini' included in Samuel Rogers' *Italy* which was published with illustrations by Turner in 1830. However, this theory has now been discounted[38] and no other appropriate candidates for the role of Turner's Juliet have offered themselves. Consequently, the work continues to present a conundrum. To understand why Turner might have wanted to purposely create a problem of identification, we need to set the painting in the context of Venetian history and recall that *Juliet and her Nurse* takes its subject from history rather than contemporary life. We also need to look carefully at what Juliet herself is actually looking at.

Turner's view of Venetian history was largely formed by the historians of his day. By then Venice was a ghost of her former self, the Serene Republic having been destroyed as an independent state by Napoleon in 1797. Venice had long been in decline, however, and in its latter stages the Venetians had sought solace for their loss of power and prestige in a reckless pursuit of pleasure. This fact did not go unobserved by British moralists, of whom Turner was one. They missed few opportunities to use the city as a symbol of decadence, to point to the sad fate of Venice as a lesson to their own empire-building countrymen, as the likely end of any powerful maritime state should duty be forsworn in favour of luxury and vanity.

For over two centuries the leading annual period of festivity for the Venetians had been the famous Carnival. Until 1797 it had lasted for six or more months of the year, starting on the first Sunday in October and ending at Lent, with a short break for Christmas. (After Venice was ceded to Austria in 1805 the Carnival was resumed on a more limited scale, starting at the end of January and ending at Lent[39]). In the constant round of festivities 'effeminacy, wantonness and debauchery'[40] were greatly assisted by the use of masks and disguises. During the entire Carnival period virtually everyone wore a mask or *bautta*, a hooded silk cape worn in conjunction with a tricorne hat and a face-mask displaying a white beaked outline, which did not just cover the area around the eyes or mouth but the entire head and shoulders. It was based upon the masks of the ancients. As Maurice Andrieux has commented:

> . . . the *bautta* became almost a uniform for Carnival. From Doge to kitchenmaid, everybody wore it, man, woman and child of every age and station. Servant-girls went masked to market, mothers carried babies in masks in their arms, the lawyer wore a mask to plead in court.

When the *bautta* was augmented by a full-length domino-cloak, the *tabarro*, the identification of individuals or even of their sex could prove impossible. There were also many other kinds of disguises, some drawn from the Commedia dell'Arte, figures like Arlecchino, Pierrot, Pantaloon, Brighella and Scaramouche, as well as more exotic oriental imports, particularly Moorish and Turkish costumes. All usefully served to relax inhibitions:

> [Everyone was] determined on concealment. If a woman knew whose chatter she was listening to, whether he were a senator or her own shoe-maker, it would ill become her to give any sign of recognition. A man would never hint that he recognised a woman; she would have broken off the encounter at once. It was just not done to indicate that you had pierced a disguise, and when someone spotted a Papal Nuncio in *bautta* and *tabarro* and besought immediate blessing everybody, as Montesquieu recalls, was dreadfully shocked.

Watertight anonymity was in fact the great lure of the Carnival, the relish that made

**12** *Juliet and her Nurse*, R.A. 1836, oil on canvas, 92 × 123 cm, Private Collection, Argentina.

it what it was. Goldoni calls the mask 'the most advantageous thing in the world', and there was nothing a masker dared not do. Before him difficulties melted away. Whoever he might be, he could join any company, go into any salon, sit down to cards, take part in the conversation, pay the women extravagant compliments. Women for their part, could walk about as they fancied, enter the cafes or the lowest haunts there were, and have unmentionable adventures. Maskers could even get into the convents whenever they wanted to. Who was to forbid them, when nobody could possibly tell whether they were male, female, rogues and vagabonds or authority personified? [And priests and nuns wore masks themselves.] All the barriers were down. There were neither rich nor poor, police nor *facchini*. There was only *Sior Maschera* and who was to set limits for that faceless personage?[41]

This licence proved not only a boon to political moralists but also quite naturally drew an endless stream of visitors from all over Europe.

**13** G. Hollis after J. M. W. Turner,
*St. Mark's Place, Venice – Juliet and her Nurse*, engraving, 1842.

For obvious reasons St Mark's Square was the central forum for anonymous sociability and sexual adventure, and it is the piazza from near its south-west corner during Carnival, in some indeterminate but clearly recent past, that Turner painted in *Juliet and her Nurse*, not around 1302 when Giulietta Capuleti is thought to have died in a suicide pact with Romeo Montecchi. The square is crowded with hundreds of costumed revellers, many wearing *bautte, tabarri, zendale* and other disguises.[42] They flirt, watch puppet-shows, firework displays and, in the engraving made from the painting in 1842 (fig. 13), mill around a burning cross, perhaps a comment upon the Venetian disregard for the moral tenets of Christianity during Carnival. Juliet stands with her partially masked nurse on the right.

There is no doubt that Turner was familiar with the Venetian Carnival, if only by reputation. He depicted figures in Carnival costume in the watercolours[43] he made of Venice after first visiting the city in 1819. Equally, there is no doubt that in the years immediately before painting *Juliet and her Nurse* he came into contact with literature that linked Venice to licentiousness and disguise. For example, in the poem 'St Mark's Place' contained in Samuel Rogers's *Italy*, a book he illustrated, he would have read that the piazza

> . . . To-day 'twas full of masks;
> And lo, the madness of the Carnival,
> The monk, the nun, the holy legate masked!

**14** *Juliet and her Nurse* (detail).

Moreover, one of Turner's illustrations to the poem 'Human Life', contained in Rogers's collection of *Poems* published in 1834, appears on the very same page as this passage drawing attention to Venetian disguise:

> Now the scene shifts to Venice – to a square
> Glittering with light, all nations masking there[44]

Just two years later, in *Juliet and her Nurse*, Turner painted a square indeed 'glittering with light' and with 'all nations masking there', as well as a person whose existence was forever altered by the use of masks. Turner appears to have known his Shakespeare,[45] and he must have been aware that Juliet does not visit Venice. It would have been easy for him to depict her 'in fair Verona'; he had visited the city, made drawings there,[46] and could easily have worked up a more apparently suitable surround. We can only conclude that he deliberately chose not to. So why should he mysteriously locate Juliet in the 'wrong' city?

The answer seems clear, once we realise that Turner was thinking associatively. Juliet is looking at people who are predominantly playing with identity and disguise. She herself was to suffer from, and eventually fall brutally foul of identity and disguise. Turner placed Juliet in Venice during carnival time in order to mirror and accentuate the difficulties concerning identification that are intrinsic to her story. It is a quite straightforward associative parallel.

The balcony scene on the right contains a number of allusions to different parts of the

**15** *St. Mark's Place, Venice – Juliet and her Nurse* (detail).

play, although in the engraving entitled *St. Mark's Place, Venice – Juliet and her Nurse* that followed the painting six years later, Turner took the opportunity to add to these references.[47] In the painting (detail, fig. 14) Juliet holds a small jug, whilst in the engraving (detail, fig. 15) Turner altered this to a pair of gloves, perhaps to allude to Romeo's wish, stated in Act II, scene 3, that he were '. . . a glove upon that hand/That I might touch that cheek'. A man's hat is also placed on the balustrade in the engraving but not in the painting. It forms an exact pendant to Juliet's feathered hat behind her, a hat that similarly owes more to Watteau than Giotto.[48] Equally apparent is a black cat which, as Harold Shapiro has plausibly argued, is very probably 'a witty allusion to Tybalt, who Mercutio . . . [In Act III, scene 1] . . . calls King of cats and ratcatcher'. This allusion is supported in the engraving by the presence of two further cats – one black, the other white – on the roof beyond the balcony, the black cat hovering over the white cat's corpse. Also evident in the engraving are more details that allude to the play. The figures nearest Juliet in the piazza are a pair of lovers, as are the figures of the nearest of the sculptures adorning the distant balustrade, whilst on the stage of the puppet theatre at the opposite side of the square a puppet also attends upon a death (detail, fig. 16).

An additional clue to the meaning of the picture is provided by the nurse. She has her arms raised in visible alarm and, as the engraving makes clear (detail, fig. 17), she is holding a small unstoppered phial in her right hand. It is not fanciful to suppose that this is the phial of 'distilled liquor' Friar Lawrence gives to Juliet, and that Turner is alluding to Juliet's

**16** *St. Mark's Place, Venice – Juliet and her Nurse* (detail).

mock-suicide which will lead, in turn, to Romeo's death and finally to her own true suicide by Romeo's dagger. There, if anywhere, is a *locus classicus* of mis-identification. How better to introduce it than in the hand of the person who was perhaps most instrumental in encouraging Juliet to pursue a love that would end in tragedy, and what better locale for it than a city supremely concerned with questions of identification? (It should also be remembered that Romeo was wearing 'an antick face' when he first met Juliet.) The fact that Turner went to great lengths to fill the square not with just any staffage but so many masked and costumed revellers supports this interpretation, for why otherwise should he have taken such pains – and why else put Juliet in Venice at Carnival – if they were not meant to contribute to the overall meaning of the work? By painting them Turner was clearly capitalising upon his awareness of the importance of fakery to the city. He did not place Juliet in an inappropriate setting at all.

That this was his intention is also indicated by the quotation he added to the second state of the engraving in 1842, a rendering of lines drawn from the fourth Canto of Byron's *Childe Harold's Pilgrimage*:

> . . . but Beauty doth not die . . .
> Nor yet forget how Venice once was dear –
> The pleasant place of all festivity
> The revel of the earth, the Masque of Italy.

**17** *St. Mark's Place, Venice – Juliet and her Nurse* (detail).

The two meanings of the word 'Masque' are particularly relevant to Turner's underlying theme, as is the fact that when the engraving was advertised for sale it was under the title of 'Juliet after the Masquerade'.[49] Here, too, a double meaning may be adduced, for Juliet's balcony scene does indeed follow her return from the masquerade at which she meets Romeo, and 'the Masquerade' can equally refer to the scene in front of her. Moreover, Turner's change of one of Byron's words in the first line of the poetic quotation also seems significant. Instead of 'but Nature doth not die' he gives us '. . . but Beauty doth not die'. Another parallel is thus drawn: both the young girl and the city in which she stands are soon to die, but only in the physical sense; by means of Turner's painting they will live on, achieving some measure of immortality through the power of art. The self-referential use of a painting to extend the meaning of a subject was something Turner resorted to occasionally in the 1830s. For example, in *Watteau Study by Fresnoy's Rules*, exhibited at the R.A. in 1831, which includes a portrait of Watteau painting, Turner addresses the whole subject of the mortality of an artist and the immortality of his work of art,[50] the latter being a theme he returned to and amplified in *The Golden Bough* (fig. 144) of 1834 which also makes an indirect statement about the creative process. In *Juliet and her Nurse* Turner once again clearly made *ars longa, vita brevis* the subject of one of his works. And Juliet's wistful gaze, her head resting on the back of her hand as she surveys the square, not only appears to express her longing for fulfilment through love, but also seems to project Turner's feelings of mortality at the age of sixty-one, his sense of the impending loss of all the gorgeousness and activity of the world. The artist did not move Juliet to Venice on a whim, out of ignorance, or because 'this is where Romeo and Juliet ought to have fallen in love, for the scene is the "objective correlative" of the lovers' passion'[51] – as though the lovely banks of the Adige could not equally have served that purpose, especially in Turner's hands – but clearly because he had considered reasons for doing so. He was addressing local, dramatic and universal problems. He was also testing our associative, imaginative and interpretative faculties to the limit.

The process of association was intrinsic to the creation of much of Turner's art, and therefore it follows that failure to associate on our part will inevitably act as a barrier to full understanding. Of course it is not being advocated that whatever is suggested by the works of Turner (or any other painter) is valid or that it automatically derives from the artist; obviously, one still needs to bring to interpretation the necessary criteria of evidence, even if this can only be found within the work itself. That is why we need to understand congruity, motivation and context. But Ruskin was quite right as far as the spirit of things are concerned. There are some insights that a literal response will just not supply. And Turner's remark to a young friend that Ruskin 'sees *more* in my pictures than I ever painted' should be viewed in the light of her hasty qualification . . .

> . . . but he seemed very much pleased. It is easy to understand this, for Turner's pictures appeal so much to the imagination, that much *must* depend on the imagination of the critic.[52]

Turner's attitude was clearly that too much interpretation is better than too little, and it is a viewpoint that certainly allows a welcome degree of interpretative latitude, although one would not wish to over-indulge it. Unfortunately, though, as a result of cultural changes in the way we look at landscapes that have come about since Turner's time, and also because we frequently lose sight of Turner's historical and aesthetic context, instead of imaginative latitudes being explored, often quite the opposite happens and literalism prevails, blocking realisation of the more subtle dimensions of Turner's art.

Nothing better illustrates this failure, and the difficulties it can lead to, than various interpretative problems which have arisen in connection with what is perhaps Turner's most famous and popular picture, *The Fighting 'Temeraire', tugged to her Last Berth to be broken up, 1838* (fig. 18), exhibited at the Royal Academy in 1839. Also in passing, these problems allow us to judge exactly to what degree Turner could depart from literalism.

**18**  *The Fighting 'Temeraire', tugged to her Last Berth to be broken up, 1838*, R.A. 1839,
oil on canvas, 91 × 122 cm, National Gallery, London.

The picture depicts the towing of the great man-of-war to Beatson's ship-breaking yard at Rotherhithe on 6 September 1838, which Turner may have witnessed.[53] It was painted at a time when there was widespread concern over the declining numbers of 'wooden walls of old England' that had so successfully defended Britain during the wars with France a quarter of a century earlier.[54] The *Téméraire* herself had played an important part at Trafalgar, having been immediately astern of the *Victory* in the weather column of the battle (see fig. 48). In more recent years she had been the Guardship of Ordinary, the Flagship of the Superintendent of the Fleet Reserve at Sheerness. As such she was depicted shortly before her demise in a watercolour by E. W. Cooke, now in the Victoria and Albert Museum, London.[55]

Turner's contemporaries had no problems in seeing symbolic meanings in the sunset; as the critic of *The Athenaeum* wrote:

A sort of sacrificial solemnity is given to the scene, by the blood-red light cast upon the waters by the round descending sun, and by the paler gleam from the faint rising crescent moon, which silvers the majestic hull, and the towering masts, and the taper spars of the doomed vessel – which latter (still following this fanciful mode of interpretation) almost gives to the picture the expression of such malignant alacrity as might befit an executioner.[56]

Thackeray expressed a similar response. Writing in *Fraser's Magazine* he remarked that

The old Temeraire is dragged to her last home by a little, spiteful, diabolical steamer. A mighty red sun, amidst a host of flaring clouds, sinks to rest . . . The little demon of a steamer is belching out a volume . . . of foul lurid red-hot malignant smoke, paddling furiously, and lashing up the water round about it; while behind it (a cold grey moon looking down on it) slow, sad and majestic, follows the brave old ship, with death, as it were, written on her . . . [Turner] makes you see and think of a great deal more than the objects before you . . . .[57]

Other critics wrote of the sunset 'typifying the departing glories of the old Temeraire',[58] the setting sun being the 'emblem of the aged ship' whilst the young moon is the 'type of the petty steamer – about to assume its station in the sky'.[59] As was written in *The Art Union* when the work was exhibited again in 1844:

It is a glorious sunset, and we are to suppose that by the time the glowing disk shall rest upon the horizon, the Temeraire shall have been towed into her last resting place.[60]

As these different interpretations demonstrate, it is apparent that imaginative observers of Turner's own day experienced little difficulty in finding meanings in Turner's sky. It is possible that the artist may have linked the sun and moon directly to either of the ships as symbols of their character or fate. However, it seems more likely that he was exploiting the general associations of the coming of night, for the linking of red sunsets to scenes connected with death, and of peaceful moonrises to the state of calm after death, is encountered elsewhere in Turner's art during this period. Nonetheless the interpreters were reacting imaginatively, which must have gratified the artist, and there was never doubt that *The Fighting 'Temeraire'* addresses the passing of the age of sail. Yet people have still encountered problems in coming to terms with Turner's imaginative, or 'poetic' conception of things. These difficulties particularly concern the location of the sunset, the masting of the man-of-war and the details of the steam tug.

For a start, Turner seems to have depicted the sun setting in the east (in relationship to the warship's having to sail from east to west up the Thames to reach Rotherhithe). A controversy was begun in the London *Times* in the winter of 1877 when it was noted that the *Téméraire* was sailing in the wrong direction.[61] A later attempt to explain this anomaly suggested that 'To keep in the only deep water channel from Sheerness to London, the first three miles would be to the eastward to round the Nore Light, and it is therefore quite possible that Turner saw her with the sunset behind her as in the picture'.[62] This ingenious attempt to provide a literal explanation just will not work. If the ship is sailing eastwards in the picture then the empty north (Essex) shore of the Thames estuary would appear on the right where Turner has instead placed a conurbation. It has also been suggested that Turner might have depicted the boat being tugged up 'Lime House Reach', where the river runs from north to south for a brief stretch.[63] The sun could conceivably be seen there on the right but, as the writer who proposed this is forced to admit, the river would appear narrower than we see it here, and the left bank would be more heavily built up.

What all this overlooks, however, is Turner's total disregard for topographical accuracy and his desire to synthesize experience. Turner may or may not have witnessed the *Téméraire* sailing in front of a similar sunset on that autumn evening in 1838 but what he saw and what he imagined are two different things. We may certainly be looking at the Thames near the Nore, as the width of the river indicates. But Turner had known the area around the Nore for many years and this wide arena could only have provided some of the scenery he needed for his picture. Clearly he has sacrificed topographical accuracy (if he did not just make the setting up, as seems likely) and compressed a wide vista, so that we are looking both westwards towards London on the right *and* eastwards towards the Thames estuary on the left. Turner employed compression in other pictures[64] and there are many examples of his disregard for 'map-making', his disparaging term for topographical accuracy. On occasion he quite happily made the sun rise in the north,[65] if we check his effects against the 'real' topoi depicted, so we should not be surprised that he takes liberties here. The only surprise is that people are ever surprised by his distortions. Moreover, there is a strong possibility that Turner invented the sunset altogether. A letter in *The Times* in 1877 by someone who signed himself 'F.C.P.' says that

> I passed 3 years of childhood on board the Téméraire, being the period during which my late father was commander of the ships 'in ordinary' at Sheerness. In the autumn of 1839 [*sic*] the Téméraire, having been sold to be broken up, was towed up the Thames. Anxious to see her on the last voyage I stationed myself near Blackwell at the time appointed for her passage. As she lazily approached, towed by one of those clumsy steamtugs of those days, the scene presented was precisely that which Turner subsequently faithfully translated to canvas. As regards the sky effects, however, the painter appears to have used justifiable licence in depicting a sunset typical of the termination of the career of the vessel.[66]

Although thirty-nine years later this eye witness got his date wrong, it is quite possible that he saw the vessel being towed by a single tug, for the second tug that is known to have towed her[67] may have joined her upriver where greater manoeuvrability would have been needed. But a sunset (or lack of one) is precisely the kind of effect one does not forget.

The need to explain things in literal terms has deflected appreciation of other imaginative elements of the picture, however. Martin Davies, whose suggestion that the ship was being towed eastwards is quoted above, also tells us that

> The Téméraire's masts were removed at Sheerness and temporary masts were put on her for the journey to Rotherhithe.

This viewpoint first surfaced in the National Gallery catalogue in 1927 and continues to be stated in recent editions. Yet it is an entirely specious idea, equivalent to the notion of having a car re-sprayed before sending it to the scrap-yard. In fact, following the standing orders of the navy whereby anything salvable was removed from a vessel before it was destroyed, the *Téméraire*'s masts and rigging were taken off at Sheerness and not replaced.[68] If he had witnessed the event, Turner would only have seen the bare hull of the ship being towed upstream. There can be no doubt that the artist reconstructed the ship from his imagination. This also explains why she is so lightly rigged. A 98-gun, Second Rate ship of the line would have been far more extensively rigged than this when seaworthy. Turner clearly reduced the number of yards and shortened the masts to make the ship seem less heavy than she would have appeared in reality, and he also made the *Téméraire* ride extremely high in the water, something not possible to this extent in actuality either.[69] Similarly, he added an ethereal appearance to the vessel by depicting her in extremely light tones which are intensified by contrast with the dark, squat tug before her. The overall effect is to make the ship seem ghost-like: she glides over the water instead of cutting through it. By adding masts to the hull that he may have seen, he romanticises the ship and alludes to her days as a proud warship some forty years before.

Another misunderstood feature of the work is the tug itself. Turner purposefully made alterations to this boat. In *all* his other depictions of paddle steamers (which were a mode of transport he often used and frequently depicted) he placed masts and funnel in the correct order, i.e. foremast, funnel, mainmast and mizzenmast. In *The Fighting 'Temeraire'* he has dispensed with the foremast, moved the funnel forward and also done away with the mizzenmast. (If we look at the *Oriental* in *Peace – Burial at Sea* of three years later, fig. 54, we can see the correct structure.) Another correspondent to *The Times* in 1877 lamented that

> Turner has committed a most grievous blunder . . . he has represented the tug with only a mizzenmast instead of only a foremast . . . I beg to ask if any tug at that time existed with a single mast.[70]

This difficulty over the mast was shared by J. T. Willmore, the man who was commissioned by a London art dealer[71] to engrave the picture in 1844. Although he had worked with Turner many times and must have been acquainted with his caprices, this apparent mistake was too much for him. Without asking Turner's permission he corrected the 'error'

**19** J. T. Willmore after J. M. W. Turner,
*The Old Téméraire*, engraving, 1845 (detail).

by transposing the funnel and mast – and whilst he was about it he also 'improved' the rigging of the *Téméraire*, adding yards and shrouds galore (detail, fig. 19). Turner was understandably furious. As the *Art Journal* of 1856 tells us

> We remember when the picture was in the hands of the engraver, the latter was in the utmost embarrassment with regard to . . . the tug . . . and ventured to make the thing like a steamboat – a liberty which excited in the artist a paroxysm of wrath. What had he to do with form? What had he to do with the forms of steam-boats? . . . the steam-boat, however, remains in the plate as the engraver shaped it.[72]

A very mundane engraving it is too – as was later commented, the image was exceedingly 'weakened by this alteration'.[73] The wraith-like ship also suffered in the process.

A major reason Turner altered the tug was that he wanted a dark accent in the centre of the formal triangle made by the *Téméraire* and the ships to her right – a Thames barge, a merchantman further off and another sailboat in the far distance. Yet it is also apparent that he not only moved the tug's funnel forward; he moved it ahead of the place usually taken by a foremast, to an impossible position at the very prow of the vessel. A convincing reason for this very startling solecism was provided by Robert C. Leslie in 1884. He saw it as an alteration made by Turner to express

> his first, strong, almost prophetic idea of smoke, soot, iron and steam, coming to the fore in all naval matters.[74]

That Leslie was correct seems proven by the fact that the funnel is situated not just at the very front of the tug but also in the van of all the ships displaying sail in the painting. Such a placement appears too studied to be fortuitous. Further support is lent to this interpretation by our knowledge of Turner's powers of association and his abilities as a formalist: he could surely have found less drastic ways to add pictorial emphasis to a triangle had he wanted to. We do indeed seem to be witnessing another of Turner's rare employments of a direct visual metaphor, not his more usual type of covert conveyance of an underlying meaning.

In this picture, if anywhere, Turner demanded to be looked at imaginatively. Yet that demand is also operative in many of his other works and for good reason. Association answered a profound need in Turner, allowing him greatly to extend the imaginative potentialities of images. And a poetic imagination calls for poetic responses, which in turn require imaginative courage. Undeniably the whole nature of association and metaphor is open to ambiguity because these processes are variable: what suggests something to one person may suggest something completely different to another. Naturally there is danger of interpretative error in all this. But if we limit ourselves to possibilities and likelihoods, carefully looking for Turner's 'clues' and bearing in mind his intense awareness of the physical and social fabric of his time, his aesthetic and poetic orientations, his responsive-ness to history and his cultural intentions, we can narrow down the danger of being incorrect. Interpretation inevitably poses risks but it is better to fall foul of them occasion-ally than to lose sight of what Turner may have meant altogether. Although, arguably, without the aid of the above anecdotes we might never have known beyond doubt what Turner intended to depict by a hound coursing a hare in *Battle Abbey, the spot where Harold fell*, or why geese are being shooed in *Wycliffe, near Rokeby*, nevertheless we might have come near to appreciating what he meant by spotting incongruities, as John Pye did, or by analysing coincidences, as with the Battle Abbey picture. But being certain of the meaning of such images, and how Turner wanted us to respond, does enable us to probe with some confidence for the presence of 'sentiment' elsewhere. When we do so we shall quickly see how immensely human the Turnerian landscape really is.

# Part I

## THE ASSOCIATION
## OF IMAGES AND IDEAS

**20** *Dolbadern Castle, North Wales*, R.A. *1800*,
oil on canvas, 119.5 × 90.2 cm, Royal Academy of Arts, London.

# ONE

# A Poetic Painture

> ... sounds harmonious, Ideal beauties or connect-
> ing Metaphors are capable of receiving pictorial
> effects.
>
> *J. M. W. Turner*

IN our day perhaps nothing could seem more aesthetically remote than the notion that
painting and poetry might be interactive or 'sister arts'. In Turner's day the accepted view
was just that. The artist himself strenuously held that

> Poesy & Painting, being sisters agree entirely ... We cannot make good Painters
> without some aid from Poesy.[1]

The body of doctrine which enshrined this belief is commonly identified by the use of the
simile *ut pictura poesis* taken from the *Ars poetica* by the Roman poet Horace, meaning 'as is
poetry, so is painting'. By the late Renaissance period, if not before, it was widely accepted
that 'There are no two things in the world that have a nearer affinity and resemblance
than poetry and painting'[2] because both enjoy either parallel or even complementary
imaginative powers, and share the same cultural purpose.

   This was the notion that the aim of each discipline was to discern and make apparent
the constant and universal principles of human nature. It was thought that an artist might
best achieve such an aim by taking his subjects from history, religion or mythology, for by
definition those areas of content were held to embody the human experiences that are of
most general rather than particular import, and therefore capable of offering the maximum
moral and spiritual enlightenment. If history did that in factual terms, then painting, like
poetry, could even more directly express fundamental truths by sorting out the wheat from
the chaff of history, religion or mythology, and could also create powerful emotional
responses, involving the viewer to a much greater degree. Therein lay the especial validity
of History painting and therein also lay the imaginative and creative usefulness of a 'poetic'
imaginative approach to the History painter himself. Faced with a variety of actions within
any given subject, by treating of things as a poetic historian (such as Virgil) might, the
History painter – in theory at least – could select and order his thoughts and experiences so

as to reveal the general and even ideal aspects of human nature. A harmonious surround to which everything contributed, the gestures and expressions of the participants, which might be those external actions that could most efficiently make evident their inner feelings and responses, a respect for the complete appropriateness or decorum of the ancillary details and surroundings, and, above all, a sense of the beauty and perfectibility of the human form, would all contribute to the creation of an epic painting analogous to epic poetry. In this way the History painter could go far beyond the limitations of factual history, for the study of history usually addresses itself to particular events and responses, rather than generalised statements. Turner certainly made clear the high value he placed upon the category of History painting, for he prized his landscapes created in that mode above all his other pictures. And by addressing himself to 'history', as he did almost from the start of his career in paintings like the *Dolbadern Castle* of 1800 (fig. 24) which he presented to the Royal Academy as his Diploma Picture upon his election as a full Academician in 1802, until the end of his career in 1850, in works that drew their subject matter from that supremely poetic history, *The Aeneid*, Turner also used History painting to proclaim his belief in the moral seriousness, universality and idealism of art itself.

The equation of painting with poetry and history, and the notion that the aim of the art is to make the workings of human nature visible, not as it is in local or particular senses but as it should be universally, thus enabling the discipline to be morally and spiritually elevating as well as a means of pleasing the senses, was the direct or indirect theme of many of the books that formed the aesthetic backbone of Turner's library. We know that the artist read a number of these works in the 1808–11 period in connection with lectures on perspective he was preparing at the time, having volunteered to become the R.A. Professor of Perspective at the very end of 1807. In the three years before he delivered the first of his lectures in 1811, Turner read or re-read over seventy important treatises on perspective, aesthetics and art-history. From this reading and his own thoughts on these subjects, he formulated a set of six lectures to be delivered annually.[3] As Turner was then in his mid-thirties, his ideas were those of a fairly mature artist, and as his lectures were revised and redelivered over the next seventeen years clearly the views presented were of undiminishing theoretical importance to him. We shall frequently draw upon them throughout this book. That Turner possessed an enquiring mind and the earnest desire to educate himself was apparent from the start of his career, so it is entirely possible that he read many of the books he drew upon for his perspective lectures well before 1808–11, even possibly in the early 1790s when he was a student at the Royal Academy Schools. In any event, that he chose these books for his library or later read them is an indication of where his aesthetic interests and identifications lay.

The books in question included *A tracte containing the Artes of Curious Paintinge* by Giovanni Paolo Lomazzo, translated into English in 1598; *The Painting of the Ancients* by

Franciscus Junius, published in 1638; *The Principles of Painting* by Roger de Piles, published in English in 1743, which allows that 'views of countries' could be included within the category of historical painting[4]; André Félibien's *Seven Conferences held in the King of France's Cabinet of Paintings*, translated in 1740; Count Francesco Algarotti's *An Essay on Painting*, published in 1764, which Turner – like Reynolds before him – evidently thought highly of; and the didactic poem *De Arte Graphica* ('The Art of Painting') by Charles Alphonse du Fresnoy. This latter was written in Latin in 1637, published after du Fresnoy's death in 1667 and first translated into English by Dryden in 1695. Dryden wrote an introductory essay to accompany the poem which draws 'A parallel betwixt Painting and Poetry'. His essay also included a translation of part of an influential treatise on art by Giovanni Pietro Bellori. Turner knew Dryden's essay as well as du Fresnoy's poem in a translation imaginatively versified by William Mason in 1783. Both texts appeared in the collected edition of Reynolds's *Works* first published in 1797, the Mason translation of du Fresnoy's poem being included because it enjoys important annotations by Reynolds.[5] Du Fresnoy begins his original Latin poem both with the *ut pictura poesis* simile of Horace and an equally famous sentiment attributed by Plutarch to Simonides of Ceos stating that 'painting is mute poesy and poetry speaking painting'.[6] Such stresses at the very outset of du Fresnoy's poem indicate how the relationship of the 'sister arts' was thought to be fundamental.

Even the most minor eighteenth century poets frequently uttered such sentiments. A typical example occurs at the beginning of Walter Harte's 'An Essay on Painting'. This was available to Turner in the ninth volume of his basic source book of poetry, Robert Anderson's *A Complete Edition of the Poets of Great Britain* (hereafter known as Anderson's *Complete Poets*), a thirteen-volume compendium from Chaucer down to his own day which was published between 1792 and 1795 and which he drew upon for much of his subject matter in his poetic-historic pictures. The ninth volume was one of those Turner was most familiar with, for it contained the complete works of several of his favourite poets.[7] He certainly knew Harte's poem, for in one of his perspective lectures he cited a footnoted reference to optics made by the poet.[8] There is every likelihood he found Harte's views on the equality of painting and poetry congenial, and he definitely did think that another of the major aims of both arts was to act prophetically, as did Harte:

> Whatever yet in poetry held true,
> If duly weigh'd, holds just in painting too:
> Alike to proph't, and delight they tend
> The means may vary, but the same their end.
> Alike from heav'n congenial first they came,
> The same their labours, and their praise the same.
> Alike by turns they touch the conscious heart,
> And each on each reflects the lights of art.

Harte stressed that he had arrived at his ideas independently of du Fresnoy[9] and this demonstrates just how far his thoughts on the subject are typical of a fairly large body of poetry that constantly supported the equation of the two arts. The link was considered to be virtually self-evident.

The doctrine of *ut pictura poesis*, and thus the primacy of History painting, was again spelt out in Jonathan Richardson's *An Essay on the Theory of Painting*. This was first published in 1715 and Turner owned a copy of the 1792 edition. And Richardson was a major influence on the writer on art who probably most influenced Turner. Sir Joshua Reynolds also asserted the primacy of poetic-historic painting in his Discourses, all of which Turner owned in their 1797 collected edition, although copies of the individual lectures were undoubtedly available to him before then, each discourse being printed shortly after it was given. Naturally, considering the institution Reynolds presided over, and the tradition it represented, it was almost inevitable that the great pedagogue should declare in the thirteenth discourse that

> POETRY addresses itself to the same faculties and the same dispositions as Painting, though by different means . . .

And in the fourth of the lectures he stated that

> History Painting . . . ought to be called Poetical, as in reality it is.

The practical and aesthetic direction of virtually the whole series of Discourses was founded upon the need to meet the extensive implications of these two equations, for Reynolds sought to promote a 'Great Style' of History painting, one necessarily alive with imaginative or 'poetic' force, and of course he regarded historic-poetic painting as the supreme hierarchy of art, from the initial discourse attempting to orientate the training of the artist towards the fulfilment of its complex goals. As far as Turner's most serious statements were concerned he entirely succeeded.

Turner probably attended the last of Reynolds's Discourses, on 10 December 1790, and he had opportunities to hear similar voicings of support for the concept of poetic-historic painting in following years. He may have attended James Barry's lectures as the R.A. Professor of Painting in 1798 when, amongst other things, Barry made a 'long parallel between Poetry & Painting',[10] and he could have read them when they were published in 1809. Barry's views were cogent and he made some particularly important points regarding the need for dramatic unity in a picture, a need Turner was especially alert to, as we shall see. Henry Fuseli, Barry's successor as R.A. Professor of Painting after the unfortunate Irishman was expelled from the institution in 1799, was no less aware of the validity and expressive potentialities of poetic-historic painting. Turner was present at the first of

Fuseli's lectures on 16 March 1801, and at the lectures Fuseli gave two years later.[11] He could also have read the first set of lectures when they were published in 1801.

Turner would have also encountered the equation of poetry and painting in the 'Essays on Painting' by Edward Dayes. Some of these initially appeared in the *Philosophical Magazine* in 1802 but they were published together in book form in 1805, and the subscription list of this publication carries Turner's name. Dayes's work appears to have had an influence on Turner's watercolours between 1793–6 and it seems likely that the young artist borrowed drawings from Dayes to copy during that period.[12] Dayes, too, had decided views on the centrality and supremacy of poetic-historic painting, the fact that painting should embody 'some important moral truth for the edification of mankind',[13] the need to 'elevate' landscape painting, and the right of the landscapist to take complete poetic licence with mountains, lakes, rivers, rocks, caverns, ruins, and indeed 'the whole face of nature', in order to achieve those ends.

John Opie was another of Turner's contemporaries whose ideas on art were familiar to him. Opie succeeded Fuseli as R.A. Professor of Painting and Turner probably attended his lectures in 1807. Certainly he knew them well slightly later, for his published copy of them, dating from 1809, contains some of Turner's most memorable annotations.[14] Opie also equated poetry and painting.

It is not surprising that Turner identified so strongly with this equation. He did so for the simple reason that he was endowed with profound poetic instincts. Throughout his life Turner thoroughly immersed himself in poetry. Through Anderson's *Complete Poets* he may well have become familiar by the mid-1790s with Spenser, Pope, Mallet, Shenstone, Gray, Dyer, Collins, Langhorne and Mark Akenside (who was especially important to him), and by 1798 he had read Milton (who also appears in Anderson). He knew at least four plays by Shakespeare,[15] and perhaps above all he prized that supremely painterly poet, James Thomson. In Thomson's verse, and especially in *The Seasons*, Turner encountered poetry resplendent with exactly his kind of landscape imagery and a superb responsiveness to light and colour. Other poems by Thomson, such as *Liberty*, must have had a decisive effect on his moral and social views too. Moreover, there was also another awareness that poetry may well have heightened. The cosmic scale and grandeur of *Paradise Lost* must surely have influenced his own responses to scale and natural grandeur, as had the variety, detail and length of Thomson's *Seasons*, with its almost Romantic urge 'to embrace the world'. Turner never approached the natural universe with an unformed sensibility; from his earliest years it had been honed by poetry. Poetry opened up the world, awakening a sense of its meaning by the creation of physical, social and moral relationships. Turner was not an artist for whom the term 'poetic painting' was an empty catch-phrase. It held very real meaning for him and greatly contributed to the development of his vision and art. Furthermore, he wrote poetry throughout his life and quite naturally liked to think of himself as a working

**21** *Buttermere Lake, with part of Cromackwater, Cumberland, a Shower*, R.A. 1798,
oil on canvas, 91.5 × 122 cm, Clore Gallery for the Turner Collection, London.

poet who was thus highly able to 'Alternate change their office and their name'. And he
constantly maintained his interest in the latest poetic developments of his day, demonstrating an especial affinity with Byron, as well as an interest in other contemporaries such as
Southey, Campbell, Scott, Rogers and Shelley.

Turner was consequently well acquainted with the body of theoretical literature that
equated painting and poetry, and both arts with the humanistic approach to history, whilst
also being fully able to form his own conclusions regarding those relationships through his
understanding of poetry itself.

It was in the years between 1798 and 1800 that Turner slowly but surely came to
comprehend how painting might best *be* poetic, through realising how these arts relate and
imaginatively function. By then he had completed his formal art-education after a decade
spent mainly as a topographical artist, gradually gaining in confidence to the point where
he had progressed from exhibiting topographical watercolours to more ambitious seascapes

in oils, like *Fishermen at Sea*, sent to the Academy in 1796 (fig. 161), *Fishermen coming ashore at Sunset* (B.J. 3), displayed there in 1797, and *Moonlight, a study at Millbank* (B.J. 2), also shown in 1797. Clearly, by 1798 he was ready to progress further.

Turner's desire to achieve a poetic painting ostensibly received stimulus from the Royal Academy itself at this time. In January 1798 the institution, responding to the growing need of artists to make the literary content of their works more explicit, resolved to permit the use of supportive texts and quotations alongside picture titles in the Exhibition catalogues. Turner wasted no time in taking advantage of the change.[16] To the titles of five paintings and drawings in the Exhibition catalogue of 1798 he appended either quotations from Milton's *Paradise Lost* or Thomson's *The Seasons*. This in itself is revealing, for of all the English poets till then Milton and Thomson were the most creative word-painters of darkness and light (and colour in Thomson's case). It is a facility apparent in all the quotations Turner chose.

As Jerrold Ziff has ingeniously demonstrated,[17] in the case of at least one of these pictures the poetry in question seems to have played an important part in forming the image by decisively affecting the way Turner elaborated his basic prosaic 'blueprint-study' sketchbook material so as to convey poetic (i.e. literary and visually harmonious) responses to the scene. The painting of *Buttermere Lake, with part of Cromackwater, Cumberland, a Shower* (fig. 21) was accompanied by these slightly altered lines from *The Seasons*:

> Till in the western sky the downward sun
> Looks out effulgent – the rapid radiance instantaneous strikes
> Th'illumin'd mountains – in a yellow mist
> Bestriding earth – The grand ethereal bow
> Shoots up immense, and every hue unfolds.[18]

It is these very effects that Turner realised in his painting, arriving at his final image after trying different locations for the 'grand ethereal bow' in an intermediate watercolour[19] and showing the golden light breaking across the more distant lake and hills. By using poetry in this way Turner was not only putting into effect the idea of poetic painting; he was also heightening the power of the poetry by intensifying its pictorialism. (Obviously this reciprocity would not have been apparent if the poetry had not been cited in the Exhibition catalogue.)

Like the verses accompanying the title of *Buttermere Lake*, another of the quotations Turner employed in 1798 is a fine piece of landscape description rich in metaphors. Below the title of his oil-painting *Morning amongst the Coniston Fells, Cumberland* (fig. 22) he appended lines culled from Book V of *Paradise Lost*:

> Ye mists and exhalations that now rise
> From hill or streaming lake, dusky or gray,

**22** *Morning amongst the Coniston Fells, Cumberland*, R.A. 1798,
oil on canvas, 123 × 89.7 cm, Clore Gallery for the Turner Collection, London.

> Till the sun paints your fleecy skirts with gold,
> In honour to the world's great Author, rise.[20]

Turner's penchant for identifying with sun-symbolism can be noted, and the fact that the sun 'paints' equally seems significant.

However, the poetry accompanying three other pictures in the same exhibition either contributes more active powers or symbolic effects. A watercolour of *The dormitory and transcept of Fountain's Abbey – Evening* was accompanied by lines from *The Seasons*:

> All ether soft'ning sober evening takes,
> Her wonted station on the middle air;
> A thousand shadows at her beck –
> In circle following circle, gathers round,
> To close the face of things.[21]

Especially in the last two lines, this verse contributes a sense of the changing movement of light in time that painting cannot convey directly. Similarly, a sense of the movement of water is produced by the verses attached to an oil-painting of *Dunstanburgh Castle, N.E. Coast of Northumberland. Sunrise after a Squally Night* (B.J. 6). The lines here are again taken from *The Seasons*:

> The precipice abrupt,
> Breaking horror on the blacken'd flood,
> Softens at thy return. – The desert joys,
> Wildly thro' all his melancholy bounds,
> Rude ruins glitter; and the briny deep,
> Seen from some pointed promontory's top,
> Far from the blue horizon's utmost verge,
> Restless reflects a floating gleam.[22]

With *Norham Castle on the Tweed, Summer's morn* (fig. 23), we encounter metaphorical verse whose pictorial realisation was to give Turner problems. The following lines were also drawn from *The Seasons* and, even more than those attached to *Morning amongst the Coniston Fells*, they demonstrate Turner's attraction to poetic sun-symbolism:

> But yonder comes the powerful King of Day,
> Rejoicing in the East: the lessening cloud,
> The kindling azure, and the mountain's brow
> Illumin'd – his near approach betoken glad.[23]

We have already seen why Turner did not 'establish' in his sky the metaphor that appears at the opening of the third line of this quote. But it is established indirectly and very subtly elsewhere in the picture, for below the castle Turner depicts a large pall of blue smoke

**23** *Norham Castle on the Tweed, Summer's morn*, R.A. 1798,
watercolour on paper, 50.9 × 73.5 cm, Private Collection, UK.

emanating from a bonfire. Turner's consideration of the way that Thomson's metaphors function, in this passage and in the verses which follow it, must have played an important part in revealing to the artist how he could create pictorial metaphors, and why he should do so. Indeed, these lines and the two previous citations quoted above probably suggested how he could use poetic accompaniments in the following year.

This is apparent since the role played by metaphor in the poetic citations of 1799 is even more pronounced. Poetry could obviously be of the greatest use if it were active in expressing things that could not be seen. Of the five examples of verse accompanying Turner's picture titles in the 1799 Exhibition catalogue, all extend either the time-scale and/or the meanings of the pictures they support by their metaphorical imagery. The verse that accompanies a watercolour of *Caernarvon Castle* (W. 254) intensifies the sense of happiness afforded by sunlight. This stanza is taken from Mallet's 'Amyntor and Theodora':

> Now rose
> Sweet Evening, solemn hour, the sun declin'd
> Hung golden o'er this nether firmament,
> Whose broad cerulean mirror, calmly bright,

> Gave back his beamy visage to the sky
> With splendour undiminish'd.[24]

Yet *Caernarvon Castle* was not the only picture displayed in 1799 which depicts an evening-effect. The oil-painting *Harlech Castle, from Twgwyn Ferry, Summer's Evening Twilight* (B.J. 9) shows a calm scene of mountain and shore, with the western sky tinged with gold. The work was accompanied by a quotation from *Paradise Lost*. Here, the verse extends the pictorial time-scale greatly:

> Now came still evening on, and twilight grey,
> Had in her sober livery all things clad.
> ———Hesperus that led
> The starry host rode brightest till the moon
> Rising in clouded majesty unveiled her peerless light.[25]

Two other works shown at this exhibition were accompanied by more violent poetic imagery. *Battle of the Nile, at 10 o'clock when L'Orient blew up, from the station of the gun-boats between the battery and castle of Aboukir* (B.J. 10) has now vanished, but presumably it pictured the effects of the explosion. Its accompanying lines from 'Paradise Lost' do more than act as a visually descriptive accompaniment:

> Immediate in a flame,
> But soon obscur'd with smoke, all heav'n appear'd.
> From these deep-throated engines belch'd whose roar
> Imbowel'd with outrageous noise the air,
> And all her entrails tore, disgorging foul
> Their devilish glut, chain'd thunderbolts and hail
> Of iron globes.[26]

Turner's use of poetry to suggest sounds and movement, whilst introducing suitably fiendish associations, must have extended the imaginative impact of the painting dynamically.

The other picture accompanied by violent poetic imagery in 1798 is *Warkworth Castle, Northumberland – thunder storm approaching at sun-set* (fig. 24) where Turner depicts the great pile on the banks of the Coquet with masses of cumulus clouds rising up beyond it. The overall effect is one of calm, with fishermen at work and smoke drifting lazily in the still air. It is the poetry that introduces the necessary sense of threat:

> —Behold slow settling o'er the lurid grove,
> Unusual darkness broods; and growing, gains
> The full possession of the sky: and on yon baleful cloud
> A redd'ning gloom, a magazine of fate,
> Ferment.[27]

**24** *Warkworth Castle, Northumberland – thunder storm approaching at sun-set*, R.A. 1799, watercolour on paper, 52.1 × 74.9 cm, Victoria and Albert Museum, London.

That last word is potent in its imaginative suggestiveness.[28] Here again Turner has extended the time-scale of an image through the poetry.

But another work accompanied by a quotation in 1799 went still further than these pictures in its reliance upon a poetic concept to dictate its ultimate subject. The picture in question was a watercolour entitled *Morning, from Dr. Langhorne's Visions of Fancy* (w. 255), and here Turner clearly aimed to reinforce or create a moral, allegorical level of meaning through his choice of title and poetry. Unfortunately this work has also disappeared, so whether it really contained metaphorical imagery cannot be verified. However, the poetry linked to its title certainly does:

> Life's morning landscape gilt with orient light,
> Where Hope and Joy, and Fancy hold their reign,
> The grove's green wave the blue stream sparkling bright,
> The blythe hours dancing round Hyperion's wain.
> In radiant colours youth's free hand pourtrays,
> Then hold the flattering tablet to his eye,

Nor thinks how soon the vernal grove decays,
Nor sees the dark cloud gathering o'er the sky.
Mirror of life thy glories thus depart.[29]

It is especially unfortunate that this watercolour has vanished for it may have been Turner's first allegorical work and the first picture in which he employed a time of day and light-effect to complement and extend the meaning of a subject. Again one is struck by the fact that the poetic imagery refers to painting, as did the lines attached to the *Coniston Fells* of the previous year. Perhaps Turner even included someone painting with 'youth's free hand' upon a 'flattering tablet' in his watercolour.

What we witness, then, in 1798 and 1799, is Turner's increasing realisation that the imaginative power of painting can be enhanced by employing poetry and poetic metaphor to make up for inherent deficiencies of movement, time, sound, the moral implications of human ageing and other non-visible realities. And in the following year Turner reversed the associative roles of the two disciplines, investing his pictorial images that were accompanied by verse with metaphorical dimensions, and using poetry as a narrative medium to supply visual and historic data. (Indeed, this verse is almost without metaphorical content.) The artist had taken the next logical step and incorporated the ability of poetry to express non-visible meanings *into the pictures themselves*, thus making them 'poetical' to an even greater degree.

This reversal is apparent in the three History pictures that were exhibited at the R.A. in 1800. (Five other works Turner sent for exhibition in that year were all topographical views of Fonthill and had no literary accompaniment whatsoever.) The most overtly historical of them is *The Fifth Plague of Egypt* (B.J. 13), in connection with which the appended blank verse simply tells us that:

And Moses stretched forth his hands towards heaven,
and the Lord sent thunder and hail, and the fire
ran along the ground ———
*Exodus, Chap. IX ver. 23*

In fact this is a description of the seventh plague (which Turner's picture portrays.) Clearly the verse was included simply to remind us of the exact nature of the plague Turner was painting; it does not add to either the pictorial or the associative qualities of the image at all. Instead, Turner advances its imaginative ramifications visually, portraying the hail and fire with particularly lurid effect. The verses serve no more than a purely factual role.

This is equally true of the lines of narrative poetry attached to the titles of the two other historical pictures Turner exhibited in 1800, although we are entirely reliant upon the poetry to know that these works are historical pictures at all, for their titles fail to reveal that. In both cases, especially the first picture we shall discuss, failure to associate the verses with the pictorial imagery, or to look at the image carefully, has prevented several commentators from realising this and from making other vital connections.[30] Both works are views of Welsh castles and, in addition to demonstrating Turner's increasing development of visual metaphor, they also share an underlying connection which only emerges when we explore their subject matter, a linkage, moreover, that is shared with *The Fifth Plague of Egypt*.

The more immediately impressive of the two Welsh castle pictures, by dint of size and medium, is the oil-painting of *Dolbadern Castle, North Wales* (fig. 20), the Diploma work that Turner gave to the Royal Academy upon his election as an Academician in 1802. Turner based the painting upon sketches he had made in Llanberis pass in 1798 and 1799.

Far below the tower are four figures (fig. 25), two soldiers standing guard over a kneeling prisoner whose wrists are bound behind him, and another seated figure who is pointing at the castle. It has been suggested that the captors are simply 'banditti . . . borrowed from the imaginary, storm-wracked landscapes of Salvator Rosa'.[31] This identification is incorrect, for the figures are clearly identified by the poetry which accompanied the picture-title in the R.A. catalogue. The author of these verses is not known, leading to an assumption that Turner wrote them himself, but they seem too fluent for a poet-*manqué*:

> How awful is the silence of the waste,
> Where nature lifts her mountains to the sky,
> Majestic solitude, behold the tower
> Where hopeless OWEN, long imprison'd, pined
> And wrung his hands for liberty, in vain.

The 'Owen' referred to in the verses is the Welsh prince Owain Goch who was imprisoned by his brother in Dolbadarn Castle between 1255 and 1277 when he was freed by Edward I of England. And that is surely whom Turner depicts in his painting: what other prisoner, who is moreover clearly linked to the tower by the pointing figure, can be meant, given these verses?[32] The lower portion of the prisoner's clothing is highlit, pointing up the way that his wrists are bound behind his back and in exact vertical alignment with the light shining through the window of the tower way above him. It hardly seems possible that such precise stresses can be coincidental.[33] Linking the prisoner's physical predicament with this place of incarceration clearly draws our attention to things to come, and identifies the prisoner as Owain. By placing him on our line of sight so far beneath the tower Turner also effectively emphasises the physical dominance that the building will soon enjoy over him, and at this moment enjoys over us.

This last point leads us to the major visual metaphor that Turner enforces in the painting. We know from the preliminary sketches for the picture in the Turner Bequest[34] that the artist went to considerable lengths to work out the structure of the painting. Clearly

**25** *Dolbadern Castle, North Wales* (detail).

he ignored topographical accuracy and considerably heightened the tower as it is seen from the level of Llanberis lake, which appears on the left. The mountains are also raised, and make the whole valley seem much narrower than it appears from this spot in reality.

The reason for this seems clear. It serves to increase the sense of imprisonment, for by extending the lines of the adjacent mountains upwards, Turner dramatically projects the sense of the enclosure of the prison through surrounding it in a clearly defined and confining way. Ingeniously the device does double duty, for it also creates a vortex of light beyond the building. And here too we witness Turner's associative imagination at work, the organisation of light and, more importantly, shadow, being in dramatic accord with the subject, so that the predominant gloom projects the feelings of the protagonist. And as Llanberis pass runs along a north-west/south-east axis, and from the fact that we see the castle to the right of Llanberis lake, we can surmise that we are looking south-eastwards and at a sunrise. Given Turner's consistent observance of dramatic decorum in his use of dawns and sunsets, i.e. dawns to amplify hope or renewal, sunsets the decline of fortunes, we seem justified in thinking that the dawn light represents something hopeful here, namely liberty. At present Owain pines for this 'in vain', for he is both historically and pictorially barred from it by the castle, but eventually he will regain it. In *Dolbadern Castle, North Wales* the dramatic timing and employment of light, the distribution of light and shade, the use of colour and the pictorial metaphorical structure are all of a piece with the content. Not for nothing did Turner offer the painting to the Royal Academy in 1802.

**26** *Caernarvon Castle, North Wales*, R.A. 1800,
watercolour on paper, 66.3 × 99.4 cm, Clore Gallery for the Turner Bequest, London.

A related historical subject, the same reliance on poetry to pinpoint that subject, the comparable use of vertical alignment to stress associations, the exploitation of the associative potential of forms, and still more metaphorical elements can be seen in the other landscape Turner exhibited in 1800 with a poetic accompaniment. This is another watercolour of *Caernarvon Castle, North Wales* (fig. 26), but unlike Turner's picture of the year before it takes a distant view of the castle. It too was complemented in the Academy catalogue by verses attributed to Turner:

> And now on Arvon's haughty tow'rs
> The Bard the song of pity pours,
> For oft on Mona's distant hills he sighs,
> Where jealous of the minstrel band,
> The tyrant drench'd with blood the land,
> And charm'd with horror, triumph'd in their cries.
> The swains of Arvon round him throng,
> And join the sorrows of his song.

Given the popularity of Thomas Gray's famous poem *The Bard* of 1757 (which Turner knew well[35]) we can assume that the artist expected his audience to recognise 'The Bard' of the verses and the picture to be the last representative of those medieval Welsh poets supposedly put to the sword by Edward I in the late thirteenth century.

The work contains a number of associative elements. Here, as in *Dolbadern Castle*, and therefore for possibly only the second or third time in his career (the first being *Morning* of the previous year), Turner observes a sense of dramatic decorum in his choice of timing, employing light and shade in a way appropriate to the elegaic subject: evening mists descend in the valley and lengthening shadows fall across the bard as he sings his song of lamentation and points towards the cause of his sorrow, the fact that Caernarvon Castle had been built by Edward I to keep the Welsh under subjection.[36]

Turner emphatically separates the foreground and its figures from the mid and far distance by the sharp line of the near-hillside, and creates a repoussoir at the left. Here a pine tree (fig. 27) is distinctly angled towards the far-away castle. The direction taken by the tree is intensified by the strong contrast between the diagonal it creates and the repeated verticals of the other trees on the left. The fact that the artist so evidently made the tree and the bard respectively lean and point towards the castle suggests that he intended us to connect them and to make the tree project the sense of threat that the bard still represents for Edward. The connection between the tree and the bard is also reinforced by the curved shape of the top of the bard's harp which is repeated and amplified by the curve of the trunk immediately above it. In turn this repetition is reinforced by the curve of a smaller tree beyond it to the left. It can also be noted that the shape of the bard's pointing hand is very

**27** *Caernarvon Castle, North Wales* (detail).

**28** Thomas Jones, *The Bard*, exhibited Society of Artists 1774,
oil on canvas, 115.5 × 167.6 cm, National Museum of Wales, Cardiff.

similar to the shape of the right-hand edge of the foliage above him. And it hardly seems coincidental that one tree, which is strongly linked to the bard, so clearly stands out from the others, just as the bard stands out as a leader among his followers.

Turner's associative use of tree-forms to extend a picture of the last of the ancient Welsh bards should not surprise us however. It was a device particularly resorted to by other major painters when illustrating Gray's version of *The Bard*. They were responding to these lines in Gray's poem:

> Hark, how each giant oak, and desert cave,
> Sighs to the torrent's awful voice beneath!
> O'er thee, oh King! their hundred arms they weave,
> Revenge on thee in hoarser murmurs breathe;[37]

Such associative imagery naturally called forth corresponding imagery from painters. For instance, Thomas Jones's *The Bard* of 1774 (fig. 28) shows the bard poised to step off the edge of a precipice (which he does to conclude the poem). Above and immediately beyond him a lightning-blasted oak not only furthers the associations of death, but its few leafy

**29** Hall and Middiman after P. J. de Loutherbourg, *The Bard*. This appeared as the frontispiece of *The Musical and Poetical Relicks of the Welsh Bards* by Edward Jones, published in 1784.

**30** Thomas Holloway after Henry Fuseli, *The Bard from Gray*, engraving, 1800. The painting upon which this print was based was exhibited at the R.A. in 1800 but has now disappeared.

branches amplify the bard's gesture as he curses Edward in farewell. Other stricken trees augment the associations of the dead who litter the landscape. Jones also sets the scene at sunset, thereby drawing upon the associations of blood-red colour and dying light. Turner might well have known this work through its engraving by J. R. Smith, published in 1775. Similarly, and obviously for the same reason, de Loutherbourg's *The Bard*, which in its engraved form appeared as the frontispiece (fig. 29) to the *Musical and Poetical Relicks of the Welsh Bards* collected by Edward Jones and published in 1784, shows the bard poised above Edward on a rockface that falls diagonally from right to left; at the foot of the rocks, exactly opposite the English king and thus at the meeting point between the two, is some foliage that repeats the shapes of the bard's streaming hair. It mirrors Edward's threatening gesture and expresses the bard's implied threat. Moreover, if Turner had read Edward Jones's *Musical and Poetical Relicks of the Welsh Bards* he would have learnt at the very beginning of the book that the word '*Bardd*' itself signifies the Branching or what springs

31 John Martin, *The Bard*, 1813–17, R.A. 1817, oil on canvas, 213.3 × 154.9 cm, Laing Art Gallery, Newcastle-upon-Tyne. The title was accompanied in the R.A. catalogue by a quotation from Gray's poem: 'Ruin seize thee, ruthless King, Confusion on thy banners wait etc'.

32 Engraving after Richard Westall, *The Bard, from Gray*, *c.*1800. The painting upon which this was based was exhibited at the R.A. in 1798, and its title was accompanied in the catalogue with the quotation: 'On a rock, whose haughty brow, etc.'

from; [being] derived from *Bar*, a branch, or, the top', the term deriving from the druidical classifications 'in which the imagery and emblematical names were taken from those of oak trees . . . Thus the Derwydd; the highest class of Druid, signified Body of the Oak or, by implication Man of the Oak, the Orydd, or novitiate class meant the young shoot, growing up'.[38] Admittedly, in keeping with his Claudian *schema* Turner gives us a pine rather than an oak in *Caernarvon Castle*, but his purpose in making the tree denote something within the context of the picture is not compromised by that alteration.

Nor were Thomas Jones and de Loutherbourg (or Turner) the only artists to respond to such poetic imagery.[39] In 1800, the same year in which Turner exhibited *Caernarvon Castle*, Henry Fuseli exhibited a major oil entitled *The Bard from Gray* at the Royal Academy.

Regrettably this has now disappeared but it was engraved by Thomas Holloway (fig. 30) so we can gauge what it looked like. Although Fuseli did not include trees in his picture, he did represent a waterfall. This appears immediately behind the bard but curiously it does not reappear at the bottom of the work, suggesting that it was included for associative reasons, to symbolise the impending fall of the bard himself. Gray's tree-imagery was to reappear in John Martin's melodramatic *The Bard* of 1813–17 (fig. 31) where gnarled oaks strengthen the bard's gesture as he heaps imprecations upon Edward before throwing himself to his doom. Although Turner (like de Loutherbourg) did not openly illustrate Gray, his familiarity with Gray's poem makes it more than likely that he based his tree-metaphor on that poem and/or on other paintings of the bard.

Yet it may have been still another picture on the same subject which determined Turner's creation of a connection between the pointing of tree and bard, and the shape of tree-trunk and harp in *Caernarvon Castle*. This was Richard Westall's *The Bard, from Gray* which was exhibited at the R.A. in 1798 when its title in the catalogue was accompanied by a quotation from the poem: 'On a rock, whose haughty brow etc'. The painting is now also lost but we can judge what it looked like from an engraving (fig. 32). Westall positioned his bard upon the edge of an unconvincing chasm, locating the bisected trunk of a tree immediately above him. Although the tree-trunk is under-characterised, we can safely assume it is an oak, given its derivation from Gray's poem. One branch extends dramatically from the trunk towards the left, emphasising the direction towards which the ornate harp is pointing. From this branch the eye is also led quite naturally down to the outer line of the harp, a connection reinforced by the parallel line of the bard's arm as he plucks the strings. On the ground lie some discarded scrolls of verse, whilst a mountain that is surely Snowdon can be seen in the distance on the right. Turner knew and apparently liked Westall's art, for the only identified English painting apart from a group of portrait sketches in Turner's collection of paintings by other artists found after his death was a deposition-scene by Westall.[40] The similarity between the harps in the two bardic works is marked, as is the formal linkup of their musical instruments with the tree-shapes above them, and the associative employment of the vengeful trees themselves. Westall's use of association is less inventive than Turner's but it is undeniably present thanks to the poetic source of his imagery. It seems quite natural that Turner, while increasing the role of landscape in his version of a bardic subject, would also extend the associative linkage between the bard and the components of the setting in which he is placed.

The exact vertical alignment of the bard and the tree whose 'hoarser murmurs breathe' towards Edward in Turner's *Caernarvon Castle, North Wales* and Westall's *The Bard, from Gray* leads us to the recognition of a crucial associative device in Turner's work. In both the *Dolbadern Castle* and the *Caernarvon Castle* of 1800 we encounter Turner's most pronounced use to date of vertical alignment to bring about associations. In the course of this book it will be seen just how often the painter thereafter employed the device. Whether or not it derived from the work of Westall and/or other artists we shall never know. Turner might easily have conceived the technique of using vertical alignment to establish connections and enhance form and meaning from other sources of basic interest to a poetic painter, and to this painter-poet in particular. For vertical connections obviously exist in poetry itself.

Consonance and association through rhyming is a major source of both poetic 'sounds harmonious' and the creation of poetic meaning. Turner may well have been acquainted with the problems of poetic consonance even by 1800 – his earliest surviving drafts of (copied) poetry date from around 1793[41] – and if he did write the verses appended to the Welsh castle pictures of 1800 he had certainly achieved some fluency by then. Yet even if the verses were not his own compositions, he must surely have known how rhyming can determine poetic content. Anyone who has ever attempted rhyming verse readily appreciates that the sense and scope of each line is partly limited and directed by the available words that will rhyme with the word-ending which precedes or follows it. Turner understood the problem well, as surviving drafts of his own attempts to versify indicate.[42] His appreciation of the difficulties that rhyming engender can be gauged from the fact that in 1809 he even painted a picture and drew up verses treating of this very problem, as well as that of poetic inspiration itself. The picture, *The Garreteer's Petition* (fig. 219), shows a poet looking to his muse in vain, while the title of the work was accompanied in the R.A. catalogue by these verses:

> Aid me, ye Powers! O bid my thoughts to roll
> In quick succession, animate my soul;
> Descend my Muse, and every thought refine,
> And finish well my long, my *long-sought* line.

Turner's consideration of the problems of rhyming and the value of consonance, may have directly inspired his pictorial technique of linking things vertically. (And a great many of the other techniques by which poetry enforces consonance, structural unity and signification, such as repetition, alliteration, rhythm and internal echoes, could have been equally influential upon Turner).

This appropriation of technique from one art to its sister art was a practice encouraged by Reynolds. In the thirteenth Discourse he stated that

> . . . Whilst the Artist is amusing himself in the contemplation of other Arts, he may habitually transfer the principles of those Arts to that which he professes . . .[43]

It would have been only natural for Turner the poet to have aided Turner the painter in 1800. In these years, when we know he was actively exploring ways to make painting poetic, what more perfect method could the artist invent to effect a real congruence of painting and poetry than the 'transfer' of a vital device from one to the other? The fact that Turner so frequently used vertical alignment and repetition to extend the meanings of many of his works after creating his avowedly poetic Welsh castle pictures of 1800 suggests very strongly that poetic consonance may indeed have been the source of his pictorial consonance.

The use of vertical alignment to establish a central meaning, and the employment of light effects in the most appropriate way possible, are not the only things the Welsh castle pictures have in common however. They also share a subtler affinity: Turner also employs these works – as he does *The Fifth Plague of Egypt* – to express a deeper underlying theme, namely liberty. In *Dolbadern Castle* it is individual liberty that is being suppressed, whilst in *Caernarvon Castle* and *The Fifth Plague of Egypt* it is national liberty that is threatened or under constraint.

It is not difficult to see why Turner addressed this singular, underlying theme so wholeheartedly in 1800. The end of the 1790s in Britain saw liberty threatened or suppressed at home and abroad, so the artist was exploring a very immediate and universal issue of the day. In Britain the threatening unrest engendered by the French Revolution and the execution of Louis XVI, combined with a growing popular demand for the redress of internal social and economic ills, along with the attendant shocks of fighting a war with France inefficiently and badly, had induced a state of paranoia in the British ruling class throughout the 1790s. This manifested itself in severe curtailments of freedom of speech and assembly, basic liberties that most Englishmen held to be their birthright. *Habeas Corpus* was suspended in 1794 and remained in suspension for the next eight years, whilst 1795 saw the introduction of the Treasonable Practises and the Seditious Meetings Bills, the so-called 'Two Acts' which not only forbade incitement 'to hatred or contempt of King, Country or Government' but also the meeting of over 50 persons without the seeking of the permission of a magistrate, defiance of whose orders became a capital offence. Further repressive measures as a result of what Fox called 'Pitt's Reign of Terror' followed, some of them in the very period in which Turner was working on the Welsh Castle pictures and the Biblical painting: in 1799 the leading radical organisation, the London Corresponding Society, was banned, along with other similar groups, and the forming of trade unions was also prohibited by the Combination Act of 1799 which withdrew certain common-law rights and allowed for the summary trial of offenders. By 1800, therefore, many an Englishman definitely 'wrung his hands for liberty, in vain'. Turner's libertarian impulses became so marked in his maturity (after about 1812), being manifested in the great many paintings in which he weighs against social and political corruption (as did all those who wanted political reform in Britain in the 1790s) that it is hard not to feel that such impulses were receiving their first – if very subtle – public expression in 1800. And certainly there were a number of artists at the time in the Royal Academy who were very alert to the suppression of liberty in Britain: according to Joseph Farington and other sources, various Royal Academicians and Associates were suspected of, or known to harbour radical sympathies. The Academicians included Henry Fuseli, the Professor of Painting between 1799–1805, his predecessor as Professor, James Barry, as well as Thomas Banks, William Hodges and Robert Smirke, whilst the suspected Associates included John Hoppner and Martin Archer Shee, later to be President of the Academy. Moreover, at that time the Academy itself was considered a politically suspect institution by the King, Queen and various members of the aristocracy because of the rumoured or avowed predisposition towards 'democracy' of many of its members.[44] An indication of Turner's own sympathies at this time is furnished by the fact that in 1832, when he was invited to illustrate the poems of the banker-poet Samuel Rogers who had held fairly radical sympathies, Turner chose as one of his subjects a passage in the poem 'Human Life' which specifically treats of political repression in the 1790s (see the discussion below of *Traitor's Gate, Tower of London*, p. 125).

Liberty was also under threat outside Britain by the very end of the eighteenth century. Napoleon expelled the British from the Continent in late 1799 and in 1800 he re-invaded Switzerland. Indeed, as has plausibly been suggested,[45] *Caernarvon Castle* may allude to that invasion, Edward I standing for Napoleon. This interpretation is supported by the fact that possibly for Turner, as was certainly the case for Thomas Gray (from whom the painter originally derived the story of the bard), Edward I was as much a French king as an English one, being Norman and a member of the Plantagenet royal line which eventually would be destroyed by the Tudors, a native, Welsh descended line of kings.

Yet if this interpretation is correct, by the same token, to Owain in *Dolbadern Castle* Edward I came not as an unwelcome invader but as a liberator.[46] It is this point which suggests that Turner was exploring both the local and the wider ramifications of liberty in 1800. Of course there can be no likelihood that Turner, a staunch patriot, would have sympathised with the ambitions of Napoleon or the successes of the French. But neither should it automatically be assumed that he would have approved of the constraints upon liberty enforced by the British government in defence of national liberty at the time. The fact that in *Dolbadern Castle, North Wales*, he chose a subject in which brother imprisons brother, clearly has some bearing upon contemporary events in Britain, as does the fact that Edward I supposedly suppressed the Welsh bards for propagating political sedition. Conversely, however, the subject of invasion itself, and most especially the depiction of its effects upon the bard in *Caernarvon Castle*, clearly alludes to events abroad. By these means Turner achieved a degree of generalisation in total accord with the demands of the doctrine of *ut pictura poesis*.

*Caernarvon Castle* is Turner's first Claudian landscape, which suggests that from 1799–1800 he had started looking carefully at Claude's use of associative devices in his landscapes, a subject we shall discuss in detail below when we identify the precise Claudian image from which Turner derived the *Caernarvon Castle*. But the Welsh castle pictures of 1800 also demonstrate something else of importance in the development of the poetic painter. *Dolbadern Castle* is very much an exercise in the 'Sublime' mode, presenting a landscape that is dark, mysterious, awesome in scale and therefore sublime. On the other hand *Caernarvon Castle*, with its gentle contours, high degree of light, colour and lyricism, is a clear and conscious realisation of the notion of the 'beautiful', the aesthetic opposite of the sublime. That Turner might wish to project this aesthetic polarity, perhaps to demonstrate his range as an artist, and equally to demonstrate that range through the very different means of oil and watercolour, is not surprising. It was a differentiation that was emphasised widely in the discussion of landscape and its representation in art especially during the latter half of the eighteenth century, a period which saw the emergence of landscape painting in Britain, and the very end of which saw Turner's training as an artist. We can be sure that the differentiation between the beautiful and the sublime was debated in the cultural milieu in which Turner moved as a young man and, indeed, his concern with the 'sublime' in landscape painting – the engendering of awe and fear through rendering the darkness, immensity and sense of mystery in nature – was to find expression particularly in works painted in response to mountain scenery in the early 1800s, several of them in the same upright format Turner employed in *Dolbadern Castle*. But even by 1800 what we can determine quite clearly in the Welsh castle pictures is the degree to which Turner had come to think, in his most important public statements at least, that both sublimity and beauty should be subordinated to serving the higher moral, expressive, dramatic – and thus poetic – needs of his 'human' landscapes. The sublimity of the scene in *Dolbadern Castle* is subtly but clearly directed towards associatively furthering our awareness of the oppressiveness of imprisonment; equally through association, the beauty of landscape and evening light in *Caernarvon Castle* expresses much of what will be lost by the destruction of the Welsh sense of identity and community. Like a great many later pictures, these works afford us concrete evidence of how Turner could regard the creation of specific types of aesthetic experience as *means* to dramatic ends, rather than ends in themselves. They are indicative of how completely Turner identified with the concept of poetic painting by 1800.

In terms of pictorial development, then, *Dolbadern Castle* and *Caernarvon Castle* mark small but significant steps forward in their control of light, handling of physical space and visual elaboration of basic topographical material. Yet they testify to a big advance in Turner's thinking regarding poetic painting. Poetry supplies vital ancillary information about each of them but now we are required to participate more imaginatively than ever before. Turner had realised that by such involvement larger areas of non-visual meaning could find expression. Through the process of imaginative association by means of pictorial organisation and the shaping of details, images could communicate, say, the dominance of a prison, the claustrophobia of imprisonment, a barrier to liberty, the plaintiveness of a

Welsh harp, the threat implied in a gesture or the onset of tyranny. In gaining these meanings Turner had forged an imaginative tool that would henceforth play a vital role in his art, producing the two seminal pictures of his career as far as poetic painting is concerned.

Between 1798 and 1800 Turner had explored a number of ways in which poetry can relate to and aid painting, and vice-versa. Having employed poetry and painting recipro-cally in 1798 to heighten the imagery of both, he enlisted the aid of poetic association in 1799 to extend the impact of his pictures in various ways, increasing our awareness of time, sound, movement and the human associations of a scene. Also in 1799, he had employed poetry to add purely moral associations to *Morning, from Dr Langhorne's Visions of Fancy*. He went on in 1800 to incorporate the power of association directly into his images (if he had not already achieved this with the *Morning* picture), using verse solely to supply a narrative dimension. That he felt he had by then made an adequate survey is suggested by the fact that after 1800 he moved on to other matters, for none of the pictures in the R.A. Exhibition of 1801 were accompanied by verses and not until 1804 would Turner again quote poetry in the Exhibition catalogue.[47] When he did select verses drawn from Ovid's *Metamorphoses* to accompany his painting *Narcissus and Echo* (B.J. 53) it was to explore a further dimension that poetry can add to painting but which painting cannot reach unaided: insight into the subjective responses of the people he depicts, for the poetry in question employs the direct quotation of both protagonists.

Thereafter, throughout his career he drew upon what he had learnt from this exploration. Turner continued to include poetic accompaniments in the R.A. catalogues right up until the end of his career, in keeping with the parameters of usage he set up between 1798 and 1804, all the while ringing the changes upon the kinds of aid that an accompanying use of poetry facilitated. The type that increasingly came to dominate was poetry which strengthened the moral – and thus humanistic – dimensions of a work (as with the 1799 *Morning*). Turner's moralism becomes ever more apparent with the advent of his own poetic text, that series of disconnected fragments of poetry known as *The Fallacies of Hope* which supposedly formed an unpublished whole poem and which in 1812 he first attached to the title of the painting *Snow Storm: Hannibal and his Army crossing the Alps* (B.J. 126). Of the 46 poetic quotations employed by Turner between 1800–1850, over half may be deemed to enjoy a moral dimension and increasingly the artist came to use poetic accompaniments for moral reasons.

Fortunately, within a decade of 1800 Turner wrote and spoke extensively about poetic painting. In doing so he cast much indirect light upon the thought processes that lay behind his development as a poetic artist at this time. A passage from one of his lecture manuscripts written around 1810 describes exactly how he had dealt with the problem of converting poetic metaphor directly into pictorial metaphor around 1798. After giving the definition of 'sentiment' quoted in the Introduction of this book, and warning that art cannot be produced to a formula, he went on to discuss further matters. It was here that he wrote the sentence that prefaces this chapter, a statement which specifies what he clearly saw as the aspect of poetry of most importance to poetic painters. He warned aspiring artists not to assume automatically that

> . . . what ever sounds harmonious, Ideal beauties or connecting Metaphors are capable of receiving pictorial effects.[48]

In other words it was not sufficient merely to pictorialise passages of poetry or poetic images and metaphors. Direct translations can look unconvincing because they usually involve a negation of the real face of nature. Turner stated that 'to be certain of success' the expression of those poetic effects '. . . ought to be Pictorial'. He added:

> Poetic descriptions most full, most Incidental [i.e. full of incident] and [which] display the greatest richness of voice are often the least pictorial [i.e. least capable of receiving convincing visual realisation] and hence *hasty* practise (or choice) to use no harsher term, is lead astray . . . the most elegant, most interesting as to character, pleasing as to introductory allusions in Poetry often fail in [pictorial] representation and the appropriate extreme of truth.[49]

His emphasis of the word 'hasty' pinpoints where he saw the problem. (Quite obviously, *unhasty* practise or choice could make elegant, interesting, characterful and pleasing allusions 'capable of receiving pictorial effects', as his work demonstrates.) He went on to illustrate the pitfalls of '*hasty* practise', discussing the passage and succeeding lines from Thomson's *Seasons* which he had quoted in 1798 in connection with *Norham Castle on the Tweed, Summer's morn* (fig. 22) and analysing the problems it presents for painters. (It was here too that he analysed the cancellation of Thomson's 'kindling azure' metaphor by being 'established' which we discussed in the Introduction above).

The difficulty as he saw it was that whereas a painter might easily depict the 'rocks, and hills, and towers, and wandering streams / High-gleaming from afar' of the following part of Thomson's poem, one could only do so at the expense of 'evading the superior elegance and [poetic] truth of the foregoing lines', i.e. the passage concerning 'the powerful King of Day / Rejoicing in the East' etc. Turner was undoubtedly aware that this latter kind of imagery is capable of representation but not in any naturalistic manner. In order to do so one would have to employ a very overt kind of visual metaphor, of the type used by, say, Guido Reni or Nicolas Poussin, perhaps by showing the sun as a King sitting in a chariot being pulled into the sky. Although in 1829 (fig. 177) Turner would depict dawn in a very similar way by representing the horses of Apollo rising into the sky next to a rising sun in his painting *Ulysses deriding Polyphemus* (a device he probably derived from Poussin), he rejected that kind of metaphor in 1810. For whilst he aspired towards the creation of a poetic landscape painting, even by 1810 he felt a still greater need to master the real appearances of nature; as long as visual metaphor did not conflict with such a desire there was no problem. It did mean, though, that he was wary of giving any blatantly allegorical or emblematic slant to painting through the use of overt metaphors or fixed symbols at this time. By definition, then, if an artist aimed to match the 'elegance and truth' of poetic allusion, as did Turner, he would have to do so by indirect methods and subtle associative means that would not efface the seemingly truthful appearances of things. Unlike Guido Reni and Nicolas Poussin, Turner wanted to avoid hybrids of the sort that would have resulted had he literally attempted to pictorialise Thomson's 'King of Day'. From his discussion of the problem we can deduce that Turner had either tried to realise Thomson's metaphor in 1798 and been dissatisfied with the results, or had thought extensively about how to do so before deciding not to, and instead let the poetry in the catalogue bring about the required associations of regal stateliness, with a pall of blue smoke symbolising the adjacent 'kindling azure' metaphor.

There can be no doubt that Turner felt that the metaphors of the sister arts could and did benefit each other. In another passage found in the lecture notes made around 1810 he addressed himself to this relationship, whilst also expressing his feeling that the two arts stemmed from the same imaginative source:

> Painting and Poetry flowing from the same fount mutually by vision, constantly comparing Poetic allusions by natural forms in one and applying forms found in Nature to the other, meandering into streams by application which reciprocally improve, reflect and heighten each others beauties like the mirrors but not the inversion of conveyors of form, generally or abstractly . . .[50]

And immediately below, Turner wrote an alternative ending to this passage:

> . . . meandering into streams by application . . . that reflect and refract each others beauties with reciprocity of splendorous allusion.

These lines and their variant ending tell us much about Turner the painter-poet. From the sentence 'comparing Poetic allusions by natural forms in one' we can see he felt that painting could create allusions comparable to those found in poetry out of the associative qualities of natural forms, whilst by 'applying forms found in nature to the other' he meant that poetry could also derive much of its metaphorical imagery from natural forms and experiences. Trees and objects that resemble other objects, effects of light, meteorological forces, animal and human actions, all provide the basis of metaphor in both arts. Additionally, each art can take those means of transference directly from the other. Turner was well aware that allegorical painting often drew its imagery from iconic poetry, just as iconic poetry had itself frequently appropriated its imagery from the allegorical paintings of artists like Reni and Poussin,[51] or from codebooks of symbolic imagery like Cesare Ripa's *Iconologia*. And Turner also believed it was theoretically possible for the metaphors of each art to 'reciprocally improve, reflect and heighten each others beauties' through imaginative intensification, much as mirrors can increase the intensity of perception, although implausibly he stressed at the end of the above quotation that they might do this without 'inversion', as true mirrors do. Clearly, from the significant addition of the word 'refract' in the variant ending – '... reflect and refract each others beauties with reciprocity of splendorous allusion' – he thought that this imaginative intensification might be brought about through indirect means, for to 'refract' is to deflect from direct communication. Moreover, the image of mirrors is in itself significant, for it indicates that Turner was aware of a common neoplatonic metaphor whereby mirrors are the means of apprehending another, more elevated level of reality. It is a subject we shall return to.

The years between 1798–1800 saw far more than the public emergence of a great talent. They saw the evolution of a truly poetic painter, one who thereafter might use poetry to specify the content of his pictures or might force us to pursue that content through verbal allusion, yet who might also use visual association to extend pictorial meaning into areas of thought and feeling normally beyond the scope of images. And the Welsh castle pictures of 1800 which brought that process to maturity demonstrate another important reason for resorting to the association of ideas in this way. It derives from Turner's belief that history, poetry and painting were not only interconnected but should ultimately be stated on the broadest moral scale.

This emerges from the same letter to John Britton of 1811 in which the artist reproves the antiquarian for attempting to 'establish' his allusion in *Pope's Villa at Twickenham*. Not only did Turner plead for reticence but he also took Britton to task on another matter:

Why say the Poet and Prophet are not often united? – for if they are not they ought to be.

Turner's work, and equation of 'the sister arts', make it clear that it was necessary for him to unite painting and prophecy. This is another reason why poetry was crucial to him and why he was attracted to poems voicing strong prophetic sentiments. If those sentiments found expression in the type of verse which articulates marked responses to the natural world – like Thomson's *Seasons* and *Liberty*, or Byron's *Childe Harold* – so much the better. Naturally this outlook led to an affinity with Augustan prophetic moralists like Thomson, Gray and Blair, not surprisingly since they had contributed largely towards his poetic views in the first place. At a social level Turner readily identified with the notions of duty and self-sacrifice espoused by such poets, especially Thomson, and like them he too warned of the related dangers to society of vanity, selfishness and the cultivation of luxury. We encounter Turner addressing such prophetic themes throughout his career in his many pictures of Carthage, Rome and Venice, all great maritime empires like Britain. These themes amplifying the need for self-denial, duty towards others and the desire for social harmony were not empty ones for Turner, mere salutary gestures to conventional wisdom. He continued to address them for the whole of his life because he felt that such moral concerns were increasingly relevant and needed to be stressed as the Industrial Revolution brought greater materialism, more dramatic contrasts of wealth and poverty, and a growing class-divisiveness, frustration and anger. Evidently he was also driven to do so because he felt that painting, like poetry, had a prophetic role to play. As well as commenting upon the present he was warning of a possible future with his lessons drawn from the past. He saw this as integral to the social role of the artist, and usefully it allowed him to combine moral purpose with imaginative vision. Just as we cannot ignore Turner the poetic-painter if we are to make full sense of the artist, so too we cannot safely ignore Turner the moralist, if for no other reason than because Turner's moral sentiments evidently dictated the forms, tonalities and colours of many of his landscapes, as with the structures and lighting of the two Welsh castle pictures of 1800. And the association of ideas and responses played an integral part in the artist's activities both as a poetic painter and as a moral seer. Examples of this interchange will be examined throughout the course of this book. But having set the context from which Turner the poet-painter emerged, and suggested why and how he did so, now we need to examine those associative processes in more systematic detail, before going on to trace some of their related artistic foundations, and finally see how ultimately they served and stemmed from Turner's profound idealism.

TWO

# Between Appearances

Reason respects the differences, and imagination
the similitudes of things.

*Shelley*

ON the most basic level Turner's extreme propensity for association can be encountered in
the artist's frequently fixed connections of places with objects, events or people he had
encountered there. For instance, as Ruskin noted, whenever Turner portrayed Scarborough[1] he painted a starfish lying on the beach; he had once noticed such a creature in
that location and thereafter linked it with the town. Similarly, in his four watercolour
drawings of Richmond, Yorkshire, he introduced a girl with a dog or dogs in the
foreground,[2] while in three of his four watercolour views of Winchelsea, Sussex,[3] he
included soldiers he had probably seen in the neighbourhood around 1806–7. One of these
military scenes (fig. 65) was not drawn until some twenty years later. Similarly, because the
artist visited the major south coast naval ports in 1811 and 1813 during the Napoleonic
Wars, he represented those towns in wartime thereafter, although the war ended in 1815.[4]
Most of his Oxford street scenes included builders at work, the last of them dating from
about forty-four years after the first.[5] This fixity of association suggests that Turner may
have associated the physical act of building with the larger theme of the construction of
knowledge to which the university town was principally dedicated. Associations of place
seem never to have left him either.[6] In his very first picture of Windsor Castle, made for
engraving in *The Pocket Magazine* in 1795, Turner aligned the flag on St George's Chapel in
the distance with a pennant flying from the mast of a Thames barge in the foreground.[7]
Thirty-two or so years later he repeated this alignment in a watercolour made for the
'Picturesque Views in England and Wales' series.[8]

Naturally, Turner used overt suggestion to evoke the associations of the places he
depicted. The simplest way to do this was by the time-honoured device of placing
associative objects across the foreground of a picture. In any case Turner had a penchant for
dropping pictorial 'litter',[9] so this method clearly held double appeal for him. A good
example occurs in *Chatham* (fig. 33), made around 1830 for engraving in the 'England and
Wales' series. Strewn across the left foreground are bundles of washing, military kitbags,

**33** W. Miller after J. M. W. Turner, *Chatham*, engraving, 1832.

**34** W. B. Cooke after J. M. W. Turner, *Bridport, Dorsetshire*, engraving, 1820.

bedrolls, and a drum and sword. Clearly they belong to the washerwoman and marine seen chatting on the right but they allude also to the military and civilian support industries particular to Chatham itself.

A more inventive example of this spread of associative material across the foreground of a picture to express the economic and social reality of place is encountered in Turner's view of *Bridport, Dorsetshire* (fig. 34), made around 1813 for engraving in the 'Southern Coast' series. The original watercolour has faded badly and the image can now be seen better through the engraving. Turner visited Bridport and its adjacent coastline on a West Country tour in 1811. As the town itself stands about a mile inland from the coast, and Turner was creating the work for a series of views of coastal subjects, he got as near to the town as he could by showing the view at West Bay looking towards East Cliff and the chain of cliffs stretching away towards the Chesil Bank. Turner was well aware that the major industry of Bridport was the manufacture of rope, which was in great demand during the Napoleonic Wars.[10] The proximity of the town to Plymouth Dock (re-named Devonport in 1824) and Portsmouth, two of the three major naval bases of the time (the other one being Chatham), plus its easy access to both of them by sea, made it the major supplier of rope to the Royal Navy. Areas of the town were designed around the manufacturing process, with long alley-ways or rope-walks laid out to facilitate the twining of the cord.

Turner literally underlines what little can be seen of the place with its principal product. On the beach a group of men strain to warp (or tow) a brig towards the shore. We therefore look at Bridport, or what Turner represented as Bridport, across the very object that formed the economic basis of its existence.

As well as employing objects for their associative and pictorial value in this way, Turner also liked to employ the similarities that forms enjoy to heighten the structural unity and meaning of his works. When this occurs for purely pictorial purposes we might characterise it as visual simile; where Turner employs it to further meaning it might be classed as visual metaphor.

VISUAL SIMILE

Turner could use the association of lines or shapes to enhance pictures in their own right. Such associations can be seen in an extraordinary number of works and they are, indeed, Turner's most common means of linkage. A good representative example, and one in which the trait has been well observed, is *Aske Hall* (fig. 35), another of the 'Richmondshire' designs made around 1817. Writing of the engraving in 1891, Mrs Alfred Hunt commented:

> The sheep, all except one on the extreme right, are admirable. How plainly they enjoy their rest, panting even in the shade! We may note the skill with which another

**35** J. Scott after J. M. W. Turner, *Aske Hall*, engraving, 1821.

represented as cropping the herbage at the side of the road is linked in composition with the curve of the little bridge at the bottom of it, and how the two curved things are somewhat provided with something which is somehow related to them in the horse bending its neck to the ground on the other side. There are relations of this sort all over the design, unsought for and unlaboured by the artist, to whom they were the natural way of telling his story when once he had seized on it as a pictorial whole. Every touch, or group of touches, with or without his conscious choice, serve its purposes as well for the likeness of the fact, as for the expression of his feelings with respect to it, for there is everywhere a link or a contrast – everywhere something which his artistic feeling has dictated to soften, accentuate or ennoble.[11]

If such formal and rhythmic connections were not so frequently encountered throughout Turner's oeuvre, one might be inclined to agree with Mrs Hunt that such relations were 'unsought for', but their very proliferation must discount that view. If we look closely at this design we can see how carefully Turner developed them. The repetition of the shape of the hill by the bridge in front of it, the similar repetition of the line of the hill beyond the horse by the curve of the animal's neck, the repetition of the sudden convolution in the overhanging branch of the ash-tree by the shape of the head of the sheep lined up directly beneath it – all these and many more instances must strongly alert us to Turner's conscious association of

**36** *Bay of Naples (Vesuvius in repose), c.*1817,
watercolour on paper, 18.1 × 28.6 cm, Private Collection, UK.

lines and forms, both to reinforce pictorial unity and intensify our experience of the landscape. Another typical example of this use of similitude occurs in a watercolour (fig. 36) made around 1817 of the *Bay of Naples (Vesuvius in repose)*. Here the diagonals of the twin peaks of the distant volcano are repeated by the diagonal lines of the various lateen-rigged feluccas in the foreground. The enforced similitude serves to stress the configuration of the volcano and thus enhance our comprehension of the physical and spatial qualities of the terrain and view.


VISUAL METAPHOR

We need only cite one example of this device here, as others will be found throughout this book. In *The Lake of Geneva with the Dent d'Oche, from Lausanne; a funeral* (fig. 37), a colour-study dating from 1841, a similar conjunction to that witnessed in *Bay of Naples* appears to point to something beyond what we see, and it can therefore be termed a visual metaphor. The watercolour was created in a sketchbook[12] and is one of several depicting the rays of the setting sun falling upon the Dent d'Oche across the lake. They all seem to show the view from the same spot and the artist has in each case therefore invented his foreground

**37** *The Lake of Geneva with the Dent d'Oche, from Lausanne: a funeral,* 1841, watercolour on paper, 23.5 × 33.4 cm, Clore Gallery for the Turner Collection, London (T.B. CCCXXXIV–2).

topography and activity. In one of the versions we see labourers tending vines amid a haze of golden colour,[13] whilst in another Turner introduces a cemetery surrounded by cypress trees into the foreground.[14] In the work illustrated, though, the artist created the objects and activity so as to enforce a connection with the rhythm created by the shadows falling across the peaks of the distant mountain as it catches the last of the sunlight. Immediately below the mountain, on this side of the lake, cypresses establish a similar but somewhat more staccato rhythmic effect, and this is picked up and repeated by the funeral procession moving up the hill on the right. Although it has aptly been written of this group of drawings that, when viewing them 'the mind wanders, entirely free of material trammelings, in a landscape immense and immutable',[15] evidently Turner's mind did not wander when he made this particular study: obviously he saw a parallel between the final movement of daylight across a mountain-top and the ultimate progression of man.

### VISUAL PUN

In the above example we can detect Turner using a play upon the similarity of visible forms to advance meaning. With a number of works the artist also touched upon the similarity of visible to imagined forms to further his expressive purposes. This is through what we can term visual pun, for if a linguistic pun is a form of allusion which plays upon the similarity of words to make one word do the job of two, a visual pun does exactly the same thing with images. Visual pun clearly appealed to Turner because of his pronounced taste for verbal puns, a predilection that sometimes even led him to entitle pictures so that they punned upon the titles of works by other artists. Turner created visual puns by playing upon the power of shapes to suggest things unseen or even unseeable. Ruskin noticed this kind of pun – without characterising it as a pun – in the *Liber Studiorum* mezzotint of *Jason* (fig. 38), published in 1807. Turner based this engraving on an oil-painting (B.J. 19) dating from 1801–2 and when he created the print he took the opportunity to make the image more sophisticated. The subject is taken from Apollonius Rhodius's *Argonautics*[16] and shows Jason approaching the cave of the dragon that guarded the Golden Fleece, amid a desolate landscape strewn with shattered trees and skeletal remains, all of which inspire associations of death. Yet Turner does not depict the Fleece, nor does he show much of its dragon guardian. Ruskin marvelled at this psychological masterstroke of forcing our imagination to conjure up the *whole* beast by simply showing part of it, but he also observed that

> The painter is not satisfied even with all the suggestiveness thus obtained, but to make sure of us, and force us, whether we will or not, to walk his way, and not ours, the trunks of the trees on the right are all cloven into yawning and writhing heads and bodies, and alive with dragon energy all about us; note especially the nearest with its gaping jaws

**38** *Jason*, mezzotint engraving, published 1807 in Part I of the *Liber Studiorum*. The work was drawn and etched by Turner himself.

and claw-like branch at the seeming shoulder . . . the painter addresses thereby that morbid and fearful condition of mind which he has endeavoured to excite in the spectator, and which in reality would have seen in every trunk and bough, as it penetrates into the deeper thicket, the object of its terror.[17]

Indeed, all over the work the divided tree trunks and boughs (and even the gigantic overhanging strata of rock) are made to resemble a shape not unlike that of the jaws and head of a crocodile. It is most clearly seen in the form of the tree-trunk over which Jason climbs, and significantly this wooden mass has a knot just where we might expect to see an eye on such a creature. That Turner did intend the shapes to suggest this meaning seems evident from his deliberately reticent portrayal of the monster itself and the sheer frequency of the crocodile-like form throughout the picture.

This kind of association also explains why Turner so often repeated bifurcated shapes across the foreground of *Simmer Lake, near Askrig* (fig. 39 and details, figs 40 and 41). The work is a watercolour made for engraving in the 'Richmondshire' series around 1817. The picture depicts the view looking south-westwards over Semer Water towards Raydale and Langstrothdale Chase. In the foreground is a large stone block around which stand or recline some cattle. One animal, to the immediate right of the rock, is particularly interesting, for Turner seems to stress its close visual similarity to traditional images of the Devil in a reclining position (fig. 40). Black in colour, its rear haunch is drawn up in a very un-bovine way and Turner emphasises its long tail and upward-pointing horns. The

**39** *Simmer Lake, near Askrig, c.*1817,
watercolour on paper, 28.7 × 41.2 cm, British Museum, London.

**40** *Simmer Lake, near Askrig* (detail).

appearance of such a diabolical looking creature at this position in the picture ought not to surprise us however, for as Mrs Alfred Hunt also observed in 1891:

> The large block of limestone in the foreground . . . is known as the Carlow Stone. There is a tradition that the devil attempted to fling it from the summit of Addleborough Hill – the high hill with the large cairn on the top of it, which rises on the eastern side of the lake, to Crag End on the western. He failed, however, to do this – was there ever a legend in which his endeavours did not fail? and it fell where it now lies. Those who doubt the truth of this may improve their faith by the sight of the marks of his fingers which can be seen to this day.[18]

As Turner made the picture for engraving in a work which might have discussed these legends, we can easily see how he may have learnt about them in the natural course of events. He was probably told the story by Thomas Dunham Whitaker who commissioned the picture, although Whitaker does not discuss the stone in the final text of his history. Knowing this, though, we can readily understand why Turner made the cow look so fiendish and also why he aligned from left to right across the foreground (fig. 41) the pointed shadows on a cowgirl's bonnet, the ears of a cow immediately to the right of her, the horns of the 'devilish' cow, the twin-pronged shape of a mooring post, the two prongs of a pitchfork carried by a rustic and the double-pronged shape of the top of a horse-collar. It would also explain why Turner makes 'Simmer Lake' so simmeringly hot. That the artist knew the legend of the Carlow Stone is proven by his careful depiction of the 'finger-marks' on the rock.

**41** *Simmer Lake, near Askrig,* (detail).

**42** *Battle Abbey*, 1810, watercolour on paper, 37.5 × 55.2 cm, Private Collection, UK.

An even more complex use of such allusive visual punning may be encountered in yet another picture of *Battle Abbey* where Turner also addressed the precise associations of the place. This version (fig. 42) was created around 1810, some five years before the *Battle Abbey, the spot where Harold fell* (fig. 5) previously discussed. Here the abbey is located in the distance. Before it we see boys throwing stones at an adder which is slithering up a declivity on the roadside towards one of two rabbit-burrows that are situated above it in a side-by-side placement not unlike that of a pair of eyes. The similarity to eyes is not coincidental since eyes have a strong connection with Battle and its abbey. No doubt Turner shared in the common belief that Harold Godwinson died at the Battle of Hastings as a result of having been struck in the eye by an arrow. The suggestion that the snake will enter one of the holes evokes the idea of an eye being pierced by something horrible with superb exactitude, and this interpretation is strengthened by the fact that it is the hole on *our* left that the snake is aimed at: it was thought that the King had received the arrow in *his* right eye.[19] The force of the allusion is increased by the traditional association of snakes with pain and evil, a connotation Turner was certainly aware of. To further the association, exactly midway between the snake and the boys Turner gives us a pair of adjacent tree

**43** *Scarborough Castle, boys crab fishing*, signed and dated 1809,
watercolour on paper, 28 × 39 cm, Wallace Collection, London.

**44** *Scarborough Town and Castle: Morning: Boys catching crabs*, R.A. 1811,
watercolour on paper, 68.7 × 101.6 cm, Private Collection, UK.

**45** *The Desert of Sinai, c.*1833, watercolour on paper, 14 × 20.2 cm, Private Collection, UK.

**46** E. Finden after J. M. W. Turner, *The Desert of Sinai*, engraving, 1835.

trunks. The flat round top of the trunk on our left exactly resembles the circles of the iris and the pupil of an eye. A piercing shape is also conjured up in the picture by the V-shaped boughs of an oak-sapling on the right which resembles an arrowhead. Turner's use of similar tree-forms in the later picture supports the likelihood that this is yet another pun. Here, only slightly less so than in the later picture – for clearly the lighting effects in this watercolour are *not* organised metaphorically – Turner creates a mood of disquiet appropriate to the subject.

In other pictures Turner alludes to actions. For instance, in two related watercolours, *Scarborough Castle, boys crab fishing* (fig. 43), dating from 1809, and *Scarborough Town and Castle : Morning : Boys catching crabs* (fig. 44) which was displayed at the Royal Academy in 1811, the latter parts of both titles tell us that Turner wanted us to look as carefully at the activity of the boys in the two works as we would at their surroundings. When we do we can immediately discern how Turner might use a shape for its inherent suggestiveness. In the first drawing one boy catches the crabs whilst the other prepares to throw his hoop around them. In the second drawing the hoop formally encircles the crabs, thus 'catching' them. This is no coincidence of placement but a cleverly arranged piece of design which allows simple forms to become very inventive visual metaphors for the act of enclosure by which things are trapped.

Another ingenious use of form to further associative meaning can be seen in *The Desert of Sinai*. The watercolour (fig. 45) dates from about 1833, having been made from a sketch by a Major Felix, and it was engraved for a set of landscape illustrations of the Bible published between 1834–6. Above the plain of Rephidim we see the towering mass of Mount Sinai. In the foreground is the Stone of Moses. According to the letterpress issued with the engraving this shows the red-granite rock 'Moses is traditionally said to have struck, when the waters miraculously gushed forth, and supplied the thirsty and fainting Israelites'.[20] In the watercolour Turner therefore shows a bolt of lightning striking through a rainless sunny sky. Its trajectory is aimed towards the rock, and apparently terminates at it, even though it is taking place far beyond. In the engraving (fig. 46) Turner suppresses the lightning altogether but heightens the tonality of the reflective right-hand edge of the rock so that it assumes a brilliant sheen not unreminiscent of the downward flow of water. (The similarity between the intrinsic linework of an engraving and the flow lines of water is exploited to enhance this effect.) Turner also lightens the tones immediately around the rock, thereby suggesting the fine spray that is given off by falling water. The downward plane of that facet of the rock means that in reality it could not reflect light coming from the top right in such a manner and we may be certain that Turner, with his knowledge of both optics and geology, would have been aware of that fact.

Perhaps one of Turner's most inventive plays on the similarity of forms occurs in a gouache of *Yarmouth Sands* (fig. 47) which was probably made around 1827 for engraving in a

**47**  *Yarmouth Sands*, *c.*1827, watercolour and body-colour on blue paper,
18.5 × 24.5 cm, Fitzwilliam Museum, Cambridge.

series of prints to be entitled 'Picturesque Views on the East Coast of England' that was
never realised. It shows the view over the wide beach at Yarmouth, with Gorleston on the
right and Gorleston pier to the left of centre. The scene is dominated by the 144-foot high
Nelson Monument. Surmounted by a statue of Britannia, this was erected in 1817 both as a
memorial to the great naval hero and as a triumphal column to celebrate his victory at
Trafalgar on 21 October 1805. In front of it we see a group of Tars and their women playing
with model boats. Such a staffage clearly exemplifies the associations of the monument and
also the place, which was the home port of the North Sea fleet at the time. Yet in one
important respect the disposition of the models on the ground seems rather curious.

    Turner has placed them in two parallel lines, a distribution that clearly refers to the
traditional method of naval warfare whereby opposing fleets would sail alongside one
another to deliver massive broadsides. A ship would rarely sink its opponent by this method

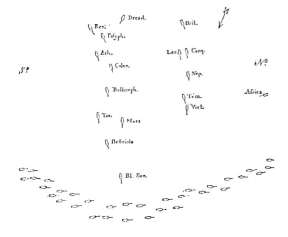

**48** Plan printed opposite page 49 in Volume IV of William James's *The Naval History of Great Britain*, published in 1826, showing the line of battle employed by Nelson at the Battle of Trafalgar.

of attack but could damage it (by shooting away sails, masts and rigging) to a point where it was incapable of manoeuvre and was forced to strike its colours.

At Trafalgar however, Nelson entirely rejected the parallel course, line-ahead tactic. Instead, he introduced his famous 'Nelson Touch', the innovation of sailing his (somewhat outnumbered) force in two columns at right angles to the combined fleets of France and Spain, thereby breaking their line into three[21] (fig. 48). The two columns were led by Nelson, on board *Victory*, whose formation aimed at the enemy's centre, and Admiral Collingwood aboard *Royal Sovereign*, whose group engaged the rear. It was a masterstroke, for it meant that the van of the enemy line ahead of the first of the two British divisions had to sail some distance before it was able to come about and re-enter the fray. The tactic bought Nelson crucial time with which to deal with the main part of the opposition.

All of this *must* have been known to Turner through his considerable researches for two earlier depictions of Trafalgar, one dating from 1805–6 which he exhibited within a year of the engagement (B.J. 58) and the other from 1823–4 (fig. 76). Yet knowing this, why has he shown us model ships drawn up in parallel alignment in front of a monument commemorating Trafalgar, and thus represented an order of battle specifically rejected by Nelson on that occasion?[22]

**49** *Yarmouth Sands* (detail).

The answer surely lies with the arrangement of figures alongside them. Turner alludes to the 'Nelson Touch' by containing his groups of people within two clearly defined triangles which are directed at right angles towards the double row of models. Indeed, an urgent sense of forward motion is imparted to both triangles by the pointing gestures of sailors, and the suggestion of propulsion is reinforced in the nearer group (fig. 49) by the straight lines of the shanks of an anchor upon which two of them are seated. The convergent lines lead the eye to the skirts of two women placed at the front of the group. These skirts are sharply pointed and look exactly like arrowheads, a resemblance Turner heightens by marking them with lines exactly like the notches commonly found on arrowheads. The two overall wedge-shapes within which the sailors and women are situated therefore thrust at the models in exactly the same direction in which Nelson's and Collingwood's columns had struck at the Combined Fleets. Turner's intimate knowledge of the tactics employed at Trafalgar is further demonstrated by the fact that the farthest triangle actually touches the line of models: Collingwood's lee division had engaged the enemy rear before Nelson reached its centre, an event that drew from the Commander the famous comment 'see how that noble fellow Collingwood takes his ship into action. How I envy him.' It is highly likely that Turner had either long known of the 'Nelson Touch' or was reminded of it by the diagram reproduced here as illustration 48. This comes from a book published in 1826 which severely criticised Turner's 1823–4 painting of *The Battle of Trafalgar* (these criticisms are reproduced on page 128) and the passage in question invites other painters from amongst its readers to use this diagram to improve upon Turner's treatment of the battle of Trafalgar in their own versions of the subject.

Certainly Turner shows us two columns of ships, the traditional lines of battle: if he had merely depicted one we would not know that he was referring to a battle *at all*, and how else was he to establish the norm from which Nelson departed? But here they are seen to represent the old order of naval procedure and the Combined Fleets, whilst the 'triangles' stand for Nelson's two columns at Trafalgar. Once again Turner brilliantly evokes the spirit of place, using the associative power of forms to allude to the supreme inspiration of the man whose victory and tragic loss lies behind the Yarmouth monument depicted.

The need to express *genius loci* inspired Turner's own genius for finding ever more imaginative ways of pictorialising it. A picture in which once again he inventively plays upon the similarity of forms, as well as other pictorial elements to express *genius loci*, is a major late oil painting entitled *Campo Santo, Venice* (fig. 50) which was exhibited at the R.A. in 1842. It shows the view immediately to the north of the city, which can be seen on the left. The island cemetery of Venice, the Isola San Michele, lies in the distance on the right. Beyond it is Murano, whilst across the horizon stretch the foothills of the Cadore. The cemetery is still very much in use – perhaps the most famous recent interment there was of Igor Stravinsky in 1971 – and to this day the stretch of water Turner depicts is called the

**50** *Campo Santo, Venice*, R.A. 1842, oil on canvas, 62.2 × 92.7 cm, Toledo Museum of Art, Toledo, Ohio.

Laguna Morta. Literally translated, 'Campo Santo' means consecrated ground; colloquially it signifies churchyard or cemetery. Turner's title specifies that the real subject is 'Cemetery, Venice'.

The picture is dominated by a twin-sail boat which glides across the water, its wing-shaped lateen sails casting long reflections on the profoundly calm water. Identically shaped sails appear in only four other pictures by Turner[23] and it is significant that he has greatly elongated them here, particularly when we see their duality repeated by two approaching columns of cirrus cloud, two dark lines of reflection cast by gondolas in the centre foreground, and two lines of light reflections issuing from the gondolas to the left and right.

Given the religious associations of the scene it is not difficult to perceive why the sails have been elongated and emphasised. Turner was stressing their resemblance to forms commonly encountered in religious art, namely the wings of angels. As we have already observed with *The Mew Stone* (fig. 7), the painter was not averse to the seeing of such forms in one of his pictures, whilst in a painting entitled *Returning from the Ball (St Martha)* exhibited at the R.A. four years after *Campo Santo*, he equated identical sail-shapes with religion in Venice. The most striking pictorial element of *Returning from the Ball* (fig. 51) is the comparison Turner creates between the twin sails of a felucca and the twin towers of a church.[24] The fact that this play upon similar dual forms is the central dramatic statement of *Returning from the Ball* suggests that the conjunction was intended to express meaning as well as draw a visual comparison. Moreover, in the same 1846 Exhibition at which *Returning from the Ball* was displayed, Turner unequivocally depicted celestial forms in a major painting entitled *The Angel Standing in the Sun* (B.J. 425), the climactic work of a series of pictures in which he included angels. So it does not seem fanciful to suppose that four years before exhibiting *The Angel Standing in the Sun* and *Returning from the Ball (St Martha)* Turner used angelic shapes in a painting showing the largest Venetian threshold to an afterlife. The horizontal alignment of the isle of the dead and the twin-sailed boat, with another similar vessel beyond, the soft light of impending nightfall, the lyricism of colour which is dominated by a range of sky blues that carry their own associations of 'the azure of heaven',[25] and the subtle hinting at celestial forms, all contribute to the unifying theme of the painting, the ineffable serenity of death.

In *Campo Santo, Venice* we encounter another of Turner's most common forms of association, the connection between timing and the content of a picture. Indeed, light, the weather upon which it depends, and even time itself, were all to be explored by Turner for metaphorical ends. Here too he relied upon our making flights of the imagination.

**51** *Returning from the Ball (St. Martha)*, R.A. 1846, oil on canvas, 61 × 91.4 cm, Oakpict Inc.

# THREE

# Decorum

As to metaphorical expression, that is a great excell-
ence in style, when used with propriety, for it gives
you two ideas for one.

*Dr Johnson*

. . . all metaphor is poetry.

*G. K. Chesterton*

TURNER is justly celebrated as a painter of light. Yet what is not so often appreciated today is how extensively the artist employed light to advance meaning. That he should have done so is clearly an indication of his commitment to the doctrine of *ut pictura poesis*.

In the aesthetic literature known to Turner, the term decorum stood not only for propriety but also for a central unity of action to which all the constituent elements such as the figures, their actions and gestures, physiognomy or age, their surrounds and even the effects of light and colour, should contribute. Advice to this effect was frequently offered in the books known to Turner. For example, Dryden reminded his readers that

> . . . the *Painter* is to take care that nothing enter into [his picture] which is not proper, or convenient to the subject . . . [All] must be of use to carry on the Main Design.[1]

And Roger de Piles wrote in *The Principles of Painting* that

> . . . objects ought not to be brought into a picture inconsiderately and without contributing to the expression and character of a subject.[2]

Naturally, given their context, such stresses usually focused upon the appropriateness of the figures and what they were doing in a picture, but there was a body of discussion that equally concerned itself with the need for dramatic decorum in a landscape-surround and its lighting. Elsewhere, in discussing the criteria for choosing subject-matter, de Piles states that

> . . . light and shade are the visible effects of nature, as well as the outlines of an human body, the attitudes, the folds of draperies, or anything else that comes into composition; all these require choice, and therefore light does the same.[3]

He also employs a suitable metaphor to underline this requirement, declaring that 'In a picture there ought to be an unity of subject for the eyes of the understanding'.[4]

A more forceful and elaborate declaration of the need for a unity of action and light, and a resulting correspondence between colour and the emotional level of a work, also emerges in André Félibien's *Seven Conferences held in the King of France's Cabinet of Paintings*. Although Turner first referred to it in a lecture manuscript dating from about 1810 (but revised around 1816), he very likely read it well before then, most probably in the late 1790s when his interest in the paintings of Nicolas Poussin was particularly marked.[5] Félibien's *Conferences* devote considerable space to Poussin's awareness of the need to impart dramatic unity and decorum in the matching of light to content in his works. For instance, on the very first page of the first conference Félibien states:

> Mr. Poussin being persuaded that the Beauty of a Picture consists in making every thing that enters into the Composition have a particular Mark of what the Work represents in general, made that his principal study. And in all his Productions, the Expression of his Subject is so generally diffused, that there appears throughout an Air of Joy or Sorrow, Anger or Sweetness according to the Nature of his Story.

Félibien then goes on to elucidate at great length Poussin's concept of a fixity of relationship between colours and the underlying central mood of a picture, 'modes' of colour which Poussin held to be equivalent to the ancient Greek modes in music. In 1810 Turner rejected such a fixity, probably because invariably he distrusted the codification of imaginative vehicles, whether they be in colour or form. But he did not in any way dispute the idea that light and colour could act as correlatives for the central emotional response of a picture. On the contrary, in 1810 Turner praised just such a correlative in one of Poussin's works, the *Deluge* of 1660–4, a picture he had seen in Paris in 1802. Turner particularly appreciated how the artist had subordinated the entire range of colour in the painting to produce an 'awfully appropriate' effect of muddiness, thus suggesting 'the residue of Earthy matter' to be deposited by the deluge. And whilst he found Poussin's painting 'deficient in every requisite of line', severely criticising its observation of events and natural phenomena, nonetheless he found its colour justly 'fitted to every imaginative conjecture of such an event'. In a fine metaphor he even ended by stating that the sun in the picture 'is not allowed to shed one ray but tears'.[6]

Elsewhere, in the sixth conference, Félibien also notes that in connection with Poussin's *The Israelites gathering the Manna*,[7] a participant in the conference, Charles Le Brun, drew attention to the figures in the picture all appearing weak whilst

> Even the Light of the Air appears pale and weak, which imprints a kind of Sadness on the Figures. And altho' the Landskip be disposed in a very elegant Manner, and fill'd with admirable Figures, the sight cannot find that Pleasure it desires, and which it commonly feels in other Pictures, designed only to represent a fine Country.[8]

In the seventh conference Sébastien Bourdon also recognised the 'dusty and melancholy Light' in *The Israelites gathering the Manna* and how in Poussin's *Christ healing the blind men*[9] Poussin

> has intended to represent a Morning, because it is likely our Saviour chose that Time as the most fit, and that wherein Objects appear with the best Advantage, that the Men might have the greater Pleasure when their Eyes were opened, and that the Miracles might be more Manifest and Evident.[10]

As Turner's response to *The Deluge* makes clear, by 1802 he had grasped how Poussin had used light and colour metaphorically,[11] and it is not difficult to see from where he might have derived that awareness. And because Poussin was the historical landscapist whose work was most associated with the idea of dramatic decorum, it seems likely that Turner derived his own strong awareness of such a need as regards light, colour and content from Félibien's elaboration of it in Poussin's work. This awareness must have been reinforced by the extensive discussions of decorum in many other theoretical and practical works in his library, or in the late 1790s by his viewing of pictures by Claude and Richard Wilson, and even by his knowledge of how poets, especially Thomson, employed associative matchings in similar ways.

Turner employed the term 'historical colour' to denote the associative use of colour because of the way that colour was frequently employed in history pictures to further meaning. He did so in conjunction with works by Poussin, Titian and others. But although the artist accepted this direction of colour towards the advancement of sentiment, he was reluctant to deploy a specific colour symbolism himself in any widespread way. There were two basic reasons for this: he felt colour is dependent upon the more fundamental values of light itself; and it is limited in the associations it can introduce.[12] He abhorred the notion of codified colour-symbolism, probably for the same reason he distrusted codified visual metaphors – they were too imaginatively limiting. However, he could use some colours for their associations – blood-red, for instance, and in *Campo Santo, Venice* (fig. 50) azure – and he certainly used the two neutrals black and white in this way. He could also quite happily employ light and darkness or the time of day in order to express things metaphorically. Naturally the sun and moon were themselves the most obvious objects with which to construct such associative meanings.

## LIGHT

Turner's observance of decorum in his deployment of light effects to advance meaning is so widespread that it disproves the notion that he was interested in light *above* all else: light for him was part of a dramatic unity and often derived from the requirements of this unity,

**52** *Caligula's Palace and Bridge*, R.A. 1831,
oil on canvas, 137 × 246.5 cm, Clore Gallery for the Turner Collection, London.

brilliantly observed though that light may be. A picture which demonstrates this is *Caligula's Palace and Bridge* (figs 52, 53) exhibited at the R.A. in 1831. Like *Borthwick Castle* (fig. 1) the work also makes clear how apparently unimportant figures can actually act as a key to unlocking the larger significance of a picture. *Caligula's Palace and Bridge* shows the 'bridge' built by the Roman Emperor across the Bay of Baia from Pozzuoli to Baia, supposedly to confound a prophecy made by the astrologer Thrasyllus that Caligula had no more chance of becoming Emperor than he had of riding a horse dryshod across the bay. According to one of Turner's probable literary sources of information regarding the structure, the 'bridge' consisted of a

> Mole of twenty-five arches, built into the sea to protect vessels from tempests and for commercial purposes . . . at the extremity of the Mole began the bridge of [the] mad emperor . . . it extended to Baiae being 3600 feet in a straight line. The difficulty of building towards the middle where the sea was too deep, caused [Caligula] to unite a prodigious number of boats, which were fixed by anchors and fastened together by chains. The road was paved and covered with sand, and had parapets on each side . . .[13]

The Emperor then proceeded over the 'bridge' in various guises for three days.

**53** *Caligula's Palace and Bridge* (detail).

Instead of depicting a bridge of boats, however, Turner elaborates the crossing into a row of mighty palaces, state and religious buildings, most of which are in ruins. As Turner moralised in a fragment from 'The Fallacies of Hope' with which he accompanied the title of the picture in the R.A. catalogue:

> What now remains of all the mighty bridge
> Which made the Lacrine lake an inner pool,
> Caligula, but mighty fragments left,
> Monuments of doubt and ruined hopes
> Yet gleaming in the Morning's ray, that tell
> How Baia's shore was loved in times gone by?

The theme of the picture is again twofold. On the one hand Turner ironically questions the fate of the grandiose aspirations of Caligula which have ended in ruin and decay. Against this he equates another sentiment through the use of the foreground figures and animals. At the lower right are a pair of lovers seated closely together, the man with his arm around the woman (fig. 53). They are looking intently at a group of household objects such as some washing and food baskets, a teapot and a child's hoop, a clear allusion to the probable outcome of their union. The association is reinforced nearby, where later Turner added some children and a nanny-goat suckling its kid.[14] The prominent, tonally spotlit and downstage placement of the lovers furthers the statement made in the two final lines of verse, that the Bay of Baia was a place much given to the pursuit of love in ancient times. Yet equally through their prominence they seem to personify a larger response which Turner evidently regarded as being fundamentally opposed to the shallow motives that gave rise to the mouldering structure beyond them. The moral seems clear: all is vanity and only love can offer mankind a means of transcending material values to create anything of permanence. And this statement of the eternal regenerative power of love is surely why in a scene of ruin Turner does not depict Caligula's palace and bridge under conditions of light symbolically appropriate to a *vanitas* theme (like a sunset), but instead gives us dawn, to symbolise the association of the Bay of Baia with love, past and present.

In another late masterpiece the time of day was dictated by the subject. When we look at the work within its historical context and the development of Turnerian metaphor, the presence of the moon also bears a metaphorical connotation.

The picture in question is *Peace – Burial at Sea* (fig. 54), exhibited at the R.A. in 1842. The title was accompanied in the catalogue by more verses from 'The Fallacies of Hope':

> The midnight torch gleamed o'er the steamer's side
> And Merit's corse was yielded to the tide.

The work is the pendant to a painting depicting Napoleon in exile, *War. The Exile and the Rock Limpet* (fig. 56), and it was Turner's homage to the memory of Sir David Wilkie. Turner had known Wilkie since the early 1800s (Wilkie was elected an Academician in 1813) and indeed, around 1806–9 he had painted a number of genre scenes in the manner adopted by Wilkie. Turner and Wilkie had not been particularly close over the years but Wilkie's death brought home to Turner, yet again, the inevitability of his own death, for at least since 1825 he had been acutely conscious of mortality following the demise of his closest friend, Walter Fawkes, only six years his senior. Turner's awareness of death had also been greatly heightened by the passing of others in following years, most notably the death of his father in 1829 and of Lord Egremont in 1837.

Turner therefore resolved to pay Wilkie suitable tribute. Wilkie had died far away from home, aboard the steamship *Oriental* on the morning of 1 June 1841 whilst returning from a tour of the Middle East, and he was buried at sea off Cape Trafalgar some forty miles from Gibraltar that same evening. Walter Thornbury recounts the genesis of the picture:

> Shortly after Wilkie's death and burial at sea a conversation took place between Turner and his friend George Jones.
> '*T.* I suppose nobody will do anything to commemorate Wilkie?
> '*J.* I shall pay a humble tribute by making a drawing representing his funeral.
> '*T.* How will you do it?

**54** *Peace – Burial at Sea*, R.A. 1842,
oil on canvas, 87 × 86.5 cm, Clore Gallery for the Turner Collection, London.

'*J*. On the deck of the vessel, as it has been described to me by persons present, at the
time that Wilkie's body was lowered into the sea.
'*T*. Well, I will do it as it must have appeared off the coast.'[15]

Wilkie had been buried at sea because the Gibraltar authorities, fearing an incursion of the
Plague then rampant in the Middle East, had closed the port to shipping. We see the
*Oriental* (whose name Turner scratched as 'Orental' over the ship's paddle) flying her flag at
half-mast whilst Wilkie's shrouded body is consigned to the deep amid a glow of golden

torchlight. This area of colour provides the only warm note in the entire work, which is otherwise distinctly cool in value, the silvery moonlight totally conveying the sensibility characterised by the title, the peace of death. Yet this is not the only way Turner used colour to express the mood of mortality connected with the picture. He painted the sails of the *Oriental* black, a departure from realism that was considered unacceptable by his more prosaically-minded fellow marine-artists (and, later, Ruskin[16]). As Thornbury tells us:

> Turner painted the sails of the steamer as black as he could make them, which occasioned a remonstrance from Stanfield who justly thought the colour and effect untrue; upon which Turner said, 'I only wish I had any colour to make them blacker'. It is very like him to have indicated mourning by this means, probably retaining some confused notions of the death of Ægeus and the black sails of the returning Theseus.[17]

That Turner did intend the colour of the sails to be symbolic, and was not merely silhouetting them against the moonlit sky, is proven by the fact that the hull of the *Oriental* is lighter in tone than the sails, which would not be the case in reality. To emphasise this point, Turner makes the area of the hull immediately below the sails even lighter.

Other metaphors are also apparent in the picture. A distress rocket is being fired from Gibraltar, not to warn off the *Oriental* because of the quarantine – then, as now, quarantine embargoes were communicated by the use of yellow flags[18] – nor is it meant to signal nautical danger in the intense calm specified by both title and image. Rather, it represents the overall distress caused by Wilkie's death. Moreover, like Wilkie the wind has just died too, for the *Oriental* can only have started using her steam engine very recently, there being no other explanation for the fact that she is still under sail and yet her sail is completely slack. Although the *Oriental* is now stationary – there is no wash – the sails will have to be struck as soon as she does resume her journey for there is no following wind – note the flag – and they will then check the forward motion of the ship, acting as a brake on its progress. And if we remember that *Peace – Burial at Sea*, was painted some three years after *The Fighting 'Temeraire'* (fig. 18) another possible meaning becomes apparent. In the earlier picture Turner's main theme was the death of Sail and its replacement by Steam, as typified by the great man-of-war and tug respectively. In *Peace – Burial at Sea* Sail has once more been replaced by Steam, and Turner may have been drawing a parallel between this demise and the death of Wilkie. Such a meaning would be extended by the fact that Turner represents the *Oriental* (which probably he never saw in actuality) as a sailing ship that has been converted to steam. This can be adduced from the fact that she displays a beak-prow, a feature of sailing vessels but not of ships built as steamers.

Nor are these all the possible metaphors in the picture. The only live occupant of the bottom half of the work is a mallard taking flight, and its diagonal sense of movement is reiterated by the diagonals of the foresails, the black smoke issuing from the funnel and the cliff-edge of the Rock on the left. Originally the picture appeared within an octagonal frame whose diagonal corner masks also supported this series of strong diagonals. Yet the inclusion of the mallard cannot simply be an incidental detail employed to give a sense of movement to the foreground or to add to the diagonal structural emphasis. From its pronounced and solitary position we may reasonably conclude that Turner placed it there for a purpose; he quite naturally isolated people, animals or objects in such prominent 'downstage' positions when he particularly wanted us to notice them.

It is not difficult to ascertain exactly what Turner may have intended to convey by putting a mallard there. Very evidently it seems to be a translation of a verbal pun into visual terms, not unlike the play upon metaphor enacted by the hare in *Battle Abbey, the spot where Harold fell* (fig. 5). We know that Turner was sometimes wont to pun upon the second of his forenames, Mallord, by representing it as 'Mallard'. For instance, he once created this pun, along with another one, in a letter to his friend and fellow Academician, Augustus Wall Callcott.[19] The letter informs Callcott that its writer had called upon a mutual acquaintance, only to find him regrettably absent. At the end of the missive, in keeping with his 'lamentations' at finding the man out, Turner changed his first name Joseph to 'Jeremiah' and replaced Mallord with a sketch of a mallard duck (fig. 55). He thereafter wrote in abbreviated form the name William he was most usually called by his friends.

Such a mallard appears in a number of Turner's works dating from the 1820–40 period and it may equally have been used as a 'hidden' signature. In *Peace – Burial at Sea*, however, Turner seems to have gone further. In addition to the fact that the bird is identical (if reversed) to the mallard in the letter to Callcott, its position and pictorial isolation may allude to Mallord Turner's own presence at Wilkie's funeral – in spirit at least – and it may even point towards Turner's awareness that he too is inevitably fated to follow Wilkie.

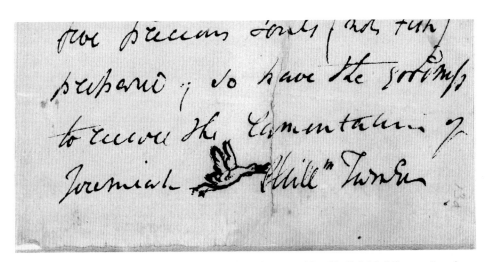

**55** J. M. W. Turner, undated letter to A. W. Callcott (detail), British Library, London.

The probable significance of the moonrise only emerges if we consider *Peace – Burial at Sea* both in relation to its pendant and within the context of Turner's frequent use of moonrises in relation to vivid sunsets at around this time. The pendant, *War. The Exile and the Rock Limpet* (fig. 56) depicts Napoleon on St Helena staring at a mollusc which, despite its lowly existence, is at least free. Napoleon's envious thoughts are made clear by another of Turner's fragments from 'The Fallacies of Hope':

> Ah! thy tent-formed shell is like
> A soldier's nightly bivouac, alone
> Amidst a sea of blood ——
> —— but you can join your comrades.[20]

It seems typical for Turner to have noticed the similarity between a 'tent-formed shell' and a 'soldier's nightly bivouac'. And Napoleonic associations are certainly advanced in *War. The Exile and the Rock Limpet*. Beneath the guns and field works rising out of the haze on the right Turner places a ship's rudder. The associations of this singular object seem relevant. It may denote either the fact that Napoleon is stranded – for no ship can sail without a rudder – or that his purposeless existence in exile is metaphorically 'rudderless'. Equally, through its close resemblance to a butcher's cleaver it could be a clever visual pun that would certainly relate to the 'sea of blood' which is both specified by the poetic metaphor and pictorialised metaphorically.[21]

Yet it is the associations of colour that are most worthy of attention at this point. As Ruskin commented, 'the lines which Turner gave this picture are very important, being the only verbal expression of that association in his mind of sunset colour with blood.'[22] But although this is Turner's only *specified* link between the crimson of sunset and blood in one of his exhibited works, the fact that he limited his use of red sunsets to pictures with subjects connected with death, decline or decay does tend to suggest that the association was a fairly constant one. Ruskin noticed this as well, stating that Turner

> was very definitely in the habit of indicating the association of any subject with circumstances of death, especially the death of multitudes, by placing it under one of his most deeply *crimsoned* skies.[23]

He also observed that 'The scarlet of the clouds was Turner's symbol of destruction'. Ruskin's interpretative instincts may have been correct in this respect, for the artist has left us a concrete example of just such an association. This occurs on page 9 of the *Boats, Ice* sketchbook (T.B. CI) of around 1806–8 where directly upon a fiery sky above a setting sun Turner wrote the words 'Fire and Blood'.

We see such bloody skies in a number of major pictures on tragic themes, such as the 1817 decline of Carthage painting (fig. 129), the 1839 *Fighting 'Temeraire'* (fig. 18) and the

**56** *War. The Exile and the Rock Limpet*, R.A. 1842,
oil on canvas, 79.5 × 79.5 cm, Clore Gallery for the Turner Collection, London.

1840 *Slavers throwing overboard the Dead and Dying – Typhon coming on* (B.J. 385) which Ruskin owned but had to sell as he found the subject too painful to live with. One of Turner's late watercolours, a view of *Goldau* (w. 1537) dating from 1843, even introduces a sky that, in Ruskin's words, employs 'scarlet and crimson, the deepest in tone of all that I know in Turner's drawings' to heighten the associations of place, the fact that the village of Goldau once situated in the foreground had been engulfed in a massive rockfall in 1806 and 457 people killed in the disaster.

If a red setting sun could allude to death, it seems logical for Turner to have extended the metaphor by exploring how a moonrise at sunset suggests the coming of night and, by association, death itself, as well as the sense of repose connected with death, as in *Peace – Burial at Sea*. The use of the moon to introduce these associations can be seen in a number of Turner's later pictures, and the symbolic conjunction of the red setting sun and rising moon that will soon replace it in the sky can even be found together in *The Fighting 'Temeraire'*. Similarly, in the 1839 R.A. show in which the *'Temeraire'* was displayed, Turner also exhibited pendants depicting ancient and modern Rome, with the moon respectively casting its light upon a dying blaze of Roman glory and the city's contemporary decrepitude. Here, too, association clearly played a crucial part in determining the choice of light effects. When the moonrise in *Peace – Burial at Sea* is connected with the sun-related blood-and-death symbolism of its pendant, as Turner intended it should be, then we can appreciate how it might hold similar associative significance. And although Wilkie was buried at 8.30 in the evening and we might therefore expect to see the moon in *Peace – Burial at Sea*, yet the placing of the orb immediately above the beak-prow of the *Oriental* hardly seems coincidental; after all, Turner could have positioned the moon anywhere in the picture. By situating it where it is he makes it lead poor Wilkie the way to watery death.

Another work exhibited two years earlier than *Peace – Burial at Sea* indicates a different but clear symbolic relationship which could exist in Turner's mind between a setting sun and a rising moon, whilst possibly denoting something else as well. This picture is both allusive and elusive, for it enjoys the most enigmatic of Turner's titles: *The New Moon; or, 'I've lost My Boat, You shan't have Your Hoop'*. The painting was exhibited at the R.A. in 1840 (fig. 57). Here Turner probably depicted a sunset at Margate and shows how a new moon can be seen to rise extremely near a setting sun, a new moon always being physically situated in the quarter of the sky between the earth and the sun. (Indeed, this writer has often observed a new moon rise above almost the exact spot where the setting sun has just disappeared over the horizon.) Yet as the title tells us, Turner was not just celebrating the beauties of a sunset and a moonrise when he named the picture. So what could be the meaning of the title, and especially its long alternative section?

An answer is not difficult to find if we consider the period during which the work was painted and the fact that such a meaning, to have been publicly understandable, would have had to refer to some fairly public event. The leading public event of 1840 in London was the wedding of Queen Victoria in February of that year. Metaphorically speaking, through his betrothal to the Queen, Prince Albert's 'new moon' can be said to have risen to her 'sun'. And this wedding gives us a clue to the meaning of the enigmatic second part of the title. The clear underlying theme of that sentence is petulant denial: 'I've lost My Boat, You shan't have Your Hoop'. A vivid demonstration of petulant denial was clearly provided by Queen Victoria at her wedding. The Whig Prime Minister, Lord Melbourne,

**57** *The New Moon; or, 'I've lost My Boat, You shan't have Your Hoop'*, R.A. 1840,
oil on canvas, 65.5 × 81.5 cm, Clore Gallery for the Turner Collection, London.

had promised the Queen an income of £50,000 per year for her consort, a move that was thwarted by the Tory Duke of Wellington in the House of Lords, who instead would only allow Prince Albert a paltry £30,000 per annum. Wellington also opposed Prince Albert's taking of precedence over the Royal Dukes. Victoria was so furious that she refused to invite Wellington to her wedding, although she relented at the last moment. The Queen's displeasure was widely reported in the Press. For example, *The Times* of Wednesday 12 February 1840 informed its readers that the duke remained uninvited until the Friday evening before the marriage on Monday 10 February and that he was excluded from the wedding breakfast and the banquet at St James's Palace which followed. Considering that in the 1840s Wellington was still the nation's leading military hero, such treatment might easily have struck Turner as petulant and an amusing demonstration of how the great luminaries of this world can become the victims of childish behaviour. If Turner did mean all this by the title of his painting, as a Royal Academician he was still well-advised to remain discreet about it.

**58** *Dudley, Worcestershire, c.*1830–1,
watercolour on paper, 28 × 42 cm, Lady Lever Art Gallery, Port Sunlight.

Turner's awareness of how a new moon can replace a setting sun in the same area of sky is also manifest in a watercolour in the 'England and Wales' series, a view of *Dudley, Worcestershire* (fig. 58) dating from about 1831. Here a new moon rises above a bleak scene of industrial activity and 'urban blight', yet the brightness of the sky does not accord with the fact that we seem to be looking at a night scene. It is more than possible that Turner has represented a new moon rising over the exact spot where the sun has just set in order to symbolically denote the coming of a new industrial order which has replaced the old order represented by Dudley Castle and Priory up on the right. This interpretation appears to be supported by the fact that to the left of the moon, in a distinctive vertical alignment, Turner places a church spire exactly above a factory chimney, thereby further enforcing the conjunction of the old and the new and suggesting a process of replacement.

The sun, the moon, even the planets – as Turner's addition to Solomon Hart's *Galileo* picture makes clear – all of these could bear hidden and sometimes very profound significance, as could the meteorological conditions that are affected by them.

**59** *Stonehenge, c.* 1825–8, watercolour on paper, 28 × 41 cm,
Private Collection, UK, on loan to Salisbury Art Gallery.

## WEATHER

Effects of weather, and particularly storms, have long been employed by artists to extend the meanings of their pictures. As we shall see later, Turner came across such metaphors in works by Titian, Poussin and Claude, as well as in mythological pictures by Richard Wilson and portraits by Reynolds. Storms as signifiers of unsettled human experience are, very naturally, amongst the most frequently encountered forms of metaphor in art. No less useful are strokes of lightning. Here Turner seems to have held some pretty constant associations. As Ruskin noted, Turner

> rarely introduces lightning [striking at a building] if the building has not been devoted to religion. The wrath of man may destroy the fortress, but only the wrath of heaven can destroy the temple.[24]

Ruskin observed an especially vivid example of such usage in *Stonehenge* (fig. 59), made for the 'England and Wales' series sometime between 1825–8. Here lightning, which has just

**60** J. T. Willmore after J. M. W. Turner,
*Temple of Minerva Sunias, Cape Colonna*, engraving, 1854.

struck dead a shepherd and several sheep, strikes again whilst we look on. Through such carnage Turner wished associatively to reinforce our awareness of the dead religion epitomised by the ruins beyond.

An identical equation between literal and metaphorical death is present in the engraving of *Temple of Minerva Sunias, Cape Colonna* (fig. 60). The watercolour upon which this print was based has vanished[25] but it is thought to have dated from about 1820. The picture shows the Doric temple to the south-east of Athens and it may illustrate lines from Thomas Campbell's poem 'The Pleasures of Hope':

> Yes, at the dead of night, by Lonna's steep
> The seaman's cry was heard along the deep.[26]

In the left distance a sinking ship can be seen, while two wolves look on in the foreground, one of them plaintively howling. To Englishmen, at least, Cape Colonna was famous in Turner's day for having been the spot where William Falconer was shipwrecked in 1750, an event which led him to compose his famous poem 'The Shipwreck',[27] re-printed no less than 83 times between 1762 and 1887. Both Campbell and Turner seem to allude to that event. Yet above the temple, on the right, we do indeed see lightning, striking in the direction of the ship but also connecting 'the wrath of heaven' and the dead religious building in the

**61** J. C. Allen after J. M. W. Turner,
*Dunwich*, engraving (unpublished but probably dating from around 1827–8).

**62** J. Horsburgh after J. M. W. Turner,
*Malvern Abbey and Gate, Worcestershire*, engraving, 1832.

**63** *Stamford, Lincolnshire, c.*1825–5,
watercolour on paper, 29 × 42 cm, Usher Art Gallery, Lincoln.

foreground, one whose original purpose had been to invoke Poseidon's help for mariners passing through the dangerous waters off Sounion where the Aegean meets the Saronic gulf.

Similarly, Turner used lightning in conjunction with contemporary religious ruins. For instance, in the engraving of *Dunwich*, made around 1827 for an unpublished continuation of the 'Southern Coast' series, he introduced lightning striking at the ruins of All Saints church (fig. 61). And when a watercolour of *Malvern Abbey and Gate, Worcestershire* came to be engraved in 1832 for the 'England and Wales' series, the artist took the opportunity once more to introduce a bolt of lightning striking from the heavens (fig. 62). Turner may also have used the device to denote the troubles of contemporary religion. In the 'England and Wales' series watercolour of *Stamford, Lincolnshire* (fig. 63), lightning strikes at St Martin's church whilst in front of it dogs bark at a gaitered cleric. This parallel may reflect the fact that during the late 1820s, when the drawing was made, the Church of England was undergoing a great deal of popular criticism for its active opposition to parliamentary reform. Turner may be alluding to that dominant political issue of the day, a supposition that is strengthened by seeing the work in the context of other statements he made about the Reform Bill in the same series during that period.

**64** *Martello Towers near Bexhill, Sussex*,
mezzotint engraved for Part VII of *Liber Studiorum* and published in 1811.
Turner was responsible for drawing and etching the plate, J. Say for engraving the print.

Turner also very appropriately coupled stormy skies with war and the military.[28] One
such connection is to be seen in *Martello Towers near Bexhill, Sussex*, a sepia design for the *Liber
Studiorum* (fig. 64). The work dates from between 1806 and 1810 while the Napoleonic war
dragged on. It shows the view across Pevensey bay, where some Martello towers formed
part of a chain of 74 defence forts built along the part of the English coast nearest to France.
In the foreground a suitable sense of aggressiveness is introduced by the sight of a man
beating an ass. Above him are a mass of storm clouds. They approach us, as do the
galloping hussars, and like them contribute a sense of urgency to the scene. Yet Turner also
addresses the theme of protectiveness, for on the ass a child is held protectively by its
mother. The deliberate alignment of the mother and child with the nearest, most prominent
of the defence towers, associatively links and amplifies that protectiveness into something
more general. In this work, too, we can perceive Turner's employment of visual simile.
There are seven Martello towers, whilst inland, between the nearest tower and Galley hill
on the right, is another building, a house on the edge of Bexhill. At the bottom left Turner
depicts a wrecked boat with a small rowing-boat lying across it. The frame-joists of the
wreck and the broken bowsprit of the rowing boat create eight uprights, matching exactly
the shapes of the Martello towers and the house beyond.

Full-blown storms could create even more appropriate associations with the military. In a work like the 'England and Wales' series watercolour of *Winchelsea, Sussex* (fig. 65), dating from some time between 1825 and 1829, Turner depicts a formation of troops making its way towards the distant town, over which a furious sky is breaking.

Turner could also invest the advance and withdrawal of storms with metaphorical significance. One such advance has already been noted in *Battle Abbey, the spot where Harold fell* (fig. 5). Another good example can be seen in *Hougoumont* (fig. 66), made around 1833 and engraved as the title-page vignette for the fifth volume of Sir Walter Scott's complete *Prose Works* published in 1834. This contains 'Paul's letters to his kinsfolk' which tells the story of the battle of Waterloo. In the picture we see the farmhouse on the battlefield, which Scotts tells us 'is (or rather *was*) a gentleman's house of the old Flemish architecture',[29] on the eve of the battle, 17 June 1815. Such a precise dating can be reckoned from the fact that, as Scott tells us, Wellington had only fallen back to the positions around Waterloo from Quatre Bras on that day in order to maintain lateral communications with the Prussians under Blucher, who themselves had retreated after having been defeated at Ligny on the 16th. Yet Turner has signally departed from the text he is ostensibly illustrating. As Scott makes clear, by the 17th it had been stormy for days in this part of Flanders and the whole area around the battlefield was sodden, 'fields of corn . . . [being] . . . reduced to swamps by the wetness of the season' whilst 'the roads, already broken up by the British artillery in their advance and retreat, were very nearly impassable.' Instead of that, however, Turner shows the scene on a dry and pleasant summer's evening, with British soldiers taking their ease on presumably dry ground while massive storm clouds are still approaching. Like the French, they too are moving up from the south, the direction indicated by the bearing upon which we are looking at Hougoumont and the nearby pall of smoke. Turner has clearly delayed the coming of this storm so as to identify it with the human storm that would break over Hougoumont the next day.[30] The inclusion of the moon in this scene of impending death is not without significance either.

It is possible that Turner obtained this storm-metaphor from Byron, for the artist's major treatment of the battle, *The Field of Waterloo* (B.J. 138), exhibited at the R.A. in 1818, was accompanied by these lines from Canto III of Byron's *Childe Harold's Pilgrimage* alongside the title in the catalogue entry:

> Last noon beheld them full of lusty life;
> Last eve in Beauty's circle proudly gay;
> The midnight brought the signal – sound of strife;
> The morn the marshalling of arms – the day,
> Battle's magnificently stern array!
> The thunder clouds close o'er it, which when rent,
> The earth is covered thick with other clay

**65** *Winchelsea, Sussex, c.*1825–9, watercolour on paper, 29 × 43 cm, British Museum, London.

**66** W. Miller after J. M. W. Turner, *Hougoumont*, engraving, 1834.

**67** *The Field of Waterloo, c. 1817,*
watercolour on paper, 28.8 × 40.5 cm, Fitzwilliam Museum, Cambridge.

**68** *The Field of Waterloo from Hougoumont, c.1832,*
vignette watercolour on thin card, 15.2 × 25.4 cm (approx.), Private Collection, UK.

**69**  *The Field of Waterloo, c.*1833, watercolour on paper, 8.3 × 14 cm, Private Collection, UK.

> Which her own clay shall cover, heaped and pent,
> Rider and horse – friend, foe, in one red burial blent!

The delay in the timing of the storm here prefigures the delay witnessed in *Hougoumont*, Byron's 'thunder clouds' also functioning metaphorically as well as literally.

Turner certainly knew that the real storm affecting the Waterloo area abated on the late afternoon of 18 June, for the sky in the oil painting of *The Field of Waterloo*, although filled with the smoke of battle, is by now very serene, with the area lit by rockets to prevent marauders, and women searching for their men by torchlight.[31] Yet just as Turner delayed the onset of the storm in *Hougoumont*, so too he held back its abatement[32] in another depiction of the scene in the aftermath of battle, a watercolour (fig. 67) probably made around the same time as the oil-painting. Here the artist once again depicts the site bestrewn with bodies 'in one red burial blent' but also with storm clouds and lightning still very much in evidence. The metaphorical storm can be seen finally breaking up (beneath the moon) in one more illustration of the battlefield from near Hougoumont (fig. 68), made around 1832 for a collection of the complete works of Byron. And an indication of Turner's attachment to this association emerges in yet another treatment of the subject (fig. 69) which probably dates from about 1833 and was made also to illustrate Scott's *Prose Works*. Here the painter shows the battlefield years after the event but appropriately with a storm again in evidence and lightning striking at La Haye Sainte farmhouse. Some horsemen are rushing towards the building, presumably to seek shelter from the lightning, and their obvious urgency exemplifies the general sense of threat. Turner also places a skeleton in the foreground to explicate other associations of the place.

Turner may also have used storms to create metaphors in marine-pictures. Three such works dating from around 1803 seem to express covert levels of meaning. For example, a desire to address contemporary preoccupations indirectly could well have motivated *Boats carrying Out Anchors and Cables to Dutch Men of War, in 1665* which was exhibited at the R.A. in 1804 (fig. 70). The artist seems to have used an incident in the Anglo-Dutch Wars of the 1660s here to warn England to be ready to repel the very real threat of Napoleonic invasion, a danger then at its height (and one only to be finally averted by the victory at Trafalgar in 1805). As Professor A. G. H. Bachrach has convincingly argued:

> After the defeat of the Dutch fleet at the Battle of Lowestoft in June 1665, the English felt so secure and complacent that they were quite unaware of how hard the Dutch were working to refit their fleet, efforts which were crowned with a number of successes culminating in their invasion of the Medway in June 1667. Turner may therefore have felt in 1804 that the threat of invasion from France was being met with a similar lack of foresight and preparation, and meant this picture to be interpreted as a warning by analogy.[33]

The mountainous seas and stormy skies, whilst on one level reflecting Turner's close involvement with, and attempts to surpass Dutch marine painting, might equally be an associative elaboration of that further meaning.

**70** *Boats carrying Out Anchors and Cables to Dutch Men of War, in 1665,*
R.A. 1804, oil on canvas, 101.5 × 130.5 cm,
The Corcoran Gallery of Art, Washington, DC.

A view of a major French port painted around the same time may contain related secondary significance. *Fishing Boats entering Calais Harbour* (fig. 71) dates from 1803–4 and was possibly exhibited in Turner's own gallery in 1804. The town is shown from the sea, framed by the twin piers of the harbour. In the centre two fishing vessels are tacking into Calais against the wind. Aboard the nearer one a sailor points warningly at the large wave sweeping up at the left. Further forward his companions are attempting to help a boy who has clambered up the mainmast to adjust a halyard.

Turner may be depicting an incident he actually witnessed. The artist had entered France *via* Calais on 15 July 1802 following the Peace of Amiens between Britain and France. This peace had come into effect on 17 March 1802 and was to last until 18 May 1803. Like a great number of his contemporaries Turner had waited a long time to visit the Continent, the war with France having lasted since 1793. We know from a sketchbook in which he recorded his arrival that his entry into France was indeed a stormy one.[34] His cross-Channel packet had had to wait off the harbour-mouth for a favourable tide, so presumably he had time to study this view. The memory stayed with him, for in 1816 he returned to the subject in a print for his set of mezzotint engravings, the *Liber Studiorum* (fig. 72), although in doing so he made some fundamental alterations to the image. The sea is calmer and the sky, although sombre, is less vehement. And whilst the pointing sailor is still to be seen, he is now gesturing with little sense of alarm, which is not surprising as the large wave is no longer in evidence and the vessel is not nearly so aslant due to the force of the wind. The boy is gone from the mast, and his helpers have been dispersed. Furthermore, the large vessel on the left seen with sails furled or flapping in the painting has lowered its sails in the print which also adds to a lessening of tension, suggesting that the ship is ready to make for sea. Given that in twelve years the tidal dangers of the harbour mouth at Calais can hardly have lessened, we are forced to find some explanation for this extreme alteration of image, nearly the most drastic change Turner made between a *Liber Studiorum* print and the earlier picture upon which it was based.

One possible reason for the modification may lie in the fact that by 1816 the stormy relations that had existed between France and Britain in 1803–4 had much abated. When the painting was made Napoleon was readying his forces in the French Channel ports and the Lowlands for the invasion of England. The large threatening wave, whilst representing the tidal bar at Calais, may also be alluding to that greater threat, which may be why the helmsman of the fishing boat is pointing to it with such alarm. Moreover, the two vessels depicted at the centre are not French boats at all but Dutch sloops, shallow-draught river and coastal vessels. Additionally, if this painting dates from early 1803, Turner may have been alluding to the threat France posed to Holland. The Netherlands had originally been invaded in 1795 by the French who set up a puppet government, the so-called 'Batavian Republic'. Although the terms of the Treaty of Amiens had specified French withdrawal

**71** *Fishing Boats entering Calais Harbour, c.*1803,
oil on canvas, 73.7 × 98.4 cm, The Frick Collection, New York.

**72** *Entrance of Calais Harbour,* mezzotint drawn, etched and
engraved by J. M. W. Turner, published in Part XI of *Liber Studiorum,* 1816.

from the Netherlands, even before hostilities were resumed on 18 May 1803, Napoleon, fearing a British invasion due to the strategic importance of the area, had begun to build up his forces there instead. It was news of this in March 1803 that set in motion the chain of events that led to renewed war between Britain and France the following May. The Dutch were caught in the middle. As the *Morning Chronicle* of 24 March 1803 commented:

> It appears by the Dutch and Hamburgh mails that the prospect of a war with England has produced the greatest alarm and despair in Holland. Those who, in defense of the ancient and approved policy of Holland for a century and a half, attached their country to the destiny of the French Empire, in preference to an equal alliance with England, now feel how frantic their conduct has been. It is impossible that the slightest misunderstanding can arise between England and France but Holland must experience the fatal effects of it . . . the Dutch contemplate a war which to them can be attended with no success, even were it fortunate for their task-masters, with the utmost anxiety. They indeed, as well as the few commercial men who yet remain in the Ports of France had, after the peace [of Amiens], laid out very large sums in equiping vessels for the different Colonies restored to them [by the treaty]. It is supposed the Dutch may have bought or fitted up above a thousand ships . . . a great part of which, in the event of a war, would immediately fall into our hands. For this the Dutch could have no compensation in military glory or national aggrandizement. Their hopes of commercial prosperity would again be overthrown. No wonder, then, they look with trembling anxiety to the result of the present negotiations.

Given Turner's lifelong interest in Dutch marine affairs, and particularly his open treatment of them in *Boats carrying Out Anchors and Cables to Dutch Men of War, in 1665* of 1804, it seems possible that he was aware of the 'trembling anxiety' of the Dutch and wished to allude to it with the large threatening wave mounting towards the sloep – and England – in *Fishing Boats entering Calais Harbour*. This hypothesis would explain why the sailor is gesturing with alarm in the painting and why, by 1816, when the war with France was ended, in the print Turner showed calmer seas and the boat with its occupants now going about their business without alarm.

A similar tempestuous allusion to contemporary events may also exist in another, more impressive view of the same port. *Calais Pier, with French Poissards preparing for Sea: an English Packet arriving* (fig. 73) was exhibited at the R.A. in 1803 and might well record something Turner had observed at first hand. Instead of waiting for the tide to change on 15 July 1802, Turner had elected to go ashore in a small rowing-boat which was 'Nearly swampt'[35] in the process. Once on land he made a number of studies of the pier and harbour, some of which contributed towards this painting.

The major dramatic event takes place at the centre-left. A large French trawler is tacking its way out of the harbour and has just avoided colliding with the English packet-boat.[36] The problem of collision is repeated in the foreground where a small fishing smack is in danger of smashing against the pier because of a strong on-shore wind. In view of the recently ended collision between Britain and France, it is very possible that the near-collision of the English ferry and French fishing vessel may embody a larger parallel, particularly when one notes that Turner made the near-collision his central nautical subject. Moreover, this meaning can be extended symbolically by the blue sky immediately above the two ships now out of danger. There we see the only area of peace in the entire picture. A strong westerly wind is blowing but we have no way of knowing whether the clouds around this patch of peaceful sky are parting or closing. However, such ambiguity may have been intentional, for it allows the implied calmer weather to be either coming or going: in the autumn, winter and spring of 1802–3, when Turner was painting this picture following his return from the Continent, there was strong public feeling that in view of Napoleon's ever-increasing bellicosity, war might easily break out again,[37] and Turner may have been allowing for that eventuality in allusive terms. In fact the war did resume just sixteen days after *Calais Pier* first went on public view at the Royal Academy on 2 May 1803, although the outbreak of hostilities had seemed certain since at least 8 March, when the King put the nation on a war footing and engendered a growing sense of crisis.[38] Turner therefore had nearly two months in which to imbue the picture with allusive sentiment. That he should have wanted to do so by showing his nautically minded countrymen what bad sailors the French could be, would have been entirely characteristic of his serious and patriotic aspirations for his art at this early stage of his career, especially at a time when war seemed imminent. It would also have made the picture of a potential enemy town more saleable. (In the event the work did not sell.)

Whether or not Turner was employing human actions and weather effects to extend the content of *Calais Pier* must remain a matter of speculation, although it seems rather odd that out of all the French subjects he could have chosen to paint, he selected Calais, and stressed local limitations whilst doing so. Perhaps he remembered how Hogarth had similarly depicted the limitations of the town in his famous *Calais Gate (The Roast Beef of Old England)*.[39] These are not merely nautical limitations either; in the small ketch by the pier a fisherman is furiously arguing with a fishwife over possession of a bottle of spirits. However, Turner's metaphorical use of weather and light effects by the time he painted Calais Pier cannot be at all in doubt, as the analysis of the Welsh castle pictures of 1800 should make clear. And although the artist may have been ready to draw attention to the loss of liberty in Britain in 1800, he never lost his patriotism either – indeed, his concern for his country emanated from his concern for liberty – so we should not be surprised if he intended to draw attention to the limitations of Britain's enemies in the years following the turn of the century.

**73** *Calais Pier, with French Poissards preparing for Sea: an English Packet arriving*, R.A. 1803, oil on canvas, 172 × 240 cm, National Gallery, London.

## TIME

The most fundamental dramatic limitation of any single pictorial image is that it does not physically operate in the dimension of time. Discussions of the concept of *ut pictura poesis* quite naturally concerned themselves with this problem, for it was in just such a respect that painting and poetry principally differ. As Henry Fuseli commented:

> *successive action* communicated by sounds, and *time*, are the medium of poetry; *form* displayed in *space*, and momentaneous energy, are the element of painting.[40]

Pictorial artists have nonetheless evolved three visual methods for overcoming the limitations of being incapable of operating in time, as well as a literary aid to doing so. The first and most obvious procedure is the creation of successive related images, as in the sequential narrative strip or cycle of images. This type of imagery had its origins in antiquity, being well exemplified by Trajan's Column, and later consecutive images, such as the Bayeux Tapestry, as well as a whole host of popular prints from the Middle Ages onwards, also typify that approach. Occasionally, major painters such as Rubens similarly overcame the limitations of time by the creation of consecutive images, as in the Maria de' Medici cycle, whilst in England the manipulation of time in this way perhaps reached its apogee in the works of Hogarth with his pictorial sequences of 'The Harlot's Progress' of 1732, 'The Rake's Progress' of 1735, 'Marriage-à-la-Mode' of 1743–5 and 'Industry and Idleness' of 1747. Turner himself did begin a narrative sequence of paintings of a visit of King George IV to Edinburgh in 1822 but the cycle was not completed. Yet partly because of its popular connotations – and hence what was considered to be its lack of artistic gravity – but even more because of its difficulty of display in the form of paintings,[41] the employment of narrative sequence was rarely resorted to by the poetic-historic painter. Instead, he or she usually brought the most important narrative moments together into a single image. Most crudely this was done in the second way of overcoming the constraints of time available to the visual artist, namely by simply ignoring those limitations altogether. For example, Turner resorted to this narrative device in *St. Julienne's Chapel* (fig. 74), a vignette made around 1832 to illustrate the third canto of Samuel Rogers' poem 'Jacqueline' (1813), where he illustrates the lines

> That morn ('twas in Ste. Julienne's cell
> As at Ste. Julienne's sacred well
> Their dream of love began)
> That morn, ere many a star was set,
> Their hands had on the altar met
> Before the holy man

Turner shows Jacqueline and her lover meeting at the 'sacred well' and, simultaneously on the left, kneeling before the monk as he later unites them.

Anachronism as regards historical appearances also occurs in Turner's work. This may be encountered in watercolours of Heidelberg dating from about 1840 where the artist depicted the town as he had recently seen it but peopled it with figures in medieval dress. Here, however, it is hard to know for certain whether Turner is referring to the past or actually depicting it, as he did in other works he made of Heidelberg during the same period.[42] Yet historically anachronistic elements are certainly present in *Rome from the Vatican. Raffaelle, accompanied by La Fornarina, preparing his Pictures for the Decoration of the Loggia* (B.J. 228) which was exhibited at the Royal Academy in 1820, the tricentenary of Raphael's death. In the work Turner portrays Raphael (born in 1483) standing in the foreground with his mistress. Amongst the artworks distributed across the foreground is a landscape that

**74** *St Julienne's Chapel*, *c.*1832, vignette watercolour on paper, 14.3 × 8.6 cm, Clore Gallery for the Turner Collection, London (T.B. CCLXXX-186).

**75** *Traitor's Gate, Tower of London*, *c.*1832, vignette watercolour on paper, 11.5 × 12 cm, Clore Gallery for the Turner Collection, London (T.B. CCLXXX-177).

looks suspiciously like a Claude, who was not born until 1600, whilst around St Peter's Square beyond them range Bernini's colonnades which date from 1656–7. However, Turner may not have cared about these anachronisms or could even have created them in order to demonstrate the point that a great artist like Raphael – or himself – transcends time. Somebody as conscious of history as was Turner cannot have been unaware of such solecisms though. Indeed, another work in which the artist manipulates events and objects in time certainly proves beyond doubt that he could consciously turn historical anachronism to dramatic effect.

*Traitor's Gate, Tower of London* (fig. 75) was made around 1832 as an illustration for the poem 'Human Life' contained in the collected *Poems* of Samuel Rogers. At the point in the poem Turner illustrates, the anonymous protagonist is being tried upon charges of treason for struggling against political oppression, and therefore we see the 'Traitor's Gate, the water-gate in the Tower of London' which Rogers characterises as

. . . that gate misnamed, thro' which before
Went Sidney, Russell, Raleigh, Cranmer, More

On the right of the gate are early-nineteenth century ships, a cutter and two merchantmen (one placed behind the other). On the left is a parade of soldiers dressed in contemporary uniform. Before the gate, however, we see a vessel whose boatmen are dressed in Tudor costume. They are rowing Sir Thomas More who is no less improbably accompanied by his executioner. Obviously Turner chose this conjunction of different periods to allude to the notion expressed by the poem that the type of despotism More had fallen foul of was alive and well and flourishing in Britain in the 1790s, the period in which the poem is set.[43] In a reverse way this may also have been the reason that historical anachronism exists in both the *Dolbadern Castle* and the *Caernarvon Castle* of 1800 (figs 24 and 26). Despite the fact that in both works we are looking at events which take place in the thirteenth century, we can also perceive the contemporary representation of a somewhat ruined Dolbadarn Castle, as well as eighteenth century shipping in Caernarvon harbour. Such an introduction of elements from the present into the past was also probably intended to point up the contemporary relevance of the contents of both pictures. A probable source for such anachronism will emerge below.

The complete ignoral of the limitations of time received Academic sanction, however. This was by means of the practice recommended by several of the exponents of the doctrine of *ut pictura poesis* that were known to Turner. For example, Franciscus Junius in his *Painting of the Ancients* of 1638 suggested (p. 311) that

> Observe onlye that the methode of a painted history must not always be tyed to the lawes of a penned historie: an historographer discourseth of affaires orderly as they were done, according as well the times as the actions: but a Painter thrusteth himselfe into the very middest, even where it most concerneth him: and recoursing from thence to the things forepart, presenting likewise the things to come, he maketh his Art all at once represent things alreadie done, things that are adoing, and things which are as yet to be done.

The notion of the painter thrusting himself 'into the very middest' was also vividly expressed by Count Algarotti in his *Essay on Painting* of 1763 where he stated (p. 89) that

> The painter . . . deprived of [the succession of time and place] must be content to depend upon one single moment. But what a moment! A moment, in which he may conjure up, at once, to the eyes of the spectators, a thousand objects; a moment, teeming with the most beautiful circumstances that can attend the action; a moment, equivalent to the successive labours of the poet.

John Opie, in his second lecture of 1807, clearly echoed Algarotti in celebrating

> . . . the critical moment, in which all the most striking and beautiful circumstances that can be imagined are concentrated, big with suspense, interest, passion, terror and action; in short, the moment of explosion, which illuminates and brings at once into

**76** *The Battle of Trafalgar*, 1822–4, oil on canvas, 259 × 365.8 cm, National Maritime Museum, Greenwich.

view the *past*, *present*, and *future*, and which, when well rendered, is often more than equivalent to all the successive energies of the poet.[44]

By 'the critical moment' Opie, like Junius and Algarotti before him (not to mention others such as Félibien and du Fresnoy) meant the key dramatic moment in any subject, mainly as presented through human gestures and postures that would create the widest possible imaginative responses in the viewer, but also by any other means that might bring this about. Certainly, Turner's adoption of 'the critical moment' as a way of by-passing the limitations of time can be seen in the largest picture the artist ever painted, *The Battle of Trafalgar* (fig. 76). This work resulted from the only royal commission Turner received, and he probably obtained the order through the good offices of his friend, Sir Thomas Lawrence, the President of the Royal Academy. The artist expended considerable effort on the picture between 1823–4, even putting in eleven days extra work on the canvas after it

**77** *The Battle of Trafalgar* (detail).

had been publicly hung in St James's Palace in order that he might meet some of the many criticisms of the picture's inconsistencies that were being offered by the public, particularly by naval viewers.

It is not surprising they had difficulties coming to terms with the work. As a naval history of 1826 tells us:

> Unfortunately for the subject which this splendid picture is meant to represent scarcely a line of truth, beyond perhaps the broadside view of the Victory's hull, is to be seen upon it. To say what time of day or what particular incident in the Victory's proceedings is meant to be referred to, we do not pretend; for the telegraphic message [i.e. Nelson's famous signal 'England expects every man to do his duty'] is going up, which was hoisted about 11h.40m. A.M., the mizen topmast is falling, which went about 1 P.M., a strong light is reflected upon the Victory's bow and sides from the burning Achille, which ship did not catch fire until 4h.30m., nor explode till 5h.45m. P.M., the fore-topmast . . . of the British three decker is falling, which never fell at all, and the Redoubtable is sinking under the bows of the Victory, although the French ship did not sink until [the next night] and then under the stern of the Swiftsure.[45]

Actually the representation of the hull of the *Victory* was originally not at all accurate either, for Turner, working from sketches of the ship made by J. S. Schetky, originally depicted her as unladen (Schetky made the sketches in Portsmouth harbour).[46] It therefore floated much too high in the water,[47] an error Turner corrected in those 'eleven days' (although clearly he remembered the effect and put it to good use in *The Fighting 'Temeraire'*). Yet this extra height may not necessarily have resulted from ignorance but instead from design, for a decorous sense of perspective can definitely be discerned in the picture. As in *Dolbadern Castle, North Wales* (figs 20, 25), the artist places our line of sight at a very low level, in this case obviously to make the battleships and clouds tower over us. Clearly it would have served Turner's dramatic purposes originally to have made the *Victory* seem as high as possible.

More certainly the work contains a number of other poetic elements, however. As John Munday has pointed out, Nelson's motto *Palmam Qui Meruit Ferat* ('He who best deserves it wins the palm') is inscribed on a spar in the water, whilst Nelson's personal flag on the fore-topmast is shown falling, as he himself had done. Turner may have taken the disposition of one of his figures from Géricault's *The Raft of the Medusa* (which he had almost certainly seen in London in 1820[48]), the man seen lying on his back at the very bottom of the work in the centre (fig. 77). He is very reminiscent of a man similarly spread-eagled upon Géricault's raft. His dead eyes and full pupils stare out at us in a way that is obviously intended to repeat the identical circles of the muzzles and barrels of the guns protruding from the hull of the *Victory*, yet another visual simile. On board the ship's boat picking up survivors in the foreground is a sailor wearing a hat inscribed with the word *Victory*. He is placed right next to a body covered in gore – a clear reminder of the price paid for that victory.

Yet if the naval historian justifiably found a great number of 'inaccuracies' in Turner's picture, he himself was partly to blame if he found it generally untruthful. For although Turner clearly departed drastically from chronological accuracy concerning the battle in his monumental masterpiece, he certainly embraced a more fundamental concept of 'truth' than was understood by his naval contemporaries. By compressing the sequence of events and subordinating them to a central theme, a more universal truth concerning the nature of warfare emerges. Turner's tumultuous and physically overwhelming view of the engagement communicates a sense of catastrophe through the glaring light, the crowds of figures struggling in the water or on shipboard, and above all through the massive cumulative forms of the *Victory*'s sails which create monstrous billowing shapes that also act as metaphorical expressions of the enormous forces unleashed by war. Turner was not allowing himself to be limited to a statement about any one particular moment in the battle; rather, he was concerned with 'taking an allowed poetical license', with compensating for 'the natural deficiencies of his art' – in short, with avoiding the constraints of time and expressing the reality at the heart of the subject. By ignoring temporal and spatial 'truth' for a wider concept of truth, Turner encompassed the whole battle of Trafalgar

**78** *Lord Ullin's daughter, c.* 1835, vignette watercolour,
12 × 10 cm, Private Collection, UK.

and equally stated something about 'the pity of war' that is as relevant today as it was in 1824.

Allusion to preceding or later events could also aid Turner in the creation of 'the critical moment' and represents the third method the artist utilised in ignoring the constraints of time. This method can be seen at work in his illustration to a poem by Thomas Campbell, *Lord Ullin's daughter* (fig. 78), dating from about 1835. The poem tells of a highland chieftain who has eloped with the daughter of Lord Ullin from whom they have been fleeing for three days. Knowing that his capture will mean certain death, the chieftain pleads with a Loch Gyle boatman to ferry them across the water to escape this fate. The 'hardy Highland wight' agrees to do so even though 'the waves are raging white'. But the storm gets worse and when Lord Ullin reaches the shore he is just in time to see his daughter and her companions being swept under, leaving him forlornly to lament her loss.

In the foreground of the vignette we see Lord Ullin's daughter and her lover who is beckoning towards the boatman on the right. High up on some cliffs not mentioned in the poem are Lord Ullin and his clansmen. They are effectively divided from their quarry by this wall of rock. The chieftain's plaid, caught by the wind, is blowing upwards and, by pointing like a tail behind him, serves to remind us of the recent pursuit. Turner may well be

**79** *Boscastle, Cornwall, c.*1824,
watercolour on paper, 14.2 × 23.1 cm, Ashmolean Museum, Oxford.

translating a verbal pun into a visual metaphor here, for in contemporary parlance a band of pursuers were called a 'tail' of followers, a term that still survives in the colloquial expression 'to tail' someone.

Both the nearest part of the bank on which the lovers stand and the waters of the loch closest to us are represented by lines that disappear with an apparent rush out of the bottom of the picture. As it hardly seems likely that any rational or experienced boatman, let alone a 'hardy Highland wight', would intentionally steer his craft towards such a vertiginous flow of water, this may be interpreted as a clear allusion to the fact that Lord Ullin's daughter, her lover and the boatman are all on the edge of an abyss into which they will soon plunge. Another possible reference may be intended by the rising moon. This is not mentioned in the poem, which describes the night as being drear, with raging skies mounting to tempests. Yet again it may allude to the imminence of death.

Naturally, given his proclivity for association, Turner sometimes went far beyond this in his desire to overcome the constraints of time. For example, in *Boscastle, Cornwall* (fig. 79) Turner brilliantly overcame the problem of how to suggest things to come. The watercolour dates from about 1824 and was made for engraving in the 'Southern Coast' series.

Turner was clearly well aware of the major navigational problem associated with

**80** E. Goodall after J. M. W. Turner, *Boscastle, Cornwall*, engraving, 1825 (detail).

Boscastle, the fact that a strong tidal flow and the confluence of two rivers within its harbour made entry into the small port very dangerous for big ships, as they ran the risk of running in too quickly and smashing into the quay. As a result, a technique was evolved whereby hawsers would be attached to large vessels from the land to check their impetus, pretty much as arrester cables operate upon aircraft on modern-day carriers.

This Turner depicts. But how was he to show that in this case the practice would probably be successful? The answer was simple – for Turner at least. Immediately in front of the partially dismasted brig the artist places a rowing-boat. Unless he were bent upon suicide no sailor worth his salt would ever put such a small vessel right under the bows of a much larger craft. We can only presume, therefore, that in this case the arresting hawsers will take up the slack and prevent the collision, perhaps by a matter of inches. Turner has invented a superbly simple device for suggesting the passage of events after the immediate frozen instant of the picture. And on the quayside at the right (fig. 80) again he hints at coming events. A woman and child are playing with a hoop; immediately beneath the object

Turner creates a simile with the identical circle of a mooring-ring. This repetition serves the threefold purpose of underlining the importance of the mooring-ring, suggesting that the brig which is moving towards it will eventually be tied to it and, metaphorically, that the mooring-ring offers the damaged vessel a measure of the same type of security that is evidently shared by the woman and child, each of whom are moored equally to their ring.

Yet perhaps Turner's most striking employment of allusion as a means of ignoring the constraints of time and of pointing to things to come occurs in one of his most inventive History paintings. Turner first began *Regulus* (fig. 81) in Rome in 1828 and re-worked it extensively in London in 1837 when the picture was exhibited at the British Institution. On that occasion the artist took great pains to add to the dazzling effect of the sunlight, scumbling white paint all over the picture. According to a contemporary he drove 'into all the hollows, and every part of the surface. This was the only work he did, and it was the finishing stroke. The sun . . . was in the centre; from it were drawn – ruled – lines to mark the rays; these lines were rather strongly marked, I suppose to guide his eye. The picture gradually became wonderfully effective, just the effect of brilliant sunlight absorbing everything and throwing a misty haze over every object.'[49]

The painting illustrates a famous story of selflessness that occurred during the first Punic war between Rome and Carthage. Marcus Attilius Regulus was a Roman consul who was taken prisoner by the Carthaginians and kept confined and chained in a dungeon. Four years later, wearying of the war, the Carthaginians sent him as an envoy to Rome after obtaining his word that he would return voluntarily. In Rome he was to plead on their behalf for a cessation of hostilities. The Carthaginians had presumed that after his ordeal he would be agreeable to such a proposition, but instead, on his arrival in Rome he urged his fellow countrymen to continue the war, even though he knew that because of his oath he must return to Carthage to sure punishment. Turner probably obtained the story from Oliver Goldsmith's *The Roman History*[50] which tells us that

> Nothing could equal the fury and the disappointment of the Carthaginians when they were informed that Regulus, instead of hastening a peace, had given his opinion for continuing the war. They accordingly prepared to punish his conduct with the most studied tortures. First, his eyelids were cut off and then . . . after some days [he was] again brought out, and exposed with his face opposite the burning sun. At last . . . he was put into a barrel stuck full of nails that pointed inwards and in this painful position he continued till he died.[51]

It has been suggested that Regulus does not actually appear in the picture,[52] and from that it has been construed that it is we, the spectators, who are instead standing in his place, gazing virtually blinded at the fierce sunlight which the artist went to such lengths to heighten in effect.[53] This is not totally correct, for as has also been pointed out, Regulus can

133

**81** *Regulus*, 1828, re-worked and exhibited British Institution 1837,
oil on canvas, 91 × 124 cm, Clore Gallery for the Turner Collection, London.

indeed be seen in the picture, a tiny figure poised on the distant quay at the right.[54] He is
surrounded by the Carthaginians[55] who are bidding him farewell as the bearer of their
fallacious hopes for peace. (This identification is further established by the title of the
engraving of the work made in 1840, namely *Ancient Carthage – the Embarcation of Regulus*.)
However, it seems certain that in addition to showing Regulus, Turner intended to allude to
the blinding of the Roman by dazzling us with light. That explains why he took such pains
to increase the glaring effect of the sunset, a timing we can reasonably infer from the tragic
subject, from the fact that under the white overpainting traces can still be made out of a
pronounced red area around the sun of the kind employed by Turner in *The Decline of the
Carthaginian Empire* (fig. 129) and elsewhere to denote sunsets, and from the painter's

characteristic need to observe decorum in the matching of light to content. As in the decline of Carthage picture – which also depicts an embarkation scene – here Turner employs the sunset to portend the more general sunset of Carthaginian power.

On the left the artist furthers the meaning of the picture by depicting the barrel in which Regulus is to suffer his painful death. The barrel is being rolled forth by four men, one of whom holds a hammer, whilst another man with his arms raised also holds a hammer. The raising of his arms suggests the act of seizure which will later befall Regulus, and the hammers obviously allude to the nails that have been driven into his barrel-coffin. The circular rim of the barrel itself reflects a line of light by being exposed to the sun, exactly as the lidless eyes of Regulus eventually will be. Turner complements this allusion to eyes by introducing a great number of circles into the picture. Principally these can be seen in the circular rims of some baskets on the boat on the left, the circular ring at the front of a boat on the left, the forms of various household objects on the right, the circles made by a great number of heads and figures above and beyond them, by the large semi-circle of the bridge on the right, and even in the numerous roundels on the buildings in the distance. Associations of conflict are introduced by means of one boy beating up another on the shore at the right. Pointing people and objects are also much in evidence, clearly to introduce associations of pointedness generally. On the right a boy points towards the sun, as does the beak-prow of a ship on the left. The piercing to come is, however, perhaps most explicitly suggested by the sharply pointed piece of flotsam at the lower left which aims straight at the circular opening of the barrel. A strong sense of forward motion is imparted to this form by a multitude of parallel diagonals on the other side of the work, and most especially by the emphatic shadow cast by a woman sheltering a little girl at the lower right. Like three other children being protected by their mothers right above her, the child is hiding her face from the sun. They are joined in their aversion by the swan-figurehead of a boat on the left and another figurehead on the right, that of a person holding a shade before his or her face. Well might they all protect their sight.

In *Regulus*, then, Turner overcame the problem of time in a very subtle and inventive way but only an awareness of the artist's reliance upon allusion and metaphor can make that transcendence clear. And of course the painter had at his disposal a fourth method of overcoming the barriers of time and one that relied solely upon association, namely the attachment of poetic quotations to the titles of his pictures. This is a completely unpictorial approach, which perhaps explains why it has never been recognised as a Turnerian way of manipulating time.

Almost from the start of his career Turner availed himself of every form of association and metaphor in order to extend the ranges of meaning in his works. But that usage did not simply grow out of his sense of self-discovery or his knowledge of aesthetic theory. Turner's development as a painter went hand-in-hand with a constant awareness of how previous artists had employed association and metaphor to further the content of their works. It is only by examining their influence on Turner, and in particular some of the greatest aesthetic and stylistic influences upon him, that we can go on to appreciate many of his more subtle means of transference, such as the use of tree, structural and topological symbolism. In doing so we can measure the full creative value of Turner's contribution to the associative tradition in landscape painting, and his apotheosis of that tradition.

# Part II

# IMITATION AND ART

**82** Martino Rota after Titian, *The Martyrdom of St. Peter*, engraving.

# FOUR

# Landscapes of Meaning

To create an epoch in the world two conditions are
manifestly essential – a good head and a great
inheritance.

*Goethe*

Immature poets imitate; mature poets steal.

*T. S. Eliot*

OF all the influences upon Turner undoubtedly the greatest was Sir Joshua Reynolds, not
in any direct painterly sense but in terms of opening Turner's mind to the influence of other
artists. Turner venerated Reynolds and the esteem in which he held the *Discourses* is not only
apparent in his own perspective lectures but, more importantly, in his art. It was Reynolds
who obviously most determined Turner's cultural aspirations concerning the status of
landscape painting and who defined the type of beauty that Turner most frequently strove
to express, as well as its means of attainment, as we shall see. By furthering the
long-established tradition of considering painting and poetry as equivalent means of
imaginative expression he must also have reinforced Turner's innate propensities. And
very evidently it was Reynolds who suggested those methods of 'imitation' whereby Turner
most fully availed himself of the lessons of the past.

Following earlier commentators, Reynolds differentiated between two related kinds of
imitation, namely artistic imitation – the absorption of the values and standards of the
artists of the past – and aesthetic imitation, the question of what constitutes appearance and
reality, and how perceptions and conceptions of such realities can be achieved and
comprehended. (The former type of imitation will be explored in this chapter, and the latter
in chapter seven.)

In the *Discourses* Reynolds leads us through the different levels of artistic imitation, to
the proposition that in its highest form artistic imitation is the creative assimilation of the
essential values of the most profound and inventive exemplars of the past. Of course
Reynolds himself 'stole' creatively from a vast number of earlier artists and in his own
wide-ranging stylistic assimilations Turner was therefore not only following Reynolds's
precepts but also his precedent. The full extent to which Turner assimilated the styles and

devices of other artists is deserving of a complete study in itself but it is not the purpose of this book to enter into such a broad investigation. What concerns us here is the degree to which Turner might have understood or assimilated methods of conveying associative meaning from the works of others.

Since the advent of Western painting, artists have frequently employed landscape elements to further the content of their works through association. Flowers, for example, could be used in this way, as in the many late-medieval depictions of the Virgin and Child surrounded by roses, where the redness of the blooms signifies the blood of Christ, and the purity of white roses the purity of the Virgin herself. Other flowers could embody a similar codified meaning, such as lilies symbolising virginity. Trees, too, appear to have been employed to introduce a metaphorical significance into Italian Renaissance religious works by, amongst others, Giotto, Ghiberti, Donatello, Piero della Francesca and Giovanni Bellini.[1] Yet it was in the works of two other Italian masters that Turner might have best discerned or indeed did discern the employment of tree-forms for their associative value.

To take the first of these masters, we can perceive that Turner looked very carefully at what was generally considered to be Titian's greatest landscape, *The Martyrdom of St Peter*. The St Peter depicted was a Dominican friar and a member of the Grand Inquisition who had made many enemies and was assassinated for his pains in 1252 midway between Milan and Como. Although this work was tragically destroyed in 1867, an idea of what it looked like can be obtained from the engraving by Martino Rota (fig. 82). Turner first saw the painting in 1802 in Paris, whence it had been removed from its original location in Venice by Napoleon, and again in 1819, on his initial visit to Venice, after it had been returned there. During the intervening period he wrote and spoke fairly extensively about its colour, fidelity to nature, pictorial organisation and impact, and he also enlarged upon the way that Titian employed the trees and light to further the underlying content of the work. In his discussion Turner employed an extremely vivid pyrotechnic simile to describe the metaphorical effect powerfully produced by Titian:

> [In the *St Peter Martyr*] the sublimity of the other arrangements of lines, by its unshackled obliquity and waved lines, obtains the associated feelings of force and continuity, that rushes like *the ignited spark* from earth towards heaven, struggling as the ascending rocket with the elements, and when no more propelled by the force, it scatters round its falling glories, seeking again its earthly bourne, while diffusing around its mellow radiance, as the descending cherub with the palm of beatitude sheds the mellow glow of gold through the darkened embrowned foliage, to the dying martyr.[2]

Obviously these 'associated feelings of force and continuity' are physical dynamics expressive of the violence being done to the protagonist of the picture, while the rush 'from earth towards heaven' was clearly seen by Turner as representing the flight of the dying man's soul towards God, as well as the returning light being 'the palm of beatitude' which accepts it. And in another passage on the painting Turner makes very clear his awareness of how the forms of the trees extend the meaning of the work:

> across [the whole picture] rushes the knotted stems of trees with dark brown foliage stretching far their leafy honors and their heads lost in the efulgence of the descending angels to crown the dying Martyr whose looks are directed and the sentiment is compleately carried upward by the imense spreading trunks rearing their expireing and wounded branches[3]

Given Turner's responsiveness here to Titian's employment of tree forms to project the violence being done to the protagonist of the picture, as well as the way those forms make apparent on a broader scale St Peter's sense of pain, fear and his expiration, it seems highly likely that Turner was equally responsive to the way that Titian employs the precise alignment, shaping and spacing of the tree-trunks to further the impact and meaning of his image, even if he did not comment upon it. Titian artfully places the right hand and sword-hilt of the assassin precisely in front of a cleft between two tree-trunks, whilst also locating his other hand, which grasps the saint's garment, exactly in front of two more cloven trunks. St Peter himself gestures upwards towards yet another cleft which 'points' straight down at him. The effect of all these purposeful alignments with pointed V shapes, as well as the shapes themselves, is to suggest very vividly the whole notion of physical penetration which is, after all, the central dramatic act of the entire picture. A sense of thrust is strongly imparted to these pointings by the line that runs down the assassin's arms to St Peter's head. In paintings produced under the direct influence of *St Peter Martyr* around 1802–3 Turner displayed little or no awareness of this metaphorical dimension to Titian's work, but by the time he came to create the two versions of *Battle Abbey* (figs 5 and 42) of just a few years later (one of which dates from 1810 when Turner wrote of Titian's use of tree forms to advance sentiment), we can see a very similar employment of pointed tree-forms to suggest appropriately piercing objects. The uses Turner made of them may well have had their origins in his appreciation of Titian's monumental masterpiece.

The metaphorical use of tree imagery in another work by Titian also appears to have been known to Turner later on in life. This is Titian's *Noli Me Tangere* or 'Touch me not', dating from about 1512 (fig. 83), a work that was bought in 1820 by Turner's friend and collaborator, Samuel Rogers. The subject is taken from John 20, 15–18. After the resurrection Christ appears before Mary Magdalene who at first takes him for a gardener (hence his hoe). However, upon perceiving his real identity she attempts to touch him. Jesus orders her not to, for henceforth his relationship with mankind will be a purely spiritual one. He pulls back his shroud from the Magdalene and the whole sense of leaning is greatly amplified by the solitary pine behind the saviour. This tree reaches up into the sky and its boughs again suggest a sense of divine protection, deliberately placed as they are

**83** Titian, *Noli Me Tangere*, *c.*1508,
oil on canvas, 109 × 91 cm, National Gallery, London.

immediately above Jesus. More clearly, though, the whole tree seems to articulate exactly what Jesus tells the woman to inform his brethren:

> I ascend unto my Father, and your Father; and *to* my God, and your God.

Turner similarly placed figures amplifying religious associations at the base of single, dominating pine trees in *The Loretto Necklace* of 1829 (B.J. 331), *Rome, from Mount Aventine* of 1836 (B.J. 366) and the 1841 *Dawn of Christianity (Flight into Egypt)* which is discussed below (fig. 150). And there are other features in Titian's work that Turner would surely have recognised. For example, beyond the penitent is a town. Titian, like Giorgione, sometimes appears to have used towns as symbols of the temporal world (for instance see Giorgione's *Reclining Venus* in the Gemäldgalerie in Dresden – in which the landscape may have been completed by Titian – or Titian's *Sacred and Profane Love* which is discussed below). The siting of the town on the same side of the picture as the Magdalene seems to fulfil that symbolic function here, especially when we see how beyond Christ on the other side of the work the landscape stretches away, 'eternally blue', towards infinity. Behind Jesus, too, we see a flock of sheep whose symbolic significance needs no elaboration, and both weather and light also add to the meaning of the work by association: just as the Magdalene had

**84** Titian, *Sacred and Profane Love* (*The Bride of Niccolò Aurelio at the Fountain of Venus*), *c.*1514, oil on canvas, 118 × 279 cm, Galleria Borghese, Rome.

repented of her sins, so too the clouds above her clear away, whilst above Christ golden morning light very evidently represents the dawning of his new dispensation.

In *Noli Me Tangere* we witness the device, commonly encountered in late medieval and Renaissance painting, of dividing a landscape background into symbolically contrasting halves in order to create a 'paysage moralisé' which augments the meanings personified by the people depicted in the work. For example, a metaphorical and moral use of contrasted types of landscapes – in this case a juxtaposition of town and country elements, as in *Noli Me Tangere* – occurs in another allegorical work by Titian that was also certainly known to Turner. This is the picture commonly entitled *Sacred and Profane Love* (fig. 84). Turner must have seen the painting initially in the Galleria Borghese in Rome, during his first visit to Italy in 1819, but he also owned a copy of it that was listed in the catalogue of effects sold from his studio in 1874 as '19 After Titian: Divine Love'. Apparently the work was never engraved in its entirety.[4] Only the nude was reproduced and that was entitled 'Amor Profano' below the image, so it cannot have been one of those prints that was sold in 1874. Unfortunately there is no way of knowing when Turner obtained his copy, nor how faithful it may have been, but the fact that he only sketched the original in a very cursory fashion when he saw it in 1819 suggests that he may have done so because he was already well acquainted with some semblance of the work.[5] Be that as it may, he can hardly have been unaware of the contrasts enforced in Titian's picture.

The precise subject of the work has been much disputed. From a limited moralistic standpoint the nude can be seen to represent profane love, as the title of the engraving testifies. The clothed figure, by her modesty, would therefore represent sacred love. This view was countered by Erwin Panofsky who offered the interpretation that the women are twin embodiments of Love in its earthly and celestial guises, the nude representing the latter.[6] The landscape would certainly support this interpretation, for again the town might stand for the temporal world, as would the finery of the seated woman, whilst the countryside stretching away to infinity on the right, with its church spire pointing towards heaven, would thus express the less transient values of the natural world, qualities embodied in the nude. She holds a flaming lamp and her raising of it heavenwards surely points to its divine origin, its contents perhaps being eternal fire. The title in the 1874 sale catalogue suggests that this dimension to the work was thought to be the case. Yet as Charles Hope has recently convincingly demonstrated,[7] the picture does not contrast sacred and profane love at all. Instead, for a variety of reasons cited by Hope, it addresses the subject of marriage, having been commissioned around 1514 by the important Venetian civil servant, Niccolò Aurelio, in celebration of his betrothal. On the left is his bride, looked at approvingly by Venus on the right. Of course in these terms the associative division of the landscape into earthly and divine aspects still works in the same way.

The picture also contains minor elements which may have appealed to Turner. On the left are two rabbits which, in Turner's day at least, were commonly thought of as symbols of fecundity or lust. In 1823 Turner introduced a rabbit into a painting exhibited at the R.A., *The Bay of Baiæ, with Apollo and the Sybil* (fig. 132), probably to signify lust as an attribute of place; the Bay of Baia was associated with ancient profligacy and the cult of Venus, to which the rabbit may also allude. On the right of Titian's painting a greyhound chases a hare which, as we have noted, Turner was to employ as a symbolic image in *Battle Abbey, the spot where Harold fell* (fig. 5) and elsewhere.

Whatever Turner's interpretation of *Sacred and Profane Love* – and he surely *did* interpret the work in symbolic terms, for it makes no sense otherwise – he cannot have failed to see how the landscape furthers the meaning of the figures by association. A less controversial 'paysage moralisé' by Titian must also have been known to him though, and may seriously have affected the way he thought about representing things in time. This is *The Three Ages of Man* (fig. 85) which Turner might have seen when it was exhibited in the Orleans collection in London in 1798–9 or after it was bought by the 3rd Duke of Bridgewater from that collection in 1798. Two years later the duke commissioned a major marine painting from Turner, *Dutch Boats in a Gale: Fishermen endeavouring to put their Fish on Board* (fig. 208), the so-called 'Bridgewater Seapiece' which caused a sensation when it was exhibited at the R.A. in 1801. Turner would have needed to visit Bridgewater House to see the picture by Willem van de Velde the Younger alongside which *Dutch Boats in a Gale* was commissioned to hang,[8] so it is likely he would have been shown the rest of the collection in view of his personal involvement with the Old Masters and the Duke of Bridgewater's concern to

**85** Titian, *The Three Ages of Man*, *c.*1509, oil on canvas, 90 × 151 cm, collection of the Duke of Sutherland on loan to the National Gallery of Scotland.

encourage such interest. He thus had every opportunity to see the Titian, and indeed may have seen it many times after 1806 when the Duke of Bridgewater's heir, the Marquess of Stafford, regularly made the Bridgewater House collection available to Royal Academicians during every London Season.[9]

The imagery of *The Three Ages of Man*[10] is relatively uncomplicated. On the right are two sleeping children, watched over by a Cupid. On the left, beneath verdant leafage, a pair of lovers gaze passionately at each other, whilst further off at the centre an old man contemplates death in the form of two skulls. These, by association, may even represent the skulls of the lovers themselves. Immediately above and beyond the old man stands a church, the mediator between this life and the next, a meaning extended once again by a landscape stretching away towards eternity. The cycle is continued by the dead tree-trunk placed above the sleeping infants. It clearly stands for death in a more general way, and this can only be kept at bay by Love, represented here by the Cupid. The children themselves may personify love, or represent the offspring of the lovers on the left, or *be* the lovers in potentia – the associative possibilities are 'open'. If the children are the offspring of the lovers then the cycle is completed, and can continue for ever and ever – exactly as it does in reality.[11]

Another work by Titian may also have suggested metaphors to Turner. In 1840 Turner produced a picture of *Bacchus and Ariadne* (fig. 186) in which he 'stole' figures directly from Titian's famous painting of the same subject in the National Gallery.[12] A notable feature of Titian's work is the ring of stars he places in the sky above Ariadne. This is an allusion to

**86** Raphael, *The Transfiguration of Christ* (detail),
1518–20, oil on canvas, 405 × 278 cm, Pinacoteca Vaticana, Rome.

future events: after Ariadne's death Bacchus will take the crown he had given her and throw it into the heavens where it will turn into a constellation. The image may very well have suggested the different but not unrelated solar device Turner introduced into Solomon Hart's *Galileo* picture (fig. 8) seven years after painting his own *Bacchus and Ariadne*. (And it should be noted that the Solomon Hart picture actually contains a copy of Martino Rota's engraving of Titian's *The Martyrdom of St Peter* hanging on the wall above Galileo, a clear allusion to the metaphorical fate of the great astronomer.)

Turner was also alert to the metaphors of another Renaissance master, Raphael. He responded with particular enthusiasm to Raphael's use of linear and light symbolism. This emerges from Turner's detailed analysis, around 1818, of a major work by Raphael, the *Transfiguration* of 1518–20, which he saw in Paris in 1802 and was to see again in Rome in 1819. The painting was completed by a pupil, being the last of Raphael's works, and in Turner's day it was widely considered to be his masterpiece. For Turner both the visible and implied linear structures of the upper part of the picture (fig. 86) were so significant that they needed to be demonstrated to his students. Accordingly he made a diagram (fig. 87) which imposed the implied structure upon the image, and he explained both the visible and the implied structures in words:

**87** *Diagram of the upper section of Raphael's Transfiguration,*
pencil and watercolour on paper, 73.8 × 53.8 cm,
Clore Gallery for the Turner Collection, London (T.B. CXCV-163).

. . . there yet exists a higher quality to the rules of perspective; as to the *designing* of the picture . . . the mere introduction of geometric forms, as in the Transfiguration, tho the laws can be traced, the art is concealed. The machinery of its rules lies hidden and it is at this point the *construction* 'of a picture being designed by the rules of Perspective, will ever be held higher in esteem by good judges'[13] and where Du Piles means 'a Picture and Perspective *are* the *same*' . . .[14] Emblems and allegorical concerns have each had their hypers[15] of admiration . . . even Raphael not excepted to indulge in the like pursuit of emblematical explicating as the circle round the heads of the Apostles: divine inspirations or the Triangle as: Divine Unity[16]

(The 'circle' referred to is the aureole of light surrounding Jesus which touches the heads of the Apostles positioned around him.)

Of particular note in this passage – along with its ending – is the way that Turner clearly responded to the subtlety, if not even the covertness of such devices for furthering meaning – 'tho the laws can be traced, the art is concealed. The machinery of its rules lies hidden . . .'[17] And the imaginativeness of his own responses is also made clear by this passage, for not many people would realise that the mere outline of an aureole touching the heads of the Apostles could impart 'divine inspirations'. He was also undoubtedly aware of

147

**88** Raphael, *The Holy Family with the Palm Tree*, *c*.1506,
oil on panel transferred to canvas, 101.4 cm diameter,
collection of the Duke of Sutherland on loan to the National Gallery of Scotland.

the traditional use of a triangle to signify the Trinity[18] but probably saw this as implicit in the concept of 'Divine Unity'. The significance of an upward pointing form at the top of a picture in which Jesus ascends to Heaven was probably not lost on him either. The profound importance to Turner of Raphael's linear symbolism will become apparent below, in discussion of important paintings of 1815 and 1817, one of which the artist considered to be his masterpiece.

Another picture by Raphael may also have made an important impression on Turner. This is *The Holy Family with the Palm Tree* (fig. 88) which Turner might have seen in the Orleans collection exhibition at the end of 1798 or after it was bought by the Duke of

Bridgewater from the exhibition (later it hung in the same gallery of Bridgewater House as the picture by Turner that the duke bought in 1801 [19]). The very shape of this picture, as well as its imagery, may have influenced Turner. One of the major reasons for Turner's attraction to circular compositions in the latter part of his life will be explored below but there can be no doubt that he was familiar with Raphael's use of these formats, for he drew attention to them in his *Rome, from the Vatican. Raffaelle, accompanied by La Fornarina, preparing his Pictures for the Decoration of the Loggia* of 1820 by reproducing Raphael's *Madonna della Sedia* in the centre of the composition and, as has recently been demonstrated,[20] structured the whole centre of the work around the circle it creates.

In *The Holy Family with the Palm Tree* (fig. 88) Raphael places the Madonna and Child beneath the palm tree itself. Palm trees are traditional symbols of the tree of life, and by its placement exactly between Mary and Jesus the tree furthers the association of the life afforded to the Holy Child by his mother, whilst through its dominating position over them it also introduces associations of maternal and divine protection into the scene. On the left the curve created by a sapling repeats the curve created by the kneeling shape of Joseph, subtly emphasising his prostration. Since Turner placed the only palm tree ever to appear in his oil paintings exactly above the Virgin and Child in his circular *Dawn of Christianity (Flight into Egypt)* of 1841 (fig. 150), it is difficult to ignore the likely influence of Raphael's picture upon Turner's work.

Turner was certainly also aware of how earlier landscapists had used metaphorical elements in their works. His comprehension of Rubens's conflation of time in one of his landscapes is worth noting, for instance. This occurs in the picture now known as *The Carters* but which was called 'Landscape with the Waggon' by Turner. He probably knew the work in reversed form through its engraving by Schelte à Bolswert.[21] In *The Carters* Rubens combines a sunny late-afternoon scene on one side of the work with a dark moonlit passage and some bats flying above a couple seated by a campfire on the other. Turner was critical that Rubens ignored 'the immutable laws of nature's light and shade'[22] by directly juxtaposing day and night in this way. Although, as we have seen, he had no objection to the bringing of widely spaced events together in one picture, compression of this kind clearly had to be effected with more rationality and much greater subtlety as far as light is concerned. Turner did not care for Rubens's landscapes in any case because of what he saw as their cavalier attitude to precise effects of light and shadow. There were certain things he was not prepared to license poetically.

Far more to Turner's taste were the landscapes of Nicolas Poussin. In one of his perspective lectures, first delivered in 1811, he extolled Poussin's 'ruling passion . . . for allegorical allusion',[23] noting for instance that in *The Saving of the infant Pyrrhus*[24] Poussin uses the emblematic image of a river-god, who is pouring water from a conch, to represent the almost insuperable physical and dramatic barrier that stands at the heart of the story.

Turner certainly agreed with Reynolds who wrote of the French master's use of codified metaphors that

> If Poussin in imitation of the Ancients represents Apollo driving his chariot out of the sea by way of representing the Sun rising, if he personifies Lakes and Rivers, it is nowise offensive in him; but seems perfectly of a piece with the general air of a picture.[25]

We know Turner felt this way from the fact that in his *Ulysses deriding Polyphemus* of 1829 (fig. 177) he depicted the horses of Apollo pulling the 'chariot' of the God up from the horizon in almost the same way that Poussin had done in his *Cephalus and Aurora*,[26] the very painting Reynolds recommended in the passage cited above.

Turner also stated his particular admiration for Poussin's *Landscape with Pyramus and Thisbe* which evidently he knew in the reversed form of its engraving published in 1769.[27] He expressed his responses metaphorically here, talking of 'the returning Thisbe' appearing in 'the . . . doubt of darkness' as she discovers the dying Pyramus 'amid gloom scatter'd foliage and broken ground' – a surround that certainly observes a sense of decorum.

Another associative aspect of Poussin's art also drew a response from Turner. One of the points he made in his perspective lectures concerns the idea that perspective can actually dictate emotional responses, as it did for him in Poussin's *Landscape with a Roman Road*[28] where 'rules [i.e. ruled lines] produce propriety even in landscape'.[29] Here, through the use of straight lines which create the striking recession of a road into the distance, and the ordering of architectural and landscape elements around it, Turner felt that Poussin had established a dignified mood throughout.

Turner not only responded to landscapes associatively in this way; he also capitalised upon associations stemming from their creators to add to the impact and import of his own works. For instance, he had the deepest respect for the land- and seascapes of Jacob van Ruisdael. On two occasions, in 1827 and 1844, he even painted pictures (B.J. 237 and 408) of a fictitious location in Holland which he named 'Port Ruysdael', to pay homage to the Dutch master and to link his own paintings directly with the tradition represented at its height by Ruisdael. The influence of the Dutch painter upon Turner is more marked in the field of seascape than landscape, although one associative feature of Ruisdael's works – lightning-smashed and dead trees – can be encountered in his landscapes. Indeed, these two similar kinds of objects were amongst the most frequently used associative objects in landscape painting between the sixteenth and nineteenth centuries, being employed to amplify moods of solitude, tragedy and death. They were especially valuable in storm-scenes and their introduction almost became commonplace. We find them in the works of a number of artists that Turner appreciated, including Titian, Salvator Rosa, Gaspard Dughet, Richard Wilson and Philippe Jacques de Loutherbourg. In a memorable image, certainly known to Turner, even Claude – who was never commonplace – resorted to the use of one such device to amplify his meaning.

**89** Salvator Rosa, *Landscape with St Anthony Abbot and St Paul the Hermit*, *c.*1665–8, oil on canvas, 67.3 × 49.5 cm, collection of Denis Mahon.

A typical picture where broken trees fulfil an associative function, to further the mood of lonely desolation and asceticism integral to the subject, is Salvator Rosa's *Landscape with St Anthony Abbot and St Paul the Hermit* (fig. 89). This work shows the meeting of the founder of monasticism and the first Christian hermit. It is not known where or when Turner can possibly have seen it.[30] Yet the great similarity between this picture and Turner's painting of *Jason* exhibited at the R.A. in 1802 (and thus the later mezzotint, fig. 38) strongly suggests that he did see it. In the Turner we see a similar overhanging rock, following exactly the same angle of fissure, and an identically placed cave, as appear in the Rosa. The associative role of the broken trees is very alike in both works, although Turner used them for slightly different purposes and later went on to fashion their forms in the print to introduce more specific associations.

The associative qualities of trees and other objects in some of the works of Antoine Watteau could also have influenced Turner. He undoubtedly knew *Oeuvres des Estampes*

**90** N. de Larmesin after Antoine Watteau, *L'Accordée de Village*, engraving.

**91** C. N. Cochin after Antoine Watteau, *La Mariée de Village*, engraving.

*Gravées d'après . . . Antoine Watteau*, the so-called 'Receuil Jullienne' (named after Jean de Jullienne, its publisher), a four-volume engraved survey of Watteau's pictures. As well as acquainting Turner with such famous images as *Le Pèlerinage à l'Ile de Cythère*, the 'Receuil Jullienne' may have brought to his attention other works that appear to have influenced him, for example *Acis et Galathé*, where the location of the one-eyed giant Polyphemus, on a hillside at the left, strongly foreshadows the location of Polyphemus and the landscape in which he is placed in Turner's own painting, *Ulysses deriding Polyphemus* of 1829 (fig. 177).[31] Also through the 'Receuil Jullienne' Turner may have gotten to know *L'Accordée de Village* (fig. 90), the original painting of which was bought by his patron and friend, John Soane, in 1802. Above the bridal couple here, two tree trunks lead the eye upwards to their intermingled foliage which, as a total form, greatly amplifies the associations of the traditional garland placed above the bride. Similarly, Turner may have known *La Mariée de Village* (fig. 91). In the engraving, which reverses the original image, we see the bride on the right and a solitary pine extending its protection from in front of a magnificent building that is obviously the church in which the wedding will be performed. The sheer magical fantasy of works like *Le Pèlerinage à l'Ile de Cythère*, as well as its colour, certainly had a profound impact on Turner, as did a number of other paintings by the French master,[32] but he must have been alert to Watteau's occasional use of metaphor as well, through both his overt symbolism, as with the cupids flying up into the air at the left of *Le Pèlerinage* – a device

**92** M. Liotard after Antoine Watteau, *Le sommeil dangereux*, engraving.

Turner employed in similar arabesque ways in a number of works – and through his not very covert symbolism. It is hard to look at *Le sommeil dangereux* in the 'Receuil Jullienne', for instance (fig. 92), and not observe how, in keeping with the theme, Watteau introduces obvious sexual symbols, such as the extremely phallic quiver resting amid garlands in the foreground in front of the sleeping women, or the tree stump on the left whose circular top resembles an open orifice. (This particular device is certainly very similar to the one Turner put to different use in *Battle Abbey*, fig. 42). Turner could also have seen Watteau's allegorical representations of the seasons in the 'Receuil Jullienne'.

Another artist not normally associated with landscape painting may nonetheless have also contributed to the development of Turner's associative procedures. This was 'the Father of the English School',[33] Sir Joshua Reynolds himself. Reynolds produced a number of allegorical works. Indeed, Turner can hardly have set foot in the R.A. without seeing his figure of *The Theory of Painting*, a woman holding a scroll bearing the inscription 'Theory is the knowledge of what is truly Nature', a sentiment Turner would have subscribed to wholeheartedly. This work hung in the Academy Library in Somerset House, the home of the R.A. for much of Turner's lifetime, and it was certainly known to him for he referred to it in one of his lectures.[34] The metaphorical dimensions of various works by Reynolds were also well understood and expounded by his contemporaries. For example, in 1813 James Northcote wrote of a picture commissioned by Catherine the Great that

> Reynolds chose to paint . . . the infant Hercules overcoming the serpents when in his cradle . . . in allusion to the great difficulties which the Empress of Russia had to encounter in the civilisation of her empire, arising from the rude state in which she found it.[35]

Similarly, in his second lecture of 1807, John Opie extolled the metaphorical subtleties of Reynolds's *Death of Cardinal Beaufort*.[36] This was engraved for Boydell's Shakespeare Gallery in 1792 and the original painting was owned by the Earl of Egremont, being hung at Petworth where Turner painted a view of it. Other pictures in which Reynolds expressed himself metaphorically may also have been known to Turner. These include *Hope nursing Love* of 1769 which hung at Bowood in Wiltshire (and which was engraved by Bartolozzi); *Recovery from Sickness, an Allegory* showing death carrying a scythe being attacked by an angel, which was in the Reynolds sale in 1796 and which was bequeathed to the Dulwich Picture Gallery after the death of Sir Francis Bourgeois in 1811; *Cupid untying the Zone of Beauty: called the Snake in the Grass* which Turner might have known in more than one of its five versions,[37] and which shows Venus being undressed by Cupid with, literally, a snake in the grass on the right; and the work that Reynolds called 'the finest picture I ever painted', namely *The Three Montgomery Sisters Adorning a Term of Hymen* (which Turner may have known in its engraved form, fig. 93). Here Reynolds depicted a married sister to the right of a term which symbolises marriage, another sister who is about to be married approaching the term, and

**93** Thomas Watson after Sir Joshua Reynolds, *The Three Montgomery Sisters Adorning a Term of Hymen*, mezzotint engraving, 1776.

an unmarried sister still kneeling. The garland that winds around the married sister adds symbolic associations of 'wedlock', as does the plentiful foliage of the landscape behind the two sisters who are committed to marriage, whilst the empty sky on the left beyond the unmarried sister equally denotes her state. If Turner knew this picture, as seems highly probable, the way that Reynolds used landscape and other components symbolically in it would not have been lost on him. (Indeed, there is even a similarity between the general layout of Reynolds's landscape and that of Turner's 1828 *Vision of Medea*, fig. 201.) And elsewhere, in famous military portraits such as those of *Colonel Banestre Tarleton* of 1782 or *Lord Heathfield* of 1788, Reynolds manipulates the elements in ways that have a direct bearing on his subjects, 'the storms of war' clearly adding to the associations of character presented. Turner could have known both of these works through engravings, as well as a great many similar instances of Reynolds's use of metaphor in his portraits. A further example will be given later. Additionally, of course, it may well have been Reynolds who first alerted Turner to the expressive, communicative and cultural value of association, for in the works of the great portraitist it is common to find an enhancement of the status of the sitter or sitters by means of a linkage with the stylistic and visual qualities, as well as the cultural and tailoring technicalities, of an earlier master. Turner was undoubtedly well aware of this.

Yet naturally it was above all from landscape painting that Turner would have learnt most about the use of association and visual metaphor in the sphere of art in which he excelled. Indeed, from the very beginning of his career he can hardly have been unaware of the role of association in such scenes. In the topographical works and 'poetic' productions of painters like Paul Sandby, Thomas Malton, Michael Angelo Rooker, Thomas Hearne, Edward Dayes, J. R. Cozens and Philippe Jacques de Loutherbourg he would often have found simple kinds of associative staffage included to further the ramifications of the landscape depicted. These artists did not necessarily place figures, animals and objects in their landscapes exactly as they had seen them. Frequently they went a stage further, introducing aspects of local life and behaviour into their scenes so as to increase our understanding of place. The indigenous industry or agriculture, the local fairs and gatherings, even the native dress, could add to the interest and charm of a scene.

Of these artists, the works of de Loutherbourg may have proven supremely important to Turner for an aspect of his use of visual metaphor, as we shall see later. Turner lived near the French-born painter in Hammersmith around 1806–11 but he first came into close contact with him much earlier than that. Walter Thornbury tells us that

> It is said that Mrs. Loutherbourg grew very jealous of Turner's frequent visits to her husband, and that at last, suspecting the young painter was obtaining all her husband's secrets from him, she shut the door in his face and roughly refused him admittance.[38]

The fact that a '*young* painter' was troubling de Loutherbourg establishes that this incident must have occurred in the 1790s rather than the mid-1800s when Turner was already an established Academician in his thirties. That supposition is supported by the fact that de Loutherbourg's influence on Turner was at its height in the early 1790s, although it remained visible well into the next decade.[39] The part of the story concerning 'secrets' appears implausible, since Turner was never much interested in technical secrets and de Loutherbourg could hardly have possessed any others that would have been of interest to him, so it must have been some aspect of de Loutherbourg's work that attracted him. Because it seems very likely that de Loutherbourg kept copies of the engravings of his works, just as Turner would later do with reproductions of his own pictures, the younger man could have not only familiarised himself with recent images by the Alsatian master but also with those made before he came to London in 1771.

One such engraving typifies the way de Loutherbourg could employ tree forms associatively. This is *The Shepherdess of the Alps* (fig. 94), the drawing of which was exhibited at the R.A. in 1776. De Loutherbourg creates a striking visual simile here between the convolution of a tree branch above a shepherdess and the shapes of the horns of a ram to which the girl is pointing. The similarity between this connection and the one Turner effected in *Aske Hall* (fig. 35) is very marked.

**94** Francesco Bartolozzi after Philippe Jacques de Loutherbourg,
*The Shepherdess of the Alps*, engraving, 1776.

**95** Philippe Jacques de Loutherbourg, *Travellers attacked by Banditti*, R.A. 1781,
oil on canvas, 67.2 × 105 cm, Tate Gallery, London.

**96** W. Bromley after Philippe Jacques de Loutherbourg,
*Lamentations*, engraving for Macklin's *Bible*, 1796.

Also worthy of note is de Loutherbourg's use of grotesquely stricken trees for their
power to extend the emotional impact of a picture through association. For example, in
*Travellers attacked by Banditti* (fig. 95), de Loutherbourg clearly extends the horror of the
scene by subordinating the human action to the ugly writhing forms of the stricken oak-tree
that is placed in the centre of the Salvator-influenced landscape. The tree itself vividly
projects the inner responses of the protagonists. Although Turner did not necessarily ever
see this work (which was exhibited at the R.A. in 1781), nonetheless similar devices appear
frequently in de Loutherbourg's many other banditti subjects.

Indeed, a large number of pictures by and after de Loutherbourg demonstrate clear
employments of metaphorical imagery and some of these could easily have been seen by
Turner in the 1790s and early 1800s at the height of his interest in the Alsatian painter. De
Loutherbourg was engaged in two major engraving projects at that time, the illustrations to
Macklin's Bible, published between 1793–1800, and Bowyer's edition of David Hume's
*History of England*, published in 1805. In the former, we can witness de Loutherbourg's
typical employment of metaphor in the illustration to *Lamentations* (fig. 96) where he renders

directly the first and eighth verses of Chapter II respectively: 'How hath the Lord covered a daughter of Zion with a cloud in his anger' and 'He made the rampart and the wall to lament'; de Loutherbourg gives us both a cloud which amplifies the gesture of the mother grieving over her child directly below it and, in a somewhat less subtle associative manner, a ruined rampart and wall. De Loutherbourg projects a thorough-going use of association in a great many of his Bible illustrations, and especially in his head and tailpiece designs he produced some of the most powerful, if today little known, of all eighteenth century 'cosmic' images, pushing the sense of the overwhelming power of God over nature to the limit and sometimes even beyond it to an imagery which borders disturbingly on the surreal. The imaginative scope of these designs may well have had an impact on Turner whose sense of the power of the cosmos was to be so powerfully developed and expressed later. On a lesser plane Turner may also have been influenced by de Loutherbourg's *History of England* vignettes, for example by the allegorical figure of malice which is depicted above a still-life of associative paraphernalia connected with the House of Lancaster. Such an image prefigures the many similar vignettes which Turner contributed to historical and topographical works later. And one image by de Loutherbourg in the Bowyer-Hume *History of England*, namely *The Great Fire of London*, where the fire is seen from beneath the arches of London Bridge, foreshadows to a startling degree the design of a vignette of *The Burning of the Houses of Parliament* (w. 1306) made by Turner around 1835.

Another contemporary landscape painter who could have contributed strongly to Turner's sense of the importance of association in landscape painting was Richard Wilson. Turner felt most intensely drawn towards Wilson in the late 1790s, prior to his own discovery of the French artist who is generally considered to be the source of Wilson's stylistic inspiration, and accordingly abandoned Wilson for his mentor. In that decade Turner travelled to Wales 'in search of Richard Wilson's birthplace',[40] literally and metaphorically, for subsequently he produced a number of oil-paintings in which Wilson's strong influence can be detected. Yet in those historical and poetic works with which Turner is known to have been acquainted, he can scarcely have been unaware of the Welsh artist's employment of the associative potentialities of forms to advance meaning, for some of Wilson's methods are strikingly obvious. This usage can typically be seen in what was and is rightly regarded as Wilson's masterpiece of Historical landscape, *The Destruction of the Children of Niobe* (fig. 97) of 1760. Here Wilson placed two shattered tree-stumps exactly midway between Niobe, and Apollo and Diana on the left. The two gods are in the process of killing off Niobe's children with their arrows for having offended their mother, Latona. The tree-stumps make evident the required association that life is being abruptly terminated, through standing beneath a large tree which spreads its foliage over them, just as Niobe stands ineffectually over her dead or threatened offspring. On the right other dead trees also show the literal effects of the storm and metaphorically enlarge upon the theme,

**97** Richard Wilson, *The Destruction of the Children of Niobe*, *c.*1759–60, exhibited Society of Artists 1760, oil on canvas, 147.3 × 188 cm, Yale Center for British Art, New Haven (Paul Mellon Collection).

whilst in keeping with the need for decorum the storm itself extends that meaning even further. As David Solkin has commented:

> The turbulent background parallels and complements the tragic narrative: just as the figures personify the elements clashing around them, so does the setting naturalise both the deities and human beings who act within it.[41]

Wilson's human landscape was surely not lost on Turner. Another good example of this reliance upon association can be seen in Wilson's *Celadon and Amelia*. The original painting dates from 1765 but it is now untraced and is represented here by the engraving made of it by William Wollett and John Browne (fig. 98). The artist took his subject from 'Summer' in

**98** William Woollett and John Browne after Richard Wilson, *Celadon and Amelia*, engraving, 1766.

Thomson's *The Seasons*.[42] Poor Amelia has just been struck dead by lightning whilst engaged upon a 'tender walk' with her lover. On the left a live tree stands above the shattered stump of a dead tree, exactly as Celadon is standing over the corpse of his beloved. On the right two intertwined saplings suggest the emotional relationship the lovers had enjoyed until only a moment before, and equally return Celadon's despairing gesture. Turner used the elements and stricken trees for their associations with death fairly frequently in this way, as in *Battle Abbey, the spot where Harold fell* (fig. 5). We shall witness such usage again.

Finally, because of Turner's knowledge of Pope's willow, we ought to consider *Lodona* by Maria Cosway (fig. 99). This picture demonstrates how widespread was the use of trees to comment upon human responses in Turner's era, and how completely nature and mankind were thought to be interactive. The original painting was exhibited in Macklin's 'Gallery of Poets' in Fleet Street in 1790 and was later engraved for the identically-named published work. Turner may easily have seen Cosway's picture, for receiving its first showing in the same exhibition was an important painting by Reynolds, the *Holy Family*

**99** Francesco Bartolozzi after Maria Cosway,
*Lodona, from Pope's Windsor Forest*, engraving, 1790.

(fig. 193) of 1788 upon which Turner seems to have based his own *Holy Family* exhibited at the R.A. in 1803 (fig. 192).

*Lodona* takes its subject from Alexander Pope's 'Windsor Forest' and shows 'a rural nymph' who, pursued by Pan, vainly implored the help of Father Thames to escape. At last she beseeches the help of Cynthia and, 'melting as in tears she lay / In a soft silver stream dissolved away'. Maria Cosway shows Lodona literally turning into water and she draws upon suitable associations of Alexander Pope by depicting Lodona weeping beneath a weeping willow. The flowing shape of the tree adds greatly to the forlorn sentiment of the work.

Maria Cosway's picture presents us with a very typical example of how association contributed to a poetic landscape of Turner's day. Yet throughout this discussion of the associative and metaphorical elements in art that may have appealed to Turner or certainly did so, only one small mention has been made of the painter who probably more than any other furthered his sense of the value of association and metaphor in landscape painting, and who in any case undoubtedly exerted the deepest painterly influence that was ever exercised upon him. But it is not through negligence that Claude Gellée, known as Claude le Lorrain, has been ignored till now. It is simply that Claude's influence was so complex in this respect that it merits two entire chapters to itself.

162

# FIVE

# The Power of Imitation

And this our life, exempt from public haunt,
Finds tongues in trees, books in the running brooks,
Sermons in stones, and good in everything.

*William Shakespeare,*
'*As You Like It*', Act II, scene 1

IN the works of Claude le Lorrain Turner perceived a completely harmonious expression of a physically ideal world that for him clearly set the standard of beauty to which all landscape painting should aspire, exactly as it had for Reynolds who proclaimed Claude the paragon of the genre in the fourth of his Discourses. Claude's idealism was matched by Turner to the end of his days and, if anything, he advanced it continuously and significantly. In this particular respect we can gauge just how deeply Turner was imbued with the artistic spirit of the late eighteenth century that had shaped him. His development of Claudian pictures, from the early *Caernarvon Castle* of 1800, through to *Dido building Carthage* and *Crossing the Brook* of that *annus mirabilis* of 1815, right up to the final four works he publicly exhibited in 1850, are a measure of the constancy of that identification. Obviously Claude's feeling for landscape organisation, as well as his sense of colour, deployment of light effects, attention to detail and advancement of expression, proved a vital stimulus to Turner's own pictorial, observational and expressive skills. More importantly, though, Claude made Turner aware of the imaginative power of painting, its capacity for articulating otherwise inexpressible responses through association, and above all its ability to project a visionary sensibility, one that Turner was himself to develop to a degree of intensity perhaps unprecedented in the history of western painting, and surely not equalled since.

Of course his identification with Claude has long been recognised. Yet are we justified in feeling that most of Turner's 'borrowings' from Claude have already been discovered? Might not an incomprehension of the associative dimensions to the works of both painters have perhaps caused us to overlook the stimulus that Turner's imagination clearly received from his recognition of associative aspects in Claude's art?

These questions obviously need answering. But before we can attempt to demonstrate the profound impact of Claude upon Turner's development of associative devices like visual metaphors – and indeed upon his whole imaginative sensibility – we will need to establish that Claude himself employed those devices in his own works, and that Turner recognised them. And before we can attempt to do that we need to establish the extent of Turner's knowledge of Claude's works, for there would be no point in analysing Claude's metaphors if there was little chance that Turner ever saw the images that contain them.

As far as we know, Turner began looking intensively at Claude's works in the late 1790s, and we are fortunate in possessing anecdotes that relate his responses to two paintings at around that time. These are set out below in connection with the pictures in question. Yet before 1814 there were no public collections in Britain and opportunities to see such masterpieces were comparatively limited. Perhaps the main way to view any quantity of pictures in the days before photography was through the medium of prints – Turner had a large print collection – and with certain artists copies of their works were collected together in bound volumes of prints. One such artist was Watteau and another was Claude, although neither painter was himself directly responsible for the engravings after their works that appeared in this way, nor for the collections themselves. Although undoubtedly Turner must have availed himself of every possible chance to see Claude's paintings on his travels, nevertheless a more readily accessible, if aesthetically less satisfying means of familiarisation, enabled him to acquaint himself extremely thoroughly with the majority of Claude's pictures.

This was through a set of engravings known as the *Liber Veritatis*. The original *Liber Veritatis* was a book of 195 drawings in which Claude recorded most of his works upon their completion. He began using this book around 1635, when he was 35 years old, and it remained in use right up until his death in 1682. There is little chance that Turner ever saw the original book even though it was in England during his lifetime. Instead, he knew the work from the set of mezzotints engraved from it by Richard Earlom which was published in 1777 by John Boydell in two volumes, each volume containing a hundred plates. In the mezzotint prints Earlom used etched lines to represent Claude's original pen lines and sepia ink for his washes. It was this same technique that Turner employed between 1807 and 1823 when he created a work based directly upon the books of engravings after Claude. His *Liber Studiorum* was originally planned to consist of a hundred plates, each allocated to a specific category – Marine, Historical, Mountainous, Architectural, Pastoral and Elevated or Epic Pastoral. Although Turner originally began his project for a reason similar to the one Claude gave for creating his own book – i.e. to establish a record of his œuvre which would prevent injurious copies from being passed off as originals – nonetheless the undertaking very soon fired Turner's imagination and he made a number of new images for the series. After appearing in fourteen parts, comprising a total of seventy-one prints (including a frontispiece), the project fizzled out due to financial problems and to a lessening of interest by the artist, leaving an additional twenty plates uncompleted and preparatory drawings for the rest.

When Turner came to make the *Liber Studiorum* he must have looked carefully at the Earlom model, as he almost certainly had done already and was to go on doing for many more years to come. For any appreciation of the dramatic range of Claude's work the Earlom *Liber Veritatis* was the logical 'book of studies' and indeed, its usage for such a purpose might suggest exactly why Turner came to title his *Liber Studiorum* as he did, particularly if we consider that during the early 1830s, when sets of the engravings were being split up for sale by dealers, Turner complained bitterly of the public who bought the prints: 'Don't they know what Liber Studiorum means?'[1] And what amongst other things Turner very evidently derived from such study was the appreciation that the mature Claude very frequently extended the meanings of his subjects by a complementary use of the landscape. Unless we share that perception then we see a good number of Claude's pictures – as we might Turner's – merely as idyllic scenes without further meanings (except of course purely sensory ones). Instead, as Michael Kitson has cogently stated,

> we ought to supplement this approach with something more. For when we take the subject into account, and above all when we know the story of that subject in some detail, we discover that what we have previously seen as a generalised 'aura of feeling' now assumes a more precise significance. We find . . . that the mood which [Claude] had created in terms of the landscape alone is at the same time perfectly adapted to express the emotions associated with the story . . .[2]

And Marcel Roethlisberger, who compiled the complete catalogues of both Claude's paintings and drawings, and one of the most perceptive writers on the artist to date, has made even more revealing comments on Claude's fusions of form and content through the interaction of figures and landscapes, offering insights that are as pertinent to Turner as they are to Claude:

> Contrary to common belief, Claude's figures are not simply an embellishment, nor are they added *a posteriori*; rather, the subject is the primordial element from which the entire composition is conceived and by which it has to be understood. All of Claude's pictures contain figures, and they provide the key to the meaning of the landscapes . . . the landscapes become more and more the pictorial equivalent of the specific literary theme and the meaning implied in it. The landscape, in other words, is composed in the mode of the subject. This correspondence . . . reveals the deepest quality of Claude's art.[3]

The correspondence is, of course, communicated through Claude's sense of colour and appreciation of light effects, but it is equally present in the disposition of his natural forms, and it is this latter correspondence that is particularly discernible in the Earlom set of prints. (And as it is being suggested that Turner initially approached many of Claude's images through that medium it therefore seems valid to examine these correspondences through the engravings.)

Claude's imaginative landscape elaborations of his human subject-matter are not difficult to recognise once one perceives the artist's acute awareness of the dramatic potentialities of association and his alertness to the ability of forms to suggest other things through similarity – exactly as with Turner. Perhaps no one since Claude's time has been in a better position to grasp this aspect of his work than Marcel Roethlisberger. In one of the most perceptive passages in the introduction to his catalogue of Claude's paintings he isolates what is probably the single most important associative element in the artist's work:

> . . . the expressive language of the trees, which for Claude became instruments of poetry, is of the greatest importance in his paintings. Each story has its specific kind of tree or combination of trees, and their shapes are in conformity with the character of the subject.

Roethlisberger then goes on to illustrate these points by noting how, for instance, in the only three Old Testament subjects with courageous heroes or heroines that Claude depicted, each work is dominated by a single large oak-tree standing apart, an isolation which appears nowhere else in his œuvre; how rough wild willow trees appear at the sides of compositions which take as their subjects stories involving some degree of dispute, force or rupture; how large noble pine trees are associated with classical, and particularly Ovidian subjects; and how in many works Claude creates parallels between the contrasting personalities of the participants in the story and the contrasting qualities of his trees. Roethlisberger also comments:

> As the varieties of the trees are in keeping with the themes, so also the movements of trunks and foliage express the action of the figures.

**100**  Richard Earlom after Claude le Lorrain,
*Landscape with the temptation of St. Anthony*
(*Liber Veritatis* 32), mezzotint engraving, 1777.

He then goes on to explore these amplifications in a number of works, some of which we shall examine below. He concludes that

> A symbolism of this kind is intuitive, never dogmatic, and has nothing in common with the farfetched interpretations of trees in the emblematic literature [of the seventeenth century].

He also adds in a note to the end of this passage that 'In many drawings of the *Liber Veritatis* the movements of the trees are even increased' (in relationship to the original models). Moreover, these are not the only devices Claude used to extend the meanings of his works. He employed line for the same purpose, as Turner undoubtedly realised, as well as the effects of light and weather.

In Claude's case, as much as Turner's, we need to establish both the pattern and extent of these associations. It is therefore worth looking at the associative devices in Claude's pictures in some detail, not least of all because Turner evidently did the same thing.

A small selection of pictures seen through the Earlom mezzotints will suffice to indicate the extent to which Claude employed associative imagery. As Roethlisberger points out, Claude's first metaphorical use of a tree occurs in *Liber Veritatis* (hereafter *LV*) 32, *Landscape with the temptation of St Anthony*[4] (fig. 100) where we see the saint looking at a divine light appearing from the top right. On the left are two barges filled with devils. Rising away from St Anthony is a willow tree which introduces associations of wildness, and upon which two forked dead branches quite clearly pun upon the great many diabolical horns placed immediately beneath them (Turner may have noticed this pun and repeated something similar in *Simmer Lake, near Askrig*, fig. 39). In *LV* 37, *Landscape with a hunting party* (fig. 101), we observe some riders, one of whom is pointing to the right, a gesture that is repeated by

**101** Richard Earlom after Claude le Lorrain,
*Landscape with a hunting party*
(*Liber Veritatis* 37), mezzotint engraving, 1777.

**102** Richard Earlom after Claude le Lorrain,
*Landscape with the finding of Moses*
(*Liber Veritatis* 47), mezzotint engraving, 1777.

**103** Richard Earlom after Claude le Lorrain,
*Landscape with Samuel anointing David King of Israel*
(*Liber Veritatis* 69), mezzotint engraving, 1777.

the huntsman standing in front of him. Their gestures, and the direction they take, are clearly amplified by the shapes of the branches and foliage of the tree that reaches out to the right-hand side of the picture. In *LV* 47, *Landscape with the finding of Moses* (fig. 102), Claude places a sleeping shepherd in the foreground, perhaps to establish by association the helplessness of the infant. On the left a broken tree stands under the shadow of a larger one whose shape also reaches over Moses. This relationship parallels the story, for had Moses stayed with his mother he would have been killed; instead, we now see him being taken under the protection of Pharaoh's daughter. In *LV* 69, *Landscape with Samuel anointing David King of Israel* (fig. 103) the anointing is taking place under a portico on the left. Exactly as Samuel raises the horn of oil above David, so too his gesture is amplified by a single tree which emerges from the ground just behind him. It leans over the sacrificial altar in the centre and extends the idea of divine benediction by association. In *LV* 88, *Landscape with the rest on the flight into Egypt* (fig. 104 and painting, fig. 153) a large oak dominates the wilder trees on the other side of the river and amplifies the suggestion of protection already afforded to the Holy Family by the angels. In *LV* 125, *Landscape with the journey to Emmaus* (fig. 105), Claude frames Jesus and a disciple at each hand with two sets of three trees,

**104** Richard Earlom after Claude le Lorrain,
*Landscape with the rest on the flight into Egypt*
(*Liber Veritatis* 88), mezzotint engraving, 1777.

**105** Richard Earlom after Claude le Lorrain,
*Landscape with the journey to Emmaus*
(*Liber Veritatis* 125), mezzotint engraving, 1777.

whilst beyond them is a triple arched bridge. Just as one of the disciples gestures towards the sun saying 'Abide with us: for it is toward evening and the day is spent' (Luke, 24: 29), so too one of the trees in each group points in the same direction, reinforcing his action. The grouping of the trees into threes, and the number of the arches of the bridge, might also be intended to allude in a traditional way to the crucifixion, a reference that would not be inappropriate here. In *LV* 141 *Coast View with Acis and Galatea* (fig. 106) we see the two lovers in the centre; on the left two trees are closely intertwined (as in Wilson's *Celadon and Amelia*, fig. 98). The lovers are seated beneath a rough awning which is supported by a branch behind Acis. The direction this branch takes initiates a strong diagonal line that leads the eye across to the one-eyed giant, Polyphemus, who is seated on the opposite hillside at the right. Polyphemus is in love with the sea-nymph and when he finds her with Acis, he will kill him. The line implies their fatal connection. Polyphemus's impending mood of jealous rage is suggested by the lowering storm-clouds and setting sun, associative effects that accord with Turner's later use of such devices. (Polyphemus was later to be the subject of one of Turner's greatest masterpieces, fig. 177.) In *LV* 158, *Pastoral Landscape with the Flight into Egypt* (fig. 107), the Holy Family have again crossed a river to the safety of Egypt, a location

**106** Richard Earlom after Claude le Lorrain,
*Coast View with Acis and Galatea*
(*Liber Veritatis* 141), mezzotint engraving, 1777.

**107** Richard Earlom after Claude le Lorrain,
*Pastoral Landscape with the Flight into Egypt*
(*Liber Veritatis* 158), mezzotint engraving, 1777

denoted by the pyramid in the distance. Above them a mass of foliage extends its cover, whilst on the near side of the river a wild willow and a broken stump associatively suggest what might have befallen Jesus had he stayed in Bethlehem. Turner was clearly to remember this juxtaposition of trees in his own *Flight into Egypt* (fig. 150), exhibited at the R.A. in 1841. In *LV 173*, *Landscape with Abraham expelling Hagar and Ishmael* (fig. 108) Abraham drives away his servant girl and the son she has borne him. They are watched by his wife Sarah on the balcony at the left. Abraham gestures towards the wilderness Hagar and Ishmael are being banished to, and the direction his gesture describes is greatly amplified by the trunk of the large tree that towers above and beyond him. This directional emphasis is strengthened by the parallel tree-trunk on the extreme right. In the foreground various bits of broken masonry suggest the break-up of Abraham's home. And in *LV 180*, *Coast of Libya with Aeneas hunting* (fig. 109) we can see Aeneas, accompanied by Achates, slaying deer to provide food for his fleet anchored on the left. The straightness of Aeneas's aim is very strongly suggested by the single straight pine tree occupying the foreground.

These few analyses should suffice at this stage to establish that Claude did employ associative suggestion to further the contents of his works. Many other examples will also be given. But it is not surprising that Claude developed such a strain in his art. Over half of his works are historical in subject and almost all are artificial landscapes in the sense that they are imaginative constructs whose details are composed of topoi, objects and effects he had observed in isolation from one another. Claude painted very few of his pictures directly from nature and therefore, like Turner, he needed an imaginative rationale with which to compose the landscapes he created in his studio. That foundation could most obviously be a

**108** Richard Earlom after Claude le Lorrain,
*Landscape with Abraham expelling Hagar and Ishmael*
(*Liber Veritatis* 173), mezzotint engraving, 1777.

**109** Richard Earlom after Claude le Lorrain,
*Coast of Libya with Aeneas hunting*
(*Liber Veritatis* 180), mezzotint engraving, 1777.

**110** Richard Earlom after Claude le Lorrain, *Landscape with the death of Procris* (*Liber Veritatis* 100), mezzotint engraving, 1777.

**111** *Procris and Cephalus*, mezzotint engraving, Part VIII of *Liber Studiorum*, 1812. The engraving was drawn and etched by Turner, and engraved by G. Clint.

subject drawn from history, religion or mythology, and it seems natural that the artist would then have adapted all the elements of the landscape to complement and increase the impact of his subject. Such an integration was not only a test of the imagination but also a means of satisfying the creative process, giving it a goal to aim for and fulfil on every level. Turner understood this procedure perfectly and practised it in his own work.

Indeed, in this respect one of Turner's pictures reveals a particularly close correspondence to a Claudian model, while also proving beyond doubt that Turner knew the Earlom set of engravings. It also demonstrates how fully he assimilated Claudian metaphor from that source. This emerges from a comparison between the Earlom mezzotint of Claude's *Landscape with the death of Procris* (*LV* 100, fig. 110) and Turner's *Liber Studiorum* mezzotint of *Procris and Cephalus* (fig. 111) which was published as plate 41 in part VIII of the work in February 1812. As Claude's original painting had long disappeared by Turner's day, he can only have known its image through Earlom's print, for although a poor copy of the painting was in England at the time, it was owned by the collector Sir George Beaumont. For reasons that will become apparent, it would therefore not have been accessible to Turner by around 1810 when he made the drawing from which the print was later developed.[5]

Both pictures depict a subject taken from Ovid's *Metamorphoses*. Procris suspects her husband of infidelity and whilst spying on him when he is out hunting at dawn, she is accidentally killed by Cephalus with the magic, unerring spear he has been given by Diana, the goddess of hunting. The hunting association, link with Diana and time of day are clearly denoted by the placing of a deer in front of the rays of dawn light immediately above Cephalus. Claude has changed the spear into an arrow, and a prominent feature of his picture is the strong diagonal that cuts right across the foreground. This forces our attention upon the dead Procris and, more importantly, associatively suggests the path that the 'fatal dart' has taken. Above Procris is another associative element, a shattered tree-stump whose top is denuded of foliage through having been struck dead by lightning, as the broken branches demonstrate. The fact that Claude places it immediately above the dead Procris hardly seems coincidental; after all, this is the only such shattered stump in the entire *Liber Veritatis* and its location cannot but point up Claude's associative intentions.

Turner created an identical diagonal line, following the same direction, and for identical associative reasons, in his *Procris and Cephalus* (fig. 111). Here again Cephalus's missile is represented by an arrow, a correspondence with Claude's image which surely proves that Turner knew the Claude. The line which denotes the path the arrow had recently taken runs across the picture from the right, although it is implied rather than stated, as in the Claude. Nonetheless it is easily visible, consisting of a sunbeam of dawn light in the distance, which the eye then connects with the base of an opening through the trees at the centre, and the arrow piercing Procris. Artfully Turner does not create any other lines in the entire work even nearly parallel to the diagonal. With one exception all the tree-trunks slant to the left or grow vertically and thus there is nothing to divert attention from the most significant line of all. The trunk that does lean away to the right, though, serves to stress the gap through which we see the distant point of light from which the line emanates, reinforcing its power as a result. A comparison of the crucial associative role of the identical diagonal line in both works helps test the merit of W. G. Rawlinson's claim that 'The death of Procris is one of the subjects in Claude's *Liber Veritatis* but his treatment of it is widely different and could in no way have suggested Turner's plate'.[6] And Turner's responsiveness to Claude's metaphor suggests that other elements of his *Procris and Cephalus* are metaphorical too. The dell, gradually darkening into the distance, rather suggests the recent darkening of Procris's mind, whilst instead of placing a stricken tree above Procris, as Claude did, Turner puts a flowering bush above Cephalus, obviously to denote his continuing power of life. This alteration serves to demonstrate Turner's awareness of Claude's use of tree-symbolism in his *death of Procris*, for although the association is reversed the parallel is so close as to obviate the possibility of coincidence.

The relationship between human responses and tree forms was also directly addressed by Claude in another painting that was known to Turner. This work had to be familiar to him by about 1801, for it hung right alongside his picture owned by the 3rd Duke of Bridgewater.[7] Naturally the Earlom engraving (*LV* 142, fig. 112) may also have served him as a useful *aide-mémoire*. In the list of contents at the beginning of the second volume of engravings the picture is entitled *Landscape with nymphs dancing. The Apulian Clown changed into a Wild Olive Tree*. The subject is taken from Book XIV of Ovid's *Metamorphoses* and tells of an Apulian shepherd who mocks a group of nymphs by jumping about in clumsy imitation of their dancing, and verbally insulting them into the bargain. For his pains he is transformed into a wild olive tree. The bitter taste of the olive is supposed to reveal traces of the harshness of his language to this day, whilst 'the shrub the coarseness of the clown retains'.[8]

Claude shows the clown actually undergoing his metamorphosis as the nymphs look on. In addition to stressing the direct anthropomorphism of the poem, Claude also makes other trees in the picture allusively reinforce the theme: a pine tree stands on the right, its graceful branches and slender trunk amplifying the grace and demeanour of the nymphs; across on the extreme left-hand side of the work, in a calculatedly opposed position, a wild-willow tree returns the now desperately unfunny gestures of the clown.

If we look at Turner's watercolour of *Colchester, Essex* (fig. 113), made around 1825 for the 'England and Wales' series, we see he used the associative suggestiveness of tree forms in a way that very strongly appears to have derived from this picture. Turner shows the view looking south towards Colchester Castle, with Middle Mill on the right. In front of the millrace, a 'mill race' takes place as children issuing from the mill chase after a hare. As the hare metaphor in *Battle Abbey, the spot where Harold fell* suggests, there seems no reason why Turner should not have taken a similar punning attitude to words here. On the left, across

**112** Richard Earlom after Claude le Lorrain, *Landscape with nymphs dancing. The Apulian Clown changed into a Wild Olive Tree (Liber Veritatis* 142), mezzotint engraving, 1777.

**113** *Colchester, Essex, c.*1825, watercolour on paper, 28 × 40 cm, Courtauld Institute of Art, London.

the pond where a horse stands drinking, its rider raises his arms to shoo the hare. To the right of him are some pollard willows, their shapes exactly mimicking his waving gestures. This repetition demonstrates Turner's penchant for visual simile once again, and the precise balance of the rider and the willows on either side of the pond establishes that the correspondence is not accidental. Turner has wittily made the trees mimic human actions, just as Claude had done in *The Apulian Clown*.[9]

The story of the unfortunate Apulian shepherd was the subject of the very work in which Turner came closest to Claude in terms of the appearance of any of his paintings. *Apullia in Search of Appullus vide Ovid* (fig. 114) dates from 1814 and Turner actually based the layout of his painting upon another work by Claude, his *Landscape with Jacob, Laban and his daughters* (fig. 115) of 1654 which has hung in the great collection of the Wyndham family at Petworth since at least 1730. The two works are virtually identical. Yet although Turner would have known Claude's painting, for he stayed at Petworth in 1809, he is not thought to have visited the house between 1813–14 when he was painting his own picture, and so it seems almost certain that he used the Earlom *Liber Veritatis* engraving (*LV* 134, fig. 116) as an *aide-mémoire* for his work.[10] This supposition is supported by the fact that although the two paintings are virtually identical in height, and were probably so originally, the width of Turner's picture conforms slightly more to the compressed width of the Earlom engraving; an engraving of the Claude by William Woollett dating from 1783 reproduced the picture in reverse, so it is much less likely to have been used by Turner.[11] It is worth analysing Claude's *Landscape with Jacob, Laban and his daughters* in terms of its own content, however, for although Turner merely based *Apullia in Search of Appullus* upon its overall design, nonetheless he must have examined the work carefully to understand its meaning, and here too he may well have detected Claude's pronounced use of association.

The subject of *Jacob, Laban and his daughters* is taken from Genesis, 29: 15–20. Jacob has served Laban for seven years in return for the promised hand of Rachel, Laban's younger daughter. However, after the period of service has elapsed Laban has surreptitiously married him to her elder sister Leah instead, as he did not want 'to give the younger [daughter] before the elder'. Jacob's realisation of the deception has just taken place, the sisters having revealed their identity by removing their veils. Leah is standing between the two men who are both pointing at her.[12] Jacob is simultaneously protesting at the deception and reminding Laban that he had kept his part of the bargain. But only after another seven years of service will he gain Rachel as his second wife.

One of Claude's associative elaborations of this narrative seems remarkably clear. Jacob has served Laban seven years: the bridge in middle distance therefore has seven arches. And the story appears to be furthered by other associative devices as well. Jacob's entrapment into marriage to a woman he did not want is amplified by the associations of the fishing net that floats across the river beyond but equally around the heads of the whole

**114** *Apullia in Search of Appullus vide Ovid*, B.I. 1814,
oil on canvas, 146 × 238.5, Clore Gallery for the Turner Collection, London.

**115** Claude le Lorrain, *Landscape with Jacob, Laban and his daughters*, signed and dated 1654,
oil on canvas, 143.5 × 251.5 cm, National Trust, Petworth House, Sussex.

group of figures. The shape it makes enlarges upon the shapes made by the women's veils which themselves allude to the fact that Jacob had been fooled into marrying the wrong woman (the Bible does not specify exactly how Laban effected the substitution). The solitary wild-willow on the left, by its isolation in relationship to the clump of trees on the right, echoes Jacob's lonely predicament while its turbulent shape projects something of his anger at learning of the fraud. The other group of trees consists of a large oak with two saplings growing at its base. One of the saplings stands forward from its parent tree, the other leans away to the right. They personify the new relationship of Laban's two daughters to their father and Jacob.[13] The large tree also dominates the grove of trees beyond, much as Laban leads his tribe.

Turner's 1814 'imitation' of this picture, *Apullia in Search of Appullus vide Ovid* (fig. 114), was painted as an entry in an annual competition for the 'best landscape' offered by the rival organisation to the Royal Academy, the British Institution, which was managed by a group of connoisseurs who included Sir George Beaumont. In 1807, when the competition began, it was a requirement that the picture entered for consideration for the hundred guinea Premium or prize should be 'proper in Point of Subject and Manner to be a Companion' to a work by Claude or Poussin. Although that demand eventually lapsed, it may have remained in Turner's mind when he came to paint his picture some years later. Turner submitted the work eleven days after the closing date for eligibility for the Premium. He failed to win the prize but it is possible that he had a more personal motive for exhibiting the picture. *Apullia in Search of Appullus* was his means of revenging himself upon Sir George Beaumont who had been an especially strong critic of his work throughout the 1800s and whom Turner detested for being the worst kind of 'connoisseur', because Beaumont laid down the law in ways damaging to artists. Beaumont was not altogether hostile to contemporary developments in literature and the fine arts, as his friendship with Wordsworth, prolonged encouragement of Constable and support for J. R. Cozens, Girtin, Wilson, Wilkie and Landseer demonstrates, and he was also a practising landscape painter who had studied with Wilson. But he became very reactionary as he got older and developed a desire 'to be supreme Dictator on Works of Art', as one of his contemporaries noted.[14] Increasingly he came to resent Turner's creative daring, particularly the heightening of his palette, as well as his influence in this respect upon Callcott. Indeed, Beaumont dubbed the two artists 'the White painters' for this very reason. It is also possible to detect elements of jealousy in Beaumont's attitude to Turner – after all, in 1796 a London newspaper had stated that 'Sir George Beaumont is unquestionably at the head of the Landscape [school]'[15] – and he was certainly active in dissuading other collectors from buying Turner's works.[16] It is therefore probably not surprising that Turner detested him.

Yet there was also an element of hypocrisy in Beaumont's attitude towards Turner which must have rankled as well. For some time before 1813 Beaumont had complained to

**116** Richard Earlom after Claude le Lorrain, *Landscape with Jacob, Laban and his daughters* (*Liber Veritatis* 134), mezzotint engraving, 1777.

people who obviously passed on his strictures to the painter that Turner 'had done more harm in misleading the taste than any other Artist'[17] and that whilst he 'acknowledged that Turner had merit . . . it was of the wrong sort and therefore on account of the seducing skill displayed should be objected to, to prevent its bad effects in inducing others to imitate it'.[18] This was richly ironic coming from Beaumont, for as one of the guiding spirits of the British Institution the connoisseur had been a prime mover in 'misleading the taste'. Principally he encouraged the copying of the Old Masters, rather than a promulgation of the kind of fruitful artistic 'imitation' or creative renewal of past styles that Reynolds had advocated and that Turner followed. Indeed, as Constable was to complain in 1822:

> Could you but see the folly and ruin exhibited at the British Gallery, you would go mad. W. Vander Velde, and Gaspar Poussin, and Titian, are made to spawn millions of abortions . . .[19]

It was obviously this problem which led Turner to out-copy the copyists by painting *Apullia in Search of Appullus*. For a long time Beaumont had been sniping at Turner, denying that he could approach Claude. Now Turner would show him how wrong he was, whilst carrying his argument into the enemy camp (for of course the British Institution was generally considered to be the rival body to the Royal Academy). Instead of creatively improving upon Claude, Turner would suspend his own sense of compositional invention to produce an almost straight pastiche, thus making it clear that if he wanted to he could follow an Old Master just as Beaumont required, and do so better than anyone. He would also choose a subject with which to revenge himself upon Beaumont in the process. In order to make his point complete, Turner invented a new character in the story of 'the Apulian clown', for nowhere in Ovid is there a female whose name imitates that of the imitative shepherd.

At the bottom left-hand corner of the work (fig. 117) Turner both identifies the dramatic protagonists and explains the exact action of the picture by writing 'Appulia in Search of Appulus learns from the Swain the cause of his Metamorphosis'.[20] Because of the use of the definite article before the word 'Swain', and from the use of the word 'Swain' itself (which means a rustic lover), we may take this title to mean that Apullia hears from Appullus himself the cause of his transformation, and equally that Apullia is the object of his affections, if not his beloved.

Above the inscription is a wild olive tree. A shepherd points at the name 'Appulus' written on its bark. We may reasonably take this man to be 'the Swain' who is informing Apullia of his own plight. Obviously we are seeing him *before* his metamorphosis. Another, seated shepherd also gestures towards the tree which equally represents Appullus *after* his

**117** *Apullia in Search of Appullus vide Ovid* (detail).

transformation. Clearly we are encountering the employment of narrative simultaneity here, as we have done already in later works like *St. Julienne's Chapel* (fig. 74). And Turner makes clear the current feelings of the transformed shepherd immediately beneath the tree. At its base is a figure seated in the traditional pose for denoting sorrow, his head resting dejectedly in his hand. Maybe this man simultaneously personifies Appullus in yet a third guise.

Apullia can be seen standing with the group of women who are located in front of the seven-arched bridge, a structure whose form also serves to underline the notion of division into two. It has been argued that the dancing girl is Apullia.[21] However, this is certainly not the case, for Apullia is hardly likely to dance upon being told of Appullus's misfortune. On the contrary, the dancer must be one of the nymphs who has been the cause of Appullus's downfall and no doubt she alludes to that fact. Surely it is the solemn-faced woman lifting her veil next to the dancer who is Apullia. She is based directly upon the Rachel in Claude's picture and physically stands in front of the dancing nymph, looking sadly at the olive tree whilst she is told the cause of her loss by the swain pointing to the tree.[22] And in the raising of her veil (which is assisted by one of the accompanying women) lies the whole dramatic point of the picture. Unlike Rachel's veil which kept the truth from Jacob, Apullia's veil has kept the truth only from herself: she has followed a fool and now realises it. But Turner also wanted to lift some veils, because for him the copyists of the British Institution who were encouraged by Sir George Beaumont were also following a fool, and sooner or later they too must realise the folly of being led by such a man. In *Apullia in Search of Appullus* Turner demonstrates that straightforward copying is not difficult, that thoughtless guying has its dangers and that blind following leads to sorrow. The painting is about the landscape it depicts, and the people in that surround, but it is no less about art and artistic identity.

In the above works we can perceive how closely Turner studied Claude and built upon his perception of the way that the French master employed both line and tree-forms to advance the meaning of his works. And other Claudes may have furthered Turner's appreciation as well. In this respect two major paintings, the so-called 'Altieri' Claudes, can be seen to have generated specific responses in such terms. It is worth examining them with their Turnerian progeny in detail.

These paintings are *Landscape with the Father of Psyche sacrificing at the Milesian Temple of Apollo* (fig. 118), and *Landscape with the Landing of Aeneas in Latium* (fig. 120). Although the pictures are pendants they were not painted together. The first work dates from 1663, the latter from 1675. Both paintings were commissioned by members of the Altieri family and they stayed in the Altieri collection right up until the late 1790s when they were purchased and sent to Britain in a man-of-war, the *Tigre*, which Nelson detached from his Mediterranean fleet. They were eventually sold to William Beckford. Turner first saw the Altieri Claudes when Beckford put them on view at his London house in May 1799. Farington recorded in his diary that upon seeing one of them (probably the *Landscape with the Father of Psyche*, fig. 118),

> Turner said He was both pleased and unhappy while He viewed it, – it seemed to be beyond the power of imitation.[23]

Turner had further, extended opportunities to study the works in detail after they were removed to Fonthill, Beckford's home in Wiltshire, which he visited for three weeks in mid-August 1799, and again in the autumn of 1800. As the degree of influence they had upon him was clearly so strong[24], it is perhaps better for us to look at the original paintings in detail, rather than the prints which were made at one remove from them.

*Landscape with the Father of Psyche sacrificing at the Milesian Temple of Apollo* and its pendant are amongst the largest paintings Claude ever produced. When Turner saw them in 1799, 1800, and perhaps again in 1816 and 1818, the works must have been considerably dirtier than we see them today, having previously hung in the same spot for about 135 years.[25] The pictures also probably suffered during transportation to England and by all accounts they were diabolically 'cleaned' in the late 1820s, although the damage has since been rectified. Marcel Roethlisberger considers them to be Claude's most beautiful works,[26] and Turner may well have rated them every bit as highly.

The *Landscape with the Father of Psyche sacrificing at the Milesian Temple of Apollo* (fig. 118) takes its subject from Book IV of *The Golden Ass* (or *Metamorphoses*) by Apuleius. The king sacrifices at the oracle of Apollo at Miletus in the hope that the god will help him find a husband for his daughter. The oracle is on the extreme left, with a statue of Apollo holding his lyre placed in a niche. The king, Psyche and their retinue surround the sacrificial altar, whilst royal servants bring up other offerings from behind the temple. Beyond them is a circular temple of Diana, and the landscape includes a mountain not unlike Monte Circeo, as seen from the Alban hills south of Rome. Its form effectively amplifies the similar shape made by the man holding down the sacrificial heifer immediately before it. On the right further supplicants approach with another heifer. Presumably they will be next to sacrifice at the altar.

Both people and animals look on expectantly. Indeed, a sense of expectation is the dominant psychological response in the work. Seated on balconies at the left are the ladies of the court and musicians, whilst a priest stands on the roof. A herd of cattle rests in the centre and the animals peer extremely intently at the proceedings, as do two shepherds who stand or sit beneath the central tree.

The picture is divided into two clearly defined sections. Those people who are about to pay homage to the god are separated from those who are not, and from the human and animal spectators. Claude differentiates the two by a subtle ellipse that begins near the bottom left-hand corner of the picture. This runs across the heads of the cattle, up to and

**118** Claude le Lorrain, *Landscape with the Father of Psyche sacrificing at the Milesian Temple of Apollo,* 1663, oil on canvas, 174 × 220 cm, National Trust, Anglesey Abbey, Cambs.

above the shepherds beneath the main tree and then across the projections of the foliage of that tree through to the top left-hand corner of the painting. The circularity of this line is reinforced by the semi-circles of the arches of the bridge, the rotundity of the temple of Diana on the left, and by the ellipses of the two major windings of the river across the plain. The more distant of these curves almost exactly repeats the shape of the ellipse of light-coloured ground around the sacrificial altar. Gradually, though, all of these shapes climactically converge at the ellipses formed by the steps leading up to the statue of Apollo, lines that give further visible expression to the sense of supplication implicit in the prayers that are being offered to the god.

There can be no doubt that Turner recognised and was profoundly impressed by Claude's use of line to denote meaning in *The Father of Psyche* (as well as its concomitant usefulness in tautening structure), for it remained in his memory for many years until suitable opportunities arose with which to 'imitate' it in the most creative way possible. And not only did he employ a somewhat similar ellipse for associative and structural reasons in the *Borthwick Castle* of 1818 (fig. 1). In another work he demonstrated his debt to Claude's *Father of Psyche* even more clearly.

This occurs in *Hythe, Kent,* a watercolour made around 1823 for engraving in the 'Southern Coast' series (fig. 119). The picture once again offers a notable example of Turner's compression of a landscape. The view from the Ashford road shows the town dominated by St Leonard's Church, with the cliffs stretching beyond Folkestone (which is hidden over the brow of the hill) towards Dover. The left half of the picture therefore takes in the vista looking due east. At the same time Turner shows the coast on the right curving around to Dungeness, the view towards the south-west.

In the centre, before the town, is the Royal Staff Corps barracks at Shornecliffe, with soldiers drawn up in front of them on parade. When Turner had first visited Hythe (probably around 1807) the barracks were the headquarters of the Royal Waggon Train, an army unit that serviced the Royal Military Canal, a defensive system built between 1804 and 1809 when fears of French invasion were still strong. It runs for twenty-eight miles around Romney Marsh, which was considered to be the likeliest spot for an invasion. A stretch of the canal can be seen under the oak tree to the right of centre. The precise association of the place is characterised by the literal depiction of a military (i.e. Royal) waggon train making its way up the hill before us. The defensive purpose of the canal is also denoted by the vertically aligned placement of a cannon pointing straight at it. On the left a sentry gestures in the direction of Calais, from whence the feared invasion would have come.

A notable feature of the work is the emphatic ellipse with which Turner underpins it, one that distinctly resembles the outer line of *The Father of Psyche*. This too runs from the bottom left-hand corner of the picture, and it continues around the side of the canal and along the skyline of the town and cliffs. Its circularity is amplified by the oak tree that dominates the drawing. This dominance is so pronounced, though, that Turner does not seem to have been using the tree simply for compositional purposes or just to create a Claudian repoussoir effect. The oak certainly offers its shade but, more importantly, the stress Turner gives it makes it seem to curve right across the picture to embrace the canal, town and coastline within its reach, thus extending a sense of protection to the town. It is this expression of a broader underlying theme, as well as the means Turner employs to bring it about, that especially makes *Hythe, Kent* seem so near to Claude's picture. After all, the underlying theme of *The Father of Psyche* is the seeking of the protection of the god, something the artist not only establishes through his subject, the expectancy of his figures and the gradual linear focus upon Apollo, but also associatively by the overriding leftwards reach of the tree which dominates the work, a tree whose placing, moreover, Turner rather follows in *Hythe, Kent*. Indeed, the resemblance between the two pictures is marked, Turner's tree even looking somewhat like Claude's tree. *Hythe, Kent* again signifies how

**119** *Hythe, Kent, c.* 1823, watercolour on paper, 14 × 22.9 cm, Guildhall Museum, London.

Turner could structure a picture around both the particular and the broadest human associations of place, and how his assimilation of lessons probably learnt from Claude certainly assisted him in that process. Yet *Hythe, Kent* is not the first work by Turner to draw heavily upon Claude's *Father of Psyche;* his *Caernarvon Castle* of 1800 (fig. 26) is very clearly a reversal of Claude's image. Turner did not have to look at either the Claude painting or the *Liber Veritatis* reproduction of the work in a mirror, however, in order to perceive the work in reverse. Instead, when making the *Caernarvon Castle* quite evidently he had at hand a copy of the engraving of *The Father of Psyche* made in 1760 by William Woollett which reverses Claude's image.[27] But characteristically Turner did not just reverse Claude's form in *Caernarvon Castle;* he also reversed the content served by that form, for whereas in *The Father of Psyche* Claude extends a sense of protection by means of his overarching tree, in *Caernarvon Castle* Turner projects a sense of threat through an arboreal vehicle, as we have indicated. And the other Altieri Claude may equally have contributed to Turner's art in specific ways as well.

The *Landscape with the Landing of Aeneas in Latium* (fig. 120) draws its subject from Book VIII of Virgil's *Aeneid*. Earlier in the narrative than the moment depicted Aeneas had

**120** Claude le Lorrain, *Landscape with the Landing of Aeneas in Latium*, 1675,
oil on canvas, 175 × 224 cm, National Trust, Anglesey Abbey, Cambs.

landed at the mouth of the Tiber but, as war broke out in the locality soon afterwards, he was overcome by anxiety. This led him to fall into a deep sleep on the banks of the Tiber. The river god himself then appeared to him and advised him to sail inland. There he would encounter a tribe, the Arcadians, with whom he must ally himself. From that alliance, and on that spot, the city of Rome would eventually arise. Upon awakening, Aeneas detached two ships from his fleet and rowed upriver. After travelling for two days he reached Pallenteum, the city of the Arcadians. This is the moment Claude depicts. Aeneas's arrival is noticed by Pallas, the son of Evander, the King of the Arcadians. Pallas comes down to the river-bank to enquire of Aeneas's identity and what he wants. To demonstrate that his intentions are friendly Aeneas greets him with an olive-branch.

Claude departs from the text in two main details. In Virgil's poem Pallas goes to meet Aeneas alone; here he is accompanied by a retinue. Claude also moves Aeneas from 'high on his ship's stern' to the prow of his vessel, to effect a more dramatic meeting with Pallas. The work contains several overt allusions: on the right are the ruins of two ancient hill towns,

Saturnia and Janiculum, which Evander will show Aeneas later that day; Aeneas's flag bears the Altieri family crest; and Claude ignores both topographical accuracy and possibility by depicting the Tiber winding all the way down to the sea. The picture may embody some covert allusions as well. Beneath the stately pine in the centre a smaller tree leans outwards, much as the king's son standing beneath it reaches out towards Aeneas. And on the left is a flock of sheep. The nearest animal is tonally spotlit, as is the clearing in which it sits. The river-god had originally prophesied that it was in a grove inhabited by a huge white sow and her thirty offspring that Aeneas would eventually found his city. The sheep Claude singles out for our attention may be a reference to this, although why he would have wanted to change the sow to a sheep is unclear (unless pigs seemed indecorous or unpoetic to him, given their common associations). Yet the extreme emphasis he gives the animal does suggest that an allusion to the sow may have been intended. In any event the sheep and shepherds certainly conjure up arcadian associations with an apt sense of decorum.

In *The Landing of Aeneas* Claude again uses a purely pictorial device to extend the meaning of his subject. The picture is structurally supported by two implied and very subtle lines that converge upon the sail-yards of the ships on the right. The upper line descends from the top-left, moves across the foliage of the smaller tree beneath the great pine in the centre and ends at the sail-yard of the further of the two vessels. The other line ascends from the points of light on the heads of two of the sheep sitting at the lower left, a point of light falling upon some bushes, and the hem of Pallas's cloak, to end at the sail-yard on Aeneas's vessel. This lower line is reinforced by the pointing gesture of the shepherd at the left. The convergence acts as a structural underpinning but, more importantly, it forces our attention towards Claude's underlying meaning. For the artist has not focused the picture upon the meeting of Aeneas with Pallas, as he might be expected to have done. Instead, he has moved our attention further to the right. But such an emphasis is not surprising. It is Aeneas's destiny to found Rome. To this end he has sailed from Troy, travelled through great dangers around the Mediterranean and loved but abandoned Queen Dido in Carthage. At last he has reached his ultimate destination. And it is from this arrival, but most specifically from the final lowering of these sail-yards that the city and empire of Rome will eventually issue. That is Claude's most imaginative dramatic perception and his most profound metaphor, and a marine artist like Turner would surely have recognised its significance. Moreover, by the linear convergence running through the picture Claude also stresses the new unity that is to ensue between the land on the left and the hitherto sea-bound Aeneas on the right. That statement is furthered by the placing of ruins immediately beyond Aeneas's vessels. They may represent Saturnia and Janiculum, but by their precise conjunction with the ships they surely also allude to Troy whose destruction had first set Aeneas upon his wanderings. Equally noticeable is the fact that the landscape on the right is wild and disorganised, in contrast to the lush and idyllic pastures of the Arcadians on the left.

The dramatic value of linear convergence as used by Claude in *The Landing of Aeneas* was very evidently not lost on Turner, for he employed it in exactly the same way in a major oil-painting he exhibited at the R.A. in 1831, *Life-Boat and Manby Apparatus going off to a Stranded Vessel making Signal (Blue Lights) of Distress* (fig. 121). The painting portrays the beach and pier at Great Yarmouth with a local invention in use. The Manby apparatus, named after its inventor Captain G. W. Manby, consisted of a lifeline which was propelled out to sea by a projectile expelled from a mortar. This mortar is just going off in the distance on the right while the vessel in distress fires a rocket composed of saltpetre, sulphur and antimony which gives off a violent blue light. Making its way out to the imperilled ship is a rowing boat. This is paying out a line attached to an anchor. On the beach are a woman and two children. To heighten the associations of the subject Turner places some wreckage immediately before us.

The work is structured by two clear diagonals, one running up the line of the beach, the other down the edge of the clouds. Both lines converge at the mortar, thus emphasising that the Manby apparatus is the technological protagonist of the picture (and the title also tells

**121** *Life-Boat and Manby Apparatus going off to a Stranded Vessel making Signal (Blue Lights) of Distress*, R.A. 1831, oil on canvas, 91.4 × 122 cm, Victoria and Albert Museum, London.

**122** *Glacier and Source of the Arveron, going up to the Mer de Glace*, R.A. 1803, watercolour on paper, 27.8 × 39.5 cm, National Museum of Wales, Cardiff.

us that). By placing it at the meeting point of the lines formed by the sky, sea and land, Turner stresses its mediant role between death and life. And through positioning the woman and children not just anywhere but immediately below both the apparatus and the anchor Turner enforces their connection as well. Maybe they are related to someone out on the shipwreck for whom the lifeboat and Manby apparatus will mean safety.

Perhaps an even more inventive use of linear convergence – although in a different direction – appears in the picture reproduced as figure 122. It has been convincingly argued that this was the watercolour shown at the R.A. in 1803 under the title of *Glacier and Source of the Arveron, going up to the Mer de Glace*,[28] for the three large mountains in the background are identifiable from left to right as the Aiguille du Dru, the Aiguille Verte and the Grands Charmoz. If this is the case then 'The subject of the picture is thus the foot of the Mer de Glace, and the source of the Arveiron'.[29] Strong diagonal lines can be seen running from midway on the left down the wall of white ice to the centre of the work at the bottom, and falling to the same point from near the top right down a line of shadow. These converging oblique lines are reinforced by the parallel treeline near the top left, and by two massive boulders on either side of the centre. The lines all lead the eye to the focal point of the whole picture, the gap between the boulders. Within that tiny space the vast column of ice sweeping around from the distant mountains turns into a trickle of water, forming the Arveiron which can be seen as the body of water at the very bottom of the picture. Here again line concentrates meaning.

**123** *Longships Lighthouse, Lands End, c.*1834–5, watercolour on paper, 29 × 44 cm, Private Collection, USA.

In addition to using linear convergence towards the right, or downwards, Turner also employed it towards the left. He did so, for similar dramatic reasons, in what is perhaps the greatest of all his marine watercolours, *Longships Lighthouse, Lands End* (fig. 123), which was drawn for the 'England and Wales' series sometime around 1834–5. Here two powerful diagonals meet on the left at the distant lighthouse, serving to pull our eye to the focal and dramatic point of the picture across a tempestuous sea bestrewn with wreckage and along desolate hillsides that are only graced by a few wreckers bearing torches and dozens of screaming sea-mews. Turner's focus serves to express his sense of irony, for lighthouses exist to prevent shipwreck. This one has signally failed in its duty. The frequency with which Turner depicted lighthouses in this way, underlining their uselessness, suggests that he may often have thought of them as representative of the failure of human aspirations.

Yet although the Yarmouth, Source of the Arveiron and Land's End pictures show Turner employing linear convergence in an ingenious manner which may have derived from Claude's *Landing of Aeneas* – and he was to use linear divergence elsewhere as well[30] – it is not in these works that he most imposingly expresses what he seems to have learnt from the Claude, just as the *Hythe, Kent* is not his most ambitious projection of what he appears to have assimilated from its pendant. Instead it is in other, more momentous works that he demonstrates his raising of the power of imitation to its highest creative level. In order to understand that more fully, we ought briefly to take into account Turner's reactions to yet another Claude. Turner's responses were recorded at second-hand long after his death by his friend George Jones and the incident in question probably occurred in 1803 in front of Claude's *Seaport with the Embarkation of the Queen of Sheba* (fig. 124), then in the collection of the London collector, John Julius Angerstein. Jones records:

> When Turner was very young he went to see Angerstein's pictures. Angerstein came into the room while the young painter was looking at the Sea Port by Claude, and spoke to him. Turner was awkward, agitated and burst into tears. Mr. Angerstein enquired the cause and pressed for an answer, when Turner said passionately, 'Because I shall never be able to paint any thing like that picture.[31]

Turner's first attempt to create a seaport subject with the sun in the centre, much as it appears in the *Embarkation of the Queen of Sheba*, dates from the late 1790s, which has led to a suggestion[32] that he created the picture under Claude's influence, and further speculation over exactly which Claude it was that Turner wept before. (*The Queen of Sheba* did not enter Angerstein's collection until 1803[33].) However, that first seaport, the view of *Caernarvon Castle* (w. 254) exhibited at the R.A. in 1799, demonstrates the influence of Richard Wilson far more than the influence of Claude, completely lacking the complexity of activity encountered in Claude's seaports; this writer is inclined to think that Turner placed his sun where it is in *Caernarvon Castle* because that is where he saw it in reality. And although Turner appears to have tinkered with the idea of creating several Claudian seaports around 1806, it was not until he was ready in terms of style and technique, that he attempted to paint them on a scale commensurate with those standards set by Claude for the representation of classical seaports. Yet when he did tackle such subjects he certainly seems to have applied the lessons he learned from the Altieri pictures.

The works in which Turner demonstrates these profoundly inventive assimilations are also pendants, and like the Altieri Claudes they too emerged from the artist's studio at different times. They are *Dido building Carthage; or the Rise of the Carthaginian Empire* (fig. 125), exhibited at the R.A. in 1815, and *The Decline of the Carthaginian Empire* (fig. 129), shown there two years later.

Turner called *Dido building Carthage; or the Rise of the Carthaginian Empire* his 'chef d'oeuvre'.[34] This valuation of the painting must not be underestimated. Turner always refused to sell the work and at the time of his death the apocryphal story was still in wide circulation that he had requested of his executors that the canvas should be used as his winding-sheet, even though Turner had bequeathed the picture to the National Gallery in the first draft of his will made over twenty years earlier. By the terms of his bequest, the

**124** Claude le Lorrain, *Seaport with the Embarkation of the Queen of Sheba*,
signed and dated 1648, oil on canvas, 148.5 × 194 cm, National Gallery, London.

painting was one of a pair he left to the National Gallery 'Provided the . . . two pictures are deemed worthy to be and are placed by the side of Claude's *Sea Port* and *Mill* that is to hang on the same line same height from the ground'. The paintings were accepted on those terms and are shown alongside the Claudes to this day. Obviously the artist prized his first truly Claudian seaport picture, and when we look carefully at *Dido building Carthage* it is not difficult to see why.

The subject is taken from Book I of Virgil's *Aeneid*. Queen Dido had fled from her native city of Tyre with the remains of her husband, Sychaeus, who had been murdered by her brother Pygmalion. On the shores of North Africa she has founded the city of Carthage. Aeneas happens across the city whilst it is being built, first surveying it from a 'lofty hill', which may be the one shown on the right. Turner also definitely includes a number of features specified by Virgil. Principal amongst these is the detail that

> Amid the town, a stately grove displayed
> A cooling shelter and delightful shade.[35]

**125** *Dido building Carthage; or the Rise of the Carthaginian Empire*, R.A. 1815,
oil on canvas, 155.5 × 232 cm, National Gallery, London.

This grove (fig. 127) dominates the right side of the picture. Below it lie some logs, perhaps to allude to the future fate of the bower. On the right of the oak is the stump of a tree that has been struck dead by lightning. The base of its shattered trunk appears from behind part of the tomb of Sychaeus, Dido's dead husband. From the location of the stump exactly halfway between the verdant oak and the tomb, and its placement immediately above a plaque bearing the name 'Sichaeo', we can safely infer that it is intended to allude to the poor man's fate. However, all is not loss, for a sapling is growing from the top of the tomb. It surely embodies an allusion to the fact that the birth of the new city stems indirectly from the death of Sychaeus. Around the tomb is a bas-relief which depicts the slaying of Sychaeus and a funeral procession, whilst below it is an arched conduit. Turner probably obtained this detail from a book he is known to have read, J. C. Eustace's *A Classical Tour through Italy*, published in 1813. There, in a discussion of ancient Roman remains, Eustace refers to the fact that 'some of these works, such as the *cloacae*, were built in the very infancy of the city, and seemed to have been considered as omens and pledges of its duration and future greatness.'[36] For Turner, basing his ideas of early Carthaginian architecture upon Graeco-

193

Roman models, they may well have conveniently served an identical symbolic purpose. By the same token, such an arched duct, when placed immediately under a tomb, may be seen as an entrance to the Underworld, Sychaeus's present abode. Again it would point to the roots of Carthage as deriving from Sychaeus's death, for it is not usual to build someone's tomb over an open drain.

On the other side of the picture in the distance (fig. 126), we see a state barge of the type Turner sketched on the Thames near Hampton Court around 1806 whilst first toying with the idea of painting a Claudian seaport subject. In front of the bustling harbour area, where men are unloading building materials and general cargo, we see Queen Dido herself (fig. 128). She is facing some architects or masons and a small boy, as well as a man in a helmet beyond them. They all kneel at her feet. Behind her stands a black slave with a fan. From a bag held by a courtier she draws the money with which to pay for all the public works.

**126** *Dido building Carthage; or the Rise of the Carthaginian Empire* (detail).

In front of Dido, with his back to us, is an imposing figure in military costume. He may very well be Aeneas. There are several reasons for thinking him so, the most obvious one being that it is through Aeneas's exploration of the newly rising city that Virgil himself conducts us around the scene in his poem, with Aeneas marvelling at the stupendous scale and diversity of it all. We should therefore expect to see Aeneas in the picture, as anyone familiar with the *Aeneid* – and a good part of Turner's original audience would have been – might naturally have looked for him here. It would be entirely characteristic of Turner to have included someone who is to play such a crucial role in determining not only Dido's fate but the destiny of Carthage as well, it being held that Aeneas's renunciation of Dido in order to found Rome was the initial cause of the fatal enmity between the two cities. Other factors additionally support this hypothesis. Alone of all the significant figures in the picture the man has his back to us, thus prompting speculation as to his identity. By this means Turner

**127** *Dido building Carthage; or the Rise of the Carthaginian Empire* (detail).

**128**  *Dido building Carthage; or the Rise of the Carthaginian Empire* (detail).

could also be suggesting that his identity is, as yet, also unknown to Dido. Equally this is why he is physically separated from her by a block of stone, whilst a mason seems to be looking up at him as though he were a stranger, for when Aeneas is wandering around looking at Carthage he has yet to meet Dido. The man is also standing in the Queen's presence, unlike the other people immediately in front of her. But perhaps the strongest support for this contention arises from the placing of the two ships' masts beyond him and Dido. They are precisely aligned with the two figures – if the lines of the masts are carried downwards they terminate at these figures – and they are the only flag-bearing masts in the whole picture. As a result, they dominate all the shipping in the harbour, just as Dido and Aeneas would naturally dominate everyone in it in terms of rank.

To the right of this group are two evidently nubile young maidens. They are gazing with more than just a hint of interest at some boys seated at the water's edge. These youths are sailing a toy boat, with another craft lying on the beach before them. The allusion here is not too difficult to fathom: the boys who are now playing with toy boats will soon sail the real vessels that will venture forth to assert Carthaginian hegemony over the Mediterranean.[37] In turn, the girls who are now looking at them will also one day bear them the children through which Carthaginian power will be further disseminated. And, given the usual care with which Turner observed the need for decorum, we may safely infer that the sun is rising, just as the city does.

Two years after exhibiting *Dido building Carthage* Turner produced a work that complements it in terms of meaning. This painting (fig. 129) enjoys the longest title of any

**129** *The Decline of the Carthaginian Empire – Rome being determined on the Overthrow of her Hated Rival, demanded from her such Terms as might either force her into War, or ruin her by Compliance: the Enervated Carthaginians, in their Anxiety for Peace, consented to give up even their Arms and their Children*, R.A. 1817, oil on canvas, 170 × 238.5 cm, Clore Gallery for the Turner Collection, London.

of Turner's works, and it was accompanied by a poetic extract in the 1817 R.A. catalogue: *The Decline of the Carthaginian Empire – Rome being determined on the Overthrow of her Hated Rival, demanded from her such Terms as might either force her into War, or ruin her by Compliance: the Enervated Carthaginians, in their Anxiety for Peace, consented to give up even their Arms and their Children*

> ****** At Hope's delusive smile
> The chieftain's safety and the mother's pride,
> Were to th'insidious conqu'ror's grasp resign'd;
> While o'er the western wave th'ensanguin'd sun,
> In gathering haze a stormy signal spread,
> And set portentous

Like the later *Regulus* (fig. 81) the picture almost certainly draws its subject from a book in Turner's library, Oliver Goldsmith's *The Roman History*, and it shows the moment between the second and third Punic wars when, as Goldsmith tells us, the Carthaginians

**130** *The Decline of the Carthaginian Empire* (detail).

had, during this long period [of nearly fifty years of peace] been only intent on amassing private wealth ... [In] no way careful for public safety [they] ... offered any reasonable satisfaction [to the Romans for peace]. To these submissions the senate only returned an evasive answer, demanding three hundred hostages within thirty days, as a security for their future conduct and an implicit obedience to their further demands. With these articles it was supposed the Carthaginians would not comply, but it turned out otherwise, for this infatuated people desiring peace on any terms sent their children within the limitted time ...

Eventually the Roman demands provoked them into war:

Now, too late, they began to see the danger of riches in a state, when it no longer had power to defend them. Those vessels therefore, of gold and silver which their luxury had taken such pride in, were converted into arms . . .[38]

This expedient was not to help them, however, for the third Punic War was to be the final one and it ended with the complete obliteration of Carthage in 146 B.C.

On the left (fig. 130) we see some of the three hundred children being torn from their mothers, with women swooning or desperately clasping their offspring in their arms. Slightly further off, children are being put aboard a boat. On the right a sorrowing mother assumes exactly the same standard pose for denoting grief that we have already witnessed Turner use in *Apullia in Search of Appullus* (figs 114, 117). Beyond her, floating on the water, is a similar, or perhaps even the same toy boat that we saw being confidently pushed forth in the earlier painting of Carthage. Now it sails forlornly into the void. In this picture Turner very definitely alludes to Aeneas, for on the left is a statue of Mercury, the winged messenger who had called Aeneas away to found Rome and, by so doing, established the antipathy between the two cities. Mercury's wand is also sculpted in low-relief on the wall above the grieving woman on the right.

The enervation of the Carthaginians, arising from their concentration upon luxury rather than duty, is established associatively throughout the picture. On either side of the semi-circular mole two figures hold up bunches of grapes, whilst other objects of pleasure are strewn across the foreground. Amongst them are musical instruments, including a tambourine and a flute, with a pan-pipe on the right, flowers and scent-bottles, a fragment of sculpture, a painter's mahl-stick (which, given Turner's profession, is naturally garlanded with flowers), an anchor, a buoy, a broken sword and an oar placed through a crown, an obvious allusion to the basis of Carthaginian power. In the distance is the setting 'ensanguin'd sun' of the supporting poem, although originally it was probably much redder than it is today, and thus more capable of effecting the required deathly associations of the tragic subject.[39]

*Dido building Carthage* and *The Decline of the Carthaginian Empire* therefore denote opposing stages in the development of a civilisation. Whether Turner had it in mind to create a second picture to express that contrast when he painted the first is unknown, but in any case *Dido building Carthage* itself contains a highly dramatic opposition of birth and death. On Dido's side of the picture all is teeming energy and dynamism, the new and the generative. Except for some distant insignificant figures located to establish scale, the other half of the work contains no live human elements at all, just nature in all her glory and mankind reduced to dust. The 'downstage' and opposed placement of Dido and her husband's tomb is particularly purposeful, and also supports the view that the 'tall dark stranger' is Aeneas, Sychaeus's successor as Dido's lover.

Yet the linear structures of both *Dido building Carthage* and *The Decline of the Carthaginian Empire* are vitally significant as well. The structure of *Dido building Carthage* consists of a number of straight lines which create overlapping ✕ and ✚ configurations. These can be seen in the line ascending the shadow cast by the boys on the left which runs across to the hillside up on the right, and the line of the edge of the river at the right which ascends to the upper parts of the buildings on the left, coupled with the cross structure to be seen in the horizontal running across the distant mole and a cornice of Sychaeus's tomb, and a vertical descending from the sun down its reflection on the water. In combination these implied or stated lines exactly resemble the linear configuration of a Union Jack. Whether Turner intended to signify the British flag is a moot point (this writer thinks not), although he can hardly have been unaware of the resemblance. Yet it is possible to discern more probable motives for his creation of this structure. In order to understand these motives fully we have to look at the work in relation to its pendant, as well as at the latter picture itself.

The most striking pictorial contrast between *Dido Building Carthage* and *The Decline of the Carthaginian Empire* resides in their opposed structural differences which reflect their opposed meanings. The essential theme of *Dido building Carthage* is the strength of the newly born city. Turner establishes this by using straight lines to create linear tautness throughout. Conversely, the underlying theme of *The Decline of the Carthaginian Empire* is enervation. How better to establish that than by suggesting slackness through the use of curved lines all over the picture? In *The Decline of the Carthaginian Empire* Turner indulges in a welter of curves. The mole in the foreground is circular, as are the temple and distant theatre on the left, whilst the octagonal urn on the right is capped by circular garlands. Beyond it the jumble of buildings very evidently does not follow any rectilinear ground-plan, thus promoting the general effect of disarray still further. By placing the urn before the very centre of this architectural mass Turner even seems to make the buildings pivot around it. Other curved forms, such as the tops of the distant trees and the back of the grieving mother on the right, add to the overall circularity. The net result is to create a distinct sense of flaccidity, a lack of structural cohesion and unity that subtly underlines the picture's theme of enervation and social disharmony. Instead of mankind aiming for a unified social goal, which all those convergent lines (and human activities) in *Dido building Carthage* so forcefully suggest, on a broader abstract level we see what happens when individual selfishness is placed above collective purpose. Very distinctly 'Things fall apart; the centre cannot hold'.

Obviously this feeling of enervation is not a fixed attribute of circularity or curvilinearity; such directions can equally evoke other, very different associations, such as the sense of protectiveness that we might see in *Hythe, Kent* (fig. 119) or the approach to a god that can be discerned in *The Father of Psyche* (fig. 118). Clearly everything depends on context, on exactly what sets in motion the required associations. *The Decline of the Carthaginian Empire* strongly determines the direction they take with its title and subject, and above all the fact that it is at a formal extreme to *Dido building Carthage*, with its dependency upon straight lines, exactly the selfsame components of a hidden 'machinery of . . . rules' that Turner discerned in Raphael's *Transfiguration*. Yet it is also possible to see in the structures of both paintings a distinct reflection of the structures of the Altieri Claudes. The circularity of Claude's *Father of Psyche* has been converted into that of Turner's *Decline of the Carthaginian Empire*, whilst the sense of opposition between two sectors of the painting in Claude's *Landing of Aeneas*, and its use of convergence, are given creative re-expression in Turner's *Dido building Carthage*. The power of imitation has been entirely recharged.

Yet it may not have been just artistic imitation which led Turner to the employment here of linear structure to denote meaning metaphorically. The use of structure in such a way had a strong theoretical basis and one that Turner had verbally made clear at some point (probably around 1812) before painting *Dido building Carthage*. As the artist stated in one of his perspective lectures:

> it must be allow'd . . . that lines have characters and that simplicity of line produces the same effect in figure and in form throughout Raphael's works and the equal interesting right lines of later days intersecting each other in Macbeth Satan Achilles and the Bard produc'd and may again produce Grandeur.[40]

200

(The works of 'later days' all appear to have been pictures by Fuseli who, as R.A. Professor of Painting, was almost certainly in the audience when Turner first delivered this lecture.[41]) In the quotation Turner makes absolutely clear his view that the structural lines of a composition can 'produce Grandeur', whilst the fact that they enjoy 'characters' by definition signifies that they can express meanings. Yet in his promulgation of the notion of line-as-meaning there also resides yet another important motive which may have found expression in Turner's 'chef d'oeuvre' and its pendant.

This has to do with Turner's teaching of perspective in the years in which both works were made. When the painter exhibited *Dido building Carthage* he had been delivering perspective lectures at the Royal Academy over the previous five years. Yet it was apparent virtually from the outset that the lectures were not a great success, for the artist did not enjoy sufficient verbal skill with which to do justice to the ideas he was trying to convey. Nor did he help himself in this respect. It might be thought that a study of optics, the laws of geometry and architecture, and the theoretical bases of the spatial interactions of forms would have provided enough material for any investigation of perspective. Not so for Turner. Unfortunately for his students but fortunately for us the artist did not limit himself to such apposite considerations. (Indeed, some critics complained that he did not discuss them at all.) Instead, in his 'discourses' Turner took the opportunity to range over a vast number of subjects: the origins and historical applications of perspective, its connection with, and development in painting, sculpture and architecture, the different modes of the science such as parallel, angular and aerial perspective, the nature of vision, light, colour and reflections, the connection between poetry and painting, and the workings of linguistic and visual metaphors. In the last of the set of six lectures, Turner discussed the role of landscape painting, a subject he clearly thought to be germane to perspective as landscapes often formed the backgrounds to poetic-historic (and thus 'Academic') paintings, so naturally they had to be spatially organised in terms of a coherent perspective. Much of this material must have baffled Turner's listeners, as when, for example, he drew analogies between perspective and anatomy. Quite simply he attempted too much. Instead of propounding some simple rules for painters, sculptors and architects to follow, he tried to trace almost everything that concerned him back to its origins. The manuscripts of these lectures are a veritable goldmine of information about the artist, and greatly help us to understand his motivations. But if the lectures mystified Turner's audiences they may also have compelled him to demonstrate pictorially what he was trying to state verbally with only limited success. For there was fortunately another method open to Turner whereby he could demonstrate the value – indeed, the very profound value – that perspective might hold for a painter. *Dido building Carthage* and *The Decline of the Carthaginian Empire* may well have been the fulfilment of that method, for they most conspicuously put into practice many of the underlying principles of perspective which the artist had been struggling to communicate verbally. For instance, we have already seen that in the lectures Turner equated perspective with linear pictorial structure and demonstrated how artists such as Raphael, Poussin and Fuseli not only lent 'Grandeur' but also meaning and 'propriety' (or decorum) to their works through the use of such linear structures. In *Dido building Carthage* and its pendant Turner raised this concept to a new level. Moreover, whilst doing so he elaborated the two fundamental principles of perspective as well. The most apparent structural feature of *Dido building Carthage* is its emphatic use of a central vanishing point upon which all of the underlying lines converge. In this respect the painting is a classic demonstration of single-point perspective, which was quite naturally the foundation of fictive representational space in a picture as far as Turner was concerned. Similarly, in *The Decline of the Carthaginian Empire* the artist demonstrates on a grand scale a multi-recessional curvilinear perspective: masses not only recede in perspective towards a single point in the distance but due to the lack of a coherent architectural ground-plan and the curvature of much of it, we also witness within the overall recession a multiplicity of other vanishing-points, in addition to the accurate depiction of many ellipses. In his lectures Turner also explored how the science of perspective is rooted in basic geometry and how recession not only modifies the perception and rendition of architecture but also the light in which it is seen, and the colours and reflections it enjoys or produces respectively. These insights are given striking expression in *Dido building Carthage* and its pendant. The works are rooted in geometric essentials, as with the implied but emphatic triangles which meet at the centre of *Dido building Carthage*. By placing the sun vertically above the centre of the painting, the artist creates and solves integral problems to do with the exact distribution of shadow in symmetric linear perspective, the modulation of light and colour in aerial perspective, the effects of reflection on water, and the consequent modifications of colour created by reflections off that water. Likewise, by placing the sun vertically off-centre in *The Decline of the Carthaginian Empire* the artist raises and solves problems of the asymmetric distribution of light and shadow, especially on the right where the complex interplay of reflections between the buildings is marked.

Of course it would be easy to see many of these technicalities as inherent to seaport subjects, especially those by Claude to which these two paintings pay such open homage. But the emphatic differences of structure between *Dido building Carthage* and its pendant, plus the rooting of those structures in the desire to further meaning, alerts us to the fact that Turner may have been elaborating ideas of basic import to his study of perspective at every level of these works. If that is so, then the two paintings are a summation of the lectures themselves. This would also explain why the artist so strongly identified with them, especially the first picture where he had originated the idea.

The rise and fall of empires – Carthage, Rome, Venice and, by implication, Britain – was to remain a favourite theme for Turner. However, although he painted other pairs of works which also contrast the destinies of great nations, he never did so again on quite this scale or with such concern to find formal structures that convey that message metaphorically. The direct comparisons of ancient and modern Italy of 1838 (B. J. 375, 374), or ancient and modern Rome of 1839 (B. J. 378, 379), are far more loosely structured and are not concerned with contrasting symmetry, to express beauty, growth and development, with asymmetry, to represent 'deformity', decline and decay, as these two pictures appear to be doing. And here, too, in the way that the pendants strongly seem to give concrete realisation to the concepts of 'symmetry' and 'asymmetry', we may even perceive yet another possible connection on Turner's part with the tenets of poetic painting. Throughout the aesthetic literature with which the artist most deeply identified the notion of symmetry was commonly equated with beauty, it being held that symmetric proportion was the ultimate type of formal harmony and therefore synonymous with beauty. Conversely, asymmetry, being disproportionate, was held to be a distortion of ideal balance, and so disfigured and 'ugly'. By extension Turner may easily have felt that balance and imbalance not only apply to architectural and pictorial relationships but to social relationships as well. Thus it is possible to see that as well as being Turner's most tautly and consciously organised statements on the grand scale – or even in the 'Great Style' – *Dido building Carthage* and its pendant may be attempts to exemplify the basic aesthetic differentiations underlying that style on the most fundamental dramatic levels.

It was surely the artistic stature of these related statements, plus Turner's realisation that in both pictures he had fully demonstrated the principles he was stating in his perspective lectures, and at last achieved the standards regarding seaport-subjects set by Claude, whilst making a moral point that offered an allegorical lesson to his own empire-building age, which initially led him to leave both works to the National Gallery to hang alongside Claude's *Seaport with the Embarkation of the Queen of Sheba* and *Landscape with dancing figures*. Later he preferred to replace *The Decline of the Carthaginian Empire* with an earlier work (fig. 213) that displayed his versatility as a marine painter in the Dutch manner. But this exchange should not blind us to the fact that Turner may have regarded both pictures as his joint 'supreme works' to the end of his life. Certainly their present separation – one picture at the National Gallery, the other in the Turner collection at Millbank – is extremely unfortunate, for the paintings belong together and should be reunited.[42] In *Dido building Carthage* and *The Decline of the Carthaginian Empire* we see the apotheosis of the concept that line plus a unifying perspective – or the lack of it – can convey meaning. Turner may well have developed these ideas from Raphael's *Transfiguration*, Poussin's *Landscape with a Roman Road* or the Altieri Claudes, as he did in part from the Claude-Earlom *Landscape with the death of Procris*, but in his 'chef d'oeuvre' and its pendant he gave them triumphantly personal expression.

**131** *The Bay of Baiæ, with Apollo and the Sybil*, R.A. 1823,
oil on canvas, 145.5 × 239 cm, Clore Gallery for the Turner Collection, London.

**132** Richard Earlom after Claude le Lorrain, *Coast Scene with
Apollo and the Cumaean Sibyl* (*Liber Veritatis* 99), mezzotint engraving, 1777.

# SIX

# Beyond Appearances

IN addition to the assimilations from the Claude-Earlom *Liber Veritatis* that we have observed in the previous chapter, the book of engravings clearly influenced Turner in a number of other ways as well. (We have in passing touched upon several of these influences in the discussion of *Dido building Carthage*.) It is worth examining them in turn.

## ANACHRONISM

The engraving which appears in the *Liber Veritatis* immediately before the *Landscape with the death of Procris* (*LV* 100, fig. 110) is the *Coast Scene with Apollo and the Cumaean Sibyl* (fig. 132). Claude shows Apollo granting the Sibyl as many years of life as the multitudinous grains of sand she proffers him. Unfortunately, however, she forgets to ask for the youthfulness with which to enjoy such longevity and is thus condemned to perpetual ageing. Claude directly alludes to this process by showing the Cumaean Oracle, and indeed all the other buildings situated around the Bay of Baia, in ruins rather than standing intact, as they surely would have done when the Sibyl was active in her early years. Turner was to depict exactly this same subject, and employ an identical allusion to the ageing process by means of anachronistic architecture, in *The Bay of Baiæ, with Apollo and the Sybil* of 1823 (fig. 131). Moreover, because Turner may have known this Claude image by the late 1790s, such a disjunction between the narrative moment depicted and the state of the buildings at the time could easily have led him to ignore the constraints of time in pictures like the *Dolbadern Castle* of 1800 (fig. 24).

## CLAUDE AND THE DECORUM OF LIGHT

Although Turner saw the Altieri Claudes hanging together as pendants in 1799, it would have been well-nigh impossible for him to have ascertained any underlying relationship between them in terms of their content, for their subject-matter incorporated private allusions to the Altieri family fortunes that were only first made clear by Marcel Roethlisberger in 1961. Yet there were other Claudes which in Turner's day were most definitely linked metaphorically in ways that have a direct bearing upon the two Carthage paintings, although it must be stressed that such connections had nothing to do with Claude as they were made long after his death. These works may have shown Turner how to extend the meaning of one image by the creation of another. The pictures in question are the so-called Radnor Claudes, named after the successive owners of the paintings since 1740, the Earls of Radnor of Longford Castle in Wiltshire, where the works hang to this day. The pictures themselves are entitled *Seacoast with the Landing of Aeneas in Latium* and *Pastoral Landscape with the Arch of Titus*. The former painting dates from 1650, the latter from some six years earlier, although the details of who originally commissioned them are obscure. In 1772 large engravings of them (in reverse) by William Woollett were published under the distinctly un-Claudian titles of *The Landing of Aeneas in Italy : the Allegorical Morning of the Roman Empire* and *Roman Edifices in Ruins : the Allegorical Evening of the Empire*. Turner may have acquainted himself with the Longford Castle paintings during the latter half of the 1790s when he was in Wiltshire at the behest of Sir Richard Colt Hoare who had commissioned a number of pictures of local subjects from him during those years. And of course the two works were represented in the Earlom *Liber Veritatis* (Nos. 82 and 122) where they were incorrectly also said to represent the allegorical morning and evening of the Roman Empire.

The supposed meanings of these engravings were elaborated a year before the appearance of *Dido building Carthage* by John Britton, the publisher of the engraving of *Pope's Villa at Twickenham* and the recipient of Turner's letter preferring allusion to direct reference:

> The . . . rise . . . or ascendancy . . . of the Roman Empire is shown by the sun rising above the horizon, in a rich and luxuriant country. Near the foreground are some vessels with several figures, intended to mark the landing of Aeneas in Italy. The decline of the empire is emblematically represented by an evening scene, or sun-set, with several Roman buildings in ruins . . .[1]

Turner may well have been acquainted with this text which appeared in Volume XV of Britton's *The Beauties of England and Wales* in 1814, for in that year a watercolour he had exhibited at the R.A. in 1798 was engraved for another of Britton's publications,[2] and he is reputed to have made 'an Emblematic Drawing . . . for a Frontispiece to one of [its volumes]'.[3] We may therefore safely assume that the two men were in close touch at that time. The appearance of pictures by Turner showing the rise and fall of a great empire, so soon after Britton had elucidated the meanings of other works also purported to do so, strongly suggests that it was Britton's moral conclusions which vitally acted upon some of Turner's choices of subject between 1814 (when he probably began *Dido building Carthage*) and 1817. Furthermore, Turner took time off in 1816 from his Carthaginian labours to paint pendants showing the ascendancy and contemporary decline of Greece (figs 141, 140).

**133** Richard Earlom after Claude le Lorrain, *Seacoast with the Landing of Aeneas in Latium* (*Liber Veritatis* 122), mezzotint engraving, 1777.

**134** Richard Earlom after Claude le Lorrain, *The Sea of Galilee with Christ calling Peter and Andrew* (*Liber Veritatis* 165), mezzotint engraving, 1777.

In the first of the two Radnor Claudes (fig. 133) – which to revert to the authentic title we should call *Seacoast with the Landing of Aeneas in Latium* – we see one of the only two partially dead trees in the entire *Liber Veritatis* (the willow in *the temptation of St. Anthony*, fig. 100, is the other, whilst the tree in *the death of Procris*, fig. 110, is completely shattered at the top). This tree stands upon the island on the right, where a few living trees also grow, a combination which perhaps alludes to the dead Troy Aeneas had abandoned (the partially dead tree points seawards) and the new life he can expect in Latium.[4] Turner would surely have realised the dramatic suitability of what was held to be Claude's depiction of a sunrise in connection with the landing of Aeneas in Italy.

Another image in the *Liber Veritatis* that appears to have acted upon Turner's sense of association is the work known in the Boydell-Earlom list of titles as *The Sea of Galilee with Christ calling Peter and Andrew*[5] (*LV* 165, fig. 134). The symbolism of this image is very transparent. Not for nothing is Christ placed directly below the most dominant feature of the whole picture, an oak-tree that crowns the rock above him. Decorum is duly observed in the pictorial effect of light: just as Jesus calls upon the two disciples to follow him, the sun also rises.

Linked to this work in its possible effect upon Turner is the *Coast View with Perseus and the origin of Coral* (*LV* 184, fig. 135). This image appears in the *Liber Veritatis* between two pictures known to Turner, *The Cumaean Sibyl conducting Aeneas to the Infernal Shades* (*LV* 183, fig. 139) and the second of the Altieri Claudes, the *Landscape with the Landing of Aeneas in Latium* (*LV* 185, the original painting of which is reproduced as fig. 120). *The origin of Coral* takes its subject from Book IV of Ovid's *Metamorphoses* and shows the scene when Perseus,

**135** Richard Earlom after Claude le Lorrain,
*Coast View with Perseus and the origin of Coral*
(*Liber Veritatis* 184), mezzotint engraving, 1777.

having slain Medusa the Gorgon, has laid her head on some seaweed on the shore to wash his hands. The blood from the decapitated 'snaky-haired monster' has caused the seaweed to harden into coral. Sea nymphs, marvelling at the transformation, test this process by casting seeds from the original corals over the waves to produce more of the organism.

In the centre is the winged horse, Pegasus. His introduction into the picture is entirely allusive, for the steed was born when Perseus slew the Gorgon, not at this point in the poem. Claude places Pegasus at the foot of an enormous rock-arch, the dominant and most arresting topographical and pictorial feature of the work. Clearly the artist may be using the springing of the rock to allude to the way that Pegasus had similarly sprung from the neck of the decapitated Gorgon, an interpretation supported by the fact that Claude places Pegasus at the very base of the rock-arch.

The supposition that Turner was acquainted with the Earlom mezzotints of *The Sea of Galilee* and *The Origin of Coral* is supported by the extreme resemblance of parts of several of his pictures to areas in the two images after Claude. For instance, *Chryses* (fig. 136) is a watercolour Turner exhibited at the R.A. in 1811. It was accompanied in the catalogue by the following quotation from the first book of Pope's translation of Homer's *Iliad*:

> The trembling priest along the shore return'd
> And in the anguish of a father mourn'd
> Disconsolate, not daring to complain,
> Silent he wander'd by the sounding main;

**136** *Chryses*, R.A. 1811, watercolour on paper, 66 × 100.4 cm, Private Collection, UK.

> Till safe at distance to his God he prays;
> The God who darts around the world his rays.[6]

Chryses was a priest of Apollo, the sun-god. His daughter, Astynome or Chryseis, had been taken by Agamemnon in the Trojan Wars. When the Greek king refused to return the girl to her father, Chryses implored the aid of Apollo, who then visited a plague upon the Greeks. This brought about the desired restoration.

Here we see Chryses seeking the aid of the god. He kneels down on the shore and, from what we may safely presume to be his temple on the cliff-top at the right, a large tree-covered rock-arch also bends to the sea-shore. Its placement immediately above the kneeling Chryses amplifies the notion of supplication by association (and it should be remembered that in addition to being considered the sun-god, Apollo was equally the god of vegetative life). But not only is the massing of *Chryses* similar in layout to *The Sea of Galilee* and *the origin of Coral*; the mountain on the horizon at the left of *Chryses* occupies the same relative pictorial position as the mountain in *The Sea of Galilee*, and resembles it. Although it is unstated whether the time of day in *Chryses* is dawn or sunset it must be dawn, if only because of the need for the dramatic appropriateness of light: Chryses would hardly pray to a sun-god disappearing over the horizon, particularly as Apollo will come to the aid of his priest. Here, as in *The Sea of Galilee*, only a sunrise can fulfil a dramatically suitable role.

**137** *Glaucus and Scylla*, mezzotint engraving,
unpublished plate (No. 73) of *Liber Studiorum*,
etched by J. M. W. Turner, engraved by W. Say.

There are strong pictorial resemblances between the Claude-Earlom *The Sea of Galilee, the Origin of Coral*, and Turner's *Chryses* in the relationship of low sun to shore, whilst in the last two works there is a particularly close connection between their rock-arches and the metaphorical use of those structures. Yet *Chryses* is not the only picture by Turner in which a rock-arch appears on the right-hand side of the work. This unusual geological formation is also evident in the unpublished *Liber Studiorum* plate of *Glaucus and Scylla* (fig. 137) and the drawing upon which it was based (T.B. CXVII–P), both of which probably date from about 1818–19. The subject is taken from Book XIII of Ovid's *Metamorphoses*.[7] Glaucus has been transformed into a triton. Seeing Scylla wandering upon the sea-shore he is filled by the desire to possess her but she spurns his advances. Later (in Book XIV), he appeals to the goddess Circe for help in attaining Scylla, but Circe herself falls in love with Glaucus and, upon being rejected, visits all manner of nasty transformations upon her hapless rival, finally turning Scylla into an extremely dangerous rock in the Straits of Messina. (The rock that was supposed to derive from her was destroyed in a powerful earthquake in 1783.) In his picture, Turner uses the light inner shape of the rock-arch to repeat and reinforce the shape Scylla makes as she turns away from Glaucus. The sense of movement of his gesture as he invites Scylla to join him is amplified by the sharp form of the rock pointing towards the sun immediately above him. This rock clearly alludes to poor Scylla's coming fate, a supposition supported by the fact that Turner shows a body of water that resembles the Straits of Messina, with what is quite possibly Mount Etna in the distance. If that is the case

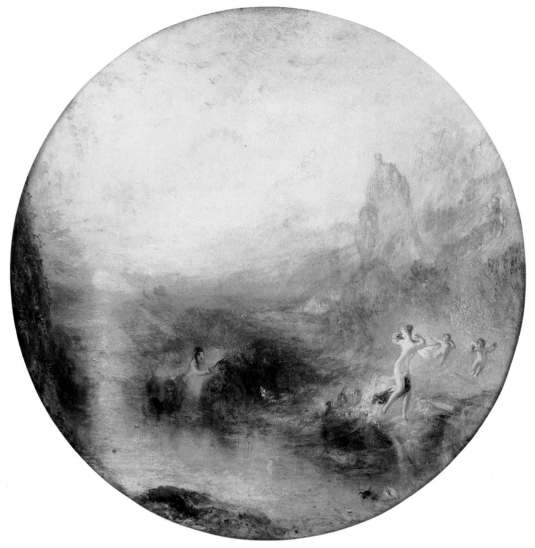

**138** *Glaucus and Scylla*, R.A. 1841,
oil on panel, 79 × 77.5 cm) Kimbell Art Gallery, Fort Worth, Texas.

then we are looking westwards and the sun is therefore setting, which is only fitting given the tragic subject.

The same sense of decorum is present in Turner's oil-painting of *Glaucus and Scylla*, exhibited at the R.A. in 1841 (fig. 138). To the left of an active Mount Etna in the distance we see one of Turner's richest sunsets beyond Glaucus, who beckons towards a dismissive Scylla once again.[8] The hapless nereid is pursued by a love that is personified here by the cupids hovering before her, impeding her escape. Uncodified metaphorical elaborations of the subject can easily be perceived as well, such as the large crab pursuing the smaller one on the beach below Scylla, and the reddish rock to the right of the sun. This clearly alludes to Scylla's eventual fate, as does the vertiginous rock above her.[9]

In addition to being visible in the Radnor Claudes and *The Sea of Galilee*, Claude's supposed or definite use of light symbolism may also have been apparent to Turner in other works. For instance, at Christie's in February 1804 he could have seen two pendant paintings that were very evidently morning and evening scenes, and both works were also included in the Earlom *Liber Veritatis*, although not connected as pendants there. The morning scene, already analysed, is *LV* 180, the *Coast of Libya with Aeneas hunting* (which was entitled in the Boydell-Earlom title-list as *Landscape with Aeneas shooting Deer*) and it will be further discussed below (fig. 109). Its pendant, a *Coast View with Aeneas and the Sibyl* was titled by Earlom *The Cumaean Sibyl conducting Aeneas to the Infernal Shades*[10] (*LV* 183, fig. 139) and Turner himself described its subject as 'The Descent of Aeneas' in one of his perspective lectures.[11] Turner painted Aeneas and the Cumaean Sibyl twice, on both occasions probably for Sir Richard Colt Hoare. The first version dates from around 1798 (figs 199, 200) and the second, which Colt Hoare bought, sometime during 1814–15. In 1834 the artist returned to the subject less directly in *The Golden Bough* (fig. 144), to elaborate an underlying theme.

Turner must have been struck by the most distinctive symbolic feature in Claude's 'Descent of Aeneas' (fig. 139), since Claude forces it upon our attention by making Aeneas's spear point directly at it: beyond the Sibyl gesturing towards 'the infernal Shades', we see the rays of the sun appearing from *below* the horizon. Like the sun, Aeneas is also beginning his descent to the Underworld.

The engravings that purported to depict the rise and fall of the Roman empire not only possibly strengthened Turner's desire to use light appropriately. They may also well have reinforced his propensity for another form of metaphorical expression.

**139** Richard Earlom after Claude le Lorrain,
*The Cumaean Sibyl conducting Aeneas to the Infernal Shades*
(*Liber Veritatis* 183) mezzotint engraving, 1777.

**140** *View of the Temple of Jupiter Panellenius in the Island of Ægina, with the Greek National Dance of the Romaika: the Acropolis of Athens in the Distance*, R.A. 1816, oil on canvas, 118.2 × 178.1 cm, The Duke of Northumberland, K. G.

PENDANTS

It is ironic that many people who are not at all sympathetic to the notion that Turner used association and visual metaphor have nonetheless been forced to recognise that by pairing pictures the painter very clearly effects the transference to further meanings. The artist had used the direct coupling of works to elaborate a greater complexity of response to topography before painting *Dido building Carthage* and its pendant between 1814–17. Examples are the pictures of Tabley House, Cheshire, dating from 1809 (B.J. 98, 99), one of which shows a view of the house under windy conditions, the other the same scene on a calm day. But with *Dido building Carthage* and the decline picture Turner also appropriated pendant painting to a moral – and thus a poetic – painterly role. And it is not only in the Carthaginian pictures of 1815 and 1817 that he did this. Two other works, possibly begun in

1814–15 and exhibited together at the R.A. in 1816, also demonstrate a profound moral connection by their complementary treatment of a subject and their opposition of effects of light with decorum; they will serve to further typify the process. The pictures also use the ruin and restoration of architecture to further their subjects allegorically. They are *View of the Temple of Jupiter Panellenius, in the Island of Ægina, with the Greek National Dance of the Romaika : the Acropolis of Athens in the Distance* (fig. 140) and a pendant of the same size, *The Temple of Jupiter Panellenius restored* (fig. 141).

For many people during the 1810s and '20s the aspirations for Greek freedom had come to replace the thwarted idealism of the French Revolution. For Turner, as for Byron, the cause was one he readily identified with, Greece being the birthplace and symbol of Liberty and Democracy. Turner either treated of or alluded to the Greek struggle for freedom in a number of pictures right up until the early 1830s when the country at last became independent. In *View of the Temple of Jupiter Panellenius, in the Island of Ægina, with the Greek National Dance of the Romaika : the Acropolis of Athens in the Distance* (fig. 140) Turner depicts what was held to be the temple of all the Greeks in ruins as it was seen at the time, under an effect of light falling from the west, and therefore in the evening, with Greek girls dancing before their Turkish masters, who sit watching or lie stupefied by drugs. In *The Temple of Jupiter Panellenius restored* (fig. 141) Turner projects the temple as it might theoretically be reconstructed in his own day, and therefore how it was originally thought to have appeared. He shows it lit from the east and thus at dawn, thereby alluding to the hoped-for restoration of Greek freedom and re-establishment of her greatness. (As Turner never visited the site, he must have made positive enquiries as to the directional alignment of the building in order to achieve these effects, an indication of the lengths he would go to in order to achieve a sense of decorum in his lighting.) The timing and meaning of *The Temple of Jupiter Panellenius restored* was also furthered in the Royal Academy catalogue by an amended quotation from a contemporary poem by Robert Southey:

> 'twas now the earliest morning; soon the sun,
> Rising above Abardos, poured his light
> Amid the forest, and, with ray aslant,
> Entering its depth, illumed the branking pines,
> Brightened their bark, tinged with a redder hue
> Its rusty stains, and cast along the ground
> Long lines of shadow, where they rose erect
> Like pillars of the temple.[12]

Here, once again, Turner employs poetry to introduce associations of time and movement, and equally to reinforce the sense of renewal afforded by the coming of day.

Other complementary meanings effected through pendant pictures can be encountered in this book, including the *Dawn of Christianity* (fig. 150) and the sun setting upon the pagan

**141**  *The Temple of Jupiter Panellenius restored*, R.A. 1816,
oil on canvas, 116.8 × 177.8 cm, Private Collection, USA.

*Glaucus and Scylla* (fig 138) of 1841, the *Peace* and *War* pictures of 1842 (figs 54, 56), and the eve of the deluge and morning after the deluge pictures of 1843 (fig. 181). This reliance upon the connection of images and the observation of a decorum of light right up until almost the end of Turner's working life demonstrates how he never lost his desire to communicate morally, associatively and dramatically, and how crucial the influence of Claude might have been in this respect.

VERTICAL ALIGNMENT

The placing of dissimilar objects in direct vertical conjunction with one another in order to enforce their association is something we can also see in *Dido building Carthage*. It was to be one of Turner's favourite methods for creating connections, for reasons of visual consonance already touched upon and because it is also a subtle but insistent way of directing the

**142** *Portsmouth, Hampshire, c.* 1824,
watercolour on paper, 15.2 × 21.8 cm, Lady Lever Art Gallery, Port Sunlight.

eye and mind to relate things. Pictorially this kind of associative relationship may have partially derived from Claude, especially from works like *The Sea of Galilee* (fig. 134) or 'The Descent of Aeneas' (fig. 139). Such vertical alignment made its first public appearance in Turner's work in the Welsh castle pictures of 1800 (figs 24 and 26). Yet *Caernarvon Castle* was also Turner's first essay in the manner of Claude and the clear influence of Claude at that time tells us that Turner had been looking intensely at the pictures of the French painter during the preceding period, probably through the Earlom *Liber Veritatis* and as a result of seeing the Altieri Claudes in May 1799. Turner's use of vertical alignment is so widespread, and is observed so abundantly throughout this book, that we need here only demonstrate the technical range it could enjoy.

One of Turner's most inventive employments of vertical alignment occurs in a watercolour of *Portsmouth, Hampshire* (fig. 142), made around 1824 for the 'Southern Coast' series, where he depicts the view across the entrance to the harbour, with the great naval station in the distance. Due to frequent movements of often very large men-of-war through such a narrow channel, access to the base had to be strictly supervised, and this was effected by signals from the Dockyard Semaphore, seen in the far distance beyond the middle of the harbour mouth. To stress its function Turner aligns two other naval guides immediately below it. These are an officer gesturing to the crew of his gig to lower sail and, below him, the rudder of yet another gig which is also under the direction of a naval officer. By this ingenious repetition Turner literally centres the whole work around the totally appropriate theme of naval control.[13]

In *Portsmouth, Hampshire* (fig. 142) Turner uses a single vertical alignment to enhance meaning. He could also employ two parallel lines of visual 'stepping-stones' for the same motive. If we return to *Hougoumont* (fig. 66) we can see how, moving upwards from the foreground, Turner aligns the letters G R (i.e. George Rex) on a baggage-wagon, with the corner of the outer wall of the farmhouse, with the pointed top of the circular haystack within its courtyard (a haystack whose firing during the battle of Waterloo was also to set the farmhouse alight), with the chimney above it, and finally with the approaching storm-clouds whose symbolism we have already examined. A parallel line leads the eye up from the shako of the seated soldier, and the rise of the outer-farmhouse wall, to the moon whose power to denote the coming of death has also been noted. The link may well allude to the fate of the soldier on the morrow. Both lines can thus be seen to remind us of the battle to come.

As well as furthering associative meaning through single and double vertical alignments, Turner could also amplify meaning by imaginatively connecting two parallel alignments. A picture which demonstrates the inventive use of this procedure is *Winchelsea, Sussex* (fig. 143). The work is Plate 42 of the *Liber Studiorum*, published in April 1812, and thus the very next image in the sequence of prints to *Procris and Cephalus* whose linear and tree symbolism we have noted earlier (fig. 111).[14] Turner's association of Winchelsea with the military has also been observed. The drawing upon which the *Liber Studiorum* print was based (T.B CXVII–P) probably dates from about 1810 at the height of the Napoleonic Wars.

In the centre a soldier talks to a woman and two children. From the look of obvious despondency on the face of the woman, and her seated position, we can infer that she is not merely a local giving directions to a passing soldier – for anyway it is the soldier who is pointing the way – but in fact his wife with their children bidding him goodbye. No other casting could account for her dejection, for it was customary to send strangers off to the wars with a rousing farewell. The soldier seems to be reluctantly gesturing towards those very shores he is going to defend, and equally towards a nearby flock of sheep, at the tail-end of which are two more soldiers: like sheep they too must obey orders (and the sheep are shown doing just that). Directly above the soldier-husband is a leafy birch tree with a sapling growing by its side. In the right-foreground, parallel to those trees, is another birch also

**143** *Winchelsea, Sussex*, mezzotint engraving,
Part IX of *Liber Studiorum*, drawn and etched by Turner, engraved by J. C. Easling.

accompanied by a sapling. The blackened branches of the nearer birch are either leafless or virtually so, for the tree has been struck dead by lightning (such electrical discharges being an association for war that Turner also used elsewhere in a Winchelsea subject, as we have seen). It is this marked parallelism of the two birch trees, each with its adjacent offspring, and the precise vertical alignment of one of the pairs of trees with the soldier, that enforces their connection and suggests the moral of the work: the soldier, as full of life as the mature tree above him, is going off to war to die, just as the other tree to which he is pointing indirectly *has* died. The wife and children now at his side will go on living and growing, just as the healthy saplings at the side of the live and dead trees will continue to live and grow. The way that the line of the stock of the soldier's rifle is carried upwards by the tree above him, and the centrality of flowering emphasis Turner gives that tree, entirely supports this interpretation. The broken rocks and ruined tower add to the sombre mood of the work, as do the long shadows cast by the late afternoon light. That choice of timing complements the sensibility of loss in the work, and all of these desolate features throw the flowering of the tree above the soldier into even greater relief by contrast.

*Winchelsea, Sussex* also prefigures *Dido building Carthage* in one important way: some five years before he painted his 'chef d'oeuvre' it shows how readily the artist employed the association of nearby but distinctly separated elements to further meaning in his works. This too is a form of organisation worthy of attention.

We have already noted in *Dido building Carthage* how Turner enforces a marked dramatic opposition between the royal retinue and bustling city on one side of the work, and the tomb on the other, thus creating a greater significance, the opposition of life and death. We can also see in that work how the artist understandably places things near to us when he especially wants us to notice them. Such placements are encountered elsewhere as well, as with the mallard in *Peace – Burial at Sea* (fig. 54). These adjacent positions may be likened to left, centre, rightstage, and downstage or midstage positions in the theatre. Turner may have derived these extremely theatrical placements of figures and objects from plays or from the very stylised theatrical tableaux of the day, and from the opera, for we know he was an avid theatre and opera-goer and that on at least two occasions he is known to have painted pictures upon themes he encountered there.[15] (Not for nothing did C. R. Leslie say of *Dido building Carthage* that 'the picture made him feel as if he were in a theatre decorated with the most splendid of drop scenes'.[16]) Moreover, it now seems fairly certain that as a teenager in the early 1790s Turner worked as a theatrical scene-painter in a London opera house.[17] Naturally he may equally have obtained the idea for such placements from any number of pictorial models where the protagonists are placed prominently in the fore or middle-grounds of landscape settings. But it was his habit of locating them in only two or three clearly demarcated left, centre and right-hand positions in the foreground or middle-distance which suggests a theatrical influence and which most easily provides the clue that an associative level of significance is present in a picture. Indeed, this positioning can sometimes reveal the most profound levels of meaning in a work.

In *The Golden Bough* (fig. 144), for instance, the location of the figures alerts us to their role as symbolic personæ. The picture was exhibited at the R.A. in 1834 but to understand it fully we have to see it as the culmination of Turner's approach to a subject. The artist had painted two earlier versions of this landscape, basing them upon sketches of Lake Avernus in Italy made on the spot by Sir Richard Colt Hoare, from which he made his own preparatory outline (T.B. LI-N). The first of the paintings (figs 199, 200), dating from about 1798, is a treatment in the style of Richard Wilson, which Colt Hoare appears not to have liked, whilst the other (B.J. 226) is a more Claudian version of around 1815, which Colt Hoare actually bought. In both pictures Turner derived his narrative from the sixth book of Virgil's *Aeneid* which he knew from translations by Dryden and Christopher Pitt in Anderson's *Complete Poets*. The Ancients considered Lake Avernus to be the entrance to the

**144**  *The Golden Bough*, R.A. 1834,
oil on canvas, 104 × 163.5 cm, Clore Gallery for the Turner Collection, London.

abode of the dead, the Underworld, from which one could only hope to return by presenting to Proserpine (the Queen of the Dead) a golden bough from a tree that grew in a vale alongside the lake. In Turner's early versions Aeneas is being shown the bough by Deiphobe, the Cumaean Sibyl, in the 1798 treatment accompanied by two companions and in the 1815 picture joined by three others, one of whom may be Chryses. (Like Chryses, Deiphobe was also in the service of Apollo.)

In 1834 Turner once again returned to the subject, not because of a commission but apparently out of choice. He still depicts the tree and lake, and appropriately gives us the Sibyl proffering the bough, although he moves her somewhat over to the left of her location in the earlier pictures and isolates her in the process. To the left of her, and at exactly the same level as the bough which promises a return from the Underworld, is a statue standing in an ultramarine blue-coloured aureole niche. Given the shape of this niche and its colour it seems very likely that this is a statue of the Virgin Mary, the blue signalling well-hallowed associations of the 'mother of heaven'. Moreover, above the niche is a painted roundel which, although indistinct, appears to contain shapes approximating the crown and crossed-key insignia of the Papacy. Furthermore, the painted decorative wall surrounds are very similar to those which appear on the Loggia of the Vatican in Turner's 1820 painting of *Rome from the Vatican*. Yet if this is the case, Turner's placing of the Virgin Mary almost alongside the Cumaean Sibyl is not an historical anachronism, such as we have encountered elsewhere in the artist's work. Instead, it is a straightforward allusion to the fact that Christian commentators from the time of Justin Martyr onwards have maintained that the Cumaean Sibyl prophesied the coming of Christ. Moreover, Virgil himself was thought to have repeated the Sibyl's actual prophecy in his *Fourth Eclogue*.[18] The Emperor Constantine, who established Christianity as the state religion of the Roman Empire in the fourth century, categorically identified Christ as the 'First-born of the New Age' spoken of by Virgil, and he was followed in this by St Augustine and other saints who also stated that Virgil had received this prophecy from the Cumaean Sibyl herself. It is therefore entirely appropriate for Turner to have included a representation of the Virgin Mary in his picture of the Cumaean Sibyl. His awareness of the connection between the two 'Virgins Divine' probably emanated from his close study of the sibyls in Michelangelo's Sistine ceiling frescoes where the Cumaean Sibyl is represented midway along the right-hand wall for exactly the reasons given above.[19]

Yet despite the inclusion of a detail which further testifies to Turner's awareness of the historical background of the Cumaean Sibyl, Aeneas and his companions are now conspicuously absent from the scene. Instead, we see some wildly abandoned dancers in the centre and, to the right, a reclining nude with a companion.[20] Strewn around them are various luxury objects including a lyre, mirrors, wine jars and the like. Through the simplest of associations, and by their prominence and isolation, we may safely take these objects to represent the vain luxuries of the world. But why should Turner have portrayed the golden bough a third time in 1834 and what could it all mean?

It is evident that Turner drew his information for the picture from Christopher Pitt's translation of this passage of Virgil's *Aeneid*, rather than Dryden's, for the latter does not specifically mention a golden bough.[21] And when we look at Pitt's version of the poem we can find a very clear reason for Turner to have returned to the subject in 1834. Aeneas sought the golden bough because he wanted to visit the Underworld to see his father again. Four years or so before Turner painted *The Golden Bough* his own father had also died, leaving him completely bereft: as the son of one of his close friends tells us, 'Turner never appeared the same man after his father's death; his family was broken up.'[22] How poignantly the lines in which Aeneas implores the Sibyl to allow him a sight of his father must have struck Turner just a few years after the demise of own much-loved father:

> Give me to view my father's reverend face
> And rush with transport to his dear embrace!

He shar'd my toils, determin'd to defy
The storms of every sea and every sky;
In hardships, cares and dangers to engage;
Nor spar'd his stooping venerable age.[23]

How truly, if figuratively, Turner's father had shared his 'storms of every sea and every sky', even well into a 'stooping venerable age'.[24] Here, surely, must have been the important imaginative starting-point for *The Golden Bough*. But where is Aeneas? He cannot be absent visiting his father in the Underworld, for if that were the case he would have taken the bough with him in order to be able to return (it will be noted that the Sibyl proffers *the* golden bough, not simply one of many). So why is Aeneas absent? Why and for whom is the Sibyl holding up the golden bough? And what exactly is the significance of the figures who are so conspicuously separated from her?

The very indifference of those figures to the Sibyl provides the answer to all these questions. The dancers and women clearly exemplify a wider indifference on the part of a vain and hedonistic humanity to the ultimate problems of life and death. They sport or surround themselves with objects of transient pleasure, typified by the articles which litter the foreground, such as vanity-goods and fragments of masonry. Turner even introduces a snake to allude to the 'infernal shades' or to denote the evils connected with vanity.

Yet one might reasonably expect that anyone who is offered the golden bough, as these people very clearly are, will take heed of it, for it affords a means of evading death. But the dancers and women clearly cannot care less. Therein lies the point. Turner has omitted Aeneas from the scene because *The Golden Bough* is not about Aeneas at all; it is about us and our indifference to a means of attaining immortality. This is in large part an indifference to the possibility of redemption afforded by religion, as denoted by the classical and modern beliefs represented respectively by the golden bough and statue of the Madonna on the left. Yet at the same time Turner may also be alluding to public indifference to his own art itself.

We have to consider *The Golden Bough* in context to understand the purport of this statement, and indeed the picture as well. Turner felt somewhat isolated during the early 1830s, as much by public indifference or even outright hostility to his work as by his father's death and the deaths of several of his friends. Quite naturally he was also intensely aware of mortality as he approached his sixties, which in those days signified old age perhaps more than they would do today. Yet Turner knew that his paintings would outlive him and in *The Golden Bough* he seems to have addressed himself in part to that subject. For if to an indifferent world the Sibyl demonstrates an object with which mankind can attain physical immortality, by a parallel process – and in the face of a similar general public indifference to his artistic offerings – so Turner may have created *The Golden Bough* as an object with which to underline the immortality of his art. All this would explain the absence of Aeneas. Turner wants us to see the golden bough and *The Golden Bough* as themselves the objects by which, respectively, mankind and himself could and would ward off death. Turner's painting is not merely a *memento mori* set in the ancient world, but is itself a projection of its subject – a Golden Bough indeed! Amid and through a landscape of unsurpassable loveliness, with its radiant golden light, and set as it originally was in a golden frame,[25] Turner's *The Golden Bough* acclaims the immortality of art and the power of the art-object to triumph over death. Given that in 1814 Turner had used *Apullia in Search of Appullus* (fig. 114) to remark upon the creative process, that in 1831 he had painted a picture of the dying Watteau in the act of painting to explore the very relationship of the artist to the notion of immortality (something he also explored in a contemporary picture of Sir Walter Scott[26]), and that in 1836 he would again apparently make a statement about the undying beauty of a work of art in *Juliet and her Nurse* (fig. 12), it does not seem fanciful to suppose that in the midst of a period of isolation and fear of mortality Turner should have wished to remind himself of the ability of his art to transcend death, exactly as in antiquity the golden bough was supposed to enable one to transcend death. And here, as elsewhere, the figures – and more especially their spatial relationships – are the vital keys which can unlock that significance.

The subtle but enforced separation of the figures is therefore an important way in which Turner elaborated metaphorical meaning. In some of his works he even coupled it with yet another device for extending what we are seeing. Here too the influence of Claude can be discerned.

## THE SYMBOLIC DIVIDE

One of the very first pictures in which Claude used the components of a landscape to further its meaning associatively was the *Landscape with the Rest on the Flight into Egypt* of about 1639 (*LV* 38) which is represented here by the Earlom *Liber Veritatis* mezzotint (fig. 145). As can

**145**  Richard Earlom after Claude le Lorrain,
*Landscape with the Rest on the Flight into Egypt*
(*Liber Veritatis* 38), mezzotint engraving, 1777.

**146** *Brinkburn Priory, Northumberland, c.*1830–1,
watercolour on paper, 29 × 46 cm, Graves Art Gallery, Sheffield.

be observed, Claude goes to extremes in the way he opposes lush vegetation on the near side of a river, which is occupied by the Holy Family and an angel, and its far side where a far less heavily wooded landscape seems quite bare by comparison, a contrast between fertility and desolation that is greatly heightened associatively by the ruined castle. Obviously this contrast is not merely intended to point up the different kinds of vegetation, and its abundance or sparsity. Instead, Claude intended the contrast to introduce associations of plenitude and dearth or even wider meanings that openly derive from the narrative. From the fact that the Holy Family are seated and accompanied by an angel, and from the extraordinary richness of their surroundings, we may confidently assume that they are safe for the time being, and that they may even have reached Egypt. If that is so, then the river clearly acts as a symbolic divide, and in any event it serves to enforce contrasts.

Turner also explored these kinds of contrasts on opposite sides of bodies of water, as we have seen with *Dido building Carthage*. Indeed, he was very strikingly to use exactly this kind of divide between plenitude and the lack of it in a watercolour of *Brinkburn Priory, Northumberland* (fig. 146), made for engraving in the 'England and Wales' series sometime around 1830. On the left side of the picture is a superabundance of natural vegetation. The other side of the work is dominated by the ruined priory. Like the building the riverbank in front of it is desolate, in strong contrast to the natural richness opposite. Turner very clearly seems to be opposing the florescence of external nature on the one hand, and the ruination of man on the other.

224

**147** Claude le Lorrain, *Landscape with Ascanius Shooting the Stag of Silvia*, 1682, oil on canvas, 120 × 150 cm, Ashmolean Museum, Oxford.

Other images in the *Liber Veritatis* which use rivers as symbolic divides were probably or definitely known to Turner. These include *LV* 88, *Landscape with the Rest on the Flight into Egypt* (fig. 104), and the similarly titled *LV* 158 (fig. 107) where the Holy Family have now definitely crossed a river to the safety of Egypt. Elsewhere Claude reversed the state: in *LV* 106, *Landscape with Hagar and the Angel* (the original painting of which belonged to Sir George Beaumont, but which entered the National Gallery collection in 1824), he used a river to signify the division between Hagar and Abraham who has banished her into the wilderness.

Claude also used a river to divide a hunter from his prey in his painting of the *Landscape with Ascanius Shooting the Stag of Silvia* (fig. 147). This was Claude's last painting, and his death prevented him from recording it in the *Liber Veritatis*; as a result it was not included in the Earlom set of engravings. Even so, Turner may have known the original picture for it appeared in the London salerooms in 1801, 1810, 1811 and 1826.[27] The work takes its subject from the seventh book of Virgil's *Aeneid* where Ascanius precipitates war in Latium by killing the pet stag of King Tyrrhus's daughter Silvia. Claude took the image from drawings he had made for an earlier picture, *Coast of Libya with Aeneas hunting* (*LV* 180, fig. 109). In one of his lectures Turner referred to 'The chace of Claude', which suggests that he meant one of these two pictures[28]. As we have seen, in the *Coast of Libya* Claude placed a solitary pine tree in the foreground, perhaps to accentuate the straightness of Aeneas's aim (and there too we encounter a prominent rock-arch). Although in *Ascanius shooting the stag of Silvia* Claude does not seem to use the trees to enlarge upon the straightness of the huntsman's aim quite as directly as he does in the *Coast of Libya*, nonetheless the tall birch tree arching out from immediately above Ascanius initiates an implied semi-circle that passes across the sky to terminate at the yews growing above the stag on the right. This line contributes to the suggestion of a link between Ascanius and the animal, and the divergence of the two yew trees reiterates the divergence of the stag's antlers below them.

All the above devices, such as the contrast between natural luxuriance and sparseness, the use of a river as a symbolic divide, the associative use of arboreal straightness to suggest a hunter's straightness of aim, and the downstage location of the protagonists of a picture, with the action taking place across the picture-plane, as witnessed in *Ascanius Shooting the Stag of Silvia*, can be discerned with especial clarity in another picture made for the 'England and Wales' series.

*Powis Castle, Montgomery* (fig. 148) dates from some time between 1825 and 1835 but most probably toward the end of that period. The castle is situated in the distance, its terraces dropping down to the river Severn. Turner places his principal protagonists, a hunter and his prey, in the foreground, on either side of the river. The prey is a heron, poised at the water's edge on the left and completely unaware of its pursuer. Immediately behind the heron are some elder trees in full leaf, whilst beyond the hunter on the right are two maples. Turner creates a strong connection between the heron and the elders by repeating and enlarging the U-shaped curve of the neck of the bird in the similar shape made by the space between the trees. And in addition to relating the bird and the trees by vertical

**148** *Powis Castle, Montgomery, c.*1825–35,
watercolour on paper, 29 × 45 cm, City Art Gallery, Manchester.

alignment and the linking of forms, Turner also connects on another level too: the extremely luxuriant flowering of the trees embodies the very quality of life enjoyed by the heron, whilst the natural vitality of those trees is intensified by the relative bleakness of the landscape opposite. Similarly, the straightness of the maples on the right suggests the straightness of the hunter's aim, something that Turner hints at by showing the hunter in the process of carefully positioning himself for his shot. In the distance, midway between heron and hunter, is another bird. From its size we may safely infer that it too is a heron. By placing this bird midway between the hunter and his prey, at the apex of a shallow triangle formed by the banks of the river as they converge in perspective, Turner seems to be suggesting that the life of the heron on the left is in the balance. Alternatively, by that process of simultaneity we have observed in *St. Julienne's Chapel* (fig. 74), the artist may be showing us the spirit of the dead bird flying off after it has been shot, or he may be indicating that the hunter will miss and the heron will escape – the associative possibilities are diverse, especially when we consider that the hunter is not wearing waders, nor is he accompanied by dogs. He would therefore encounter difficulty in retrieving his spoil. But perhaps these omissions are intentional. Turner may have wanted the river to act as a symbolic divide in the life and death situation that the hunter is creating.

This work is not the only 'England and Wales' series watercolour in which Turner employs hunting imagery, and a river which clearly acts as a symbolic divide, in order to point up the difference between life and death. In *Chain Bridge over the River Tees* (fig. 149) of around 1836 he places a hunter and some birds once again in linked opposition across a river, within a similarly polarised context of bleakness versus rich foliage.[29]

**149** *Chain Bridge over the River Tees, c.*1836,
watercolour on paper, 27 × 43 cm, Private Collection, U K.

**150** *Dawn of Christianity (Flight into Egypt)*, R.A. 1841,
oil on canvas, circular, diameter 78.5 cm, The Ulster Museum, Belfast.

And these are not the only pictures in which the influence of Claude upon Turner's use of a river as a symbolic divide can be detected either. A fine late painting demonstrates Turner's creation of the same kind of river-divide symbolism that we encounter in Claude's work, along with trees used as metaphors and light handled with decorum. The picture is Turner's treatment of the same subject as that recorded by Claude in *Liber Veritatis* drawings and the Earlom engravings numbers 38, 88 and 158, namely the Holy Mother and Child on their flight into Egypt, and it might well have drawn upon the latter images (or, in the case of *LV* 88 possibly even a knowledge of the original painting) for some of its associative devices, although it seems to owe something also to Raphael's *The Holy Family with the Palm Tree* (fig. 88).

*Dawn of Christianity (Flight into Egypt)* was shown at the R.A. in 1841 with the quotation 'That Star has risen' from the poem 'Spring' by the Rev. Thomas Gisborne appended in the catalogue. On the right (fig. 150) are the Virgin and Child, preceded by an angel, who make their way up a riverside road which comes around towards us. Although there is no way of knowing for sure whether they have crossed the river or not, it seems likely that they have, for the river effectively divides them from the human evil symbolised by the snake opposite. And although the serpent is linked to them visually by a strong diagonal, the broken bridge associatively assures their safety. Moreover, the gap it emphasises effectively symbolises the gap that exists between Christianity and 'the old religion'. On the left, beyond the snake, we see dawn breaking. This accords with Gisborne's text, for it is whilst dawn 'crimson'd' the 'impatient East' that the coming of Christ as a 'Day-Star' had taken place. The blinding white brilliance of the sky on the right, above Jesus and Mary, suggests the new and radiantly pure dispensation that the Child will bring, whilst the redness of the dawn could also conveniently symbolise the blood-letting that is now taking place in Bethlehem. Gisborne's metaphorical rising 'Star' is directly rendered by Turner who links Jesus and the star with a strong beam of light.[30] The palm-tree in front of the star can clearly be seen to conjure up a conscious orientalism and a sense of protection, as do similarly placed trees in Claude's treatments of this subject and the palm-tree in Raphael's painting. Indeed, the placement of the 'Day-Star' of Jesus immediately *beneath* the sheltering leaves of the palm-tree renders that sense of protection beyond doubt. Moreover, the fusion of star and palm tree, which may equally stand for the tree of life, suggests that the star will in turn afford protection to others. Another metaphorical level to the work may reside in the fact that the picture was painted as a pendant to *Glaucus and Scylla* (fig. 138).[31] The pictures enjoy polarised colour contrasts, *Glaucus and Scylla* being hot and rich, *Dawn of Christianity* cool and unsullied. Because the 'dawn' of the *Dawn of Christianity (Flight into Egypt)* is both a literal and a metaphorical time of day, we may equally be correct in seeing the sunset of *Glaucus and Scylla* as representative of a larger 'sunset' as well: more generally *Glaucus and Scylla* and the *Dawn of Christianity (Flight into Egypt)* may respectively represent the death of paganism and the birth of the religion that replaced it in the West.

In *Dawn of Christianity*, as with its probable Claudian models, we appear to be witnessing protagonists separated from danger by a physical and metaphorical divide. In other works Turner seems also to have imbued the fording of such divisions with meaning.

## CROSSING A DIVIDE

The symbolism of *Abbotsford* (fig. 151) grew directly out of Turner's experience, for life virtually imitated art here. In 1831 Turner visited Abbotsford in Scotland to stay with the mortally ill Sir Walter Scott in order to gather material for a number of watercolours which were to be engraved to illustrate a complete edition of Scott's *Poetical Works*. On one level

*Abbotsford* undoubtedly incorporates the memory of an outing made during that visit from Scott's great house by Turner and the Edinburgh publisher of the edition, Robert Cadell. Scott was too ill to join Turner and Cadell on the drive, and he was perhaps wise to stay at home, for it was a long and tiring day. Turner, Cadell and a servant boy who acted as their coachman travelled around in a gig for some '12½ hours in the open air'[32] whilst Turner gathered material for his watercolours. Turner made a number of sketches of Abbotsford from different positions at the end of the day before they forded the Tweed to return home.

Yet although Turner subsequently projected the experience of crossing the river into his view of Abbotsford, he may have intended the figures to represent Scott with an entourage, rather than the servant, Cadell and himself. For although it is impossible to identify the people in *Abbotsford* individually, so small are they, Turner must have been aware that the public, knowing nothing of his own peregrinations, would have been likely to think that one of the men seated in the gig was Scott, particularly in a view of Scott's house. By raising one of the men in the gig slightly above the other, and vertically aligning him with the summit of White Law far above him in the distance, it is suggested that the person seated nearest the house may be Scott. Turner never confined himself imaginatively to his own physical experiences, and certainly we know the picture to be a projection anyway, inasmuch as he did not witness the river-crossing but actually took part in it, so there is no reason why one of the figures in the gig might not represent Scott. Turner lends dignity to

**151** H. Le Keux after J. M. W. Turner, *Abbotsford*, 1834, engraving.

the crossing by including two outriders. Neither of them are mentioned by Cadell in his diary of the tour so we can safely infer that they were products of the artist's imagination, introduced to add to the stateliness of the procession. The nearest of the outriders conveys a feeling of fatigue as he leans over his horse, a very appropriate response in a picture of the dying poet. The way Turner leads the eye up to the moon at the left also increases the sense of slow, dignified motion across the river. And with the moon once again we encounter Turner's strong sense of association. When he made *Abbotsford* in July 1832[33] Turner was well aware that the great poet and novelist did not have long to live. Indeed, Scott was to die just two months later, on 21 September. Turner shared similar apprehensions regarding his own fate in the years following his father's death, so it may have seemed natural to him to introduce a valedictory note into *Abbotsford* (which was, in fact, the last of his contributions to Scott's *Poetical Works* to be engraved). Of all the illustrations made for the series, the subject of this picture was naturally most closely associated in the public mind with Scott and therefore it could easily have been the image through which Turner wanted to address himself most directly to the subject of Scott as a person. How could he do that more appropriately in the twilight of Scott's life than by showing Scott crossing a great divide, at the end of day, with a moonrise stressing the proximity of night? Moreover, to see this event as a symbolic river-crossing, carried out beneath a moonrise that associatively denotes the coming of death, is supported by the fact that although Turner originally surrounded all of his illustrations to Scott's *Poetical Works* with architectural designs that were '. . . clearly derived from contemporary funeral wall plaques or tablets',[34] only one of them survived the transition from watercolour to engraving. That picture is *Abbotsford* and it is not difficult to see why. Even before Scott died Turner had framed his picture of the great house with a cartouche showing Scott's writing desk and chair now vacant. As Gerald Finley has commented:

> That the author is not represented in these interior glimpses makes the mood more poignant and the commemorative element more pronounced.[35]

Turner definitely knew that Scott was not long for this earth when he made *Abbotsford* and he took the opportunity whilst creating the work to transform his own personal experience into an image more pertinent to the subject. The result is a picture that imparts a haunting sense of sadness.

Yet it is to 1815, the year in which Turner separated life and death elements in *Dido building Carthage* by means of a river, that we must return to encounter perhaps his most subtle use of a river as a divide to be crossed. For in that year Turner was not only concerned with proclaiming the growth of a nation; he seems to have been equally interested in expressing the growth of the individual, and even of life itself.

*Crossing the Brook* (fig. 152) was also exhibited at the R.A. in 1815, but it is not a picture

**152** *Crossing the Brook*, R.A. 1815, oil on canvas, 193 × 165 cm, Clore Gallery for the Turner Collection, London.

that has been much explored in terms of imagery, probably because it is usually considered representative of Turner at his most Claudian and, since we have somewhat lost sight of Claude's use of associative elements, a purely 'visual' picture. Indeed, one commentator recently wrote that in *Crossing the Brook* 'form [is] significant, but there [is] no content'.[36] That dubious statement needs to be tested.

Probable Claudian models for *Crossing the Brook* are easy to find. The work enjoys a striking correspondence with two images by Claude. Evidently one of them was known to Turner from its Earlom engraving, *LV* 47, the *Landscape with the finding of Moses* (fig. 102) which *Crossing the Brook* greatly resembles. The other is the nearly identical *Landscape with the rest on the flight into Egypt*, *LV* 88 (fig. 153). As Turner might have seen the painting of the latter at Holker Hall, near Windermere in Cumberland, either in 1797 or 1801, or (as is more likely) on his tour of the area in 1809, the picture is represented here in its original guise. Although the work was reproduced in the *Liber Veritatis*, it appears there in a somewhat altered form.[37]

Turner obviously had these landscapes in mind when he synthesised the panorama that appears in *Crossing the Brook* from sketches he made on a West Country tour in 1813. On that visit he based himself in Plymouth and took excursions into the surrounding countryside. In the picture we can recognise stretches of the river Tamar, with Calstock bridge in the centre and Plymouth Sound faintly discernible in the distance. On the right is a grotto with a lane in front of it. The banks of the brook converge midway between two girls, whilst at the very point of convergence is a small, deeply clefted rock which is placed immediately above a dog. Thereafter the brook meanders off beyond the rock into the centre-distance and runs parallel with the river far below it on the left. The protagonists are aligned across the foreground and their location creates a sense of sequence to the 'crossing', the eye being pulled from the empty area on the right, *via* the seated girl, the dog crossing to the left, and the girl who has crossed the brook, to the repoussoir on the left. A friend of Turner's[38] later recognised the standing girl as being the artist's elder daughter, Evelina (his younger daughter being named Georgiana).

Yet there are a number of reasons for believing that *Crossing the Brook* is not merely an expression of Turner's regard for a part of the world once characterised by a friend of the artist as an 'English Eden',[39] which has been treated in the manner of Claude with some ancillary figures thrown in. Foremost amongst these reasons is the picture-title itself. *Crossing the Brook* is virtually alone amongst the several hundred pictures publicly exhibited by Turner (and thus entitled by him) to enjoy a title which describes an *action* that is unrelated to any specific person, place or time, 'the Brook' in question clearly being a generalised one, as is made clear by the use of the definite article.[40] It is clear, then, that in choosing the title of his Devonshire-inspired landscape Turner wanted us to consider the *crossing* of the brook as the primary subject of his work. The fact that the artist gave the

**153** Claude le Lorrain, *Landscape with the rest on the Flight into Egypt*, oil on canvas, 208 × 152.5 cm, The Cleveland Museum of Art, Cleveland, Ohio.

**154** C. Guerin after Philippe Jacques de Loutherbourg, *Le Passage du Ruisseau*, engraving.

picture a generalised title rather than call it, say, 'View near Plymouth' or 'West Country Scene', certainly underlines that stress.

The inspiration for the title – and perhaps even the subject itself – could have derived from three identically named pictures by other artists. The first is a print after de Loutherbourg (fig. 154). This was probably an early work[41] made in France well before de Loutherbourg came to England but he may easily have had copies of the engraving in his London studio where Turner could have seen them. Although the title (reproduced here) appears in French, even Turner with his limited French would have been able to understand that a 'ruisseau' is not a 'rivière'. The image of one girl being carried by a young man across a brook, whilst another looks on and prepares to cross, could well have contributed to Turner's imagery in *Crossing the Brook*.

Another *Crossing the Brook* was by Henry Thomson, R.A. This picture was exhibited in 1803 at the R.A. where it was particularly well received. It was bought by a fellow patron of Turner's, Sir John Leicester, during the Academy Dinner, at which Turner himself was present.[42] Leicester subsequently hung Thomson's *Crossing the Brook* in the gallery of his house at 24 Hill Street, London, very near to Turner's *The Shipwreck* (fig. 229), so there can be no doubt that Turner knew it.[43]

The other *Crossing the Brook* was by Sir Joshua Reynolds and comprised a portrait of Hester Cholmondeley.[44] This was displayed in the major exhibition of Reynolds's works that was held at the British Institution in 1813, the grand opening of which was attended by both Turner and Thomson.[45] In de Loutherbourg's, Thomson's and Reynolds's *Crossing the Brook* the imagery of girls traversing a body of water – in the Thomson a child being helped across stepping stones by its mother, in the Reynolds a four-year-old carrying her dog – may have inspired Turner to take the idea much further as regards the figures and landscape, and to think through what the universal ramifications of the subject of a girl crossing a brook could be.

For there are several 'clues' which alert us to the fact that there is more than meets the eye in Turner's *Crossing the Brook*. First there is the bag under the arm of the girl on the left (fig. 155). She is holding up her dress to prevent it from getting wet but as a result the bag, which appears to be full and is therefore presumably quite heavy, looks completely unsupported. Moreover, between her feet on the water is a totally inexplicable vertical reflection. This cannot be cast by the bag as the object would have to be placed behind her to reflect off the water at that level, and as the rock behind her is in shadow it can hardly be creating such a reflection itself. Then there is the grotto[46] with a well-worn road connecting it with the brook. Why should a grotto enjoy what in early nineteenth-century terms would have been a major thoroughfare leading up to or away from it? Grottoes were fairly common in picturesque landscape gardens – although the scenery in *Crossing the Brook* looks positively wild – but for roads to terminate at, or start from grottoes was less common, if not extremely unusual. And in any case the road apparently leads nowhere at this end. Moreover, why should the road be so rutted? What kind of heavy usage could produce such rutting? Indeed, what can all of these curiosities point to, in addition to many other details in the work? Could the stress of the unusual title, the disposition of the staffage and the arrangement of the landscape, as well as perhaps the direction of the light, indicate that Turner may have wanted to convey something covert in *Crossing the Brook*? Might some underlying theme unite all of the constituent elements of the picture?

An extremely convincing answer, if not a detailed argument to support it, was provided by Jack Lindsay in 1966:

> The girls [Turner's daughters who would have been in their early teens around 1814–15] were now growing up. We may accept Trimmer's recognition of the girl in *Crossing the Brook* as Evelina. Turner had completed his idea of [the] picture when he merged the delicate great vista and its Claudean flanking trees with the episode of the girl wading through the water. He probably got the idea of the girls from Thomson's

*Crossing the Brook* . . . There is no aesthetic relation between the two pictures; but possibly Turner took from Thomson the idea of girls crossing water, which he then developed in his own way. Knowing the way his fancy worked, we may take Evelina's brook-crossing to symbolize her arrival at womanhood. Another girl (Georgiana) remains on the bank; Evelina steps into the flowing waters and crosses into the new life of maturity.[47]

This interpretation turns out to be convincing, for it is supported by the pictorial details and by our knowledge of Turner's associative processes. Moreover, such human motivation to the picture would be particularly extended by the landscape.

*Crossing the Brook* indeed seems to be an allegory of female puberty. Reading the picture from right to left, as the direction taken by the dog and the standing girl suggests we should, we first see the grotto. Turner was thoroughly acquainted with a body of literature either pointing out that in classical times such structures were considered to be sacred well-springs and sources of life, or giving poetic expression to such associations. He was certainly familiar with the grotto that stood in the grounds of Pope's villa at Twickenham (which still survives) and he might easily have been as well acquainted with the grotto at Stourhead in Wiltshire, Colt Hoare's country seat. There the grotto containing a white marble river god denoting the source of the river Stour actually bore the Latin inscription '. . . the home of the nymphs' above its portico.[48] That Turner may have shared such an association is suggested by the fact that the only grotto ever to appear in his exhibited output occurs in this picture of two young girls. From the womb-like opening of the grotto the well-worn road then leads the eye to the seated girl (fig. 155). Judging by her facial features she appears to be younger than the girl on the left and like her she too has a bag. These bags may be Turner's metaphors for the womb, particularly as the older girl's bag – now that she has 'crossed the brook' – is red, whilst the younger girl's bag is white. Moreover, next to the younger girl's bag is a red, stoppered bottle, which could easily denote that she has yet to reach puberty. This would also be conveyed by the fact that both bag and bottle are placed slightly apart from her. Even more significantly, a white cloth is draped across her lap. The fact that she is sitting, whilst the other girl stands, does not seem insignificant either.

Next we see the dog. Jack Lindsay interpreted this as a reminder of 'the animal life of [Evelina]', an interpretation that is supported by the immediate vertical alignment of the dog with the clefted rock. The similarity of this cleft to the female sexual cleft is marked.

Finally we see the elder girl herself (who may be Evelina). The abundant bag that she is holding unconvincingly points downwards and terminates immediately in front of her lap. The bag is wet, a fact denoted by the highlights upon it. The inexplicable reflection on the water between her legs is, moreover, red in colour and phallic in shape.[49]

The landscape contributes to this overall meaning. Beyond the older girl the bridge furthers the associations of 'crossing'. Above the seated girl are saplings whilst above the

**155** *Crossing the Brook* (detail).

standing one are tall, stately plane trees whose fertility and elegance makes them the perfect and most appropriately organic means of associatively expressing the burgeoning natural forces that are at work within the maturing girl. And in the sky beyond them we encounter, yet again, Turner's sense of decorum regarding the distribution of light, for we are looking southwards towards Plymouth, and the sun which catches the tops of the trees and casts long shadows is therefore rising.

Of Turner's receptivity to the idea that a body of water can represent a significant divide to be crossed in life there can be no doubt. In 1845 he linked exactly such a metaphor with this very painting. After a bout of illness he wrote to an acquaintance of

> . . . the Crossing the Brook Picture
> (Thank Heaven, which in its
> kindness has enabled me to
> wade through the Brook) – it I
> hope may continue to be mine –
> it is one of my children[50]

Although Turner referred to a number of his pictures as his 'children'[51] – as indeed any artist might – nonetheless he may clearly also have been remembering the portrait of Evelina here.

Given that art history – or at least British art history – is a profession that tends to be dominated by men, the interpretation of *Crossing the Brook* as a celebration of the awakening of female fertility might easily be scoffed at. Yet Turner certainly knew contemporary literature on sexual religious symbolism and may well have been acquainted with writings on biological processes.[52] And in any event there seems no reason why, say, some eighty years before Edvard Munch painted puberty openly, another artist, and one with two growing daughters at that, should not have treated the same subject, if somewhat more optimistically and circumspectly.

Turner's affirmation of the processes of biological growth of one half of our species should not surprise us, however. It seems a perfectly healthy and obvious concern for a painter to whom all aspects of the natural world were of absorbing interest. For instance, we know from some surviving drawings and from the regrettable fact that Ruskin inexcusably destroyed certain sexually explicit sketchbooks (which might conceivably have had some connection with this picture) that Turner had a strong sexual curiosity.[53] Such an interest inevitably found expression in his art, not necessarily through bawdiness – although he could be every bit as bawdy as Shakespeare or Mozart – but through the creation of beauty.

For *Crossing the Brook* is much more than merely one of Turner's major 'imitations' of Claude, a picture that possesses itself of both the manner and spirit of the great French master. It also expresses Turner's awareness of the organic existence that mankind shares with the rest of nature. In that sense *Crossing the Brook* is a completely human landscape. In addition to drawing upon fundamental areas of our experience to impose a sense of order upon the external world, it also shows that Turner was determined to give pictorial realisation to our *inner* life and that surround. Association and metaphor were the vital means of effecting such ends.

*Crossing the Brook* is a picture which demonstrates the exact meaning of Turner's statement that 'sentiment' can be created as much from 'the perceptions gained from nature and her works' as with 'the application of interlectual feeling' derived from poetic and historic awarenesses. The heightened beauty of natural forms is used here to illuminate both the non-visible quality of life inherent in those forms and the selfsame quality of life existing within woman. And this use of the visible to render the invisible takes us to the next stage of our enquiry because it did not receive expression in Turner's work by chance. Rather, it manifests the conceptual basis of his art, his conscious distinction between appearance and reality. For within every equation of painting and poetry known to Turner, and serving equally as the theoretical foundation of both, lies a single unifying concept, the complete meeting-place of 'imitation' and style, imitative reality and 'true' reality. This concept is given clear pictorial expression in *Crossing the Brook* and it had a vital and life-long impact upon Turner. By studying it we shall at last be able to see why the artist so frequently pushed the imaginative realms of his art beyond appearances.

# Part III

# IMITATION AND REALITY

**156** *Venice, the Bridge of Sighs*, R.A. 1840,
oil on canvas, 61 × 91.5 cm,
Clore Gallery for the Turner Collection, London.
The title was accompanied by the following verse in
the R.A. catalogue when the work was first exhibited:

I stood upon a bridge, a palace
And a prison on each hand – *Byron*

# SEVEN

# The Paths of Mutability

... all we need is to affirm that Turner ... was a worshipper, that he bowed down before, and therefore exalted himself in the contemplation of, the invisible within the visible. This is why there is in his work a beauty that nature cannot show; a beauty, one must hasten to say, not surpassing but different from that of nature, no mere imitation of what nature sets before us ... Is not every artist, consciously or unconsciously, a Platonist, seeking everywhere the types of which visible things are but the imperfect forms? Could Plato have seen a Turner landscape would he not at once have given to painting a place in his Republic?

*J. E. Pythian, 1910*

... the Idea (the noblest part of art).

*J. M. W. Turner*

IT will be remembered that Turner equated 'sounds harmonious, Ideal beauties or connecting Metaphors'. What might he have meant by the second of these?

Turner subscribed to the belief that the 'Ideal beauties' of poetry and painting are expressions of some quality of perfect beauty that is either present or conceivable throughout nature. It is not surprising he should have done so, for this was the major tenet of the doctrine of *ut pictura poesis*. The view was commonly held that every living thing or category of object is an imperfect or 'deformed' variant of an ideal archetype which either enjoys an eternal existence in the mind of God, independently of man, or that it exists as a notional perfection within the human imagination. The former concept originally derived from Plato's Theory of Ideas or Forms, the latter from more recent idealism. Such a difference of opinion enjoyed a fundamental and necessary cause. Plato had argued that the Ideas and the absolute beauties they embody are transcendental immaterialities and that man can only begin to comprehend them through an ever more mystical contemplation. (For him they could never be represented at second remove through art.) Naturally, these views gave theorists of representational painting a very real problem, for how could an artist portray absolutes of beauty if they were so far removed from normal human ken? Thus of necessity a number of major proponents of the Ideal in art rejected Plato's location of the Ideas. For example, by drawing upon du Fresnoy, Dryden and Algarotti, Reynolds located his concept of absolute beauty entirely within, rather than beyond the mind and imagination of man, and just hived off the transcendental realm beyond human conception. For him 'the beauty of which we are in quest' would be 'an idea that subsists only in the mind'. Because this 'great ideal perfection and beauty are not to be sought in the heavens but upon the earth. They are about us, and upon every side of us', constant visual enquiry could lead the artist to the possession of 'the idea of that central form' or archetype.[1]

Evidently without being aware of any contradiction, Turner felt that the Ideas exist both independently of man as immaterial abstractions and that they are simply the products of our imagination. But amongst the writers on poetic painting known to him, and especially those from Dryden onwards, the latter outlook prevailed. It was commonly asserted that it was the duty of the artist to form a comprehension of the Ideal by observing the individual characteristics of all the objects before his gaze and, through synthesis of their most perfect features, to arrive at an approximation of those imagined archetypes. As Dryden vividly stated:

> Both [poetry and painting] . . . are not only true imitations of Nature, but of the best Nature, of that which is wrought up to a nobler pitch. They present us with Images more perfect than the Life in any individual; and we have the pleasure to see all the scatter'd Beauties of Nature united by a *happy Chymistry*, without its deformities or faults.[2]

Just how the artist should do this was spelt out by du Fresnoy in *The Art of Painting* (given here in Mason's translation):

> When first the orient rays of beauty move
> The conscious soul, they light the lamp of love;
> Love wakes those warm desires that prompt our chase,
> To follow and to fix each flying grace;
> But earth-born graces sparingly impart
> The symmetry supreme of perfect art:
> For though our casual glance may sometimes meet
> With charms that strike the soul, and seem complete,
> Yet if those charms too closely we define,
> Content to copy nature line for line,
> Our end is lost. Not such the Master's care,
> Curious he culls the perfect from the fair;
> Judge of his art, through beauty's realm he flies
> Selects, combines, improves, diversifies . . .[3]

Throughout the literature on poetic painting perhaps the most frequently quoted example of culling 'the perfect from the fair' was that of the ancient painter Zeuxis who, in order to produce a picture of Helen of Troy, had observed the most beautiful traits not of one but of five models, from whom he had selected, combined, improved and diversified the features he used in his final image. From such empirical enquiry and assimilation it was presumed that an artist would then progress to the formation of a totally imaginative conception of perfect beauty. Only in this way could he or she transcend the arbitrary or singular and arrive at universals. As Reynolds stated in his third Discourse, delivered in 1770:

> The whole beauty and grandeur of the art [of painting] consists . . . in being able to get above all singular forms, local customs, particularities, and details of every kind.

> ALL the objects which are exhibited to our view by nature, upon close examination will be found to have their blemishes or defects. The most beautiful forms have something about them like weakness, minuteness, or imperfection. But it is not every eye that perceives these blemishes. It must be an eye long used to the contemplation and comparison of these forms; and which, by a long habit of observing what any set of objects of the same kind have in common, has acquired the power of discerning what each wants in particular. This long laborious comparison should be the first study of the painter, who aims at the greatest style. By this means, he acquires a just idea of beautiful forms; he corrects nature by herself, her imperfect state by her perfect . . .

> THUS it is from a reiterated experience, and a close comparison of the objects in nature, that an artist becomes possessed of the idea of that central form . . . from which every deviation is deformity.[4]

He restated this aspiration dogmatically but poetically around 1783 in one of his annotations to Mason's translation of du Fresnoy's *The Art of Painting* (two lines of which he quotes at the end):

> There is an absolute necessity for the Painter to generalise his notions; to paint particulars is not to paint nature, it is only to paint circumstances. When the Artist has conceived in his imagination the image of perfect beauty, or the abstract idea of forms, he may be said to be admitted into the great Council of Nature, and to

> > Trace Beauty's beam to its eternal spring,
> > And pure to man the fire celestial bring.[5]

This was imitation proper, the expression of that 'central form' or 'image of perfect beauty', and it should not be confused with the purely artistic imitation – the absorption of the values and standards of the artists of the past – that Reynolds and others also propounded in the aesthetic literature known to Turner.

Naturally, given the humanistic orientation of their common aesthetic, for Bellori, de

Piles, du Fresnoy, Dryden, Richardson, Algarotti and Reynolds, ideal 'imitation' supremely concerned the human figure, something we shall return to. But because of idealisation Reynolds, for one, allowed that landscape painting could rise above its otherwise fairly low place in the accepted hierarchy of artistic concerns. He did so principally because of Claude. In the fourth Discourse Reynolds praised Claude as a model landscapist because of the very synthetic process by which he arrived at his final images:

> CLAUDE LORRAIN . . . was convinced, that taking nature as he found it seldom produced beauty. His pictures are a composition of the various draughts which he had made from various beautiful scenes and prospects . . . . That the practise of Claude Lorrain, in respect to his choice, is to be adopted by Landschape Painters, in opposition to that of the Flemish or Dutch Schools, there can be no doubt, as its truth is founded upon the same principle as that by which the Historical Painter acquires perfect form.[6]

The key phrase here is 'taking nature as he found it'. Like his predecessors, Reynolds was disturbed by the randomness of experience: art had to triumph over the arbitrary. And the landscape painter is especially beholden to chance, for he sees his subjects at different times under constantly varying conditions of weather, and thus with an ever-changing light, colour and dependent human or non-human behaviour – what Reynolds (appropriating a phrase from de Piles) called the 'Accidents of Nature'. Merely accepting those preconditions – the 'representation of an individual spot, and each in its kind a very faithful but very confined portrait' – might suffice for a 'low' type of landscape, i.e. 'the Flemish and Dutch Schools', but for the genre to aspire to any serious consideration the landscapist must exercise the same kind of choice or control over the elements as the history-painter did over the components of his pictures. Indeed, this exercise of choice was seen to be central to the validity of landscape painting in the literature on poetic painting. Roger de Piles, in *The Principles of Painting* (from which Reynolds took the phrase 'Accidents of Nature') stated the principle quite clearly in the section of his work entitled 'the necessity of making a Choice in Painting':

> The painter seldom finds satisfaction in casual nature, as being generally short of what he aims at. He must, by the help of art, make as good a choice of her as possible, in all her visible effects, in order to bring her to some perfection. Now light and shade are the visible effects of nature, as well as the outlines of an human body, the attitudes, the folds of draperies, or anything else that comes into composition; all these require choice, and therefore light does the same.[7]

By definition, the control of 'Accidents' by the exercise of choice was crucial to bring nature 'to some perfection' or to express the Ideal, for it was only by this means that an artist could convey the essentials which underlie 'casual Nature' and thus generalise to the greatest degree possible. Throughout his life Turner never took nature as he found it but exercised exactly this kind of control over the elements and light, as well as all the forms and phenomena that are affected by them. And naturally, the need for dramatic aptness that is implied by de Piles in the foregoing passage may also have influenced Turner's thinking regarding the decorum of light.

That Turner thought ideal generalisation to be vital to landscape painting is attested by a statement in one of his lecture manuscripts:

> To select, combine and concentrate that which is beautiful in nature and admirable in art is as much the business of the landscape painter in his line as in the other departments of art.[8]

There can be no doubt why he felt this. As he stated in a passage from Reynolds's final Discourse which he paraphrased in one of his own lectures:

> . . . it is necessary to mark the greater from the lesser truth: namely the larger and more liberal idea of nature from the comparatively narrow and confined. namely that which addresses itself to the imagination from that which is solely addressed to the Eye.[9]

Nothing could more precisely define where Turner's lifelong priorities as an artist lay than this paraphrase and the identification it embodies. Such an emphasis of the ascendancy of universals over particulars, and of imagination over perception, reveals what was undoubtedly his dominant creative outlook. And he also left us a specific indication of the primacy he accorded to conceptual archetypes or Ideas. This appears in a draft for his first perspective lecture where he states that from the beginnings of the revival of painting in the modern era its practitioners had not looked for 'the most indescribable and inscrutable cause which produces the Idea (the noblest part of art)' – i.e. spent time enquiring into the sources of inspiration – but had concentrated their energies upon realising the 'immediate effect and application of such Ideas . . . by giving them a local situation and to each its form and color, Light, shadow and gradation'.[10] His capitalisation of the initial letter of the word 'Idea' and stress of its artistic status are particularly revealing, for respectively they demonstrate that he realised the meaning of the term and agreed with its creative implications.

It would be absurd to deny that Turner spent his whole life studying and capturing the appearances and values of particular nature, the precise characteristics of places and the conditions in which they were seen. His observations, in the thousands of pencil and pen studies of 'particular' nature, mainly in the sketchbooks of the Turner Bequest, formed the entire basis of his art. Clearly the painter wanted to comprehend the particularities of nature to as great a degree as anyone had ever done before him, if not even more so. But *basis* is the crucial term here, for the painter constantly endeavoured to overcome arbitrary experience as embodied in the sketches by developing his landscapes away from that material to varying degrees. His imaginative elaborations might incorporate a modicum of topographical accuracy or range to total fantasy. No less than Claude, Turner was capable of merging several viewpoints, conflating or widening vistas, raising or lowering mountains and hills or taking other topographical liberties. His frequent enormous spatial expansion of things grew directly from the doctrine of poetic painting, for a basic requirement of the doctrine was that a painter should strive to bring about an epic art by creating the greatest dramatic impact possible. Naturally, spatial expansion also fulfilled another requirement of the doctrine of poetic painting by making the essential physical values of the original scene more dynamically apparent.

Memory, too, could serve the purposes of ideal synthesis, for the faculty provides a ready means whereby the essential is sifted from the unimportant. There can be no doubt of the enormous capacity of Turner's memory, as from it were provided almost all of the effects of weather, light, colour and human or other behaviour which appear in his works. Certainly he used sketching as a means of enforcing the act of looking, and equally he employed the sketches as a storehouse of information. But behind all this it is very apparent that for Turner, sketching from any given subject was merely a means of serving the process of artistic synthesis, and always an activity which trained the act of memory. For although the artist avowed that he used every glance as an opportunity with which to study appearances, nonetheless he also completely identified with the notion proclaimed by the poet Mark Akenside, that 'memory her ideal train preserves': for him, as for Akenside, that was a major means of arriving at a conceptualisation of the Ideal on all levels. (For the evidence for these assertions, see footnotes 23 and 28 below.)

In addition to employing memory as a means of addressing 'the larger and more liberal idea of nature', Turner also frequently synthesised his works from several preliminary sketches, for like Claude he could as happily create landscapes 'from the various draughts which he had made from various beautiful scenes and prospects'. And this is not just true of works like the historical compositions; it can apply equally to pictures specifically made for topographical schemes where one might expect complete faithfulness to topography, as the many complaints about Turner's 'inaccurate' rendering of topography attest. Moreover, even when the artist remained faithful to topography he often imaginatively altered the weather, light-effects and colour that he had originally seen. It is doubtful that very many of Turner's final land- or seascapes reach us as the artist originally saw them, for most of them are imaginative constructs. Unlike the Impressionists, Turner rarely painted from nature. Instead, as Claude and the advocates of the doctrine of *ut pictura poesis* recommended, Turner nearly always regarded the study of nature as a means to an end – albeit a vital one – rather than as an end in itself. For although it may appear that he went to greater lengths than any previous landscapist had done in representing 'casual nature' – the appearance of the sea or clouds, for instance – nonetheless, as will be argued below, his rendering of these and other natural forms was affected by the requirement, stated by proponents of the Ideal, that an artist should convey essentials and exercise 'choice' over particular nature. If we look through the whole of Turner's public output, which includes not only his exhibited works but also the topographical pictures intended ultimately for viewing by a wider audience through the medium of engraving, and at his literary illustrations, as well as a good deal of his finished private work, we perceive that the artist strove constantly for an expression of the imaginative essence of a place in associative terms – his awareness of its history or culture – and/or the projection of it in physical terms, to express its material essence. To serve this latter end Turner often originally explored a landscape from a number of viewpoints, in order to gain the maximum comprehension of its physicality.[11] Sometimes he then made exploratory studies in watercolour in which he returned 'to an idea many times, refining colour harmonies and formal relationships, with the intention of extracting a pictorial essence from the observable facts',[12] a process which includes expression of the truth of place in physical terms (and perhaps also in associative terms as well). Even where costume is concerned, Turner appears to have aimed for a modicum of generalisation, for whilst he was never so indecorous as to portray, say, Dutchmen dressed in kilts,[13] nonetheless he still ignored literalism in an attempt to project the essential flavour of a locale by means of apparel. For example, kilts are obviously intrinsic to the Scottish Highlands but in lowland views such as *Borthwick Castle* (fig. 1) and other works, he introduced kilted figures where they would not normally be seen. This type of discrepancy indicates that Turner employed costume for its associative ability to conjure up the most general sense of geographical identity (in this case the generality of Scotland). We have already noted how he could project the broadest statements about human behaviour in such local contexts.

Most aspects of Turner's art were subordinated to his concern with essentials, and association played a key part in arriving at them. For example, in addition to the Shakespearian, historical and art-historical associations of Venice, Turner evidently felt two, more subtle associations for the city. The first was a moral one, the fact that the city had once been a place of enormous material wealth and sumptuousness; for Turner, as for others, its predilection for self-indulgence in luxury had led to its downfall. Because of this association, in most of his highly finished paintings of the city from the mid-1830s onwards, as well as in a great number of watercolours, the artist crowds the canals with shipping heaped to the gunwales with an extraordinarily brilliant and profuse display of objects (fig. 156), a sight he could rarely if ever have witnessed in reality, especially in the 1830s and '40s when the city was so visibly in economic decline.

Turner's further association for Venice was a physical one. A common feature of a great many of his representations of the place dating from after 1833 – but increasingly so after 1840 – is the way that Turner subtly explores not only the nature of visual appearances but also that of material reality in his views of the city. In watercolour the buildings are frequently roughed in with the most delicate washes, over which the architectural structures are then principally indicated in line. The approach in the oil-paintings is very similar, except that here the artist occasionally builds up some of the general architectural masses with a subtle but pronounced impasto, thus making the materiality of the buildings particularly tangible. He then draws over these areas largely in line. Both in watercolour and oil-paint Turner raises the tonality of the buildings to a very high level and merges the buildings with their reflections to an inordinate degree. These reflections are usually much lengthier than they could have been in reality even in Turner's day when the water was far less disturbed by passing boats than it is today. Such approaches easily capture the effects of optical dazzle that are caused by damp surfaces glistening in very bright light. Yet a great many of the buildings rendered in this way are not brilliantly lit at all; indeed, one of Turner's favourite moments in Venice is that evening period when the light is on the wane. A typical example of the watercolour approach is *Venice: the Grand Canal* (fig. 157), whilst a good example of the oil-painting treatment is *Campo Santo, Venice* (fig. 50). The identical outcome of these overlapping approaches is to de-emphasize the weightiness of Venetian architecture, to produce buildings that look completely immaterial, floating as they do amidst an ethereal and disembodying radiance. This is not how we normally see Venice, nor was it the way Turner saw it either, judging from the large number of precise, objective line-drawings in his sketchbooks. But what the artist saw and what his concept of the essential reality appertaining to the place suggested to him were very different things. Although he knew beyond question that Venice is built of solid, heavy masonry, he evidently came to feel that the transcendent physical apprehension of the city is its sense of floating upon the waters. He subordinated everything to the communication of that 'poetic' view of things, enlarging upon his awareness of what is perhaps the most celebrated and nearly unique urban experience that Venice has to offer. This representation of the city clearly derived from his own physical responses, and is perhaps equally intended to call upon our associations, for undeniably the principal way in which we all approach Venice in reality is by floating through it. Moreover, because the painterly processes used to achieve this effect involved a softening of outline Turner was also able to communicate the sense of atmospheric moisture which is a very real quality of Venice. Certainly this is not a literal representation of Venice at the time, for none of Turner's contemporaries depicted the city floating and glistening as he did, and nor did they distort its topography with comparable freedom. Neither are these shining and pellucid images mere exercises in stylistic invention or painterliness. Rather, Turner's late projections of a floating, ethereal Venice express directly what the artist had come to feel was the underlying physical truth of place. Here, as in his moral-historical conception of the city, we are confronted with a profoundly imaginative idealism that discloses some essential reality.

Naturally, this sacrifice of literal truth to 'poetic truth' also occurs in works where the

**157** *Venice: the Grand Canal, c.*1840,
watercolour and bodycolour with pen-work on paper, 21.5 × 31.5 cm, Ashmolean Museum, Oxford.

artist was not amplifying any associative levels. And Turner's idealism was not limited to Venice. Throughout his career the painter increasingly evoked a 'visionary' or conceptually idealised world of light, forms and colours, beyond the material realm yet utterly rooted in it, projecting what for him were essential qualities of beauty or the truth of place.

This takes us to the very heart of the matter. Turner's idealism was the well-spring of his art, and for him imaginative reality constantly transcended the prosaic reality of arbitrary appearances. Such a transcendence was formed and fed by his determination to meet the requirement of the theory of poetic painting that an artist express his apprehension of ideal or essential reality. Turner evolved three ways of meeting this demand for idealisation. Firstly, in order to state his conception of the historic and cultural essentials that lie beyond appearances he explored the processes of association and visual metaphor to the utmost. Secondly, he created imaginary landscapes which project an ideal world, this being the most direct way for a landscapist to express the notion of a perfect, generalised and timeless beauty. Thirdly, Turner addressed what might be termed the ideality of form underlying appearances. This ideality may be detected in the components of his land- and seascapes, and in such subsidiary but perfected forms perhaps more than anywhere we can witness Turner's response to the injunctions of Reynolds and others that a poetic painter should idealise. Frequently Turner would combine two of these kinds of idealisation, sometimes all three. We must examine the last two kinds in greater detail, however, before we go on to explore the observations that Turner organised a good many of his landscapes around his conception of an essential or ideal meaning, and that he was anxious to distinguish between appearance and reality.

IDEAL LANDSCAPE

A major part of Turner's work was openly devoted to projecting the world as a perfect place. This perfection derived in no small measure from the associations of art itself, being dependent on the linking of certain kinds of landscapes and pictorial structures with certain painters. Naturally the influence of Claude was paramount in this respect, because for Turner the French artist was the paragon of ideal landscape, just as he had been for Reynolds. Turner certainly regarded his own Claudian idealised landscapes as the most important of his works, the artistic core of his œuvre, and this was surely not for stylistic reasons alone.

We can recognise this identification, and the related transcendence of the actual by the ideal, from almost the very start of Turner's career. Quite naturally he identified with the works of Richard Wilson, the first artist to have treated British subjects in the manner of Claude, in the process making them look both Italianate and ideal. But he went directly to the Master once he had assimilated Wilson, as *Caernarvon Castle* (figs 26, 27) testifies. In that work of 1800 he even used 'some perfect state of nature' to project the imperfect behaviour of man, just as Claude had occasionally done, which indicates the lessons on the use of visual metaphor that he had learnt from Claude by that time. And from 1800 onwards, right up until the last time he exhibited in public in 1850, Turner painted a vast number of ideal landscapes in a manner obviously drawn from Claude.

Other artists contributed stylistically to Turner's idealisations of landscape also. He was especially receptive to the ideal element in Dutch marine and landscape painting, the representation of serene light, particularly as exemplified by the 'golden colour of ambient vapour'[14] in the works of Aelbert Cuyp. The influence of Cuyp can easily be discerned in the 1807 (fig. 213) and 1809 versions of the *Sun rising through Vapour* or the 1818 *Dort or Dordrecht, the Dort Packet-Boat from Rotterdam becalmed* (B. J. 137) which shows Cuyp's home town at dawn and contains specific references to the painter.

From about 1819 another artist contributed stylistically towards Turner's idealisation of landscape. Indeed, Turner later stated that he had learnt more from Antoine Watteau than from any other painter.[15] Even if this was manifested more in terms of colour than form in his work, such a remark might also clarify Turner's attraction to Watteau's projection of

**158** *Mowbray Lodge, Ripon, c.*1815,
watercolour on paper, 27.7 × 39.4 cm, Lady Lever Art Gallery, Port Sunlight.

idyllic human behaviour, something that Watteau also expressively extended through the complementary use of landscape and light, and a quality we shall return to in the next chapter. Turner's response may reflect nostalgia on his part for the courtly behaviour Watteau depicts, as it was something he especially singled out for representation in the Watteauesque works *What You Will!* of 1822 (B. J. 229), *Boccaccio relating the Tale of the Birdcage* of 1828 (B.J. 244) and *The Palace of La Belle Gabrielle* (W. 1049), a watercolour dating from about 1832.

Turner also paralleled his projections of a perfected natural and/or social world in the styles of Claude, Cuyp and Watteau by other kinds of idealised landscapes, notably the large group of very finished Thames pastorals he painted between 1806 and 1809. These reveal another, sub-related form of Turnerian association, the artist's tendency to idealise certain types of scenery. One does not have to indulge in any psychoanalytic speculation to appreciate that for the young Turner, who had grown up in the dingy warren of buildings, courts and streets around Covent Garden, his removal at about the age of ten to Brentford, outside London, following the death of his sister, may have proved one of the most decisive experiences of his life. Instead of hubbub, squalor and decay, at Brentford and on the nearby reaches of the Thames between Hammersmith and Windsor he must have perceived an idyllic world. It certainly contributed to Turner's life and work, for in addition to residing at Isleworth, Hammersmith and Twickenham later, he always thereafter depicted the area in idealised terms.

Upstream of Westminster the Thames was an obvious subject for pictorial idealisation. No less idyllic were the Welsh, Scottish and Swiss mountains, and the Yorkshire Dales, at least in their more peaceful aspects. Amidst the dramatic grandeur of such surroundings Turner readily appreciated an ineffable serenity. In a number of topographical works like *Mowbray Lodge, Ripon* (fig. 158) of about 1815 and *Gibside, County Durham* of 1817 (w. 378), the painter not only idealised the landscape but also introduced women dressed in neo-classical garb to bring contemporary associations of the Ideal into play. And judging from the prosaic 'blueprint-study' sketches upon which they were based, landscapes like *Wycliffe, near Rokeby* (fig. 6), with its radiant dawn, and *Bolton Abbey, Yorkshire* (fig. 171) made for the 'England and Wales' series around 1825, seem idealised in every sense. In a good many of Turner's very late Swiss watercolours, such as the 1842 dawn and dusk views of Mount Rigi from across Lake Lucerne (w. 1524–5), panoramas of Lake Lucerne from above Brunnen (w. 1526–8), and a group of Swiss lake scenes that may date from as late as 1846–50 (w. 1560–4), it is also easy to discern the forcing of reality into a more perfect mould of form and feeling. And these pictures, like all the other works that are either specified or implied in this section, were to some extent landscapes 'selected, combined and concentrated' from an amalgam of memories and 'various draughts made from various . . . prospects', fused together in the crucible of the artist's imagination. They may lean somewhat closer towards particularity than Reynolds might have wished for, since with a few exceptions they are not entirely imaginary composites of the most beautiful characteristics of *several* places. Yet even so, they are both fictive and imaginatively perfected enough for all that, and they immeasurably improve upon the realities on which they were based.

## THE IDEALITY OF FORMS

Ideal imitation was thought by proponents of poetic painting to be the highest kind of representation open to the artist. As Count Algarotti eloquently stated:

> an ideal Painter, and such alone is a true Painter, resembles the Poet: instead of copying he imitates; that is, he works with his fancy, and represents objects, endued with all that perfection which belongs to the species and may be conceived in the Archetype.[16]

Turner also encountered similar advice elsewhere; as he recommended to others in one of his lecture manuscripts:

Dryden in his preface to Fresnoy gives a saying of Cicero[17] as therefore in forms and figures there is somewhat which is excellent and perfect to which imagined species all things are referred by imitation . . . which imitation of nature is the groundwork of our art . . . by immitation of which imaginary forms all things are represented which fall under human sight.[18]

That quality of perfection residing in 'imaginary forms' was characterised by Reynolds in his third Discourse as 'Ideal Beauty'. It was clearly from the term 'Ideal Beauty' that Turner derived the phrase 'Ideal beauties' which he used to identify archetypes stated in poetry that might similarly be stated by the poetic painter. For Reynolds it was equally incumbent upon the artist to discern the truth or underlying principles governing appearances and behaviour, as Ideal Beauty was 'formed on the uniform, eternal and immutable laws of nature' and was therefore by definition synonymous with truth. By grasping such laws one would automatically state the ideality of things, the essential, immutable truth shared by each 'species' of form. Reynolds also equated beauty with nature, and both with the inner life of man, for he stated that

> My notion of nature comprehends not only the forms which nature produces, but also the nature and internal fabrick and organization, as I may call it, of the human mind and imagination. The terms beauty, or nature, which are general ideas, are but different modes of expressing the same thing . . .[19]

Here in particular we can witness the intense humanism that underlay the whole principle of poetic painting, as well as perhaps a source of the humanisation that Turner developed in employing the external forms of nature to express the inner life of man.

For Reynolds beauty, truth, nature and human nature were indivisible. And whilst Turner continually contrasted the beauty of external nature with the external lack of beauty in man (for reasons we shall come to), there is conclusive evidence that in all other respects he totally accepted Reynolds's aesthetic. Certainly he felt that 'Ideal beauties' could only be created by an imaginative synthesis of the most perfect characteristics of individual models; as he declared in a lecture manuscript of around 1810:

> Ideal forms combining [are] conveyed by vision to the mind to enable it by an analytical and comparative enquiry as to form, endeavour to modify conjecture into Theory, to express harmoniously and represent practically.[20]

Elsewhere he stated categorically the need also

> . . . to balance well the line between deformity and truth.[21]

For Turner, like Reynolds, 'deformity' and variation upon an imaginary 'central form' were synonymous, as, conversely, were truth and the Ideal. An artist therefore had to synthesize a universal concept of Ideal Beauty from observations of particular nature and from his imagination.

Yet whilst Turner subscribed to the view that 'Ideal beauties' reside in '*imagined species*' of form to which 'all things are referred by imitation', he also envisaged them to be eternally extant, transcendental actualities, as Plato had suggested.[22] Ultimately this contradiction did not matter, for Turner was not seeking a path to philosophical enlightenment. On the one hand he was looking for a way to create order out of arbitrary experience, as the doctrine of poetic painting demanded. He saw a means to that end in an imaginative art founded upon

> . . . contemplating and defining qualities and causes, effects and incidents, and . . . [developing] . . . by practise the possibility of attaining what appears mysterious upon principle . . .[23]

On the other hand he believed that archetypes do actually enjoy an independent existence beyond the mind of man.

This emerges equally from his lecture notes on perspective. One underlying concern clearly preoccupied Turner throughout his perspective lectures, namely a desire to arrive at fundamentals. This concern is evinced by his having linked perspective to the Academic poetic-historical tradition of aesthetics, with its emphasis upon 'beauty is truth', and its comprehension that 'Laws . . . regulate the appearance of *form*.'[24] The main point of analysing forms, and their visual modification through perspective, was to grasp such fundamentals. It was a view Turner expressed with fervour in a final draft for the conclusion of the first lecture:

> . . . the true basis of Perspective: namely *Geometry*, as well as the course of pictorial immitation to Nature in all varieties of form, particular or circumstantial, combined or comparative, *all tell us*, tells one great cause, and in the words of Akenside presents
>
> In matter's mouldering structures
> The pure forms of Triangle, Circle, Cube or Cone[25]

By this stress upon pointers to 'one great cause' and the quotation from Akenside, Turner emphasized the importance that geometry held for him. Unlike Cézanne, who almost a century later wrote to Emile Bernard 'you must see in nature the cylinder, the sphere, the cone',[26] Turner felt that the selfsame structures are far more than just useful pictorial devices; they are pointers to the existence of a supernal reality.

The lines of poetry with which Turner ended his lecture are quoted from Book II of Mark Akenside's long didactic poem 'The Pleasures of the Imagination' which was written in 1744 and originally entitled 'The Pleasures of Imagination'. Thereafter it was considerably revised, and republished in an expanded and incomplete form between 1757–1770.

Turner owned both versions of the poem, as they appeared in Volume Nine of Anderson's *Complete Poets*, and he read them most likely before 1802.[27] The work is based upon papers by Joseph Addison which constitute his *Essay on the Pleasures of the Imagination*, published in successive issues of *The Spectator* in 1712, and it also draws upon related aesthetic discussions by Francis Hutcheson and Lord Shaftesbury. Akenside follows Addison in suggesting that the 'Pleasures' of the imagination derive essentially from our experiences of greatness, beauty and novelty, which is, of course, a value that can be present in either greatness or beauty, rather than one which exists independently; he also explores the power and importance of association and memory in the imaginative process.[28] Yet there are strong affinities with Platonic thought running through the poem and, indeed, it opens by setting forth the Platonic concept that the universe and all its material manifestations of beauty are generated from archetypes enjoying an everlasting existence in the divine mind, an existence that Akenside characterises as 'Eternal Form'.[29] Turner's citing of lines from 'The Pleasures of the Imagination' to identify some of the forms issuing from that prime source shows that this concept proved especially attractive to him, as does the fact that in his lecture manuscripts he drew upon these lines concerning archetypal forms no less than seven times, usually with their preceding verses.[30] Here is the maximum extent of Turner's quotation, to which have been added the following lines in square brackets to complete the meaning:

> . . . Such the rise of forms
> Sequester'd far from sense and every spot
> Peculiar in the realms of space and time;
> Such is the throne which man for Truth amid
> The paths of mutability hath built
> Secure, unshaken, still: and whence he views,
> In matter's mouldering structures, the pure forms
> Of triangle, or circle, cube or cone,
> [Impassive all: whose attributes nor force
> Nor fate can alter. There he first conceives
> True being, and an intellectual world
> The same this hour and ever . . .[31]]

Yet whilst Turner believed that such fundamental geometry enjoys a metaphysical existence 'sequester'd far from sense' and generated by 'one great cause', he also discerned that to some degree it can be perceived in the real world. In 1818 he drew attention to its existence in animal, vegetable and mineral structures, pointing out that bone structures – which he called 'the *machinery of all form*' – share with vegetable and mineral structures, such as the cells of bees and bysaltic rocks respectively,

> the like Geometric form, of whose elementary principles all nature partakes.[32]

For Turner this universal geometry manifested itself even in the consciousness of 'primitive' peoples like the South Sea islanders, the ancient Britons and the American 'savages' who displayed intuitive 'notions of geometric form' in their body-decorations. And in architecture could be perceived a discipline that

> moves steadily and uniformly towards geometric form by principle, toward geometric form by judgement, towards geometric form by propriety, towards geometric forms to render them practical, for every design partakes of geometry, and evinces the more power by the arrangement of fewer forms than in the other departments of the arts.[33]

Indeed, it was through a consideration of architecture that Turner may first have arrived at his suppositions concerning 'the pure forms'.

This emerges from a passage in one of the lectures where he connected some simple conclusions posited upon the spatial distortions enforced by perspective, with Akenside's verses concerning archetypal geometry. The passage even tells us when and from whom Turner may have gained such an association with architecture. Whilst discussing the principles of vertical perspective, he asked his listeners to consider the west towers of Westminster Abbey and the fact that although 'we know their proportions are nearly equal . . . at the top as at the base', nonetheless as one approaches them they appear to 'rapidly decrease upwards and . . . even . . . incline towards each other'. He went on to point out that just as 'Horizontal perspective is allowed' to vanish at 'an immaginary vertical point', so too 'vertical parallel lines diminish'. This observation had surprised Turner when it was first communicated to him by Thomas Malton, junior, who, 'during the progress of his work of London and Westminster', had mentioned[34] to Turner the difficulty he had initially encountered by putting in all the perpendicular lines in a parallel rather than recessional way when drawing those towers. It was only by rejecting preconceptions and trusting to 'nature' (i.e. observation) that Malton had overcome these difficulties. Turner then went on to state that Malton's

> mode of instruction was divested as much as possible of prolixity and much improved the matter by useful abbreviation which he most readily imparted and exulted in recommending whatever he saw in nature Incontravertable
> as in the words of Akenside
>
>> For such is the Throne for Truth amid the
>> paths of mutability hath built, secure, unshaken, still
>> and whence he views in natures mouldering structures the
>> Pure forms of circle triangle cube or cone[35]

Malton's 'Picturesque Tour through London and Westminster' was published in 1792[36] and Turner is known to have worked with him by 1789; the incident referred to therefore probably occurred around 1790. Although it is not absolutely clear whether it was Malton who made the connection between Akenside's poetry and the need to ignore preconceptions because of contrary visual evidence, or whether it was simply Turner quoting the verses from memory to strengthen Malton's point, nonetheless it is readily apparent that Turner sensed in geometry the existence of a universal truth underlying appearances: evidently he knew that vertical lines, if continued in perspective, would meet at 'an imaginary vertical point' and thus, in conjunction with a base-line formed by the ground, create a triangle: 'whence he views / In matter's mouldering structures, the pure forms' indeed, especially if they can be perceived underlying such a mouldering structure as Westminster Abbey. Yet if Turner did receive this lesson from Malton he clearly gained more than conventional insights from a conventional architectural topographer. And this may have occurred before he became a student at the Royal Academy Schools!

There is further clear evidence of Turner's belief in the existence of archetypal forms underlying appearances in his other lecture discussions of geometry. Whether such forms have their origins in the individual imagination or whether they enjoy an eternal transcendent existence is irrelevant: in either case they found expression in Turner's art, both in the subtle geometric linear structures that often underpin his works or in other related ways. And his comprehension of fundamentals was enormously advanced by his analysis of architecture itself, for this must be regarded as one of the major intellectual bases of his art. Through his early training as an architectural topographer Turner quickly attained a thorough grasp of the masses, volumes, stresses and structural interactions which underlie the forms of buildings, as well as an understanding of the effects of light upon surfaces, spatiality and the mechanics of perspective. Yet it was not only the representation of human architecture that benefited from this knowledge. For an artist who discerned a universal 'Geometric form' in man-made and natural architecture, the logical outcome of his interest was an enhanced understanding of geological forms and structures, as well as the attendant effects and conditions under which they are seen. Wherever we look amongst Turner's renderings of mountains and hills, rocks or stones, we perceive his grasp of the truths of geology, the perception of an internal logic and order amidst all 'the rubbish of Creation'. Even in his early studies of Welsh, Scottish and Swiss mountains a strong analytical process is visibly at work alongside dramatic responses, constantly seeking out and comprehending the pressures, masses and densities of rock formations, their fracturings, stratifications and pointings, as well as the effects of weathering and the spatial interplays of form. The artist who so punctiliously examined both the particularities and underlying generalities of man-made architecture did no less for the architecture of nature. If we look again at the 1803 *Glacier and Source of the Arveron, going up to the Mer de Glace* (fig. 122) we instantly recognise Turner's grasp of how the glacier forced its way through the terrain, how the distant mountains differ from each other in terms of rock-formation and stratification, how

**159** S. Middiman after J. M. W. Turner, *Moss Dale Fall*, 1822, engraving.

the ice is forced up under intense pressure to form rhythmic patterns, how the lesser slopes beneath the glacier have been incised by the constant fall of water, how the boulders in the foreground have been shaped by exposure – and without losing any of their sense of veracity all of these perceptions are subordinated to the 'greater' imaginative truth, the subtle metaphorical line that directs our eye to the source of the Arveiron. Or if we turn our attention to *Moss Dale Fall*, we can readily perceive the extent to which Turner was able to fashion his profound understanding of geology into the very stuff of art itself. The watercolour (w. 572) was created around 1817 for the 'History of Richmondshire' but because it has faded the engraving made from it in 1822 under Turner's close supervision is reproduced here (fig. 159). In this picture, which represents the waterfall that descends from Sandy Hill into Great Gill in Mossdale, Yorkshire, the artist does not create his normal dialogue between man and natural forces, for this is one of the few topographical pictures in which Turner omits humankind completely, and only a goat on the right denotes the animal world at all. Instead, he imparts a profound tension to external nature, filling the rocky landscape with a feeling of immense space by exaggerating the relative size of its forms, and creating a sense of tremendous energy through the dynamic interplay of the

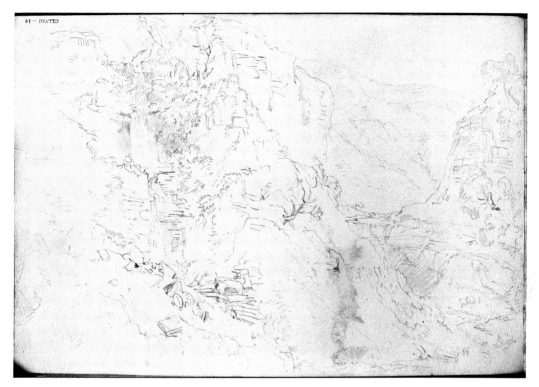

**160** Pencil drawing of Mossdale Falls in the *Yorkshire 5* sketchbook, T.B. CXLVIII, p. 16.

movement of water, geological strata-lines, late-afternoon light and shadow effects, contrasts between areas of pictorial complexity and vacancy and a superbly rhythmic set of overlapping linear arabesques. At the rockface on the left, he controls the 'Accidents of Nature' in no uncertain way, forging the original jumble of objects and phenomena into a tremendously coherent unity. Yet this imparting of coherence does not compromise either the feeling of natural wildness nor the statement of essentials in any way. On the contrary, it brings them into focus, especially the latter. Not only do we perceive the rock-steps of the waterfall much more clearly than they appear in the pencil-drawing upon which the work was based (fig. 160), and see more fully the stratifications of limestone which are only summarily indicated in that study, but we can also detect a grasp of fundamentals that is quite remarkable: every pressure of the rock is understood, each fracture, fissure and erosion can be traced to a cause, all the strata are differentiated in terms of weight and volume. For instance, note in the centre of the main mass of hillside how all the large boulders – none of which are indicated in the sketch – rest and weigh down upon those beneath. Turner renders visible their sense of balance and thrusting tension, something he emphasises subtly through visual attraction and intellectual association by making the area

259

**161** *Fishermen at Sea*, R.A. 1796,
oil on canvas, 91.5 × 122.4 cm, Clore Gallery for the Turner Collection, London.

below them respectively lighter in tone and downwards-pointing in shape. In this work we encounter with particular clarity Turner's total knowledge of the architecture of natural forms. Yet as the sketch shows, he has drawn almost entirely upon memory and under-standing for his information. Nothing can better indicate the degree to which imagination fed upon assimilated knowledge in Turner's art than *Moss Dale Fall*, for it is a picture in which the painter exhaustively manipulates the visible appearances of nature for expressive reasons whilst simultaneously making clear his complete grasp of the ideality of forms: Turner has very nearly portrayed the vast forces themselves which once brought such rocks into being. We are virtually present at the Creation.

Turner's sense of the ideality of geological forms was undoubtedly reinforced at the start of his career by his study of architecture, and it was developed more directly too. For example, around 1811, whilst preparing to take a trip around the southern and western coasts of England in search of suitable subjects for the projected 'Southern Coast' series of watercolours and engravings, Turner wrote extensive analyses of geological data in one of his sketchbooks.[37] Over some four closely written pages he discusses the stratification of the

Purbeck hills and the ridges of the South Downs, the structural composition of the coastline between Beachy Head and the 'Ile of White', and even an investigation of the process whereby Britain had been gradually sundered from the continental mainland of Europe by the incursion of the sea upon the isthmus that once joined the two. Throughout this lengthy passage Turner makes evident his desire to comprehend the fundamentals underlying the landscapes he intended to investigate.

Naturally, such concern extended to seascapes as well. Indeed, in this important area, an awareness of the ideality of forms had been necessary from the start of his artistic career. In the supreme age of sail it was insufficient just to make the sea look suitably watery or wavy and the clouds visibly scud; cause and effect had to be demonstrated fully, and the more effectively the better. Moreover, such natural phenomena, being subject to laws of behaviour, could easily be considered to harbour an 'imagined species of form'. As any marine engineer or meteorologist can testify, there is a typical pattern of wave motion usual to each specific set of weather conditions, just as there is, say, a typical cirrus cloud, no matter how varied or 'deformed' any individual example may appear. And the depiction of seas and clouds is always dependent on some sense of imagined form anyway, for both seas and clouds are in constant flux. Certainly Turner was too inventive and self-demanding ever to be satisfied with painting merely serried rows of waves, or conventional stylisations of clouds, except during a short period at the start of his career. His need to perceive 'qualities and causes' was fundamental. Faced with such conceptual demands, and by constant observation, he soon developed the imaginative ability to summon forth seas and skies that not only may express his own inner emotional turbulence, and project the verities of appearance, but appear to embody a firm understanding of their underlying truth of behaviour, their ideality of form.

Even by the mid-1790s Turner had developed his keen and soon-to-be unrivalled awareness of the active and dramatic principles of the motion of water, its reflectivity, and the mechanics of wind and wave interaction. A full understanding of the movement of the sea can be witnessed in the first oil-painting he ever exhibited, *Fishermen at Sea* of 1796 (fig. 161), a fine moonlit view of the Needles off the Isle of Wight. The artist very precisely distinguishes between the heavy swell in the forefront, representing the turbulent motion of the Solent, and the calmer waters of the English Channel beyond the Needles. And here too we find evidence that Reynolds's injunction to address the imagination, not merely the eye, had already taken hold of Turner, for we encounter total topographical licence: the Needles are at the western end of the Isle of Wight and run along an east-west bearing. In the picture we are looking simultaneously due south at the rocks, and due east along the Channel coast of the Isle of Wight stretching around to St Catherine's Point in the far distance, and thus in two directions at once. It might also be noted that the clouds are stylised somewhat in the manner of de Loutherbourg.

**162** *Fishermen upon a Lee-Shore, in Squally Weather*, R.A. 1802,
oil on canvas, 91.4 × 122 cm, Southampton Art Gallery.

Turner's grasp of wave-motion grew in accuracy from this time onwards. In a picture like *Fishermen upon a Lee-Shore, in Squally Weather* of 1802 (fig. 162) we witness its development. The work shows the recurrent nightmare of all sailors before the advent of Steam, of being propelled onto a shore towards which the wind is blowing, from which there is no means of escape. By placing the vessel immediately beneath a break in the clouds the artist dramatically directs the eye to the fishermen's plight, whilst the stylisation of the clouds ceases to be apparent. Turner's representation of the breakers is particularly vivid. Breakers are extremely hard to portray but here they not only seem outwardly convincing; we also get a very real sense of what is propelling them. And this mastery continued to grow, even though in two pictures painted around 1803–4 (*Boats carrying Out Anchors*, fig. 70, and *Fishing Boats entering Calais Harbour*, fig. 71) Turner tried to short-cut his method of drawing the sea by using a palette knife to apply thick white paint, to represent white water. He was heavily criticised for this[38] and evidently agreed, realising that the violence of the sea could not adequately be stated by a subjective painterly equivalent; the results indeed look clumsy. Thereafter he reverted to a more careful delineation of form, tedious to paint but more visually convincing and emotionally expressive. The results of this reversion can be

**163** *The Wreck of a Transport Ship, c.*1810,
oil on canvas, 172.7 × 241.2 cm, the Fundaçao Calouste Gulbenkian, Lisbon.

seen in *The Shipwreck* of 1805 (fig. 229) where the ebb and flow of the tides is stated with a phenomenal accuracy and power. By some five or so years later, in *The Wreck of a Transport Ship* (fig. 163), Turner added a new dimension to this realism by a dramatic exaggeration of form which made one naval contemporary comment that 'nothing could survive in such a sea'.[39] Indeed, the work projects a catastrophic violence completely unprecedented in the history of marine-painting. Yet everywhere in the maelstrom we perceive Turner's grasp of the ideality of the sea, its truth of motion and charged energy. This comprehension, now fully attained, never left him.

Turner's awareness of the laws of cloud formation and motion took longer to develop. As already stated, in the 1796 *Fishermen at Sea* the clouds are rather clumsily stylised, and even by 1803, as seen in *Calais Pier* (fig. 73), Turner still occasionally accumulated forms which look more like theatrical drop-curtains than clouds. But within a few years this artificiality or superficiality had completely disappeared. In a work like the 1809 *Trout Fishing in the Dee* (fig. 164) Turner's grasp of cloud forms and the underlying forces affecting their motion seems complete: we can easily perceive an updraught meeting the rain-clouds passing over the Berwyn hills, a sense of circular movement that Turner heightens

**164** *Trout Fishing in the Dee, Corwen Bridge and Cottage*, Turner's Gallery 1809,
oil on canvas, 91.5 × 122 cm, The Taft Museum, Cincinnati, Ohio.

associatively by forming semi-circles around the backs of a kneeling fisherman on the left
and a bending fisherman in the centre. And although the sky is filled with 'vapour',[40] it is
also imbued with coherent movement and dynamism, something we witness in reality but
rarely encounter in art.

Turner's awareness of the ideality of clouds was apparent ever afterwards and could be
expressed with even greater subtlety than here. Yet perhaps the ideality of form in his
landscapes is usually rendered most immediately visible by his trees, not surprisingly, since
trees are frequently the dominant forms in a picture. From the very start Turner had
perceived the 'qualities and causes' inherent to trees, as a vast number of sketches and
studies in the Turner Bequest prove, but it was not until around 1810 that the artist seems to
have felt that the ideality of such forms could be better expressed by attempting to articulate
underlying principles rather than by stylisation in works taken to an advanced stage. In
early Claudian compositions like *Caernarvon Castle* of 1800 (figs 26, 27) or *Macon* of 1803 (B.J.
47), trees are stylised in the manner of Claude. And in the majority of his topographical
watercolours between 1790–1810, a very eighteenth-century mannerism is apparent in the

**165** *Oak tree, Hampton Court, Herefordshire, c.1796,*
pencil and watercolour with some body-colour on paper, 30.5 × 41.3 cm,
Whitworth Art Gallery, University of Manchester.

**166** *North-west Front, Cassiobury, c.1807,*
watercolour on paper, 28 × 39.4 cm, Private Collection, USA.

**167** *Willows beside a Stream, c.*1806–7,
oil on canvas, 86 × 116.5 cm, Clore Gallery for the Turner Collection, London.

trees. Particularly at the ends of branches, the leaves are gathered into those kinds of clusters that earlier landscapists like Wilson and de Loutherbourg so often created. This approach is seen in *Oak tree, Hampton Court, Herefordshire* (fig. 165), dating from about 1795, where Turner communicates the spatial relationship of foliage to branches by differentiating between them clearly, yet also conveys a sense of the overall tree-form and its structure. Turner's grasp of form – which derived from his sense of architecture – is never in doubt, but he is less successful at expressing the sense of living growth within the organism; we are looking only at a plausible rendering of externals, at leaves which sit on branches instead of flowering from them. For Turner the architectural topographer leaves are something which merely embellish the form. This limitation is still apparent in many of Turner's water-colours a decade later. For example, the trees on either side of the view in *North-west Front, Cassiobury* (fig. 166), dating from about 1807, demonstrate that selfsame fault, with the separation between wood and foliage still visible.

Around 1806–10, however, a more probing enquiry into the dynamics of foliage took over. This may have resulted from sessions of working directly from nature. During this period, Turner employed a boat as a floating studio to travel the Thames and its tributaries, painting as he went. It was not the first time he had worked directly from nature, nor was it to be the last, although he seems to have rarely if ever undertaken the procedure after 1813. There can be no doubt that he indulged in what was for him an unusual painterly practice in order to further his comprehension of reality and to analyse natural forms, for many of the studies are directly or indirectly of trees (for an example see fig. 167) and these demonstrate an increased understanding of, and responsiveness to, the organic sense of trees than was hitherto evident in his works.

However, the artist's ability to project the organic 'qualities' of trees by a more pronounced expression of their 'causes' manifested itself after about 1810, and reached fruition around 1815. Another indirect cause for this development is not hard to find. Turner's close consideration of aesthetics and fundamentals between 1808 and 1812 in preparation for the perspective lectures clearly influenced his art, suggesting how he could transcend realism to give expression to the idealism that the lectures openly supported. Certainly, a marked if subtle change in Turner's depiction of trees becomes apparent in these years and it can best be perceived if we compare two pictures.

*Mercury and Herse* (fig. 168) was exhibited at the R.A. in 1811 and takes its subject from Book II of Ovid's *Metamorphoses*. Its title was accompanied in the catalogue by these lines:

> Close by the sacred walls in wide Munichia's plain
> The God well pleas'd beheld the virgin train.[41]

Herse is returning from having paid homage to Minerva, whose votive day it is. A bas-relief beneath the temple on the left seems to allude to the event, for it shows two women kneeling at an altar before two priests. Prior to the moment depicted Mercury had been flying over Athens and, falling instantly in love with Herse, had wheeled about and placed himself before her. This confrontation is the event Turner depicts. Herse is in the centre, at the head of 'the virgin train', with Mercury to the right of her. The sudden turnabout of the god after seeing Herse is the subject of an extended simile by Ovid and Turner may allude to that reversal by locating a sweeping chain of highlights upon a conch at Mercury's elbow. Their circular motion suggests the descending movement of the god which has just taken place.

On the left appears to be another possible example of Turner's use of narrative simultaneity. In order to woo Herse, later in the narrative Mercury will entreat the help of her sister Aglauros, but Aglauros will be persuaded by a hideous woman who personifies Envy to deny him access to Herse. Mercury will then turn Aglauros to stone for her effrontery. Ovid describes the metamorphosis as Aglauros slowly feels her limbs becoming so heavy that she cannot rise from a sitting position.

A woman reclining on the left is accompanied by an ugly old crone who is speaking to her, whilst to the left of her is another similarly dressed woman who is extremely rigidly

**168** *Mercury and Herse*, R.A. 1811, oil on canvas, 190.5 × 160 cm, Private Collection, U.K.

seated and who stares out at us. Surrounded as they are by quantities of fallen masonry it may be that we are looking at Aglauros 'before and after'. Turner also seems to be using each of the trees nearest to Herse and Mercury to amplify their present physical relationship associatively. Above and to the left of Herse a delicate pine stands at the head of a line of pines, much as Herse leads the procession of maidens. Similarly, the slight curve of the trunk of the tree behind Mercury repeats the proud curve made by his body as he presents himself to Herse.

*Mercury and Herse* is a supremely idealised landscape which clearly demonstrates Claude's influence upon Turner's style and methods of elaborating meaning. But it also shows that even as late as 1811 Turner thought of natural objects such as trees in merely external terms, for although the trees in this work are convincingly represented they have no organic feel to them. Their foliage still forms conventional clumps resembling the amorphous masses of foliage one frequently encounters upon Claude's trees.

Just four years later, though, in the equally Claudian *Crossing the Brook* (fig. 152), we see a complete transformation, a really vivid expression of the ideality of trees. The sense of their inner life actually extends the meaning of the picture. Instead of the opaque foliage we saw in *Mercury and Herse*, a new transparency of leafage, as well as a graceful linearity of trunks and boughs, combine to strongly communicate a sense of organic vitality. But although the trees on the left of *Crossing the Brook* have frequently been labelled 'Claudian' simply because they act as a repoussoir, in fact they bear no resemblance to any of Claude's trees. Like Turner's trees in *Mercury and Herse*, Claude's trees are always more literally rendered, and although their upper leafage can certainly look very ethereal when depicted under conditions of morning or evening light, such foliage is far more solid than the leafage of Turner's mature works. The difference in this respect between Claude and Turner is nowhere better illustrated than by a comparison between the trees in *Crossing the Brook* and those on the left of Claude's *Rest on the Flight into Egypt* (fig. 153) upon whose design it was partly based.

Another indication of Turner's increased awareness of the organic life of tree-forms by 1815 emerges from a consideration of the interrelationship between branches and foliage in *Crossing the Brook*. If we look carefully at the pine on the left in *Mercury and Herse* we see that Turner has not bothered to interrelate them at all: the foliage sits on the branches almost like cotton-wool. In *Crossing the Brook* he effects a new and much finer correspondence between each tree and its leafage, and he expresses much deeper insights into the anatomy of such organisms. Indeed, with these trees we witness the creation of perfected forms that seem to be the sylvan equivalent to the kinds of idealised human forms we encounter in, say, the works of Praxiteles or Michelangelo.

Turner made apparent his awareness of the underlying life-force of trees very frequently from about 1815 onwards. It is evident in *Mowbray Lodge, Ripon* of around that date

**169** *England: Richmond Hill, on the Prince Regent's Birthday*, R.A. 1819,
oil on canvas, 180 × 334.5 cm, Clore Gallery for the Turner Collection, London.

**170** *Mortlake Terrace, the Seat of William Moffatt, Esq. Summer's Evening*, R.A. 1827,
oil on canvas, 92 × 122 cm, National Gallery of Art, Washington, D.C.

**171** *Bolton Abbey, Yorkshire, c.*1825,
watercolour on paper, 29.2 × 39.3 cm, Lady Lever Art Gallery, Port Sunlight.

**172** *Durham Cathedral, c.*1834–5,
watercolour on paper, 29 × 44 cm, National Gallery of Scotland, Edinburgh.

(fig. 158), as well as in *The Temple of Jupiter Panellenius restored*, dating from 1814–16 (fig. 141) where the quotation from Southey draws attention to the aptness of dawn light and stresses the similarity between human and natural architecture, the trees rising erect 'like pillars of the temple'. We also see it in *Aske Hall* (fig. 35) where the entire image pulsates with energy due to this communication of the inner life of the trees and foliage that frame the view.

The same qualities of ideality are also expressed by the trees in many of Turner's other idealised landscapes, and for identical reasons. They can be seen in the supremely elegant, idealised trees in *England: Richmond Hill, on the Prince Regent's Birthday* of 1819 (fig. 169), and in the effulgent foliage and graceful branches of the plane-trees in the *Mortlake Terrace* paintings of 1826 (B.J. 235) and 1827 (fig. 170). Equally idealised trees appear frequently elsewhere, particularly in watercolours of the 'England and Wales' series like *Bolton Abbey* (fig. 171), *Richmond Terrace* (w. 879) and *Durham Cathedral* (fig. 172), all dating from the 1825–35 period. In the latter work Turner opposes graceful birches with the powerful bulk of the great building just catching the last rays of evening sunlight across the river Wear. This contrast between delicacy and solidity adds to our sense of the solidity and strength of the cathedral. In both trees and building, though, Turner projects his complete comprehension of the underlying structure.

It was about the trees in *Durham Cathedral*, and in several other works where Turner also expressed the ideality of tree-forms, that Ruskin wrote:

> These two characters, the woody stiffness hinted through muscular line, and the inventive grace of the upper boughs, have never been rendered except by Turner; he does not merely draw them better than others, but he is the only man who has ever drawn them at all.[42]

Although in some of his later works Turner resorted to an extreme stylisation of trees which perhaps reflected his fatigue at painting them,[43] nonetheless such objects are always underpinned by a certainty of form. Of course Ruskin devoted enormous space to this grasp of 'truth' in *Modern Painters* (where he also analysed Turner's 'realism' in depicting mountains, seas and skies at great length), and there seems little point in further expatiating here about the ideality of Turner's trees. Ruskin recognised that as far as such forms are concerned, Turner

> constantly . . . adheres to this principle of nature; taking in his highest compositions the perfect ideal form, every spray being graceful and varied in itself, but . . . invariably hinting at the constant tendency in all; and thus, in spite of his abundant complexity, he arranges his trees under simpler and grander forms than any other artist . . .[44]

Not even Reynolds could have asked for more than this expression of 'the constant tendency in all'. And for Turner that constancy did not merely concern forms but also a more common fundamental. Since his earliest works, especially in the field of marine painting,

**173** *Falls of the Rhine, Schaffhausen, c.*1841,
watercolour with some pen on paper, 22.7 × 28.4 cm, Courtauld Institute of Art, London.

Turner had been preoccupied with expressing energy. As we have seen, it was his eventual grasp not only of the forms of transient phenomena such as seas and clouds but also of the energy activating them that makes his mature depictions of them so compelling and, indeed, so unequalled in the history of western painting; other artists may reproduce the external appearance of sea and clouds with greater verisimilitude but none rival, let alone surpass Turner's grasp of what impels them. Not surprisingly, in time this sense of energy emerges from behind the individual appearances of things to ever greater degrees, finally coming to visibly pervade almost everything on the outside. Such an increase in the appearance of fundamental energy can be especially discerned in Turner's late water-colours where material distinctions frequently dissolve altogether. For example, in a water-colour like *Falls of the Rhine, Schaffhausen* (fig. 173) of about 1841, the immense flow of energy through the falls, and the spray they give off, bounds up into the atmosphere, whilst also seeming to appear behind the figures and objects sketched out in the foreground. In *Sion,*

**174** *Sion, near the Simplon Pass, c.*1846,
watercolour on paper, 37.4 × 55.3 cm, City Art Gallery, Manchester.

**175** *A Swiss Pass, c.*1848–50,
watercolour on paper, 35.9 × 50.8 cm, Victoria and Albert Museum, London.

*near the Simplon Pass* (fig. 174) of about 1845, only the dark blue sky and mountain shadows that butt up against the church or the line of hillside on its right, as well as the cliff beneath the church, refuse to share in the general breakdown of form: everywhere else the barriers between material objects disappear entirely. And in *A Swiss Pass* (fig. 175) which may date from as late as 1850, or *The Lauerzer See, with the Mythens* of about 1846 (fig. 179), the energy-flow seems all-pervasive. Everything here is interactive, dynamic and flowing. The unity of earth and sky is complete, bound by the energy which underlies them. For Turner rocks are no longer merely hard, static objects. They can share in a flux that seems universal. In some of Turner's late watercolours crowds of people even appear to be caught up in such encompassing physical energy. Yet the dissolution of form in these and similar works does not diminish our sense of reality; if anything it convinces us that we are perceiving a higher reality. Turner has conceived and stated a unifying ideal reality which underlies all visible things, for one does not see the material world like this. Energy became the underlying subject of many of Turner's late works because it was virtually the ultimate ideality for him.

Yet there came to be another, even more fundamental power than that. This was the source of most earthly energy and nearly all of its light, and an object almost certainly regarded by the artist as divine.

## THE SUN IS GOD

The statement ascribed to Turner that 'The Sun is God' seems so completely borne out by his later work that it is difficult to believe he did not utter it, or that he did not hold it to be completely true. But how likely is it that Turner did state such a belief?

It is Ruskin who tells us:

> The Sun is God said Turner, a few weeks before he died with the setting rays of it on his face.[45]

This passage needs to be broken down into three parts: Ruskin's quotation of Turner's words; the passage concerning 'a few weeks before he died'; and the time of day at which Ruskin tells us the demise took place.

Initially it might seem that Ruskin could not have been present when Turner made the statement, for he was not in London 'a few weeks' before Turner died on 19 December 1851. He had left for Venice (where he spent the subsequent autumn and winter) on 1 August 1851, and clearly three months or so is not just 'a few weeks'. But Ruskin wrote this passage in September 1874 and the lapse of time could easily account for his error of memory. The fact that he was absent from London when Turner died might account for his solecism that the artist expired with the rays of the setting sun upon his face, for Turner actually died at around 9 o'clock in the morning. Ruskin was obviously romanticising Turner's death. Yet the mistake does not invalidate the quotation, for it is unlikely that he romanticised that too. Ruskin had too much respect for 'truth' to have invented the quote. (Alternatively he may have obtained it from someone else, such as his father, who could have heard Turner make the remark.[46]) But there are strong circumstantial reasons for accepting the quotation as true. One reason has to do with Ruskin's overall perception of Turner just before the artist's death. Ruskin tended to stress Turner's unhappiness, telling us for example that 'the end of Turner's life had been a very sorrowful one',[47] that as the painter grew older he would burst into tears as his hands ceased to obey him,[48] and that 'the old man's soul had been gradually crushed within him, leaving him at the close of his life weak, sinful, desolate – nothing but his generosity and kindness of heart left'.[49] This emphasis has even led to speculations as to whether Ruskin was not even projecting his own sense of pessimism onto Turner.[50] However, there is no real reason to doubt the truthfulness of this testimony, for clearly it refers to the period 'at the close' of Turner's life when he was no longer capable of painting at all, i.e. between about the spring of 1850 and the very end of 1851.[51] But the truthfulness of Ruskin's observations is supported rather than disproved by the remark concerning the sun as God, for here is an affirmation of belief amidst Turner's understandable anguish at the loss of his powers; and the thought of extinction strengthens the case for accepting the quotation, and Ruskin's other testimony, as true. If Ruskin had wanted to make us believe that Turner was totally nihilistic at the end of his life, he would surely have suppressed the remark concerning the sun as God.

Further support for the Sun as God story emerges from a consideration of Turner's known cultural identifications. The notion of the sun as the embodiment of the Deity may have been present in Turner's mind from the beginning of his career, for it is vividly established in the literature that he prized most highly. For instance, in the passages that precede or follow the very first poetic quotations he ever used in conjunction with his pictures, those verses by Milton and Thomson he appended in 1798 to the titles of his paintings *Morning amongst the Coniston Fells, Cumberland* (fig. 21), and *Norham Castle on the Tweed, Summer's morn* (fig. 22), there are clear references to the sun as a spiritual force, a pointer to the existence of God. The lines from Milton's *Paradise Lost* accompanying *Coniston Fells* are preceded by verses that declare the sun to be 'of this great world both eye and soul' and which recall its divine origin. In the Thomson poem the identification is even more strongly stated. Right after the verses about 'the powerful King of Day' that Turner quoted in 1798 to support his picture, and the lines concerning the 'rocks, and hills, and towers, and wandering streams/High gleaming from afar' that he subsequently discussed in 1811, we discover the following passage:

> Prime cheerer, Light!
> Of all material beings first and best!
> Efflux divine! Nature's resplendent robe,
> Without whose vesting beauty all were wrapt
> In unessential gloom; and thou, O Sun!
> Soul of surrounding worlds! In whom best seen
> Shines out thy maker! May I sing of thee?
>    'Tis by thy secret, strong, attractive force,
>    As with a chain indissoluble bound,
>    Thy system rolls entire . . .[52]

The poet then continues over the next hundred or so lines to link the solar system to the sun, to trace the dependency of the vegetable and human world upon it, to probe how the minerals which are used to make the tools of both war and peace were formed by its powers, how diamonds and other precious and semi-precious stones 'all its native lustre let abroad', and how all landscapes (i.e. 'the precipice abrupt', 'desert joys' and 'Rude ruins' of the passage that accompanies the *Dunstanburgh Castle* of 1798) are transformed by its appearance. Given Turner's familiarity with this whole section of the poem and the demonstrable impact it had upon him, as well as his responsiveness to light and his constant concern to trace things back to their origins, these sentiments encountered early in life might certainly have sowed the seeds for a later emergence of pantheistic belief, a conviction which can only have been continually strengthened by his activities as a landscapist.

This type of sentiment was by no means rare in the poetry of Turner's youth. Thomson expresses related sentiments in *Liberty* when, in Part II of the poem, he discusses the rise of liberty and thought in ancient Greece:

> O'er all shone out the great Athenian sage,
> And father of philosophy – the sun,
> From whose white blaze emerged each various sect
> Took various tints, but with diminished beam.
> Tutor of Athens! he in every street
> Dealt priceless treasure – goodness his delight,
> Wisdom his wealth, and glory his reward.
> Deep through the human heart with playful art
> His simple question stole, as into truth
> And serious deeds he smiled the laughing race,
> Taught moral happy life, whate'er can bless
> Or grace mankind . . .[53]

Such re-tracing of human thought and moral goodness back to the sun could easily have led Turner to consider the orb as a source of moral inspiration as well as one of physical power.

The symbolism of the sun as the divine well-spring of life was no less firmly expressed in other poems published in Anderson's *Complete Poets* and available to Turner. One such example is a poem inspired and influenced by Thomson's *Seasons*, David Mallet's famous work, 'The Excursion', of 1728. As we know, Turner attached lines taken from Mallet's 'Amyntor and Theodora' to his watercolour of *Caernarvon Castle*, exhibited at the R.A. in 1799, so he could easily have read this poem too. In the first canto of 'The Excursion' Mallet describes a sunrise as 'The King of Glory', and the whole theme of the poem is an excursive survey of the vastness and complexity of the earth and heavens. In the second canto the poet goes on to exalt the sun as the 'Fairest of beings! first created light!' and the 'Prime cause of beauty!' before re-tracing all things to their 'unfailing source of splendour' in a passage clearly derived from Thomson.[54] And earlier poets published in Anderson, such as Abraham Cowley, Thomas Parnell, Elijah Fenton and Thomas Yalden expressed similar identifications in their various odes to the sun and hymns to morning or light.[55] Clearly, the dazzling sun in Turner's later works did not hold the central, dominating position because the artist was unconsciously prefiguring Impressionism. It is rather more likely that we are looking at the attainment of something that Turner had long been striving for, namely a pictorial expression of those metaphysical correlations between the sun and active spiritual powers so prevalent in the literary works that shaped his poetic vision of things.

These correspondences between the sun and the spirit were not unknown in the writings on *ut pictura poesis* which so vitally contributed to his deeper view of the world either. For example, in Lomazzo's *A Tracte containing the Artes of Curious Paintinge*, the section entitled 'On the Nature of Light' states that

> First and principally this word Light signifieth the image of that divine nature which is the sonne of God, and the brightness thereof; which the *Platonickes* call the image of the divine minde. Secondly the confortable operatio of the holy ghost. Thirdly that divine vertue, which being diffused through all the creatures, is in men their divine grace; and in all other living creatures, that powre whereby they are preserved and defended . . . Fourthly, that intelligence in the Angels . . . Fifthly in the heavenly bodies it causes abundance of Life, signifying an effectual propagation and visible brightnesse in the fire, with a certaine accidental powre proceeding from the same. Sixtly it is taken in man, for the light of their *agent* understanding, which illuminateth their patient or passible understanding; (in a word) for the discourse of reason and the knowledge of divine things. Last of all it signifieth a quality proceeding from the Sunne or the fire, which so discovereth colours, that they may be seen . . .[56]

Such metaphysical dimensions to light are not only present in Lomazzo's semantic definitions of the term. They are also introduced into his investigation of the actual workings of light itself. He divides light into primary and secondary kinds, i.e. that which is given off directly and that which is merely passed on. He then also further subdivides primary light into three species. The first is primary *direct* light, the type that emanates from a powerful physical source like the sun. Then there is *divine* light, 'that which is caused by the divers apperitions of Angels &c. whether it be by day or night', and which in turn exists as '3 sorts; *Direct, Reflected* and *Refracted*'; in this connection he cites examples of how artists like Titian and Correggio represented divine light in works showing 'quiers of Angels, Patriachs, Prophets and all other blessed soules', pictures such as Nativity and Resurrection scenes where pictorialisations of divine light are by definition metaphorical. Naturally, Turner would have encountered no difficulties in accepting the existence of such light (at least in pictorial terms), as his confident appreciations of the representations of divine light in Titian's *St Peter Martyr* (fig. 82) and Raphael's *Transfiguration* (fig. 86) make clear. Finally, for Lomazzo there is primary *artificial* light, the kind that is given off by 'a fire, a candle, torch, fornace etc'. Turner was familiar with this whole passage of Lomazzo, as is demonstrated by a précis he wrote carefully in ink in a small pocket sketchbook he was using around 1809:

> Light
> Primary Light that which is received direct
> Second Primary Lights into 3 direct Reflected and refracted
> Lomazzo gives this to emanation of the Deity or adoration of Glory
> Third Primary Light to artificial light . . .[57]

It hardly seems likely that Turner would have taken the trouble to especially note Lomazzo's hypothesis that light is invested with divine powers unless it was at least useful to him in his thinking about the pictorial function of light for his perspective lectures, and perhaps it even held a metaphysical significance for him as well. Indeed, in view of his receptivity to Akenside's Platonism it seems most probable that he did accept Lomazzo's opinion that light exists primarily as an 'image of the divine minde', particularly since the initial and revised versions of Akenside's poem treating of the pleasures of imagination liken the workings of 'the Divine Mind' to the workings of the sun.[58] And from feeling that light derives *from* the Deity, given Turner's propensity for fundamentals it would easily have been a short step for him to think that the overriding source of earthly light *is* the Deity; surely it was more than artistic intuition that led Ruskin to state that the painter had definitely made that step. Moreover, evidence directly stemming from Turner suggests that he did so.

Naturally, Turner was well aware that the Ancients had regarded the sun as divine. The sun-god Apollo appears in both *Chryses* (fig. 136) and the *Apollo and Python* of 1811 (B.J. 115), a year when Turner's concern with fundamentals was at its height. And Apollo also rises up in the chariot of the sun in *Ulysses deriding Polyphemus* of 1829 (fig. 177). Of course, for someone as preoccupied as Turner was with tracing things back to their origins, and as conscious of the interdependencies of nature, the notion that the sun is the 'Prime cheerer' of the world may have appeared obvious. Moreover, we are fairly certain that the artist rejected conventional religion. There is no pattern of worship in his life,[59] although he may have been attracted to Deism around the time of Humphrey Boyle's trial in 1822. According to Ruskin, Turner was 'without hope' of redemption or of an after-life,[60] a view lent credence by his 'poem' on the fallaciousness of hope as well as by a number of his paintings. But given the central role and significant emphasis Turner places upon the celestial orb in many of his later works, as well as the verbal statement of the sun's divinity which he almost certainly made, there cannot be much doubt that he considered the sun to be in some sense the 'Soul of surrounding worlds', rather than merely a physical object. If such was the case then the all-pervasive energy that appears in many of Turner's late pictures is far more than the simple expression of physical force in the world; it is the embodiment of his belief in some unifying metaphysical power of the sun itself.

And yet another profound ideality in Turner's art definitely emanated from that source: colour. Turner definitely knew that light is the basis of colour and the embodiment of it prismatically, and that in colour, too, may be perceived universals – what he called in one of his lectures

> a natural kind of Trigonometry in vision.[61]

By this he meant that the three primary colours – red, yellow and blue – are 'of the essence of natural structure, of the same order as the basic geometrical forms'.[62] Such a comparison is not surprising; as has also been noted, for Turner '. . . the ideal, the scientifically "primary" and the "primitive" came to be identified'[63] with one another wherever they were encountered.

Some of the literature on poetic painting also touches upon this ideality of colour. For example, Turner would surely have read in the part of Giovanni Pietro Bellori's essay on 'The Idea of the Painter, Sculptor and Architect' which was available to him, that the duty of an artist is

> . . . to represent [Nature] as it was first created, either in colour or in lineament.[64]

This stress upon the primary, and therefore essential and ideal qualities of colour, was also articulated in Turner's own day by John Opie who stated in his fourth lecture, delivered in 1807, that

> The grand style consists . . . in supplying the defects, and avoiding the redundencies of individual and imperfect forms; and colouring is not less capable, by rejecting what is merely accidental, and copying only the general and characteristic hue of each object, of being elevated to the same ideal standard.[65]

Such a recommendation to seek out essential colour-values could well have contributed to the greater purity and separation of individual colours that appears in Turner's work over the years. It would certainly account for the increasing stress that Turner placed upon the primaries.

Opie was not Turner's only contemporary to touch upon an ideality of colour. The philosopher and colour-maker George Field went even further, perceiving in colour proof of the existence of the Deity. Around 1811 Field wrote a book entitled *Chromatics, or an Essay on the Analogy and Harmony of Colours*. Although it was not published until 1817, the author submitted the manuscript to 'Farington and other Artists' in 1814.[66] In it Field stated that

> If *all* reason be allied to the *universal*, then must the development of reason, in a sensible object, indicate the universal reason or intelligence to which it belongs. Dull of consciousness therefore will be the mind that in contemplating a system so simple, various and harmonious, as that of colours, should not discover therein a type of that TRIUNE ESSENCE WHO COULD NOT BUT CONSTRUCT ALL THINGS AFTER THE PATTERN OF HIS OWN PERFECTION. For this reason, the Divine Wisdom that framed the world, gave *His image* not to man alone, but . . . *filled the world with symbols of Himself*. And since of all sensible things colour is pre-eminent, for it gives value and distinction to whatever is visible, we may wonder the less that the perfection of form and system belongs supereminently to colours, or that they constitute a type of Universal Intelligence Himself.[67]

That Turner probably did read Field's book in manuscript in 1814 is suggested by a passage in Thornbury's biography of the painter:

> Mr Field having sent Turner his treatise on 'Chromatics', when they next met, asked him his opinion of it. 'You have not told us too much', was Turner's dry remark.[68]

According to the same source Turner later went on to denounce Field's book as 'fallacious', and it is not difficult to deduce why. Field posited analogies between colour and sound, something that Turner had rejected in 1810–11 when he dismissed the analogies that Poussin had posited between colours and the classical modes in music. It is not surprising that Turner thought Field unoriginal. Yet it should not be supposed from this that Turner would necessarily have rejected Field's notion that colour enjoys a divine origin. Certainly, Field might have reinforced Turner's identification of the major source of earthly light with the Deity, colour being wholly identified with light by the artist who declared in one of his lectures that 'Light is . . . colour'.[69]

Of course it is particularly as a colourist that Turner is thought to have developed a kind of proto-Impressionist response to the world, being seen to have moved away from the sombre chiaroscuro and limited colour-ranges of his early work to brilliance in his later art because he wished to express the outward appearances of nature with greater fidelity and

**176** *Cologne, the Arrival of a Packet Boat. Evening*, R.A. 1826,
oil on canvas, 168. 6 × 224.1 cm, The Frick Collection, New York.

**177** *Ulysses deriding Polyphemus – Homer's Odyssey*, R.A. 1829,
oil on canvas, 132.5 × 203 cm, National Gallery, London.

freedom. However, such an explanation is inadequate, for it ignores the degree to which the painter manipulated the 'Accidents of Nature' in colour as much as in form: where in Turner's art is there ever much use of bright green to denote the colour of grass for instance? The concept of ideal or perfected colour would not have restricted Turner expressively in any way; if anything it could only have enhanced his ability to give meaning, emotional value and beauty to the world of appearances, just as the realisation of the ideality of forms certainly did so. Here, too, he may well have been responding to a specific cultural imperative of his time, for the gradual lightening, greater purity, increasing brilliance and ever-more subtle interplay of Turner's palette after about 1810 could easily have resulted from a desire to achieve in colour an equivalent to the ideal forms he was simultaneously developing (and what better way could there be to attain in painting a correlative for the 'sounds harmonious' of poetry?). Certainly it seems unlikely that Turner would have wanted to express an ideality of form without an ideality of colour as well. In this sphere, too, the artist could match and surpass normal appearances. The sense of freedom that derives from the ability to go beyond what is literally seen, to state an imaginative, perfected concept of things, would certainly account for Turner's imaginative development as a colourist. Indeed, in a great number of his works we can perceive ranges of colour that seem quite magical, Turner employing combinations which are never encountered in normal visual experience, and subtleties that only an idealising imagination could discover. In some pictures he even creates harmonies of colour that appear unearthly, a kind of visual equivalent to those other-worldly modulations we encounter in the late music of Schubert for instance. It would be impossible to reproduce such subtleties of colouring in a book; they are far beyond the power of imitation through printing. But anyone who has ever had the good fortune to see pictures like the gorgeous *Cologne, the Arrival of a Packet Boat. Evening* of 1826 (fig. 176) in the Frick Collection, New York, the *Ulysses deriding Polyphemus* of 1829 in the London National Gallery (fig. 177), the miraculous *Bally-burgh Ness* of about 1835 (fig. 178) in the Fogg Art Museum, Cambridge, Massachusetts, the *Glaucus and Scylla* of 1841 (fig. 138), the topographically unidentified *Alpine landscape* (w. 1511) of the same period in the Fitzwilliam Museum, Cambridge, England, the *Lauerzer See, with the Mythens* of about 1846 in the Victoria and Albert Museum, London (fig. 179), and indeed a whole host of late oils or Venetian and Swiss watercolours, will certainly be in a position to consider the possibility that Turner not only *imagined* a perfect world of colour – which we certainly know he did – and rendered such imaginings in harmonies that most other painters have never even dreamt of, but also that he was inspired to do so by the idealising concept of poetic painting.

Yet we do not have to rely entirely upon subjective responses to test the validity of this hypothesis; in a number of pictures the artist affords us some visual evidence that he did indeed evolve an ideal colouring. Turner underpins many works with a single primary

**178** *Bally-burgh Ness, c.*1835,
watercolour on paper, 7.9 × 15 cm, Fogg Art Museum, Cambridge, Mass.

**179** *The Lauerzer See, with the Mythens, c.*1846,
watercolour on paper, 33.7 × 54.5 cm, Victoria and Albert Museum, London.

**180** *Cologne, from the river*, signed and dated 1820,
watercolour on paper, 30.8 × 46.3 cm, Seattle Art Museum, Washington.

colour over which he then places tonal variants of that colour. In this connection witnesses of Turner's working processes in watercolour at Farnley Hall before 1825 attest to seeing the artist preparing papers with overall red, yellow and blue washes and hanging them on a clothes-line in his room to dry.[70] Such a dependence on the three primary colours also appears in his frequent explorations of the expressive potential those colours enjoy when used in conjunction with one another, and this again is a process we see clearly emerge in the years after 1810. The colour range of *Dido building Carthage* (fig. 125) revolves around the fundamental polarities of red, yellow and blue, whilst in a watercolour like *Cologne* of 1820 (fig. 180) we can see Turner deploy yellow and blue throughout the work, with small touches of red for the figures. (The ideality of Turner's liquid and cloud-forms is particularly evident in this picture.) Perhaps the classic example of this basic conjunction of primaries occurs in *The Fighting 'Temeraire'* (fig. 18) where the entire colour-range revolves around their polarities. And this range is also a feature of many pictures which enjoy either a circular format or a circular or semi-circular stress in their composition, paintings such as the *Peace* and *War* pendants of 1842 (figs 54, 56) or *Glaucus and Scylla*[71] and *Dawn of Christianity* of 1841 (figs 138, 150) where each paired work opposes the most dynamic contrasts of primaries. Upon seeing the latter two pictures David Roberts commented that 'Turner as usual is primitive in colour, having confined himself to three prismatic colours, Red, Blue and Yellow'.[72] A similar response was projected by the painter himself in connection with *Light and Colour (Goethe's Theory) – The Morning after the Deluge – Moses writing the Book of Genesis* (fig. 181) of 1843, a painting of which Turner would say no more to Ruskin than 'Red, blue and yellow' after the critic had lifted a curtain hanging over the work in the artist's studio.[73]

The circular composition or format of these pictures, when combined with this 'trigonometry' of colour, can be seen to represent yet another aspect of Turner's attraction to fundamentals, and possibly the most subtle of all his responses to Raphael as well. When Turner reproduced Raphael's circular *Madonna della Sedia* (Pitti Palace, Florence) in *Rome from the Vatican. Raffaele, accompanied by La Fornarina, preparing his Pictures for the Decoration of the Loggia* of 1820, he not only indicated the values he prized in Raphael's work but also pointed to one of the most important formats by which Raphael had created structural and symbolic unity, something Turner was attracted to in Raphael's work, as his analysis of the *Transfiguration* (fig. 86) shows (and it will be remembered that *The Holy Family with the Palm Tree*, fig. 88, is also a tondo). Naturally, it is not difficult to see why Turner was drawn to such unities of form and meaning, but his painterly celebration of a great master's choice of a circular format may also reflect another aspect of his preoccupation with essentials, for of all the basic geometric forms the circle is perhaps the most important in human terms. Not only is our world circular but so, too, is our field of vision, the primary area of concern to any painter. For Turner such a shape, of all the shapes available to him, may well have come to represent something even more fundamental than the other 'pure forms'. Moreover, another essential can exist in the circle as well, for Turner was undoubtedly aware of the colour-circle, wherein each colour leads imperceptibly to the next in progression. And in formal terms there also resides in the circle an implied dynamic which Turner evidently felt to be profoundly basic: the vortex. This form of revolving movement around the centre of a picture has long been celebrated in Turner's work and it was undoubtedly the most effective way for him to involve us dramatically and dynamically in the fictive space of a picture; as he once advised an amateur painter, it is important to 'Centre your interest'.[74] Naturally, the most efficient way to achieve this is by funneling our attention towards the centre of the work by means of the shape of the picture-format itself. Moreover, the ensuing sense of being at the very heart of things in the fictive physical space introduces associations of the infinite, the sense that the space we are looking at extends outwards for ever.

In *Light and Colour (Goethe's Theory) – The Morning after the Deluge – Moses writing the Book of Genesis* (fig. 181) of 1843, Turner brought all of these realisations together into one picture: the use of primaries and their progression in a colour-circle, a strong vortexical movement within a circular pictorial structure to effect a 'cosmic' dynamic, and the use of that circular

**181** *Light and Colour (Goethe's Theory) – the Morning after the Deluge – Moses writing the Book of Genesis,*
R.A. 1843, oil on canvas, 78.5 × 78.5 cm, Clore Gallery for the Turner Collection, London.

structure itself to augment the content of the work metaphorically. The picture enjoys a
pendant, *Shade and Darkness – the Evening of the Deluge* (B.J. 404), and the titles of both works
demonstrate Turner's sense of decorum regarding the suitably timed relationship of
light-effects to content, for the passage in Genesis that tells the story of Noah says nothing of
the times of day when the Deluge began or ended – evidently these timings are symbolic,
although they are hallowed by tradition. The title of *Light and Colour (Goethe's Theory) – The
Morning after the Deluge – Moses writing the Book of Genesis* was accompanied by these verses
from Turner's 'Fallacies of Hope' in the R.A. catalogue:

> The ark stood firm on Ararat; th'returning sun
> Exhaled earth's humid bubbles, and emulous of light,
> Reflected her lost forms, each in prismatic guise
> Hope's harbinger, ephemeral as the summer fly
> Which rises, flits, expands, and dies.

This verse needs some analysis. The meaning of the first line is clear but the second is ambiguous until we realise that the word 'emulous' does not necessarily mean 'imitative of' or 'envious of' but can also signify 'greedy of power',[75] the sense in which Turner uses it here: the sun is not 'envious *of* light' but greedily wants to increase its power, and visibly does so. We can interpret the verse to mean that after the Deluge the returning sun, as it grows in brightness, causes the earth to exhale 'humid bubbles' which shine with prismatic colours and reflect forms, i.e. the images of the drowned populace who appear in the painting. Yet such resurrected images do not act as 'Hope's harbinger', the prefigurations of an eventual Resurrection. Instead, they point up how fallacious the hope of Resurrection really is, for like the may-fly the bubbles will quickly die. Turner's rejection of a final Resurrection is doubly expressed in the painting, for we see Moses and a serpent in the sky. Their appcarance there is explained by the imagery of St John, chapter 3, verses 14–15:

> And as Moses lifted up the serpent in the
> wilderness, even so must the Son of man be lifted up:

> That whosoever believeth in him should not perish,
> but have eternal life.

However, given the verses that Turner quotes from the 'Fallacies of Hope', he is evidently refuting the notion that the 'Son of man', symbolised by the snake which appears before Moses, promises eternal life.

Turner had used bubbles as symbols of ephemerality long before the appearance of Goethe's book *Farbenlehre* to which he alludes in the title of the painting, although naturally Goethe may have pointed up the continuing usefulness of such images to the artist. Goethe's book was translated into English, published in 1840 under the title of *Theory of Colours* and annotated by Turner. Goethe had observed that colour-sequences to be seen around the edges of bubbles of foam on drinking-chocolate follow the order of the primaries and are necessarily ephemeral. Yet Turner not only represents bubbles within the painting – the circle within which all of the forms appear is itself a large projection of a prismatically coloured bubble. Turner creates this parallel by his choice of a circular surround, his distribution of primary colours around the edge of that circle and by the placement of highlights – a brilliant sun and its reflection – as well as areas of darkness towards the centre. Once again the artist's propensity to create parallels between the content of a painting and the object itself (as in *The Golden Bough*, fig. 144, *Juliet and her Nurse*, fig. 12, and others), can be discerned.

Given its visual intensity, obviously the sun is the dominant force in the picture. But Turner's sun is not just a physical object, any more than the man in the sky is simply a hovering figure or the snake a mere reptile: the very fact that for Turner the sun causes the earth to exhale 'humid bubbles' which reveal images of the drowned inhabitants of the world surely implies that the artist has covertly represented the sun as God here, for only the Deity can resurrect images of the dead. The metaphorical status of the sun in the picture can also be supported associatively by the figurative light imagery in the part of St John's gospel from which the serpent-symbol image is drawn. As verses 18–21 of St John, chapter 3 tell us:

> And this is the condemnation, that light is come
> into the world, and men loved darkness rather than
> light, because their deeds were evil.

> For every one that doeth evil hateth the light,
> neither cometh to the light, lest his deeds be reproved.

> But he that doeth truth cometh to the light, that his
> deeds may be made manifest, that they are wrought in
> God.

Equally, Turner may be expressing the realisation that the white light created by the sun that fills the major part of the picture would exist in reality as the essence of colour, for he knew well that, as a prism reveals, white light synthesizes all colours, although white paint does not; as he stated in his examination of light, 'white [paint] is the substitute of light, as [white in reality] is the compound of aerial light'[76] (and therefore of colour).

Naturally, if Turner really did verbally state that 'The Sun is God', then we might expect him to have expressed such a conviction in a religious work. But there is no reason to believe that he would have confined his identification of the sun with God simply to religious pictures. Since Turner constantly stressed essentials in his perspective lectures, and above all *metaphysical* essentials, it is likely that he depicted the sun as the divine basis of life and energy everywhere in his mature works, for he must readily have appreciated that the celestial orb is the ultimate ideality and essence of the material world, being the fundamental source of all life on earth. Turner may well have considered the sun 'an image of the divine mind', if not the very embodiment of that mind, and pictured it as such. Indeed, it seems certain that he did, for the statement that 'The Sun is God' fits the pattern of metaphysical belief that Turner is known to have held. And if the artist did represent the sun as God, then we can easily appreciate that the blinding orb must be his all-surpassing 'splendorous allusion', a veritable 'King of Day' indeed. Because everything that Turner held most dear – light, colour, nature and thus art – derives existence from that star, it is not at all surprising that he should have accorded it divine powers and made it burn with increasing, life-giving intensity as he neared his end.

IDEAL BEAUTIES OR CONNECTING METAPHORS

The doctrine of poetic painting was carefully explored by Turner between 1798 and 1800, and again for long after 1808. From the first such an investigation gave rise to works in which the artist realised pictorial correlatives for poetic effects, increasingly generating images equal to the 'sounds harmonious' of poetry in their felicities of form and colour. Equally, the doctrine of poetic painting gave direction to a profound dramatic sense and an innate concern with fundamentals, leading Turner to explore more fully what are meant by artistic imagination and 'vision', beauty and truth, and universals of form, natural structure, energy, colour and light. The desire to arrive at underlying associative meanings took a natural, often central place within this nexus of concerns, and the use of metaphor and association provided imaginatively rewarding aids for the construction of pictures. The term 'Ideal beauties' – whether applied to poetry or painting – harboured two meanings which could be interconnected, representing the idealisation of externals through artistic stylisation and/or choice of subject, as well as an imaginative concentration and projection of the inner values of objects and phenomena. The constant need to pursue such essentials acted decisively upon Turner's sense of form and ensured the most readily if subtly visible quality in all his work, namely its expression of some inherent truth of form and behaviour respectively present in physical objects such as trees and rocks, and physical phenomena such as the movement of the sea or the shapes of clouds. The ideality of form which gradually pervades Turner's work and becomes apparent everywhere after about 1815 adds immeasurably to the values of beauty it expresses. By building upon these values Turner the poetic-painter created an art that addresses the broadest and most essential levels of reality in nature, including human nature.

Turner not only felt that poetry and painting draw imagery from nature with which to create metaphors, and that 'splendorous allusion' in one art is sometimes capable of enriching the expressive range of the other, but that their shared concept of archetypal beauty also enlarges the potential of metaphors to convey meaning. And so we finally ascertain why the artist seems to have thought of 'Ideal beauties *or* connecting Metaphors' as conjoined alternatives. In a number of his works certain objects or natural phenomena, such as trees, clouds and effects of light, express both the artist's conception of their principles and perfected forms whilst equally functioning as transferences to further our comprehension of human experience: trees expressive of their own ideality can also convey a sense of the general florescence of animal (including human) or avian life, as in *Crossing the Brook* (fig. 152) and *Powis Castle* (fig. 148) respectively, or convey a sense of human protectiveness as in *Hythe, Kent* (fig. 119); clouds whose ideality is very apparent can denote 'the storms of war', as in *Hougoumont* (fig. 66), *The Field of Waterloo* (fig. 67) or *The Battle of Trafalgar* (fig. 76); idealised morning light and the effects it creates can advance associations of human birth and generation, as in *Dido building Carthage* (fig. 125), or of human maturity, as in *Crossing the Brook*; and idealised evening light can similarly extend the meaning of subjects connected with decay or extinction, as in *Caernarvon Castle* (fig. 26), *Pope's Villa at Twickenham* (fig. 9), *The Fighting 'Temeraire'* (fig. 18), *Peace – Burial at Sea* (fig. 54), *The Decline of the Carthaginian Empire* (fig. 129) and *Abbotsford* (fig. 151). Equally, the earthly geometry that for Turner reflected supernal models can also serve to fortify the underlying meaning of pictures, as in *Lifeboat and Manby Apparatus* (fig. 121), *Glacier and Source of the Arveron* (fig. 122), *Longships Lighthouse* (fig. 123), *Dido building Carthage* and other works, just as the lack of it also serves metaphorical ends in *The Decline of the Carthaginian Empire*. In all of these works we see the creation of 'sentiment' on interactive levels. Yet what these pictures also have in common is Turner's dissatisfaction with mere outward appearances. For him it was more important to conceive and state fundamental realities existing beyond the visible sphere than it was just to reproduce the appearances of things faithfully, and much of his life's work was devoted to achieving that realisation, an ambition obviously formed by the theory of poetic painting. The artist's writings expound his belief in the need to differentiate between reality and appearance, or to distinguish 'the greater from the lesser truth', and so do his works. Indeed, in one picture he not only provides us with evidence of how highly he valued the crucial difference between appearance and reality but he also singled out the image to act as a specific key to that distinction, thus supplying a vital insight to the central imaginative dynamic of his art. The picture in which he gave us this key is therefore one of the most significant in his entire œuvre.

Turner began the *Liber Studiorum* in 1806 but not until some six years later – and hence a year after he began to lecture on perspective and the fundamentals underlying appearances, and at about the time he produced metaphorical images like *Procris and Cephalus* or *Winchelsea* for the *Liber Studiorum* – did he produce a Frontispiece for the scheme. This consists of a picture of *Europa and the Bull* (fig. 183) set amidst a decorative surround (fig. 182). Visually the work is unremarkable but its importance lies in its content and few attempts have been made to explore that dimension. Ruskin saw the image as a typical Turnerian comment upon the brevity of civilisations, for we see the city of Tyre on the left, whose 'beauty [is] passing away into terror and judgement' (to which he added cryptically '. . . Europa being the mother of Minos and Rhadamanthus'[77]). Later, the Rev. Stopford Brooke, in his book on the *Liber Studiorum*, commented that Turner chose this picture to preface his work

> . . . with a deliberate meaning. He painted the passing away of Tyre, and symbolised it by the story of Europa; and in it he expressed all his own sorrow, both grim and pitiful, for the decay and death of human works and glory and beauty. He had a special

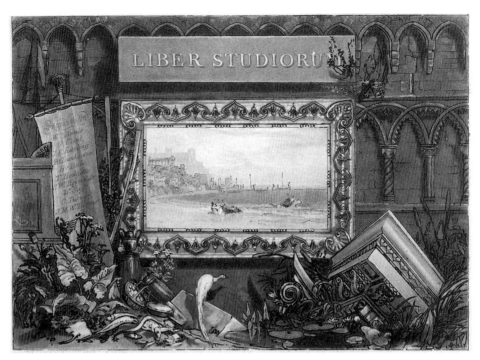

**182** *The Frontispiece* for the *Liber Studiorum*, mezzotint engraving, 1812,
drawn, etched and the centre image engraved by Turner,
the surround engraved by J. C. Easling.

attraction towards great sea-empires, gathered perhaps from his silent love of England,
and he illustrated their rise and fall in the two pictures – for which he seems to have had
the most personal love – the Rise, and the Fall of Carthage. Therefore, if he wished to
represent in the most striking manner his sense of the sadness of humanity, he would
choose to do it under the image of the fall of a Queen of the sea. Here he has chosen
Tyre.[78]

Given the overt pessimism of many of Turner's titles, picture subjects and accompanying
poetic quotations, this explanation of his choice of subject to introduce the *Liber Studiorum*
might seem convincing. But some thirty-three years after creating the image Turner
returned to it (Frontispiece) as the subject of one of the group of paintings he created in the
mid-1840s in which he re-worked various images from the *Liber Studiorum*. In none of these
later pictures does Turner impart any feelings of pessimism whatsoever; on the contrary,
the entire set projects Turner's radiant idealism with the utmost subtlety and power. As the
artist was more likely to have intensified an inherently pessimistic statement as he neared
death rather than lessened it, this somewhat discounts the view that he chose a subject
linked to the decline of Tyre in *Europa and the Bull* in order to address the passing of
civilisations (a theme he certainly dealt with during the years he re-worked the *Liber*

**183** *Frontispiece* for the *Liber Studiorum* of *Europa and the Bull*.

*Studiorum* images). And in any case, in the late picture the city of Tyre has disappeared altogether and been replaced by a haze of colour. So why did Turner choose this subject to introduce and make an essential statement about the *Liber Studiorum*?

The answer may well reside in Turner's literary source for the picture. He probably obtained the story from Joseph Addison's translation of sections of Ovid's *Metamorphoses* in volume seven of Anderson's *Complete Poets*.[79] Ovid tells how Jupiter, desiring Europa, changed himself into a bull and mingled with cattle on the shores of Tyre. Europa, drawn to him by his friendliness and beauty, mounts his back to ride him and is thereupon carried off. As Ovid and Addison conclude:

> Through storms and tempests he the virgin bore,
> And lands her safe on the Dictean shore,
> Where now, in his divinest form array'd
> In his true shape he captivates the maid,
> Who gazes on him, and with wondering eyes
> Beholds the new majestic figure rise,
> His glowing features, and celestial light.
> And all the God discover'd to her sight.[80]

In this account of the story of Europa and the bull there exists not only the equation of a god with light but also a clear statement concerning the difference between appearance and reality. Beneath a title that proclaims Turner's homage to the *Liber Veritatis* it would seem natural for him to allude to that crucial poetic awareness he most fully prized and perhaps first discerned visually in Claude's work. Yet it may be that Turner chose the subject of Europa and the bull for the introductory image of the *Liber Studiorum* because through associative parallel it says something fundamental about the nature of art itself. We too are transported by a great work of art into a different and often more illuminating reality than the one we normally enjoy. In an image chosen to be the frontispiece of a set of pictures in which he summed up his achievements to date (and through which he was perhaps to do so again), as well as to preface a scheme he proposed as the subject of creative study, such a statement seems most apposite. For Turner imaginative or poetic reality was true reality, not simply the world of transitory appearances. To fix and frame that perception was the task he set himself throughout his life. Like Jupiter with the object of his attentions, and through the power of association and other imaginative enhancements, Turner carries us away with him to another, greater reality beyond the visible sphere. We owe it to ourselves as well as the artist to cross with him into that realm.

## THE IDEALITY OF MAN?

Throughout this chapter one aspect of the Ideal has been consistently overlooked. This is the area of form where Turner very clearly did not project the ideal of beauty that was required by the doctrine of poetic painting. To have fulfilled that doctrine completely he would not only have had to represent the perfected appearances of external nature but, more importantly, those of man. Clearly, he failed to do so. Turner may have created beautiful land- and seascapes, and imbued them with profound insights and meanings, but his figures are rarely beautified and idealistic as the doctrine of poetic painting required; indeed, Turner's figures seem a joke to most people. How then might we reconcile Turner's stated aspirations towards the expression of an 'Ideal Beauty' in his landscapes, with his evident failure to create 'Ideal beauties' in the people who inhabit them? Is there an explanation for this discrepancy? That is the final question we must face.

# EIGHT

# Turner's Human Landscape

Is not the caricaturist's task exactly the same as the classical artist's? Both see the lasting truth beneath the surface of mere outward appearance. Both try to help nature accomplish its plan. The one may strive to visualise the perfect form and to realise it in his work, the other to grasp the perfect deformity, and thus reveal the very essence of a personality. A good caricature, like every work of art, is more true to life than reality.

*Annibale Carracci*

Much of what the public were most pained by in Turner's figure drawing arose from what Turner himself had been chiefly pained by in the public.

*John Ruskin*

Man is Nature's sole mistake!

*W. S. Gilbert, 'Princess Ida'*

OF all the features of Turner's art, his figures are perhaps the least highly regarded. 'Misshapen', 'deformed', 'doll-like' or 'vulgar' are epithets frequently levelled at them. The phenomenal powers of observation and expression which the artist brought to the depiction of landscapes, seas and skies do not seem, in general appreciation at least, to have found their match in the human beings who inhabit those surrounds. Even Ruskin shared this judgement:

Notwithstanding his deep sympathy and imaginative power, there was, throughout Turner's later life, an infirmity in his figure conception which has always been to me, out of the whole multitude of questions that have come across me concerning art, the most inexplicable. With the most exquisite sense of grace and proportion in other forms, he continually admits awkwardnesses and errors in his figures which a child of ten years old would have avoided . . . all that I can guess respecting it is, that he had got so much into the habit of weaving natural forms – rocks, boughs, and waves – into exactly the shapes that would best help his composition, that when he came to an unsubdueable form in man or animal, he could not endure the resistance, and lifted features out of their places as he would have raised or dropped one window in a tower whose equalities tormented him; and wrung a neck as remorselessly as he would have twisted a bough, to get it into the light or shade he wanted.[1]

There is undoubtedly much truth in Ruskin's assertion that Turner manipulated human forms for compositional reasons. Yet such a conclusion does not explain why Turner's figures should also look 'doll-like' or 'vulgar'.

More recently Adrian Stokes has attempted to account for the apparent deficiency of Turner's human forms by borrowing the terminology of Melanie Klein to argue that the artist's 'variegated dolls' are merely 'part-objects', the painter's awareness of the felicities of human form having been subconsciously 'transferred' to the shapes with which he ordered his landscapes.[2] Alternatively it has been suggested, principally by Ruskin, that Turner quite simply could not *draw* the human figure, although this inability does not show up elsewhere, and the artist was very adept at portraying other animals such as fawns, pigs and donkeys with great accuracy, as Ruskin was forced to admit.

Naturally, nobody could argue that Turner's depictions of the human frame are as noble or elegant in conception as, say, those of Poussin or Watteau. On the other hand, they do manifest many virtues which balance this supposed shortcoming. To the same extent as people in the works of Poussin and Watteau – or indeed, of any other great master – Turner's figures can and usually do play a crucial role in his pictures, enforcing balance, scale and pictorial effect, whilst also externalising their precise human motivations. Yet although we can readily understand what compels Turner's men, women and children, and recognise their pictorial importance and expressiveness, this does not explain why those people frequently appear so deficient in form and lacking in 'refined' social qualities. With his acute powers of observation, enormous memory and painterly skills Turner could easily have created a more anatomically convincing or handsome human staffage had he wanted to. Surely the artist's many fine mature sketches of nudes, or of classical and modern statues, tell us that he had the power to do so. But without losing sight of the very real problems of figure-drawing, might it not be that Turner's 'failure' in this area resulted from conscious choice?

Certainly, if one judges how assiduously Turner studied the human form from the relatively few life drawings he made as a student that have come down to us in the Turner Bequest, one might conclude that he did not give such study much attention. And indeed, an early history of the Royal Academy, written within living memory of the artist, would seem to verify such a conclusion, for it tells us that Turner

> . . . did not follow out the prescribed course of teaching in the life and antique schools.[3]

Yet although Turner may not have been a very assiduous student, it is clear that he must have given the major part of his attention at the Schools to the analysis of antique casts, judging from surviving attendance books,[4] and this would seem to indicate that he destroyed most of his student exercises, for very few antique-cast drawings survive compared to the large numbers of drawings he must have made during the lengthy period he studied from the antique: Turner spent all his time in the Schools in 1790 and 1791 drawing from the antique and did not move on to draw from the live model until mid-1792. (However, he may even then have been disbarred from studying the female form, for the Schools regulations forbade male students under the age of twenty or unmarried to draw the female nude. But since discipline was lax at the time[5] he may have been able to evade the restrictions. And if he was disbarred from attending for some of the time until 1795, attendance would not have been difficult thereafter, especially after he was elected an Associate Academician in November 1799.) Perhaps Turner's involvement in life-drawing as a student was at its greatest in the winter of 1792–3, although the Academy attendance record books indicate that he went on occasionally frequenting the life class until near the end of 1793.

But even if Turner was not the most ardent student in the life schools during the 1790s, some of the extant figure drawings do demonstrate a ready comprehension and expression of the human form. For example, as a fairly typical life study of around 1797 demonstrates (fig. 184), the figure is well-modelled and convincingly proportioned, whilst the play of light across the form is felicitously rendered. In his maturity Turner made a great number of

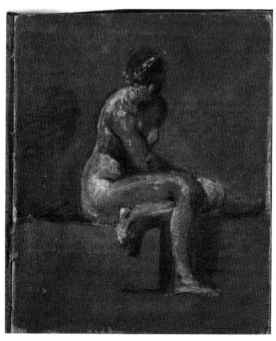

**184** *Seated nude*, p. 19 of the *Wilson* sketchbook,
T.B. XXXVII, *c.* 1797, Clore Gallery for the Turner Bequest, London.

**185** *The Deluge*, exhibited Turner's gallery 1805?,
oil on canvas, 14.3 × 23.5 cm, Clore Gallery for the Turner Collection, London.

sketches of nudes and figures (the nudes almost certainly when he was a Visitor in the R.A. Schools), and he employed these as the basis of the figures in his painted works. Sometimes he would even cut out such sketches, paste them onto paintings, and paint over them. And in a few paintings an unusual degree of accuracy in the way the figures are represented strongly suggests that Turner may even have occasionally employed a live model or models in his studio. For example, the figure of the eponymous priest in *Chryses* (fig. 136) appears to have been drawn from life. The detailing of the body, the rendering of the clothing and its shaping, the distribution of light and shadow, and the totally accurate grasp of the volume of the underlying form make it apparent that Turner certainly could portray the human figure as well as anyone when he particularly cared to. (One of the legs of this figure seems unusually elongated, however, but there may have been a pictorial reason for that exaggeration, as we shall see.) Similarly, in *The Deluge* (fig. 185), a picture painted around 1805, we again see people whose poses and representational qualities suggest that they were created from life. In particular, the depiction of the black[6] man heroically supporting the body of the unconscious girl on the right, suggests that this was the case. There are tell-tale indications that Turner had recourse to models here, in the obvious pinnings of the drapery covering the lower half of the black, and the exact and intricate modellings of the muscles of his back. Similarly, the girl who has fainted and the woman kneeling before her also seem entirely convincing in form, as do most of the other figures in the picture. Turner undoubtedly began this work around 1804 as a creative 'imitation' of Poussin's *Deluge*, which he saw in the Louvre in 1802, so it may be that he took unusual care over the figures in his *Deluge* because he wanted to equal the high standards set by Poussin in his version of this subject.[7]

Doubtless there may have been other pictures for which Turner used live models, and the attested recognition of actual people in works like *Frosty Morning* (B. J. 127) and *Crossing the Brook* (fig. 152), where one of the artist's daughters has been recognised, certainly makes it seem likely. But with these few possible exceptions, it is clear that Turner rarely painted from a live model. Indeed, except for two early self-portraits (B.J. 20 and 25) there is no incontrovertible evidence that he ever did so. Most of the figures that appear in his land- and seascapes were very obviously carried over from sketches made from the life or were the product of memory and imagination. Obviously the bother involved in setting a pose, and the time (and expense) it took, which could seriously limit or inhibit creative spontaneity, led Turner to take short-cuts in the creation of his figures. When one considers that even an artist as adept at figure representation as David Wilkie could spend up to a week simply looking for his models before devoting a long time to painting them,[8] one easily sees why Turner might have taken short-cuts. Moreover, just as he sought out the essentials of a landscape through memory and imagination, so too those faculties could have helped him to sort out and express the essential dramatic roles of the staffage. Yet although this method may suggest why Turner ended up with a less than convincing human staffage by notional standards of anatomical accuracy, it does not explain why he should have allowed such an 'infirmity' to exist and flourish, frequently doing little or nothing to correct it. He can hardly have been unaware of it, as exceptional works like *Chryses* and *The Deluge* would tend to prove.

Obviously there have to be other reasons that account for the 'awkwardnesses and errors' in Turner's figures. Turner's critic, Sir George Beaumont, may unwittingly have identified one of them to Joseph Farington in 1803, when he stated that

> Turner finishes his distances & middle distances upon a scale that requires *universal precission* throughout his pictures, – but his foregrounds are comparative *blots*, & faces of figures witht. a feature being expressed.[9]

Beaumont meant this as a condemnation but evidently Turner had anyway come to feel long before then[10] that by such inexactitude in his foreground figures and details a quality of appropriateness, immediacy and even movement could be conveyed which might otherwise be limited were those people and objects to be represented in more detail, and thus appear to be over-defined or too static.

**186**  *Bacchus and Ariadne*, R.A. 1840,
oil on canvas, 79 × 79 cm, Clore Gallery for the Turner Collection, London.

**187**  *Thomson's Æolian Harp*, Turner's Gallery 1809,
oil on canvas, 166.7 × 306 cm, City Art Galleries, Manchester.

Yet in passing Adrian Stokes put his finger upon another very appreciable and positive aspect of Turner's rendering of human forms, and even unknowingly touched on one of the main reasons for their frequent 'deformity':

> Turner could both record and improvise figures or groups in any attitude and in *a variety of styles* [italics mine].[11]

It is the latter talent which ultimately indicates that Turner *purposefully* created a distorted physiognomy and anatomy for a large segment of mankind, rather than simply arrive at them through ineptitude or psychological blockage. For even though Stokes did not explore the subject further, quite rightly he recognised that there is not just one type of Turnerian human figure but many. Exactly as the artist 'imitated' the styles of other painters when creating his land- and seascapes, so, too, he adapted their ways of portraying the figure to suit his own expressive needs. And because manifold stylisation was clearly a conscious creative process for Turner, and because through its dramatic and expressive use he makes it clear that he did not imitate the ways other artists had represented their figures simply for stylistic reasons, it is therefore possible to detect meaning in the way he imposed differing but precise characteristics upon the human form. By placing different types of stylised figures in different contexts Turner hoped to enhance the meanings of his works in a positive way. We are, in fact, witnessing yet another form of Turnerian association.

Most obviously these relationships are encountered in Turner's precise matchings of the artistic styles of his figures to the artistic styles of the pictures they appear in, and the painter was certainly not averse to stealing the forms of his figures from other artists. This can be seen most strikingly in Turner's *Bacchus and Ariadne* (fig. 186), exhibited at the R.A. in 1840, where he stole figures directly from Titian's picture of the same subject. The Titian was hanging by 1839–40 in the National Gallery which then shared the building in Trafalgar Square with the Royal Academy. Since Turner was a Visitor in the R.A. painting Schools in 1839, he may actually have painted his work next to the Titian in order to demonstrate the creative side of imitation to his students, for he reverses Titian's figures and jumbles up their relationships.[12] Certainly the copying of Old Masters played a central role in the training of students at the R.A. at the time, and indeed it was one of the major reasons the Academy came to be housed in the same building as the National Gallery after 1837.

No less obviously Turner also appropriated the figure-style of his favourite landscapist. For example, as Michael Kitson has noted, in overtly Claudian works such as *Macon* and *Thomson's Æolian Harp* (fig. 187, and detail fig. 188) we encounter elegant figures with 'swinging dresses, serpentine poses and tripping gait'. These figures are clearly based upon similar elongated figures by Claude, their 'attenuated forms [echoing] the tall, swaying trees occurring in the landscape'. Yet Turner did not introduce Claudian-type figures into

301

**188** *Thomson's Æolian Harp* (detail).

all of his Claudian-style pictures. Instead, he restricted them to works containing certain types of subject matter. As Kitson also remarks:

> He [Turner] seems to have considered Claudian figures to be appropriate almost exclusively to mythological subject-matter. He did not use them for religious subjects . . . or, which is more surprising, for scenes from ancient history; his 'Carthage' pictures, both from the 1814–17 period and the last year but one of his life, contain figures which bear only the vaguest resemblance to Claude's . . .[13]

This process of selection readily demonstrates how conscious Turner could be of both the stylisation of his figures and the need for some manner of aptness in their usage. The degree to which Claude projected stylisation rather than straightforward anatomical correctness in his figures, and increasingly so as he got older, did not escape Turner's notice and, indeed, may have contributed greatly to his desire to evolve a personal, perhaps even an equally idiosyncratic identity for his own figures.

Turner also matched the stylisation of his figures to the conscious stylisation of works painted in the manner of Van Dyck. In *Lucy, Countess of Carlisle, and Dorothy Percy's Visit to their Father Lord Percy, when under attainder upon the Supposition of his being concerned in the Gunpowder Plot* (B.J. 338), exhibited at the R.A. in 1831, as well as the contemporaneous *A Lady in Van Dyck Costume* (B.J. 444), Turner appropriated both the artistic manner of Van Dyck and the figures themselves directly from works by Van Dyck at Petworth where he may very well have painted the pictures.[14]

Human elegance of a similar power was assimilated by Turner from Watteau. The elegance and sensuality of many of Watteau's figures greatly appealed to him and one aspect of Watteauesque human form – the viewing of the bare shoulders, necks and heads of women from behind – was a physical feature that Turner especially emphasized. It can be

189 *Music at East Cowes Castle*, *c.*1827–46,
oil on canvas, 121 × 90.5 cm,
Clore Gallery for the Turner Collection, London.

190 *Two Women with a Letter*, *c.*1827–46,
oil on canvas, 122 × 91.5 cm,
Clore Gallery for the Turner Collection, London.

very clearly seen with the women in *England: Richmond Hill, on the Prince Regent's Birthday* of 1819 (fig. 169). The same stress on elegance and sensuality appears in other works created after that date, including another panoramic view from the same spot made in 1825 (w. 518), and it is dramatically apparent in works like *Music at East Cowes Castle* (fig. 189), which may have been begun in 1827 or 1832 but which was probably re-worked in the mid-1840s. This influence is equally to be seen in *Two Women with a Letter* (fig. 190) which may well have been painted and/or re-worked simultaneously. Quite naturally, Turner depicted women in Watteauesque dress and postures in his French scenes of the 1820s and '30s, obviously in order to capture associations of Gallic elegance. (His introduction into *Thomson's Æolian Harp* (fig. 188) of a Watteauesque young man may also be noted.)

Other artists also influenced the formation of Turner's figures or affected his attitude towards them. Naturally, at the beginning of the 1790s we can discern the influence of Thomas Malton Jr with whom Turner studied for possibly two or three years after 1789. Malton's influence makes itself felt by a certain elongated stylised elegance of the figures.

And Turner's thinking about staffage was stimulated by the marked influence of Michael Angelo Rooker around 1791–92. Rooker's impact was principally upon Turner's representation of building surfaces, the great tonal variety and patternings of stone and brickwork, plaster renderings, timbers and tiles that Rooker gives us (fig. 191) being assimilated by Turner who began to elaborate with great care, subtlety and ingenuity, a complex mosaic of tonal differences over the surfaces of his buildings. But along with this representational assimilation, Turner can hardly have failed to notice that Rooker habitually creates figures who possess an 'anti-heroic' quality, by which they 'act as a psychological counterweight to the architectural subject'. As Patrick Conner has also written, in terms almost as fully applicable to Turner as they are to Rooker, from this time onwards

> In the case of Rooker's pictures of antiquities, the powerfully built rustic figures, conspicuous and carefully drawn, are not simply observers, as are the elegant touring gentlefolk who are to be seen in many contemporary views: they are inhabitants, participators, possessors of the scene. Instead of directing the spectator's attention towards the antique subject, they bring that subject within their own terms of existence.[15]

As we have seen with a number of works in this book (i.e., *Borthwick Castle*, figs 1 and 2, and *Battle Abbey*, fig. 42) this is exactly what Turner does. Moreover, Rooker would sometimes take this 'anti-heroic' quality to extremes, populating the interiors of ancient buildings with the most mundane inhabitants in ways that Turner may have known.[16] Although in time Turner went on to elaborate and use the mundane quality of his figures for a higher purpose and for more pointed reasons than Rooker, nonetheless the notion of offering a dramatic counterbalance to imposing subjects may well initially have derived from Rooker. Some idea of the especial attraction that Rooker's work must have held for Turner is indicated by the fact that when he was still only a struggling artist of twenty-six, he obtained a batch of pencil sketches by Rooker at the auction following the artist's death in 1801, quite an unusual thing for Turner to have done unless he continued to feel strongly drawn to Rooker's work.[17]

Another type of Turnerian figure derives from Reynolds. We can perceive this particularly clearly in Turner's *Holy Family* (fig. 192) of 1803 where he modelled his figures more upon Reynolds than upon Titian from whom he had initially derived the idea for the picture. The clear prototypes for the protagonists were the softly-rounded figures of Reynolds's *Holy Family* of 1788 (fig. 193) which Turner could have seen prominently displayed in Macklin's gallery in 1790, the show in which Maria Cosway's *Lodona* (fig. 99) was also on view.[18] Reynolds's work was subsequently engraved by William Sharpe and published in 1793. Yet a wider-reaching assimilation of the style of Reynolds's figures can be detected later on in Turner's career, and would seem to stem from the particular

**191** Michael Angelo Rooker, *Battle Abbey*, signed and dated 1792, R.A. 1792,
watercolour, 41. 9 × 59.7 cm, Royal Academy of Arts, London.
Turner made copies of this drawing in the Academy exhibition (T.B. XVII-Q, R).

**192** *Holy Family*, R.A. 1803, oil on canvas, 102 × 141.5 cm, Clore Gallery for the Turner Collection, London.

**193** Sir Joshua Reynolds,
*The Holy Family with the infant St. John*, 1788,
195 × 146 cm, Tate Gallery, London.

**194** Sir Joshua Reynolds, *King George III*, c.1779,
oil on canvas, 274 × 183 cm,
Royal Academy of Arts, London.

influence of two pictures, Reynolds's portraits of King George III and Queen Charlotte, dating from 1778–80, which hung for the major part of Turner's career in the Council Room of the Royal Academy, to whom they still belong. These portraits demonstrate a degree of scumbling and glazing that is almost unique in Reynolds's output and which prefigure a similar technique we commonly encounter in Turner's work from the late 1820s onwards. There is also a swirling linearity to the portrait of the King (fig. 194), and a flattened modelling of the forms of his body, which again seems to have influenced Turner: some passages of Reynolds's painting could almost be from Turner's hand, so marked is the similarity of modelling, drawing, scumbling and glazing. As Turner must have spent a great many hours in the presence of these paintings it is perhaps not surprising that he should have emulated their technique and 'imitated' certain effects in them, as well as appropriated something of their modelling of the figure.

A more continuous influence on the shaping of Turner's figures was not Reynolds, however, but one of his own contemporaries. It is perhaps not surprising that Turner should have come under the sway of Henry Fuseli. As Professor of Painting at the R.A. between 1799–1805, and again between 1810–25, Fuseli was very active in propounding the Academic values previously upheld by Reynolds. Turner attended the lectures in which Fuseli emphasized the very qualities of imitation and the Ideal that Reynolds had praised, and Fuseli had been a Visitor in the R.A. life class in 1792 when Turner's attendance began, as well as in 1795, 1796, 1798 and frequently thereafter. Fuseli himself entertained high opinions of Turner's landscapes and his figures. Privately he called him 'the only landscape-painter of genius in all Europe'[19] and in 1801 he not only praised the 'Bridge-water Seapiece' (figs 208, 210) as the best picture in the R.A. Exhibition but emphasized that its figures were 'also very clever'.[20]

Turner's attraction to Fuseli arose from the fact that Fuseli was a profoundly dramatic painter, one as capable of creating theatrical pictorial effects as he was himself. Andrew Wilton has suggested a good reason for this attraction:

**195** *Kneeling Figure with upraised head and arm,*
*c.*1792, black, white and red chalk on brown
paper, 46.9 × 29.8 cm, T.B. XVIII-B, Clore Gallery
for the Turner Collection, London.

**196** Henry Fuseli, *Thor, in the boat of Hymir, battering*
*the Midgard serpent* (detail), 1790,
oil on canvas, 131 × 92 cm,
Royal Academy of Arts, London.

The Academy was dominated by artists who exploited histrionics and the history-painter who carried most conviction to his contemporaries [i.e. Fuseli] is the most explicitly theatrical of them all . . . But Fuseli could teach the young artist, in whatever field he worked, that exaggeration, to the point of utter fantasy, is a legitimate tool of expression. Turner must have studied with care the means by which the influential Fuseli achieved his results . . .[21]

Here Wilton puts his finger on one of Turner's essential motivations, for 'exaggeration, to the point of utter fantasy' was not only 'a legitimate tool of expression' but also a fulfilment of the requirement to express things dramatically as set out by the theory of poetic painting. Turner's responsiveness to theatricality might also have derived from a childhood spent in the theatre-conscious Covent Garden area (as Wilton points out) but it was a sensibility that must have been sharpened by contact with both Fuseli's art and his aesthetic concerns. Yet it was obviously not only Fuseli's commitment to a deeply imaginative and intensely dramatic poetic-historic painting that influenced Turner's work. The high level of expressiveness manifested by Fuseli's figures also clearly made a strong impression upon him. Its effect can most readily be appreciated in Turner's representations of women, especially nudes, although as some life drawings dating from between 1792–98 demonstrate,[22] the influence can also be detected in studies of the male nude. Indeed, the similarity between one of these male nudes (fig. 195) and the figure of Thor in Fuseli's Diploma picture of 1790 (fig. 196) is particularly striking.[23] The pose of Jason in both Turner's painting and mezzotint (fig. 38) is also very Fuselian.

One of the most obvious characteristics of Fuseli's depictions of women is their excessive curvilinearity, an emphasis that, as *The Nightmare* (fig. 197) of 1781 makes clear, the artist used as a means of heightening content, in this case the feeling of mental strain and sexual abandon. Yet the woman in *The Nightmare* can be considered static when compared

**197** Henry Fuseli, *The Nightmare*, R.A. 1781, oil on canvas, 101 × 217 cm, Detroit Institute of Art.

**198** W. Bromley after Henry Fuseli,
*Venus appearing to Ulysses*, 1803, engraving.

to many of Fuseli's other females. A swirling continuity of limbs and dress is a particular feature of such women (fig. 198) and we see this in many of Turner's women as well. For instance, the exaggerated, rounded forms of the Sibyl in *Æeneas and the Sibyl, Lake Avernus* (fig. 199 and detail, fig. 201) of 1798 demonstrate something of that curvature of line as do, much later and far more, the forms of almost all the women in *Vision of Medea* of 1828 (fig. 200). And perhaps nowhere in his many works does Turner's stylisation of human forms come closer to Fuseli than in *The Parting of Hero and Leander* of 1837 (fig. 203 and detail, fig. 202). Here the waving figures on the terrace and the embracing protagonists beyond them strike a particularly Fuselian note, as does the rhythmic interweaving of figures and architecture.[24]

**199** *Æneas and the Sibyl, Lake Avernus, c.*1798, oil on canvas,
76.5 × 98.5 cm, Clore Gallery for the Turner Collection, London.

**200** *Vision of Medea,* 1828, oil on canvas, 173.5 × 241 cm, Clore Gallery for the Turner Collection,
London. Note Turner's visual simile between the waving arms of Medea,
to the left of centre, and the branches of a distant tree, to the left.

**201** *Æneas and the Sibyl*
(detail).

**202** *The Parting of Hero and Leander*
(detail).

**203** *The Parting of Hero and Leander – from the Greek of Musæus*, R.A. 1837,
oil on canvas, 146 × 236 cm, National Gallery, London.

Moreover, Turner may have employed a subtle distortion of physiognomy and anatomy for metaphorical ends, pretty much as Fuseli did in both of his versions of *The Nightmare* and elsewhere. Fuseli was undoubtedly aware of a correlation between physiognomy and character, for he was a lifelong friend of Johann Kaspar Lavater whose widely-read *Physiognomische Fragmente* he illustrated. This was translated into English, accompanied by Fuseli's designs, under the title of *Essays on Physiognomy* between 1789–98. In his book Lavater propounds a direct relationship between individual appearances and inner character. Naturally he drew examples from art with which to illustrate his theory, finding correspondences between, for example, the personalities of Raphael's staffage and their forms, and those of Rembrandt and Hogarth, although in the case of the latter two artists Lavater deemed the correspondences to be ugly and evil respectively. Fuseli distrusted the idea of a fixed relationship between physiognomy and character in reality, but undoubtedly felt that some degree of correlation might actually exist, and that naturally any degree of correspondence was communicatively helpful. Turner may have followed him along these lines even as early as the 1790s when he first came into contact with Fuseli.

Clearly, one way in which an artist can create correspondences between outer form and inner character is by emphasising or distorting externals. Fuseli's frequent, instantly recognisable exaggerations and distortions could easily have led Turner to dramatically distort his own figures for similar dramatic and expressive ends. For example, in *Windsor Castle from the Thames* of around 1805 (detail, fig. 204), Turner seems to have purposely elongated the arm of a boatman pushing on his pole, the torso of his companion as he pulls on the rudder, and the arms of a bending shepherdess; this physical lengthening of the girl's arms may have been intended associatively to strengthen the idea that the shepherdess is protecting her sheep. A similar distortion for associative ends perhaps can also be seen in the figure of *Chryses* (fig. 136) where the leg of the priest resting behind him is unnaturally elongated, thereby augmenting the line which leads the eye up from the shadow at the bottom-right, along Chryses' wand, to the sun-god, thus emphasising the priest's act of supplication whilst also directing our attention towards the central power in the picture. Another, most Fuselian distortion can also be seen in *Calais Sands, Low Water, Poissards collecting Bait* of 1830 (fig. 205) where the neck of a bending 'Poissard' in the foreground is very evidently elongated in order to emphasise her tiredness as she leans over her work at the end of the day. The curvature of her body is subtly reinforced by a purely visual association, the creation of a similarly circular shape in the rounded shapes of the cloud-mass above and slightly to the left of her, and in the barrel on the right.[25] And whilst the ugly physical distortion of Scylla in *Glaucus and Scylla* of 1841 (fig. 138) undoubtedly reflects the fact that the poor nymph has already begun her metamorphosis, the extreme curvilinearity of her body again seems to draw directly upon Fuseli. Moreover, another aspect of Fuseli's portrayal of the human form clearly found expression in Turner's work.

**204** *Windsor Castle from the Thames* (detail), *c*.1805,
oil on canvas, 91 × 122 cm, National Trust, Petworth House.

**205** *Calais Sands, Low Water, Poissards collecting Bait*, R.A. 1830,
oil on canvas, 73 × 107 cm, Bury Art Gallery and Museum, Bury, Lancs.

This is the same kind of elongation of the bare female head and neck when viewed from behind that we see in the work of Watteau, although it is probable that Fuseli arrived at such forms independently. However, the representation of these features, and Turner's attraction to them, obviously heightened his identification with both Watteau and Fuseli.

If borrowings from Claude, Van Dyck and Watteau lent eloquence to Turner's renderings of figures, and Rooker, Reynolds and Fuseli added greater dramatic tension and point, then it was to an even more consummate painter of the human frame that Turner looked for other distinctive qualities.

Today Rembrandt is thought of as one of the most elevated painters of human appearances but in Turner's day the reverse was usually true. Indeed, many of Turner's contemporaries considered Rembrandt to be a painter of 'common nature' and of the most vulgar types of figures. For example, in the seventh Discourse, Reynolds followed earlier writers like de Piles and Jonathan Richardson in blaming Rembrandt for painting 'individual nature just as he finds it' instead of improving upon it as any self-respecting academic idealist should do. And Turner certainly also knew the opinion of Rembrandt formed by Martin Archer Shee whose *Elements of Art: A Poem* of 1809 he annotated and where (p. 214) Shee asked rhetorically: 'How are the magical effects of Rembrandt degraded by the gross vulgarity of his character, and the revolting deformities of his design?' John Opie also berated Rembrandt for his 'disgusting forms' (i.e. his figures).[26] Fuseli went even further, characterising Rembrandt's figures as 'swampy excrescences', 'uniform abstracts of lumpy or meagre deformity'.[27] Turner himself had a very high regard for Rembrandt's handling of light and shade but he was also undoubtedly aware of contemporary appraisal of the Dutch painter's 'vulgarity', for the vulgarisation of humanity is a marked feature of crowd-scenes he painted under the influence of Rembrandt, works like *Pilate washing his Hands* of 1830 (B.J. 332) or *Shadrach, Meshech and Abednego in the Burning Fiery Furnace* of 1832 (B.J. 346).

Turner was also responsive to the garb as well as the types of figures represented by other painters who were regarded as vulgarisers of the human form in his own day. This can especially be witnessed in his seascapes. Where the overall style of his early seascapes is concerned, he came under the thrall of Dutch marine-painting, particularly the influence of Ludolf Backhuizen, Jacob van Ruisdael, Willem van de Velde the Younger and Aelbert Cuyp. Yet it was not a Dutch but a Flemish painter who stands out as having stylistically affected the figures in these works.

David Teniers the Younger was enormously popular in Turner's day and was very well represented in British collections by the end of the eighteenth century. In Turner's immediate circle the Duke of Bridgewater, for instance, had bought a number of works by Teniers from the Orleans collection, whilst Benjamin West owned four pictures that he is likely to have seen.[28] Moreover, in the 1790s Turner was in contact with de Loutherbourg, who was unusually aware of Teniers' figures, as we shall discover shortly. Works by Teniers were also frequently engraved. A close friend and confidant of Turner's, James Holworthy, was not only quite possibly the owner of Watteau's *L'Isle enchantée*, from which Turner clearly derived a number of figures in the *Richmond Hill* of 1819, but he also owned over two hundred prints after Teniers, a collection that was described after his death as 'one of the finest in the Kingdom'.[29] Turner probably knew Holworthy by 1805, although the influence of Teniers upon Turner's figures can be seen well before then.

One of Teniers' standard personæ is a man wearing a flat Flemish cap, with a somewhat hunched back, who is seen from behind. Such a figure can be seen twice in a very typical engraving after Teniers of the kind that might well have been known to Turner (fig. 206). Here we see the man immediately to the right of the woman at the well, and another man who is dancing in the centre is also viewed from behind and again has a rather hunched back, above which appears an identical type of cap but without any discernible area of neck appearing. The combination of this type of figure, posture and cap can be witnessed literally dozens of times in Teniers' work, and far more so than in the pictures of any other Flemish or Dutch painter of the period. He is very much a stock character in Teniers' art. Other good examples appear in a typical painting of a *Kermesse* (figs 207, 214). Turner may have seen this painting when it came up for sale in London in 1794, or known the engraving made of it by Le Bas. There can be no doubt that he knew it by 1810, for it hung at Ashburnham Place in Sussex, which he visited and painted in that year[30].

This selfsame type of figure, usually seen from behind, who displays precisely the same high shoulders, and who is always wearing a flat *red* Flemish cap which appears low above the line of the shoulders (exactly like the man in the Teniers' *Kermesse*, figs 207, 214), can be witnessed in a number of Turner's seascapes from about 1800 onwards. He can be seen as

**206** P. L. Surugue after David Teniers the Younger, *Divertissements de Paysans Hollandais*, 1748, engraving (detail).

the helmsman of the main vessel in *Dutch Boats in a Gale* of 1801 (the 'Bridgewater Seapiece', fig. 208 and detail, fig. 210), as the helmsman of the foreign fishing boat which is taking evasive action to avoid ramming the incoming English packet in *Calais Pier* of 1803 (fig. 73), as the helmsman of the small boat in *Boats carrying Out Anchors and Cables to Dutch Men of War, in 1665* of 1804 (fig. 70), as a figure on the right of *A Coast Scene with Fishermen hauling a Boat ashore* of around 1803 (fig. 209 and detail, fig. 211), and as a figure seated in the central lifeboat in *The Shipwreck* of 1805 who seems strangely indifferent to his fate (detail, fig. 230). Most strikingly of all he appears standing with his hands behind his back at the right-centre of *Sun rising through Vapour; Fishermen cleaning and selling Fish* of 1807 (fig. 212 and detail, fig. 213). Indeed, this man seems to have been lifted directly from Teniers (compare him in the detail, fig. 213, with the man taking a similar stance on the left of Teniers' *Kermesse*, detail, fig. 214). Several of the men on the right and left of Turner's picture also wear Flemish dress and similar flat caps, whilst another figure wearing the same kind of headgear sits with his back to us on the pier at the right. Yet it was not just this one stance and type of person that derived from Teniers. In all of the marine-pictures by Turner we have cited, the influence of the lowlands painter can be discerned in the individuality of the figures, their rough characters being brought out by their raw, almost caricature-like exteriors.

That Turner did prize this quality of individuality in the figures of Teniers seems to be apparent from a statement he made regarding the Flemish painter in the sixth of his perspective lectures, the talk on 'Backgrounds':

> Without affecting to do anything, Teniers has given us that individuality, which the great genius of Rubens in his Flemish Fête and pastorals always seem'd in search of. Artfully arrang'd and exquisitely touched tho looking careless, bearing a freshness and silvery tone pervading everywhere thro' all the diversity of colours, tho' scattered upon the innumerable figures of the Flemish Marriage Feast at Louther Castle,[31] yet all the tones tend by his consummate management, concentrated, to one figure in white and grey which binds the whole together.[32]

Quite naturally Turner always reserved his highest praise for those painters whose observation and control of light accorded most nearly with his own, and his receptiveness to Teniers' subordination of tone to the production of a climactic effect is particularly noteworthy. Of equal value is his appreciation of the balance Teniers effected between the 'Artfully arrang'd and exquisitely touched' with the expressively 'careless': Turner the virtuoso always prized the insoucient painterly virtuosity of others. Yet above all it is the word 'individuality' in this quote which seems revealing, for quite clearly Turner was not using the word disparagingly in the Reynoldsian sense here, but as a means of praising the characterisation and quality of motivation in Teniers' figures. Given the way he places Teniers above Rubens in this respect, such a construction upon what he meant cannot be in doubt. And that Turner devoted a whole paragraph to Teniers in this lecture, whereas he

**207** David Teniers the Younger, *Kermesse*, signed and dated 1648,
oil on canvas, 115 × 178 cm, Staatliche Kunsthalle, Karlsruhe.

**208** *Dutch Boats in a Gale: Fishermen endeavouring to put their Fish on Board* ('The Bridgewater Seapiece'),
R.A. 1801, oil on canvas, 162.5 × 222 cm, Private Collection, UK.

**209** *A Coast Scene with Fishermen hauling a Boat ashore, c.*1803,
oil on canvas, 91.4 × 122 cm, The Iveagh Bequest, Kenwood.

**210** *Dutch Boats in a Gale*
(detail).

**211** *A Coast Scene with Fishermen*
(detail).

**212** *Sun rising through Vapour; Fishermen cleaning and selling Fish*, R.A. 1807, oil on canvas, 134.5 × 179 cm, National Gallery, London.

**213** *Sun rising through Vapour* (detail).

**214** David Teniers the Younger, *Kermesse* (detail).

**215** *The Unpaid Bill, or the Dentist reproving his Son's Prodigality*, R.A. 1808, oil on panel, 59.4 × 80 cm, Private Collection, USA.

**216** *The Unpaid Bill, or the Dentist reproving his Son's Prodigality* (detail).

lumped Cuyp, Paulus Potter and Adriaen van de Velde together in one following shorter paragraph, does not seem insignificant either.

In 1807 Turner began to compete with the painter whom Sir Walter Scott called 'The Teniers of Scotland'. David Wilkie had caused a sensation at the R.A. in 1806 with his Teniers-like *Village Politicians* and promised to do so again. Accordingly, in 1807 Turner stressed his own identification with Teniers in the staffage of pictures like the *Sun rising through Vapour*, and in more Teniers and Wilkie-like works such as *A Country Blacksmith disputing upon the Price of Iron* (B.J. 68). But although the emergence of Wilkie in 1806 may have intensified Turner's identification with Teniers after that time, and motivated him to produce a number of Teniers-like pastoral interiors, his leaning towards Teniers was undoubtedly apparent well before then in his marine pictures, the predominantly lowlands-orientated works he had created so far. And subsequently Turner used these Teniers-like people – albeit in contemporary dress and observing more local behaviour – in very un-Flemish rustic scenes, because those droll figures could be used to further sentiment. For example, in *Pope's Villa at Twickenham* of 1808 (fig. 9) there is a subtle but marked difference between the characterisation of the labourers discussing the fragments of the ruined house, the young couple who look on, and the fishermen on the right. Through a sly, Teniers-like emphasis of their clumsiness of character the labourers acquire a comic air that is both indebted to lowlands genre-painting and something that is particularly useful to Turner's moral, for it adds greatly to the irony of the situation: it is doubtful whether such 'rude mechanicals' can have read Pope but nevertheless they alone are immediately aware of the value of the precious building that is being destroyed.

A large number of Turner's works display the influence of Teniers after 1807, either in their choice of subjects, arrangement of objects and interior lighting, or in their Teniers-inspired figures. One picture in particular assimilates all of these elements, as well as testifies to Turner's wide acquaintance with Teniers' imagery. This is *The Unpaid Bill, or the Dentist Reproving his Son's Prodigality*, exhibited at the R.A. in 1808 (figs 215, 216). It shows the cluttered interior of a dental surgery, not unlike the many similarly cluttered interiors containing dentists, apothecaries, surgeons and alchemists painted by Teniers. Indeed, it is now thought that when Turner's picture was commissioned by Richard Payne Knight, it was to act as a pendant to another work Knight owned and believed to be by Teniers, *The Alchemist's Laboratory*.[33] Moreover, Teniers was also famous for his numerous anthropomorphic representations of monkeys, and in *The Unpaid Bill* we see a monkey immediately in front of the dentist, possibly to add satire to the work, for what dentist keeps a monkey, or even a parrot like the one on the left, in his surgery? In this context it is perhaps unsurprising that Turner also includes a few visual puns: upon the dentist's chair at the right he has fashioned a cushion to resemble the shape of a canine tooth, whilst the feet of a low bench in front of it, as well as the shapes of papers and jugs, all resemble molars. And Turner's title

**217** *Isis*, mezzotint engraving, Part XIV of *Liber Studiorum*, 1819, drawn and etched by Turner and engraved by W. Say. The design closely follows that of the painting entitled *The Thames at Weybridge* (B.J. 204) dating from around 1807–10.

**218** William Woollet after William Hogarth,
*Frontispiece to Joshua Kirby's 'Perspective of Architecture'*, 1761, engraving.

may also point to a satirical intent, for the picture could allude in a veiled way to the prodigality of the Prince of Wales, later Prince Regent and then George IV, who during the period in which this picture was painted was still a constant source of paternal and public dismay due to his prodigious spending and immense debts. Certainly Turner's references to an 'Unpaid Bill' and fatherly reproval of 'Prodigality' were very topical in 1808 and can hardly have been coincidental with what was then widespread public knowledge and concern, for the artist could have simply entitled the work something like 'The Dentist and his family' had he wished to avoid such a connection being made. Given that within just a few years Payne Knight was to publicly manifest a pronounced dislike of the Prince of Wales, the likelihood of this interpretation being correct seems almost certain.[34] If that is the case then the empty dentist's chair may symbolise the throne which was intermittently vacated by George III during his periodic bouts of insanity. Furthermore, the head and shoulders of the young man standing before his father are placed in front of a wall-mounted frame, which suggests that he is looking closely at himself in a mirror, an allusion to the notorious vanity of the Prince of Wales. Through the window the rough outline of a building not unlike Windsor Castle can also be seen.

It is not surprising that Turner identified with such a 'low-life' painter as Teniers, for he had been exposed to satirical imagery since childhood. Within a mile or so of his birthplace there were around two hundred satirical printsellers and publishers[35] operative between 1772–1810. Even in Turner's day the prints were not considered to be of an inferior nature; they were often regarded as pictorially valuable, highly sophisticated designs, incorporating all manner of visual puns, allusions and metaphors, especially when made by major artists such as Hogarth, Rowlandson and Gillray. Indeed, the first of these great satirists appears to have influenced Turner considerably, although the landscapist also assimilated qualities from Rowlandson,[36] as we shall see.

Turner may have been familiar with Hogarth's engravings and a number of his paintings. He most definitely knew Hogarth's writings, for some verses in a poetry notebook that Turner was using around 1808–09 refer to 'the line of Beauty',[37] a concept Hogarth developed in his book *The Analysis of Beauty*, published in 1753. Turner probably read the book in 1808 in preparation for the perspective lectures. In view of this quotation it is even possible to surmise that Turner's increasing use of subtle serpentine lines after about 1810 may have stemmed in part from Hogarth's much-derided notion that such lines are the major psychological source of our experience of beauty. And a painting by Turner that is now entitled *The Thames at Weybridge* (B.J 204), as well as a *Liber Studiorum* drawing and print of the same subject (fig. 217), all demonstrate a marked resemblance to Hogarth's Frontispiece for Joshua Kirby's *Perspective of Architecture* of 1760 (fig. 218) which Turner had also read in connection with his lectures between 1808–11, a period from which both the painting and drawing appear to date. Although in Turner's picture the opposite riverbank is quite different from Hogarth's scenery, and there is a far less elaborate foreground staffage, the locations of the circular rotundas are extremely similar in the pictures of both artists, as are the directions of the light. No less alike are the angles at which the model of Hogarth's 'new' architectural order and Turner's foreground sarcophagus lean; here, the similarity is so pronounced as to be beyond coincidence. Clearly, Hogarth's image filtered into Turner's imagination and was transformed into an inventive 'imitation'.

Nor is this the only connection that exists between Hogarth and Turner at this time. The influence of Hogarth upon the figures in *The Unpaid Bill* (fig. 215) has also been detected,[38] whilst the device of aligning a head with a picture-frame which appears in the work, perhaps to make a moral point concerning mirrors and vanity, was also used by Hogarth in *The death of the Earl* in the 'Marriage-à-la-Mode' series. Yet perhaps Turner's most obviously Hogarthian work is *The Garreteer's Petition* (fig. 219) which he exhibited at the R.A. in 1809. Clearly the picture was based upon Hogarth's *The Distressed Poet* and shows a poet similarly invoking the aid of the poetic muse whilst sitting in impoverished surroundings, even though Turner does not satirise his poet as Hogarth does, but presents him merely as someone in search of inspiration. The influence of Teniers and Wilkie upon the appearance of the garret in which the poet languishes can also be discerned.

Turner would undoubtedly have been easily capable of recognising the numerous visual puns and similes in Hogarth's work. In addition to sharing a penchant for this kind of visual play, Hogarth and Turner enjoyed other mutual enthusiasms as well. For example, in the sixth image of the 'Marriage-à-la-Mode' series, *The Death of the Countess*, above the

**219** *The Garreteer's Petition*, R.A. 1809,
oil on panel, 55 × 79 cm, Clore Gallery for the Turner Collection, London.

dying countess Hogarth places a Teniers-like picture of a flat-capped man seen urinating from behind. In 'The Four Times of the Day' set there is naturally a sense of appropriateness in the relationship of content to light, whilst Hogarth's manipulation of time in his *Before* and *After* pictures could conceivably have contributed towards Turner's creation of complementary images like the Carthaginian and Grecian pendants of 1815–17. Turner's watercolour of *Northampton* (fig. 220), made but not engraved for the 'England and Wales' series around 1831, is clearly linked to Hogarth's 'Election' series, the paintings of which were in the Soane collection. *Northampton* also shares much in common with Hogarth's picture of *The Industrious 'prentice Lord-Mayor of London*, for both works portray coaches being pulled through swirling election crowds.[39] In another image in the 'Industry and Idleness' series, to which this industrious apprentice picture belongs, Hogarth also shows the idle apprentice playing upon a grave, a dramatic situation which Turner may have restated in a somewhat different but related way in some of his watercolours. The idea of using ships' models to demonstrate the order of battle employed by Nelson at Trafalgar in *Yarmouth Sands* (fig. 47) could easily have derived from *Canvassing for Votes* (fig. 221) in Hogarth's 'Election' series, where two men argue over the tactics employed at the Battle of Portobello, using pieces of tobacco-pipe laid out in a semi-circle to demonstrate Admiral Vernon's manoeuvre at that battle. And naturally, Hogarth's frequent theatrical deployment of figures into left, centre and right-stage locations may also have influenced Turner.

It is wrong to regard Hogarth's art as merely comic. Instead, it reflects the painter's profoundly serious anger at the weakness, stupidity and vanity of mankind. This under-

**220** *Northampton, Northamptonshire*, winter 1830–1,
watercolour, 29 × 44 cm, Private Collection, USA.

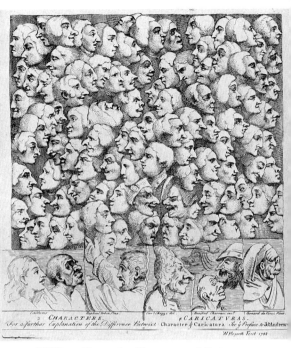

**221** William Hogarth, *Canvassing for Votes* (detail),
1757, etching and engraving.

**222** William Hogarth, *Characters and Caricaturas*, 1743,
etching (The subscription ticket
to 'Marriage-à-la-Mode').

current of anger compelled Hogarth to express himself satirically and it is that anger which still gives his art its cutting edge. No extraordinary powers are needed to recognise Hogarth's anger and we can be fairly certain that Turner, with his finely tuned emotional responsiveness and attitude of underlying pessimism towards the human race, was acutely aware of it. Moreover, he may have known that Hogarth intended his art to reveal the *inner* character of his persona, rather than merely satirise their external features. This difference was emphasized by Henry Fielding in the preface to his novel *Joseph Andrews* of 1742, to which passage Hogarth drew attention with the legend at the bottom of his subscription ticket to 'Marriage-à-la Mode' (where he also differentiated visually between character and caricature, fig. 222). In the preface Fielding first equates caricature in painting with burlesque in writing, and then distinguishes Hogarth's art from caricature:

> He who should call the Ingenious *Hogarth* a Burlesque Painter, would in my Opinion, do him very little Honour: For sure it is much easier, much less the Subject of Admiration, to paint a Man with a Nose or any other Feature of a preposterous size, or to expose him in some absurd or monstrous Attitude, than to express the Affections of Men on Canvas. It hath been thought a vast Commendation of a Painter, to say his Figures *seem to breath*; but surely, it is a much greater and nobler Applause, *that they appear to think*.[40]

326

In no small part this communication of the inner life of Hogarth's characters is effected by the way that their physiognomy reveals correspondent qualities in their nature. Indeed, one crucial element of Hogarth's genius as an interpreter of the human condition lay in his ability to find and express such correspondences with enormous insight and exactitude: looking at any person by Hogarth can immediately tell us what kind of underlying personality they enjoy. Whilst Turner never addressed himself to the diversity of mankind as did Hogarth, nonetheless it was just this principle of correlation between physiognomy and character that most mattered to him in the creation of his own figures, and it was a well-established principle in the art that was known to him.

Similar correspondences to those existing in Hogarth's works were also enacted, and often in landscape settings, by another painter who directly influenced Turner and who had himself come under the sway of Hogarth. Indeed, he may even have provided the link between Turner and Hogarth. This was de Loutherbourg. Soon after arriving in England de Loutherbourg produced a set of satirical prints entitled 'Caricatures of the English'

**223** N. Ponce after Philippe Jacques de Loutherbourg, *Men ditching*, 1773, engraving. The figure in the centre particularly demonstrates the influence of Teniers the Younger. The engraving was one of several illustrating Rosset's poem 'L'Agriculture', published in Paris in 1774.

**224** J. F. Foulquier after Philippe Jacques de Loutherbourg, *Un Archinoble Espagnol qui va faire Sieste pour aider la digestion*, etching, date unknown. The influence of Teniers upon the figure in the background is particularly marked.

which demonstrate the marked influence of Hogarth, as well as of Pier Leone Ghezzi, an early practitioner of caricature definitely known to Hogarth. And de Loutherbourg also most certainly knew the work of Teniers. In a number of de Loutherbourg's very early prints we find the same Teniers-like hunched men, viewed from the rear and wearing flat Flemish caps, that have already been seen frequently in Turner's marine pictures. For example, in the centre of a print dating from 1773 that shows men ditching (fig. 223), we see one of these figures, whilst in the background of an even earlier caricature (fig. 224) we again witness this type of man, standing with his hands behind his back in almost the exact pose of the prominent lone figure in Turner's *Sun rising through Vapour* (fig. 212). And in yet another caricature, of a country toy-seller (fig. 225), not only do we see just such a Teniers-like man sketched in the background, but at the bottom of the picture are drawn the same kind of variations upon 'deformity' that are to be found in Hogarth's subscription ticket to 'Marriage-à-la-Mode'. Such physiognomical variations could easily have derived from Hogarth, or even from similar portrayals by Annibale Carracci, at once an idealising figure-painter and a founding-father of modern caricature, whose views on the ability of caricature to reveal the underlying essence of human personality are placed at the head of this chapter.

**225** Philippe Jacques de Loutherbourg,
*A country toyseller*, etching, date unknown.
Note the figure in the background on the right.

**226** Philippe Jacques de Loutherbourg, *Travellers outside the Bull Inn, with a rainbow in the sky (The Rainbow)*, 1784, oil on canvas, 101.6 × 127 cm, Yale Center for British Art, Paul Mellon Collection.

Yet like Carracci, de Loutherbourg was capable of both profound earnestness and caricature, so that in his work we can witness the elaboration of very different kinds of character in the figures. These vary according to the seriousness of the images in which they appear. For instance, in his History pictures and battle pieces de Loutherbourg created fairly unstylised figures and emphasized their heroic qualities. Here there is little or no sense of anatomical or physiognomical deformation at all (for an example see fig. 96). In his topographical works, however, the figures are almost completely caricatured, as the artist stresses their clumsiness or physical crudeness (for an example see fig. 227). This near-satirical element clearly stemmed in part from de Loutherbourg's development of a new genre of painting which combined the serious, expressive representation of landscape with the ironic observation of mankind in the tradition of Hogarth. Here he forged a link between two entirely different areas of content in painting. Indeed, because a pair of such pictures were reproduced in the late 1770s through the polygraphic process by Matthew Boulton's picture manufactory in Manchester, de Loutherbourg became fairly well-known for this kind of imagery. These pictures are *A winter morning, with a party skating* and *A summer evening, with a view of a public road*. The complementary nature of their content is obvious from their titles alone and it would undoubtedly have appealed to Turner were he acquainted with the pictures. In these images de Loutherbourg brings together his serious responses to landscape and his humorous responses to mankind, satirising the figures to a marked degree (including possibly himself in the skating picture, a work that was copied by Rowlandson[41] when hanging in its original form in the R.A. in 1776). An even more expressive landscape appears in *The Rainbow* of 1784 (fig. 226) where the conjunction of seriousness and wit is again apparent, de Loutherbourg conveying a marked sense of satire through the characteristics of the boys and their dogs who harass a cat on a boat as it crosses the pond on the left, whilst some men and travellers look on at the right.

Whether Turner was familiar with these pictures is not known but he was almost certainly acquainted with de Loutherbourg's sets of topographical coloured aquatints entitled 'The Picturesque Scenery of Great Britain' of 1801 and 'The Picturesque and Romantic Scenery of England and Wales' of 1805[42]. Here once again the artist populates his landscapes with figures whose physiognomy projects caricature. This can be seen very typically in a view of Ramsgate (fig. 227) which was based upon a painting[43] dating from around 1785. There is no doubt that de Loutherbourg intended to convey the underlying character of these figures by such physiognomic and anatomical distortion, for he was demonstrably a painter who could draw and paint figures with absolute accuracy, likeness and seriousness when he wanted to. Since these pictures can have had no satirical purpose but were simply created as topographical works, they demonstrate how de Loutherbourg extended the human range of topographical pictures, as well as the range of humanity in

**227** William Pickett and John Clark after Philippe Jacques de Loutherbourg, *Entrance of Ramsgate Harbour*, coloured aquatint, Plate III of *The Romantic and Picturesque Scenery of England and Wales*, 1805. The same image was engraved earlier by J. C. Stadler and issued as Plate I of Loutherbourg's *Picturesque Scenery of Great Britain* and published in 1801 under the title of *Ramsgate in a high gale*. A painting of the same image dates from around 1785.

**228** *Sailors taking pigs on board a boat during a storm* (detail), *c*.1794, pencil, pen and brown ink and watercolour on paper, 21.6 × 27.5 cm, Clore Gallery for the Turner Collection, London, (T.B. XXIII-T). Note the extreme resemblance that Turner creates between the facial features of the boy on the left and the piglet he is holding.

them. Yet even before de Loutherbourg expressed such a satirical response to character via the figures in these published sets of engravings, the same qualities were apparent in individual reproductions of his works and in original pictures like those cited above, so the crude but purposeful qualities of de Loutherbourg's figures could have provided lessons for Turner in the 1790s when he is known to have been attracted to de Loutherbourg's work. Indeed, both in respect of his contribution to the development of topographical painting *per se*, and his development of human physiognomy in landscape settings, de Loutherbourg must have been a major influence upon Turner. It is not surprising that the young artist frequently called on him, or that Turner's high regard for de Loutherbourg continued: as late as 1833 he bought drawings by de Loutherbourg at auction, along with works by Dayes and Girtin who had also acted as important early influences upon him.[44] Nor is it surprising that Rowlandson was equally influenced by de Loutherbourg, given his own desire to place his humorous figures in straightforward landscape settings. Moreover, Turner was also attracted to Rowlandson's work, for in a number of early drawings we can perceive the marked influence of that artist as well. It can be detected in pictures like *Sailors taking pigs on board a boat during a storm* (fig. 228), a watercolour dating from about 1794, and in other sheets in the Turner Bequest from about the same time, like *Fishermen on a Stormy Shore* (T.B. XXIII-w) and a study of fishwives, boats and carts (T.B. XXIII-Y). Turner's apparent identification with Rowlandson shows that in the early 1790s he was experimenting with the creation of a characterful physiognomy for his figures, and this supports the view that the caricatural distortion frequently encountered in his later work was intentional. And of course Turner's identification with Rowlandson may have led to, or reinforced his identification with de Loutherbourg himself.

Thus there were two vital processes in de Loutherbourg's art which were probably of great import to Turner. These were the matching of the level of seriousness in a given subject with the serious treatment of the figures or, alternatively, the emphasis of the seriousness of a landscape by contrasting it with the comicality of the figures. The latter approach achieved a major augmentation of the dramatic range of a picture. And such an augmentation was very necessary to Turner, for it paralleled and supported a larger process that was of central importance to him, namely the profound expansion of the entire cultural and artistic range of landscape painting upon which he was anyway embarked. In order to achieve such an expansion Turner clearly called upon every means available to him, and one was the manipulation of the style or styles of his figures.

This leads us to the basic question of whether Turner's allegedly weak figures were intentionally arrived at by the artist. The answer seems clear. We have discerned already that Turner was emphatically aware of the need to match light to the central dramatic subject or theme of a picture. And this keen sense of decorum is the clue to much else in Turner, for it would not have been limited to the distribution of light-effects. It is utterly impossible that Turner was unaware of the need to match the appearance, demeanour, social status and emotional responses of his figures to the underlying content of the pictures in which they appear, for this appropriateness was given far more stress in the doctrine of *ut pictura poesis* than any concern with the matching of light-effects to dramatic content, being virtually the entire theoretic meaning of the term decorum itself. We can therefore be completely certain that Turner purposely created the crudeness and 'doll-like' appearance of his figures, if not even that he thought of such crudity as being compatible with decorum. And an essential component of the artist's outlook suggests both that he did consciously choose to ignore the demands of the concept of *ut pictura poesis* regarding the representation of man as an idealised physical type and why he did so, instead preferring to 'deform' mankind out of conviction. This is the fact that one simple moral relationship can be constantly witnessed throughout Turner's work: the contrast between the imperfection of man and the perfection of external nature, between our essential vanity and vulnerability, frequent physical ugliness, insignificance and mortality, and the power, beauty, immensity and eternal renewal of the world around us. Turner might diminish this contrast by making his figures a degree less ugly or more heroic but he rarely dispensed with it altogether, for as

**229** *The Shipwreck*, Turner's Gallery 1805,
oil on canvas, 170.5 × 241.5 cm, Clore Gallery for the Turner Collection, London.

far as man is concerned it is the fundamental dramatic statement of his entire art. The physical 'deformity' of our species was clearly not rejected by Turner; instead, he exaggerated it, for by that means he could greatly extend the moral value and emotional range of landscape painting. To this end he evolved his own typical kind of figure from an amalgam of sources, but principally Fuseli, Teniers, de Loutherbourg and Rowlandson. At the same time he went further than de Loutherbourg in the matching of figure-types to types of subject by employing artistic association to broaden the concept of decorum in the creation of figures, through directly reproducing the figure-styles of other artists as well. Here is surely the ultimate cause of the stylistic diversity of the figures in Turner's work.

It is not difficult to comprehend how such a diversity could serve Turner's artistic ends. For example, in *The Shipwreck* of 1805 (fig. 229 and detail, fig. 230), we can see that the Teniers-like character of the figures greatly extends the impact of the picture. Unless we consider these people to be mere stylistic or associative exercises in the manner of Teniers – which hardly allows Turner any genuine dramatic purpose in the work at all – then we are forced to recognise that the moral, emotional and dramatic range of the picture is pushed to the limit by the extreme contrast Turner effects between the humble, even crude character

**230** *The Shipwreck* (detail).

of the victims of the storm, and the terrifyingly awesome context in which they appear. After all, the artist could just as easily have portrayed noble-looking figures sporting a variety of heroic postures in such a surround. But obviously he made them as he did because of both his dramatic sensibility and his love of truth: shipwrecks are not noble or heroic events, even if they do call forth qualities of nobility and heroism; they are terrible, painful tragedies and Turner clearly realised that such a tragic sensibility could be greatly furthered by making the victims of his catastrophe look as un-heroic as possible. How better to convey the fear and primal state of childlike dependency that we often become subject to when we are confronted by threatening events beyond our control than by fashioning a staffage which is primitive and childlike. For such Teniers-like 'deformed' human beings seem immensely vulnerable; heroic figures do not. And our vulnerability is quite obviously the essential human message of *The Shipwreck*, as indeed it is of a great many of Turner's other pictures.

In this connection Turner's views on the dramatic relationship of the sublime and the ridiculous are highly pertinent. In his *Cockermouth* sketchbook, which was in use in 1809, Turner noted some remarks of Tom Paine's in *The Age of Reason*, wherein Paine had stated that

> The sublime and the ridiculous are often so nearly related that it is difficult to class them separately. One step above the sublime becomes ridiculous and one step above the ridiculous makes the sublime again.[45]

Clearly, in pictures like *The Shipwreck* Turner brought together the sublime, as represented by the immense power of the elements, and the ridiculous, as seen in the pathetic attempts of mankind to deal with those elements, a wholly moral contrast. What better means was

334

there at Turner's disposal to portray human ridiculousness than by 'deforming' his staffage, in the same way that 'low' painters such as Teniers and Hogarth had done. It is clear that the caricature-like physiognomies and anatomical deformities in *The Shipwreck* are in no way the result of an inability to draw. Even a cursory inspection of the painting reveals that Turner went to considerable trouble in painting these people, for they are extremely detailed and skilfully modelled: quite obviously the artist *wanted* to make his staffage look absurd. Moreover, the frequent crudeness of both his assimilated and his own types of figures could intrinsically serve a further vital end as well, for it could easily express the artist's regard for mankind on the social level: by means of these caricatured figures Turner could comment upon the ignorance, incomprehension and brutalised physical development of the greater mass of mankind at a time when education, the refinement of manners and healthy physical development were the privilege of only a comparative few. Turner represented men and women like this quite clearly because essentially that was how a great number, if not *all* of us appeared to him because of his moral view of the vanity of mankind, exactly as we had been viewed by Teniers, Hogarth and de Loutherbourg in such a socially detached manner. Turner was well aware of the realities underlying most human life in his day and gave them forthright expression, whilst also proclaiming the infinitesimally small part that we play in the universal scheme of things. Of course he did not literally perceive such miscellaneous human oddities on his travels, although he did explore some of the more socially deprived parts of Europe. By representing the people he saw in this way he was creating an outer form that could reveal an inner quality of character which could not otherwise be portrayed. Indeed, he was simply doing what he had perceived other artists had done in order to display their conceptions of underlying human character. When Turner wanted a beauty of human form in certain types of pictures he would look to Claude for a suitable kind of figure; through both association and their intrinsic elegance these people could greatly advance his purposes as far as the communication of feeling and content are concerned. Similarly in other kinds of pictures he would look to Fuseli or Watteau, or whoever. When he wanted the maximum physiognomical or anatomical rectitude he could even employ models, as perhaps he did in *The Deluge* (fig. 185) and elsewhere. But in most cases he preferred to state the 'deformity' of mankind. We may reasonably conclude that for the most part Turner's figures are doll-like and 'vulgar' not because the artist was unable to draw the human figure, or because he did not wish to take the same time over his figures that he did over the often far more intricate forms of his land- and seascapes, nor because he suffered from some psychological blockage vis à vis his fellow human beings, but quite simply because that was how he wished to show us. Turner's 'comic' figures were his way of commenting upon the human comedy itself. It is only our failure to recognise the basic Turnerian contrast between man and the external natural world that has blinded us to this comment.

And by creating an absurd, generalised type of mankind Turner did project an archetype, albeit one at an opposite physical remove from the type of divine or semi-divine figure that Reynolds and his predecessors had called for. Most certainly God did not create man in his own image to Turner. For someone as convinced as he was that man is merely a small part of creation and not the lord over it, that could not be the case. Rather than transcend the ugliness of mankind, Turner embraced it, so as to widen his art and to say something about the human condition, just as Teniers, Hogarth and de Loutherbourg had done. Turner *did* state what for him was the essential in man. And this was surely the main reason he refused to follow the injunction of *ut pictura poesis* to create an archetypal beauty of human form. Reynolds and the other exponents of poetic painting had advocated the representation of imagined and/or synthesised models of perfect physical beauty of the kind that earlier artists such as Phidias, Praxiteles, Zeuxis, Michelangelo and Raphael gave us. But if Turner had done so not only would he have severely compromised what for him were the fundamental statements of man's moral and physical place in the universe; he would also have compromised his expression of the essential fact of our social existence. This is because, to judge by his work, for Turner human life rarely enjoyed the advantage of being beauteous: even though it had its comic side, it was frequently dangerous, usually impoverished and almost always filled with toil. Instead, Turner went beyond the central tenet of *ut pictura poesis*, disregarding the call for an ideal beauty of human form in quest of some different and more profound ideality of our existence. For sure he wanted to reveal the essence of things, but human life as it is in all its fullness of experience, not simply how it looks on some imagined, materially perfect physical plane. Moreover, by intentionally representing the crude features most common to common mankind Turner also encompassed something more: he cast his net socially over the greatest range of humanity, thereby achieving the related idealistic goal of maximum generality, whilst depicting mankind in the widest behavioural terms. By these means he created our archetype. It may be an inverted archetype but it is an archetype nonetheless. With their simplified features and apparent crudity of being, how can we fail to recognise Turner's models of humanity for ourselves?

Certainly no contradiction exists in Turner's moralistic view of our species: he was in no way anti-human. The artist just regarded the human within a larger perspective (as do all great idealists), and celebrated every aspect of it, from the tragic and joyous, to the noble-minded and bawdy. Yet above all the painter remained a moralist whose poetic and prophetic sensibilities supplied a framework of ultimate things. Beyond doubt that moral perspective made him feel that man is fundamentally vain and foolish, with our self-deluded 'fallacious' pretensions of 'hope', as though God and the whole universe revolve around us. Turner wanted to point up such hubris. His 'weak-looking' figures were the supreme and most direct means available to him of ironically underlining that immense vanity.

Occasionally, as in *Crossing the Brook*, he stressed what we share physically with external nature. He might even depict our strength in standing up to our surroundings, as in *Borthwick Castle*. But more frequently the painter emphasized the strong contrast between man and the external world, for increasingly he took a tragic view of human existence, and made use of external nature to intensify that sense of tragedy. The moral point of such utterance is heightened, not diminished, by the ever-greater beauty and radiance with which he surrounds us.

The theme that 'all is vanity' is hardly an original one in western art but it governed Turner's view of mankind. And this is not conjecture but something that the artist expressed in concrete ways. It can be witnessed in the subjects and contents of a great many pictures, in the very title of 'The Fallacies of Hope' that he gave to the disparate fragments of verse which he appended to the titles of pictures between 1812–50, as well as very frequently in the poetic fragments and titles themselves. In addition, his interconnected depreciation of our physical smallness in relation to the world can also be confidently deduced. Evidence of such thinking may be found in a draft for the very first of his perspective lectures. Whilst examining the effect that vertical lines and the dominating height of ruins may have upon our imagination, Turner stated his awareness of human limitations quite explicitly:

> . . . however colossal man may be in interlect he must draw some scale of his inferiority and in the words of Rousseau feel all the "littleness of man" before the immense fragments of marble . . .[46]

Turner constantly drew the scale of our inferiority by the way he represented us, and not merely in relationship to our own architectural ruins and other 'Fallacies of Hope': throughout his art the immensities of mountains, seas and skies constantly point up all the 'littleness of man' in far greater terms.

In sum, then, Turner's weak-looking figures were overt metaphors for the human condition itself. Their creator was a profound moralist and humanist, as well as arguably the greatest landscape painter ever. The moralist, the humanist and the landscapist were one, however, being subsumed within Turner the idealist, and the humanism found its most vital, complete and subtle expression in a crucial aspect of Turner's work that has historically either been lost, ignored or misunderstood, namely the process of imaginative association. From his twenty-second year, if not before, the artist embarked upon an analysis of the relationship of painting to literary forms and ideas because he wanted to imbue landscape painting with the same degree of complexity regarding the statement of internalised human thoughts and responses that literature and poetry usually express. By doing so he could also elevate the cultural status of the genre. From 1808–11 he augmented this search by identifying or re-identifying with the concept of the Ideal which formed the foundation of the doctrine that urged this identification between painting and literature. As a result he not only elevated his expression of the internal world of man onto another plane but, perhaps more importantly, did the same for landscape, imbuing all the forms and phenomena outside of man with an intensified sense of beauty that enjoys as its basis the expression of essentials. By this means he took us to the very heart of things as far as the world that surrounds us is concerned. And eventually he imparted this ideal quality to everything beyond man, including light which he considered to be a divine emanation. Only man struck Turner as less than perfect and he stressed this essential imperfection through his figures. Yet if the pessimism he was prey to gave him his ultimate human measure of things, within that perspective he explored every aspect of human experience and it is this, as much as his celebration of the beauty and power of external nature, that gives his art its ever-increasing relevance to mankind.

The concept of poetic painting, along with the pictorial, aesthetic, moral, physical, imaginative and associative considerations it gave rise to, therefore stands at the very centre of Turner's art. That concept also harnessed the artist's political, social and prophetic sensibilities as well, for these bore no less crucially upon the formation of his pictures and imagery. In order to justify these conclusions we have had to traverse a vast landscape, one made broader by the need to establish that Turner did not use association in a cultural vacuum but as part of a long and well-hallowed tradition in landscape-painting. Turner's contribution to that tradition was huge, even if it is not much recognised today. We must simultaneously step backwards historically and forwards imaginatively to be able to explore that realm to the full, as we need to. Only then will we be able to recognise that this by no means neglected genius is even more immense in creative stature than perhaps we ever suspected.

# Afterword and Acknowledgements

> There is something very strange and sorrowful in the way Turner used to hint only at these under meanings of his; leaving us to find them out, helplessly, and if we did *not* find them out, no word more ever came from him. Down to the grave he went, silent. 'You cannot read me; you do not care for me; let it all pass; go your ways.'
>
> *John Ruskin, 1856*

AS the reader will doubtless long ago have realised, a fundamental contradiction lies at the very heart of this book. Turner wanted *you* to guess his meanings, not someone acting on your behalf; anyone who undertakes an explication of his work must do so at the expense of subverting the artist's stated intentions. *Mea culpa.* My only justification for assuming this role is that hopefully it will inspire others to make the necessary associative connections in the vast number of pictures which have not yet been dealt with, or further apposite ones in those that have.

I wish especially to thank three people who have been of particular help to the writing of this book. The first is John Gage. In addition to the vital contribution his published work has made to the development of the book, I also owe him an immense amount on a personal plane, for he has never made me feel that my intellectual insufficiencies were irredeemable and, indeed, has always endeavoured to correct them with great patience and tact. He read both the penultimate and final drafts of the book with extraordinary thoroughness, and his many suggestions have made a major contribution to the final results (although I take full responsibility for any deficiencies in those results). I cannot adequately express my gratitude to him for his help and interest, both of which greatly sustained me over the three and a half years it took to write this book.

I must also single out Nick Robinson for gratitude. He encouraged me to undertake the project and set in motion the finding of a publisher for it. To him, too, I am grateful for the initial impartation of any basic writing skills I may possess, and my debt is therefore a continuing one.

And on a practical level I wish to express my gratitude to Steve Bury, the librarian of Chelsea School of Art, London. He has borne my constant bombardment of requests for books and other material over this long period with endless patience, and been of the utmost usefulness in tracking down the most obscure matter at all times and without ever questioning its relevance.

I must also thank Professor Michael Kitson of the Paul Mellon Centre for Studies in British Art, London, for making available the considerable resources of that institution; the particular interest he has taken in this book has proven especially encouraging. I should equally like to thank Mrs Evelyn Newby of the Mellon Centre for her great help in garnering photos for the book.

Others whom I must thank are Martin Butlin, the Keeper of the Historic British Collection of the Tate Gallery for allowing me to make study-photographs which have been of great value in interpreting various works, and for his immediate and invariably helpful replies to all my queries; Andrew Wilton, the Curator of the Clore Gallery for the Turner Collection, London, for exactly the same reasons; Evelyn Joll and Sue Valentine of Messrs Thomas Agnew and Sons, Ltd, for help in obtaining photographs of works in private collections and for assisting me in perusing books from Turner's library still in the Turner family collection; Mrs Rosalind Turner; David Posnett of the Leger Galleries; Reginald Williams of the British Museum Department of Prints and Drawings and his staff; Brian Allen of the Paul Mellon Centre for Studies in British Art; Dr Francis Ames-Lewis, Professor A. G. H. Bachrach, John Bird, Rodney Burke, William Chubb, Jane Churchill, Carole Conrad, Robert Cumming, Martha Mel Edmunds, Michael Kauffmann, Paul Goldman, Professor E. H. Gombrich, Professor Louis Hawes, Adele Holcomb, Charles Hope, Sidney C. Hutchison, Denis Mahon, Barbara and Don Malin, Professor John McCoubrey, Hector Medora, Peter van der Merwe, Ruth K. Meyer, John Munday, Edgar Munhall, Constance-Anne Parker, Dr Nicholas Penny, Cecilia Powell, Grace Ritchie, Professor Eric Sams and F. Eldon Smith (the very best of headmasters and history teachers); Anne Tennant, Stanley Warburton, Henry Wemyss, Dr Selby Whittingham, Robert and Edward Yardley, and Patrick Youngblood, who has also proven a fount of readily accessible knowledge on a great number of occasions. Equally I am indebted to Professor Jerrold Ziff, not only for his personal encouragement but also indirectly for his work. Although I may differ in my conclusions, nonetheless his essay on Turner's thought processes between 1798–1800, and even more so his earlier essay on Turner's connection of painting with poetry, made seminal contributions to the development of this book.

Thanks must be accorded to Barry Venning and Nicholas Reese, both of whom read the manuscript and made useful suggestions for improving it. I owe an especial debt of gratitude to Helen Fraser of William Heinemann for at long last cutting through the Gordian knot of problems concerning the publication of the book, and Faith Evans for aiding her in doing so. Roger Smith of Heinemann has also been unfailingly helpful, and Elisabeth Guss did much valuable work copy-editing the book. I must also thank Tony Kitzinger both for designing the book and for keeping his eyes open for errors and improvements whilst doing so. Jane Cocking typed the manuscript with indefatigable patience and efficiency, and Jacky Darville has been, is, and ever shall be my supreme source of strength. Finally, and most importantly of all, I must thank my two children, Anna and Mark, who have been denied a great many juvenile tricks whilst 'the Turner book' prevented me from fully exploring the landscapes of their childhood.

*Acton,*                                                                                                     *E.S.*
*January 1985*

# Short Chronology
## of Turner's Life and Works

Due to the need to discuss works out of their chronological sequence in this book, the following short chronology might help the reader to establish a sequential framework for the pictures discussed in the text. For purposes of space many of the picture titles have been abbreviated. All works are in oils unless stated otherwise and the following conventions are used: w denotes watercolour, E indicates engraving and *L.S.* signifies *Liber Studiorum*. A question mark after a title denotes that the exact date of the work is uncertain.

WORKS DISCUSSED IN THIS BOOK

**1775** **23 April** Joseph Mallord William Turner born at 21 Maiden Lane, Covent Garden, the son of a wig-maker and barber.

**1787** First signed and dated watercolours, some made in and around Margate.

**1789** Probably begins studying with Thomas Malton Jnr at around this time.
**11 December** admitted as a student at the R.A. Schools.

**1790** Exhibits first work at the R.A., a watercolour of *The Archbishop's palace, Lambeth*.

**1791** Travels through the West Country, visiting Bristol and Bath etc.

**1792** Visits southern and central Wales. Attends Life Academy regularly in latter half of year.

**1793** **27 March** awarded the 'Greater Silver Pallet' for landscape drawing by the Society of Arts.

**1794** Publication of first engraving from one of his drawings. First tour of Midlands. Also forays into north Wales. Begins attending the 'Academy' of Dr Monro on winter evenings, along with Girtin and others, to copy drawings by J. R. Cozens and other artists at around this time, and continues to be so employed for about three years.                     *Sailors taking pigs on board*, w.

**1795** Tours southern England and south Wales.

**1796** First oil-painting at the Royal Academy.     *Fishermen at Sea*; *Oak Tree, Hampton Court*, w.

**1797** Tours north of England and Lake District.     *Elgin Cathedral, Morayshire*, E.

**1798** Tours Wales extensively.

*Æneas and the Sibyl*;
*Morning amongst the Coniston Fells*;
*Dunstanburgh Castle*; *Buttermere Lake*;
*Fountains Abbey*, w; *Norham Castle on the Tweed*, w.

**1799** **May** sees Altieri Claudes at William Beckford's house in London. Probably studies the Earlom *Liber Veritatis* at around this time.
**August–September** stays three weeks with Beckford at Fonthill, enjoying further opportunity to study Altieri Claudes.
**September–October (?)** visits Lancashire and North Wales.
**4 November** elected an Associate of the Royal Academy.

*Harlech Castle*; *Battle of the Nile*;
*Caernarvon Castle*, w with verses from Mallet;
*Morning, from Dr. Langhorne's Visions of Fancy*, w;
*Warkworth Castle*, w.

**1800** First verses by Turner himself appended to titles of pictures in the R.A. catalogue.

*Dolbadern Castle, North Wales*;
*Caernarvon Castle, North Wales*, w; *Fifth Plague of Egypt*.

**1801** **June–August** first tour of Scotland, returning through the Lake District.

*Dutch Boats in a Gale* ('The Bridgewater Seapiece').

**1802** **12 February** elected Royal Academician. First visit to France and Switzerland, studies in the Louvre in Paris, sees Poussin's *Deluge* and Titian's *St. Peter Martyr*.

*Fishermen upon a Lee-Shore*;
*Jason*.

**1803** Serves on the R.A. Council during stormiest year in Academy's history.

*Macon*; *Calais Pier*; *Holy Family*;
*Coast Scene with Fishermen* (?);
*Fishing Boats entering Calais Harbour* (?);
*Glacier and Source of the Arveron*, w.

**1804** **15 April** death of Turner's mother after long mental illness.
**April** completes own gallery in Harley St. Stays regularly at Sion Ferry House, Isleworth, either in this year, or by next.

*Boats carrying out Anchors*.

**1805** **May** first exhibition held in Turner's Gallery at 64 Harley Street, closes 1 June.

*The Shipwreck*; *The Deluge* (?);
*Windsor Castle* (?).

**1806** Exhibits two oils at the opening exhibition of the British Institution. Stays at Knockholt, Kent, with W. F. Wells who suggests the *L.S.* project.
**October** takes second house at Hammersmith.

*Windsor Castle from the Thames* (?).

**1807** **11 June** first part of *L.S.* appears. Probably visits Sussex in summer.
**2 November** elected R.A. Professor of Perspective.

*Sun rising through Vapour*;
*The Thames at Weybridge* (?);
*Willows beside a Stream* (?);
*Northwest Front, Cassiobury* (?), w;
*Jason, L.S.*

**1808** **July** visits Tabley House, Cheshire, and forays into Wales. First visit to Farnley Hall, the home of his great friend and patron, Walter Fawkes.

*Pope's Villa at Twickenham*;
*The Unpaid Bill*.

**1809** Visits Petworth House, Sussex for first time. Also revisits Farnley and does so again almost every year until 1824.

*Thomson's Æolian Harp; Trout Fishing in the Dee; The Garreteer's Petition; Scarborough Castle,* w.

**1810** Visits Sussex to make drawings to be engraved on behalf of John Fuller, M.P. Also occupies house in Queen Ann St.

*Battle Abbey,* w; *Wreck of a Transport Ship* (?).

**1811** **7 January** first perspective lecture at the R.A.
**July–September** visits West Country to obtain material for 'Southern Coast' series. Gives up house in Hammersmith, stays at Sun Ferry House, Isleworth before building house at Twickenham.

*Mercury and Herse; Chryses,* w; *Martello Towers near Bexhill,* L.S.; *Scarborough Town,* w.

**1812** First quotation from Ms. poem 'Fallacies of Hope' in R.A. catalogue.

Frontispiece design of *Europa and the Bull,* L.S.; *Procris and Cephalus,* L.S.; *Winchelsea, Sussex,* L.S.

**1813** Completes Solus (later Sandycombe) Lodge, Twickenham.
**August** makes second tour of West Country, staying principally in Plymouth, again in connection with the 'Southern Coast' series.

**1814** **June** visits Portsmouth to sketch Review of the Fleet.

*Apullia in Search of Appullus; The Mew Stone at the entrance of Plymouth Sound* (?), w.

**1815** Tours Yorkshire, summer.

*Dido building Carthage; Crossing the Brook; Battle Abbey, the spot where Harold fell* (?), w (E pub. 1819).

**1816** **July–September** tours north of England to gain material for the 'Richmondshire' series.

*Temple of Jupiter Panellenius restored; View of the Temple of Jupiter Panellenius; Entrance of Calais Harbour,* L.S..

**1817** **August–September** visits Belgium, the Rhine between Cologne and Mainz, and Holland. Returns via County Durham and Farnley.

*The Decline of the Carthaginian Empire; The Field of Waterloo* (?), w; *Bay of Naples (Vesuvius in repose)* (?), w; *Simmer Lake, near Askrig,* (?) w; *Aske Hall* (?), w; *Moss Dale Fall* (?), w; *Bridport, Dorsetshire* (?), w. *Borthwick Castle* (?), w.

**1818** **October–November** visits Edinburgh to discuss illustrating Scott's 'Provincial Antiquities'.

**1819** **April–June** Walter Fawkes publicly exhibits over sixty of Turner's watercolours at his London residence (and again in 1820).
**August–1 February** (1820) First trip to Italy, visits Turin, Como, Venice, Florence, Rome, Naples, returns via Switzerland.

*England: Richmond Hill, on the Prince Regent's Birthday; Isis,* L.S..

**1820** Enlarges Queen Ann Street house.

*Rome from the Vatican; Temple of Minerva Sunias, Cape Colonna* (?), w; *Cologne,* w.

**1821** Visits Paris, Rouen, Dieppe, etc.

**1822 August** visits Edinburgh for George IV's
State Visit.

**1823** Commissioned to paint *The Battle of*
*Trafalgar.*

*Bay of Baiæ;*
*Wycliffe near Rokeby,* E (w dates from *c.* 1816);
*Hythe, Kent* (?), w.

**1824 Summer and Autumn** tours east and
south-east England.

*The Battle of Trafalgar;*
*Boscastle, Cornwall* (?), w;
*Portsmouth, Hampshire* (?), w.

**1825 28 August** sets out on tour of Holland, the
Rhine and Belgium. Begins 'Picturesque
Views in England and Wales' series.
**25 October** Walter Fawkes dies.

*Bolton Abbey* (?), w;
*Colchester, Essex* (?), w.

**1826 10 August–26 November** visits the
Meuse, the Moselle, Brittany and the Loire.
Probably re-visits Petworth and stays there
frequently until 1837.

*Cologne, the Arrival of a Packet Boat.*

**1827 July–September** stays at East Cowes
Castle with John Nash.

*Mortlake Terrace;*
*Yarmouth Sands* (?), w; *Dunwich* (?), E.

**1828** Delivers last lectures at R.A.
**August–February 1829** second visit to
Italy, travels to Rome via Paris, Lyon,
Avignon, Florence, returns via Loreto,
Ancona, Bologna, Turin, Mont Cenis,
Switzerland and France.

*Vision of Medea; Salisbury* (?), w;
*Stonehenge* (?), w;
*Stamford* (?), w;
*Winchelsea* (?), w.

**1829 Early June–July** seventy-nine 'England
and Wales' series watercolours exhibited at
the Egyptian Hall, Piccadilly.
**Summer** visits Paris, Normandy and
Brittany.
**21 September** death of Turner's father.

*Ulysses deriding Polyphemus.*

**1830 Late August** tours the Midlands to obtain
further material for the 'England and Wales'
series.

*Calais Sands;*
*Malvern Abbey* (?), w; *Chatham* (?), w;
*Brinkburn Priory* (?), w.

**1831 July–September** tours Scotland to obtain
material for illustrations to Scott's poems.
Stays with Scott at Abbotsford.

*Life-Boat and Manby Apparatus;*
*Caligula's Palace and Bridge; Dudley* (?), w;
*Northampton,* w.

**1832 September** visits Paris, possibly meets
Delacroix.

*Abbotsford,* w; *St. Julienne's chapel* (?), w;
*Traitor's Gate, Tower of London* (?), w;
*Field of Waterloo* (?, Byron), w;

**1833** Travels to Copenhagen, Berlin, Dresden,
Prague, Vienna and Venice, returns via
Austria, Germany and possibly Holland or
Belgium.

*The Field of Waterloo* (?, Scott), w;
*The Desert of Sinai* (?), w.

**1834 Late July** visits the Meuse, the Moselle and
the Rhine.

*The Golden Bough;*
*Powis Castle, Montgomery* (?), w;
*Longships Lighthouse* (?), w;
*Durham Cathedral* (?), w; *Hougoumont* (?), w.

**1835 Summer** possibly tours Germany.

*Bally-burgh Ness* (?), w;
*Lord Ullin's daughter* (?), w.

**1836 Summer** tours France, Switzerland and the
Val d'Aosta.

*Juliet and her Nurse;*
*Chain Bridge* (?), w.

**1837** **11 November** Lord Egremont dies.
**28 December** resigns as R.A. Professor of
Perspective.

**1838** **September 6** possibly sees *Téméraire*
being towed upriver.

**1839** **June 18** 'England and Wales' series
engravings sold off at auction, Turner buys
entire collection, series uncompleted with
only about 100 of the original 120
watercolours having been made.

**1840** **22 June** meets Ruskin for the first time.
**August–October** visits Venice, travelling
via Rotterdam and the Rhine and returning
through Munich and Coburg.

**1841** **August–October** visits Switzerland.



**1842** **August–October** visits Switzerland

**1843** First volume of Ruskin's *Modern Painters*
appears, stoutly defending Turner against
his critics.

**1844** **August–October** visits Switzerland,
returning via Heidelberg and the Rhine.

**1845** **May** visits northern France. Acts as
President of Royal Academy during illness
of Martin Archer Shee.
**September–October** visits Dieppe and the
coast of Picardy. Probably begins late
'Liber' series of oil-paintings.

**1846** Moves to Chelsea at around this time.




**1848–9** Growing infirmity.

**1850** Exhibits last four paintings at the Royal
Academy

**1851** **19 December** dies at his house, 119
Cheyne Walk, Chelsea. Buried at St Paul's,
30 December.

*Regulus* (begun 1828);
*Parting of Hero and Leander.*

*Phryne going to the Baths as Venus;*
*Modern Italy; Ancient Italy.*
*The Fighting 'Temeraire';*
*Ancient Rome;*
*Modern Rome.*

*Venice, the Bridge of Sighs; The New Moon;*
*Bacchus and Ariadne;*
*Venice, the Grand Canal* (?), w.

*Dawn of Christianity; Glaucus and Scylla;*
*Falls of the Rhine, Schaffhausen* (?), w;
*Lake of Geneva,* w.
*Campo Santo, Venice; Peace – Burial at Sea;*
*War. The Exile and the Rock Limpet.*
*Goldau,* w;
*Light and Colour (Goethe's Theory).*

*Returning from the Ball (St. Martha);*
*Europa and the Bull* (?); *Music at East Cowes*
*Castle* (?);
*Two Women with a Letter* (?);
*Sion, near the Simplon Pass* (?), w;
*The Lauerzer See, with the Mythens* (?), w.

*A Swiss Pass* (?), w.

# Notes

### INTRODUCTION

1 Ronald Paulson, *Literary Landscape: Turner and Constable*, London and New Haven, 1982, p. 69.

2 W. G. Rawlinson, *The Engraved Work of J. M. W. Turner, R.A.*, Vol. I, 1908, p. 'I'.

3 T. B. CLXVII, pp. 75a and 76.

4 British Library, *Add. Ms. 46151*, N, p. 8. The spelling – or more accurately mis-spelling – is represented here as it appears in the original manuscript. To avoid wearying the reader with the interpolation of the term *sic* after every instance of Turnerian or eighteenth and nineteenth century idiosyncratic spelling, throughout this book all spellings will be given as originally written.

5 Sir Walter Scott, 'Provincial Antiquities and Picturesque Scenery of Scotland', London and Edinburgh, 1826, p. 35.

6 Thomas Miller, *Turner and Girtin's Picturesque Views Sixty Years Hence*, London, 1854, p. xix.

7 *Views in Sussex* sketchbook, T. B. CXXXVIII, *c.* 1810.

8 William Bell Scott, *Autobiographical Notes*, London, 1892, Vol. I, p. 84. 'Thomson' was John Thomson of Duddington (1778–1840), a Presbyterian minister and landscape painter. Clearly, Turner has here confused King Harold I Harefoot (died 1040) with King Harold II (?1020–66) who was the king killed at the Battle of Hastings.

9 This transition in the state of the trees was first pointed out to the author by Prof. John McCoubrey, to whom he is most grateful. See also John McCoubrey, 'Time's Railway: Turner and the Great Western', *Turner Studies*, Summer 1986, Vol. 6 No. 1, p. 38.

10 R. R. Reinagle, *Views in Sussex*, letterpress.

11 Ruskin, *Modern Painters*, Vol. II, in *Works*, Vol. IV, p. 298.

12 This discussion is recorded in a hand-written memorandum by Dr John Percy dated 11 April, 1869 stating that he had been given the information that day by John Pye. It is kept with the impression of the *Wycliffe* engraving discussed above, in the collection of the British Museum Department of Prints and Drawings.

13 Miller, *op. cit.*, 1854, p. xix.

14 Both clearly emanated from Pye and details were doubtless selectively emphasised either by Pye or in the re-tellings by Percy and Miller.

15 Jack Lindsay, *J. M. W. Turner*, London, 1966, p. 140.

16 David Hill, *Turner in Yorkshire* (exhibition catalogue, York City Art Gallery, 1980) p. 87.

17 Dr Percy states in his memorandum (*loc. cit.*) that he was informed of this by Pye and Halsted, a London printseller. It is not known whom Turner presented them to.

18 Richard Carlile, *Report of the Trial of Humphrey Boyle indicted at the instance of the Constitutional Association as 'A Man with name unknown' for publishing an alleged Blasphemous and seditious Libel . . . with a narrative of the proceedings against the defendent before Trial*, London, R. Carlile, 55 Fleet Street, 1822, p. 5. That the author was Richard Carlile himself is indicated by the signed 'Dedication to the dying Vice Society and the defunct Constitutional Association'.

19 G. M. Trevelyan, *British History in the Nineteenth Century*, London, 1922, p. 162.

20 *Suppressed Defence, The Defense of Mary-Anne Carlile*, published by Richard Carlile, London, 1821. The first two sections of the *Wycliffe* inscription were almost directly quoted by Turner from page 15 of this pamphlet (which was re-

published under the title of *A New-Year's Address to the Reformers of Great Britain* early in 1822). Here is the passage as given by Carlile, with only the sections that were *not* quoted or slightly amended by Turner given in italics:

> . . . in the second year of Henry the Fifth, a law was passed by which . . . *whatsoever* they were that should read the scriptures in their mother tongue, (which was then called Wickleu's Learning) they should forfeit land, cattle, body, life and goods, from their heirs for ever, and be condemned for heretics to God, enemies to the crown, and most errant traitors to the land. In *the year 1543, an act of Parliament was obtained against Tyndal's Bible, and the prefaces and notes of all other editions.* It was *therefore* enacted 'that no women, (except noblewomen, who might read to themselves alone, and not to others, and for which indulgence they were indebted to the courtesy of Cranmer,) nor artificers, 'prentices, journeymen, serving-men, nor labourers, were to read the Bible or New Testament in English, to himself or to any others privately or openly, upon pain of one month's imprisonment.'

The section in quotation marks was itself quoted from Townley's *Biblical Anecdotes*, London, 1813, p. 156. This was in turn derived from *The Complete Collection of State Trials*, vol. I, London, 1730, pp. 49 and 189.

21 E. P. Thompson, *The Making of the English Working Class*, London, 1968, p. 797. Thompson's remark is proven by the fact that Boyle, a self-taught flax-dresser from Leeds, had only come down to London in December 1821 'for the sole purpose of making one that should battle the Constitutional and Vice associations, through the medium of Mr. Carlile's shop'. (Carlile, *loc. cit.* 1822). He was arrested on 27 December 1821.

22 Walter Thornbury, *The Life of J. M. W Turner, R.A.*, second edition, London, 1877, p. 541.

23 *The Mustering of the Warrior Angels* (w. 1264, now untraced but engraved by R. Brandard, 1835, R. 598), *The Fall of the Rebel Angels* (w. 1265, similarly lost but engraved by E. Goodall, 1835, R. 599) and *The Temptation on the Pinnacle* (w. 1268, Private Collection, UK).

24 No. 385. The title and inscription as given in the catalogue were as follows:

*John Milton visiting Galileo when a prisoner to the Inquisition near Florence in 1638.*

> There it was that I found and visited the famous Galileo, grown old, a prisoner to the Inquisition, for thinking in astronomy otherwise than the Franciscan and Dominican Accusers thought.

25 *Reminiscences of Solomon Hart, R.A.*, London 1882, pp. 94–5.

26 Quoted in Walter Thornbury, *The Life of J. M. W. Turner, R.A.*, 1862, Vol. II, pp. 45–46.

27 John Ruskin, *Modern Painters*, Vol. V, in *Works*, Vol. VII, p. 435n.

28 F. G., *Notes and Queries*, series VII, Vol. 10, July–December, 1896, pp. 21–22.

29 Most certainly Turner does not portray the construction of the new house '. . . of Lady Howe that is being built on the ruins of Pope's demolished villa' as stated by Ronald Paulson, *op. cit.* 1982, p. 78. The new villa was not built until 1812. Possibly Turner recorded the villa in the course of demolition on page 35a of the *Greenwich* sketchbook, T.B. CII, of around 1806–7. The book also contains extensive draft verses '. . . upon the Demolition of Pope's House', on pp. 11a–14a.

30 John Britton, *The Fine Arts of the English School*, London 1812, n.p. (pp. 19–20). The passage is dated 'December, 1811' but was obviously drawn from John Landseer's comments on the painting published in 1808.

31 R. S. Cobbett, *The Memorials of Twickenham*, London, 1872, pp. 235–6. An indication of just how completely Pope's Willow has become forgotten is demonstrated by the exhibition catalogue *Alexander Pope's Villa*, Marble Hill House, London 1980, p. 13 where the compiler, Morris R. Brownell, states that 'The 1790s began to worship a new icon, a weeping willow associated with the poet no more reliably than Shakespeare's mulberry' but gives no reason for that worship at all. The otherwise excellent catalogue does, however, reproduce a number of views in which the willow (or willows) can clearly be seen.

32 John Gage (ed.), *The Collected Correspondence of J. M. W. Turner*, Oxford, 1980, letter 43, pp. 50–1.

33 British Library, *Add. Ms.* 46151, N, p. 9. This manuscript was possibly revised around 1812 and certainly so in 1818.

34 J. Ruskin, *Notes on the Turner Gallery, at Marlborough House, 1856*, in *Works*, Vol. XIII, p. 108.

35 See also the *Vision of Medea* (fig. 201), R.A. 1831, Clore Gallery for the Turner Collection, London (B.J. 293) and *Light and Colour (Goethe's Theory) – the Morning after the Deluge – Moses writing the Book of Genesis*, R.A. 1843, (B.J. 405) which is interpreted below and reproduced as fig. 181. Turner refers to 'the bubble pleasure' in an early poem on an inside cover of his *Salisbury* sketchbook, T.B. XLIX.

36 *Blackwood's Edinburgh Magazine*, October 1836, pp. 550–1.

37 Jerrold Ziff, *Art Bulletin*, LXIII, 1980, p. 170.

38 Harold I. Shapiro, *Art Bulletin*, LXIII, 1981, p. 346.

39 Even by 1819, when the artist first visited Venice, the celebration of Carnival was in decline. Although he could not have seen any large-scale Carnival celebration when he visited the city in 1819, 1833 or 1840, of course it is quite possible that people did frequently venture out in Carnival costume, especially for masked balls and the like. However, *Murray's Handbook for Travellers in Northern Italy* (London, 1842, p. 326) tells us that by the time of its publication Venetian . . .

> Sky, air and water continue the same, but all the actors who peopled the scene are gone; for the Venetians have cast aside in despair all the peculiarities which marked their nationality in their day of independence. The national dresses, the red *tabarro* of the men and the black *zendale* of the women, so often mentioned in Goldoni's plays, have entirely disappeared. The masks, the saltinbanks, the soothsayers, the motley crowds which enlivened the piazza, have followed the fate of doges and senators. The gondolas alone linger in their ancient form, gliding, as in the days of yore, on the canals in ghostly and funeral silence.

40 John Chetwode Eustace, *A Classical Tour through Italy*, London, 1813, Vol. I, pp. 179–80. Turner referred to this book in a letter of 7 January 1826 (see Gage, *op. cit.*, 1980, letter 112).

Turner probably read the book before visiting Italy for the first time in 1819. (See John Gage, 'Turner and Stourhead: the making of a classicist?', *Art Quarterly*, XXXVII, 1974, p. 77 and note 54).

41 Maurice Andrieux, *Daily Life in Venice in the time of Casanova*, London, 1972, pp. 120–1.

42 The same viewpoint of the square, although from much lower, is depicted in an engraving by Domenico Louisa (dates unknown but probably early eighteenth century) entitled *Veduta della Piazza di S. Marco dell'ultimo giorno di Carnevale* (fig. below). It could well be that Turner saw this print on sale in Venice.

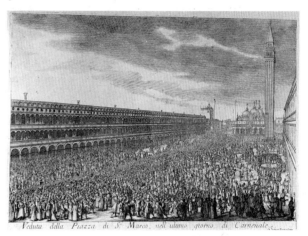

*Veduta della Piazza di S. Marco, nell'ultimo giorno di Carnevale.*

Domenico Louisa, *Veduta della Piazza di S. Marco dell'ultimo giorno di Carnevale* ('View of the Piazza of S. Marco on the last day of the Carnival'), engraving, date unknown, published in *In Venetia per Domenico Louisa*, Volume I. The view is from the selfsame location in St Mark's Square as *Juliet and her Nurse*, although lower in height.

43 For example, *The Rialto, Venice*, *c.*1820 (W. 718), Indianapolis Museum of Art; *The Salute from the Academy Quay*, *c.*1820 (unlisted by Wilton but reproduced in colour as Plate XII in A. J. Finberg, *In Venice with Turner*, London, 1930, p. 73); and in the even earlier *The Rialto, Venice* (W. 700, R. 144, untraced) made around 1818 as an illustration to Hakewill's *Picturesque Tour of Italy* before Turner ever went to Italy. In this latter image a woman who appears in a window on the right curiously foreshadows the figure of Jessica in the 1830 oil painting of that name, B.J. 333.

44 Samuel Rogers, *Italy*, London, 1830, p. 59; Rogers' *Poems*, London, 1834, p. 95, contains Turner's vignette of *Venice, The Rialto – Moonlight*, R. 386; and T.B. CCLXXX–196 (W. 1190).

45 He referred to Bassanio's ballad from *The Merchant of Venice* in one of his perspective lectures (see main text above), and referred to the play through quotations attached to the titles of *Jessica*, exhibited at the R.A. in 1830, and *The Grand Canal, Venice*, shown there in 1837. He also adopted the alternative title of *Twelth-Night; or What you Will* as the title of a painting exhibited at the R.A. in 1822.

46 For instance, see pp. 23–31 of the *Milan to Venice* sketchbook (T.B. CLXXV) of 1819, or pp. 58a–59, 62a, 65a, 67, 67a and 73–75 in the *Lintz, Salzburg, Innsbruck, Verona and Venice* sketchbook of 1833 (T.B. CCXI).

47 In fact, as a comparison of the preliminary etched state of the print with the first proof state demonstrates, Turner added the refinements in the engraving referred to in the main text below only *after* the painting had initially been copied by George Hollis, the engraver. Copies of both the etched state and first proof state are in the Print Room of the Victoria and Albert Museum.

48 On page 5a of the *Perspective* sketchbook (T.B. CVIII) of around 1809 Turner noted Giotto's dates (1266?–1377) and discussed the artist.

49 *The Art Union*, March 1842, p. 38.

50 See Gerald Finley, '*Ars Longa, Vita Brevis*: the *Watteau Study* and *Lord Percy* by J. M. W. Turner', *Journal of the Warburg and Courtauld Institutes*, Volume 44, 1981, pp. 241–247.

51 Shapiro, *op. cit.*, 1981.

52 'M.L.' (Mary Lloyd), *Sunny Memories*, London, 1880, pp. 34–5, reprinted in *Turner Studies*, Vol. 4 No. 1, Summer, 1984, p. 23. Other contemporaries of Turner also record the artist as having stated that Ruskin over-interpreted his works. For instance, Solomon Hart in his *Reminiscences* (p. 48) noted that 'Turner confessed to me that Mr Ruskin often accredited him with motives that never actuated him. He was, however, evidently alive to the value of that writer's remarks, as from their appearance, may be dated the increased appreciation of his art'. Lovell Reeve, in his obituary of Turner in the *Literary Gazette* for 1852 (p. 20) relates Turner

complaining that 'He [Ruskin] knows a great deal more about my pictures than I do . . . he puts things into my head, and points out meanings in them that I never intended'. Ruskin refuted this charge in Volume V of *Modern Painters*, first published in 1860 (*Works*, Vol. VI, pp. 274–5), stating that 'Foolish people are fond of repeating a story which has gone the full round of the artistical world, that Turner, some day, somewhere said to somebody (time, place, or person never being ascertainable), that I discovered in his pictures things which he did himself not know were there. Turner was not a person apt to say things of this kind; being generally, respecting all the movements of his own mind, as silent as a granite crest; and if he ever did say it, was probably laughing at the person to whom he was speaking'. Turner's friend, the Rev. William Kingsley, stated that 'No greater nonsense can be uttered than the story of Turner's saying that Mr Ruskin saw things in his pictures that he himself had not thought of' (to which Ruskin added 'I'm so glad of this bit. Nothing ever puts me more "beside myself" . . . than this vulgar assertion'). Kingsley added that the statement '. . . must have been invented for the purpose of disparaging both Turner and Ruskin by someone who knew neither' (see Ruskin, *Works*, Vol. XIII, pp. 535–6). However, Mary Lloyd and Solomon Hart most certainly did not invent the remarks they recorded and Lovell Reeve may well have been party to such a statement as well. Yet without knowing exactly *what* statements Ruskin made about *which* pictures it is impossible to ascertain the degree of over-interpretation Turner complained of, whilst to use those complaints as a pretext to dismiss *all* interpretation of Turner's works is clearly invalid.

53 See Amy Woolner, *The Life and Letters of Thomas Woolner, R.A.*, London, 1903, Vol. 2, pp. 260–1. Woolner's daughter records an anecdote that Woolner apparently received from the sculptor W. F. Woodington who supposedly saw Turner on board the same steamer on which he was returning from Margate and making 'little sketches on cards' of the ship being towed up-river 'in the midst of a great blazing sunset'. For a contradiction of the existence of this sunset by a direct eye-witness, see main text and note 66 below.

54 See Louis Hawes, 'Turner's *Fighting Temer-aire*', *Art Quarterly*, XXXV, 1972, pp. 23–48.

55 Victoria and Albert Museum, accession number 177–1889, catalogued as *Ships of War in the Medway, off Sheerness* and signed and dated 1 July 1833. The identification of the main vessel in the watercolour as the *Téméraire* was made public by John Munday at the Turner Symposium, Alcuin College, York, summer 1980.

56 *The Athenaeum*, 11 May 1839.

57 *Fraser's Magazine*, June 1839, p. 744.

58 *The Spectator*, 11 May 1839.

59 *The Art Union*, 15 May 1839.

60 *The Art Union*, September 1844, p. 294.

61 The controversy was started by a statement on 14 December 1877 in a review of Christmas books that the *Téméraire* was sailing in the wrong direction. For various letters responding to this statement see main text below.

62 Martin Davies, *National Gallery Catalogues: The British School*, 1946, p. 97.

63 Hawes, *op. cit.*, p. 43 n. 6. To be fair, Hawes also states that 'Turner . . . would have felt free to place the sun where he did regardless of what he actually saw'.

64 For an example see *Hythe, Kent*, discussed below in chapter five.

65 For examples see *Torbay, seen from Brixham, Devonshire* and *Hasboro Sands*, discussed and reproduced as Nos 34 and 88 respectively in Eric Shanes, *Turner's Rivers, Harbours and Coasts*, London 1981.

66 *The Times*, 20 December 1877, p. 6.

67 *The Times*, 13 September 1838, p. 6.

68 I am indebted for this information to Peter van de Merwe of the National Maritime Museum who is preparing a paper on the subject. Also see the letter from Henry Liggins to R. N. Wornum of 22 July 1878 (National Gallery archives) who states that he often saw the *Téméraire* whilst she was being dismantled and that 'The Masts etc. were not in her when towed up – They were removed at Sheerness 28 August 1838'.

69 Turner shows the foremast with only course and topsail-yards; the mainmast appears only to have a coursesail yard, whilst the mizzenmast

displays only driver and topsail yards (E. W. Cooke's watercolour demonstrates that the *Téméraire* at Sheerness had no yards at all by 1833).

70 Thomas Austin Jnr., letter to *The Times*, 18 December 1877, p. 10.

71 J. Hogarth, who also took the opportunity of exhibiting the painting at his premises at 60 Great Portland Street, London, in the late summer of 1844. Interestingly, Hogarth also wrote to *The Times* on 18 December 1877 stating that he saw the *Téméraire* towed out of the Medway on her last voyage.

72 *The Art Journal*, 1856, p. 289.

73 R. C. Leslie, letter to John Ruskin of 15 June 1884, reprinted in Ruskin, *Works*, XXXV, p. 574.

74 *ibid.*

## CHAPTER ONE: A POETIC PAINTURE

1 British Library, *Add. Ms.*, 46151, BB, p. 22. This lecture appears to date from around 1818 and was revised in 1827.

2 Robert Wolseley, 'Preface to *Valentinian, a Tragedy*' in *Critical Essays of the Seventeenth Century*, ed. Spingarn, Oxford, 1909, Vol. III, p. 16.

3 For a list of the books in Turner's collection see Andrew Wilton, *Turner in his time*, London, 1987, pp. 246–7. A number of them are still in the ownership of a member of the Turner family.

The first R.A. Professor of Perspective was Samuel Wale but he died in 1786. Thereafter the post remained vacant, although Edward Edwards gave private tuition in the subject. However, Edwards died in 1806, which prompted Turner to volunteer his services in May 1807. He was elected 'R.A.P.P.' in December 1807. Evidently he slightly regretted his decision to volunteer, for after three years preparation he joked at the beginning of his first lecture that 'Alacrity should have appeared earlier on my behalf' (British Library, *Add. Ms.* 46151, K, p. 2). In fact Turner went on delivering the lectures until 1828, and finally resigned the Professorship in February 1838.

A list in British Library *Add. Ms.* 46151, B, tells us that the subjects of the perspective lectures were:

1 Introduction: Its origin use. How far connected with Anatomy. Painting architecture and Sculpture. Elements . . . Parallel Angular Aerial Perspective.

2 Vision. Subdivision of the Elements and Forms of Perspective . . . Parallel . . . Perspective the cube by the old Masters.

3 Angular Perspectives

4 Aerial Perspective Light and Colour

5 Reflexes Reflexions and colour.

6 Backgrounds Introduction of Architecture and Landscape.

This course was amended in 1818 to a series of lectures comprising:

1 Introduction

2 Lecture on the language of perspective

3 Vision

4 Light and Shade

5 Reflection

6 Colours

However, individual lectures within each lecture-series – which were given in 1811, 1812, 1814, 1815, 1816, 1818, 1819, 1821, 1824, 1825, 1827 and 1828 – may have been revised in 1812, 1814, 1816, 1818, 1819 and 1827, which demonstrates how seriously Turner continued to take the ideas presented therein.

4 Roger de Piles, *The Principles of Painting*, London, 1743, p. 33.

5 The 4th edition of this publication, dating from 1809, was in Turner's library. However, he must have read the *Discourses* well before then, judging from the value he placed upon them.

6 Ut Pictura Poesis erit; similesque Poesi
Sit Pictura, refert par œmula quœque
sororem,
Alternantque vices et nomina; muta Poesis
Dicitur hæc, Pictura loquens solet illa Poetæ

The statement was attributed to Simonides of Ceos by Plutarch in his *Moralia*, 364 f.

7 The volume consists of the complete works of Swift, Thomson, Watts, Hamilton, Philips, West, Collins, Dyer, Shenstone, Mallet, Akenside and Harte.

8 British Library, *Add. Ms.* 46151, C, p. 5, where Turner wrote that 'Baptista Porta had discovered the Camera according to Harte which [can?] play upon the gloomy wall . . .' This is a reference to lines 386–393 of Harte's

'An Essay on Painting' (Anderson, Vol. IX, p. 823).

9 On page 819 of Anderson, Vol. IX, Harte states that 'I had finished the whole [of "An Essay on Painting"] before I ever saw Du Fresnoy; as will appear by comparison'.

10 *The Diary of Joseph Farington*, ed. Garlick and Macintyre, Vol. III, London and New Haven, 1978, p. 968, Monday 15 January 1798.

11 Farington, *op. cit.*, Vol. IV, 1978, p. 1523 (16 March 1801), p. 1529 (30 March 1801), Vol. V, 1979, p. 1987 (28 February 1803) and p. 1998 (21 March 1803).

12 For the influence of Dayes on Turner, see A. J. Finberg, *The Life of J. M. W. Turner, R.A.*, 2nd ed., Oxford, 1961, pp. 22, 26, and 37. Dayes himself mentions in the section of his *Essays in Painting*, London, 1805, devoted to 'Professional sketches of modern artists' that

> The way [Turner] acquired his professional powers, was by borrowing, where he could, a drawing or picture to copy from; or by making a sketch of any one in the Exhibition early in the morning, and finishing it at home. By such practises, and by a patient perseverance, he has overcome all the difficulties of his art. [p. 352]

As Finberg comments (*loc. cit.* p. 19). 'It may not be unjustifiable to assume that Dayes himself was probably one of those from whom the youthful Turner borrowed drawings'.

13 Dayes, *op. cit.*, 1805, p. 228.

14 See Barry Venning, 'Turner's Annotated Books: Opie's "Lectures on Painting" and Shee's "Elements of Art" (I)' in *Turner Studies*, Vol. 2 No. I, Summer 1982, pp. 36–46.

15 *The Merchant of Venice*, with which he was fairly familiar judging by his citations from the play in connection with paintings (see Introduction, n. 45); *Romeo and Juliet*, judging by *Juliet and her Nurse*; and *Twelfth Night; or What you Will!*, the subtitle and imagery of which he employed in a painting of 1822. In addition he also knew *The Tempest* (see Thornbury, *op. cit.*, 1877, p. 353 on Turner's enthusiasm for Macready's production of the play).

16 This was decided by the R.A. Council on 20 January 1798. As the Exhibition opened to the

public on 23 April (Turner's birthday) the artist had plenty of time to take advantage of the change and this argues against any notion that Turner 'added' poetic quotations to his pictures after they had been painted merely to exploit the change.

17 Jerrold Ziff, 'Turner's First Poetic Quotations: an Examination of Intentions', *Turner Studies*, Vol. 2 No. I, summer 1982, pp. 2–11.

18 Turner here conflates passages from lines 189–205 of the poem (see The *Complete Poetical Works of James Thomson*, Oxford, 2nd edition, 1951, p. 10).

19 T.B. XXXV–84. As Ziff notes, the watercolour indicates Turner's testing of the placement of the rainbow in the final painting, for the work shows two rainbows at odds with each other.

20 Lines 185–8. In Milton's original, the fourth word in line two of this quotation is 'steaming'.

21 'Summer', lines 1648–50 and 1653–54. The watercolour of *Fountain's Abbey* is w. 238, Private Collection, UK.

22 'Summer', lines 163–170. Turner alters the first word of the second line to 'Breaking' from 'Projecting', and the second word of the penultimate line becomes 'from' instead of 'to the blue horizon's utmost verge'.

23 'Summer', lines 81–6. Turner omits three words from line 85.

24 Lines 170–5 (on p. 698 of Anderson, Vol. IX).

25 Book IV, lines 598–9 and 605–8.

26 Book VI, lines 602–7.

27 'Summer', lines 1103–5 and 1109–11.

28 As Jack Lindsay notes (*J. M. W. Turner*, London, 1966, p. 59), Turner cuts out Thomson's images of chemical combustion in the intervening lines between the beginning and end of his quote, obviously because they are too limiting in imaginative effect in relation to his picture.

29 This is a compilation of lines drawn from John Langhorne's 'The Visions of Fancy' of 1762; the verse is drawn from the Fourth Elegy, stanzas six and seven, and the Second Elegy, stanza three, line one. The poem was available to Turner in Volume XI of Anderson's *Complete Poets*. For an analysis of the influence of this

poem upon Turner, and particularly upon his formation of the title 'The Fallacies of Hope', see Jerrold Ziff, 'John Langhorne and Turner's "Fallacies of Hope"', *Journal of the Warburg and Courtauld Institutes*, Vol. 37, 1964, pp. 340–2.

30 For example, Andrew Wilton in *Turner and the Sublime*, London, 1982, p. 40, states that there are only two figures in the picture, where four are clearly visible. However, at least this is two figures more than were seen by Jack Lindsay (*op. cit.*, 1966, p. 60) who declares that in the picture 'the human actors are not shown' at all. Wilton repeatedly fails to connect the verses with these figures as well, which is hardly surprising (see also the following footnote and the catalogue *Turner in Wales*, Llandudno and Swansea, 1984, No. 98, p. 69).

31 Wilton, *op. cit.*, 1979, p. 65.

32 Of course it might be that we are looking at an allegorical figure, perhaps symbolising 'liberty' (for reasons which will become apparent below). Turner was to symbolise Greek liberty and its loss under the Turks by means of a fettered nude woman in the 1822 watercolour of *The Acropolis, Athens* (w. 1055). It will be remembered that he had already painted an allegorical subject in 1799.

33 As pointed out by Martha Mel Edmunds, Turner was also vertically to align an apparent allusion to a prisoner and his prison in the 'England and Wales' series watercolour of *Launceston, Cornwall*. See Martha Mel Edmunds, 'Picture Note' on the work in *Turner Studies*, Vol. 4 No. 2, Winter 1984, pp. 59–60.

34 For examples of the watercolours see T.B. LXX–B, C, D, E, O, X, Y and Z; for the pastels see the *Studies for Pictures* sketchbook, T.B. LXIV, pp. 103, 104, 108, 109, 112 and 113.

35 At least to judge from the fact that as late as 1843 Turner based lines from the 'Fallacies of Hope' (which he appended to the title of *The Sun of Venice going to Sea* in the R.A. catalogue) upon verses from Gray's 'Bard' (see Butlin and Joll, *op. cit.* 1984, No. 402, p. 251). In 1809 he quoted lines from Gray's 'Ode on a distant prospect of Eton College' in the R.A. catalogue to support the title of *Near the Thames Lock, Windsor*, B.J. 88, Petworth House.

36 We can determine this time of day from the

fact that we are looking northwards at Caernarvon and the shadows are falling from the left.

37 Canto II Lines 9–12. The poem was available to Turner in Volume X of Anderson's *Complete Poets*, pp. 220–2.

38 Edward Jones, *Musical and Poetical Relicks of the Welsh Bards*, London, 1794, p. 2.

39 In 1761 Paul Sandby exhibited a painting of *The Bard* at The Society of Artists, of which William Mason (who had probably commissioned the work) wrote in part:

> Sandby has made such a picture! such a bard! such a headlong flood! such a Snowdon! such giant oaks!

The painting is now lost. (See Bruce Robertson, 'In at the Birth of British Historical Landscape Painting', *Turner Studies*, Vol. 4, No. I, Summer 1984, pp. 44–6).

40 See *Catalogue of Ancient and Modern Pictures . . . late the property of J. M. W. Turner*, Christie, Manson and Woods, 25 July 1874, lot 28. The portrait sketches were probably by John Jackson RA (see John Gage, *op. cit.*, 1969, note 100, p. 244). For Westall see Richard J. Westall, 'The Westall Brothers', *Turner Studies*, Vol. 4 No. I, Summer 1984, pp. 23–38.

41 See A. J. Finberg, *A Complete Inventory of the Drawings of the Turner Bequest*, London, 2 Vols, 1909, Vol. I, p. 23 (T.B. XVII–S, where Turner scribbled some verses from Blair's 'The Grave' onto the back of a drawing on card). As Jerrold Ziff has pointed out, Turner's activities as a poet (but only as far as drafts in his sketchbooks are concerned) really started in earnest around 1808 (see Jerrold Ziff, 'J. M. W. Turner on Poetry and Painting', *Studies in Romanticism*, Vol. III, No. 4, Summer 1964, pp. 193–215).

42 And additional evidence of this examination may be adduced from a passage written on pp. 66a–7 of the *Derbyshire* sketchbook (T.B. CVI):

> a musical close requires with the Last syllable of the last but one to be a long syllable. Words of short ones are seldom as *particular* and [? are seldom] harmonious unless a Long syllable proceed them . . .

43 Sir Joshua Reynolds, *Discourses on Art*, ed. Robert Wark, London 1959, p. 234.

44 It has been thought 'highly unlikely' that Turner was commenting upon contemporary affairs in *Dolbadern Castle* because at the time of its creation the artist would have been wary of proclaiming any political sympathies whatsoever on account of his anxiety to gain election to the Royal Academy (see Wilton, *op. cit.*, 1984, p. 28), an ambition he achieved by being elected an Associate R.A. at the very end of 1799 and a full Academician in February 1802. However, this viewpoint excludes any perception of just how politicised the R.A. was at the time, the demands for 'Liberty' and the 'Alarmist' reaction against these demands having found their expression as much within that institution as they did outside it during the period. Amongst the R.A.s, A.R.A.s, exhibitors and persons linked to the R.A. who held, or were suspected of harbouring a sympathy for 'democracy', were Thomas Banks R.A., William Hodges R.A., Henry Fuseli R.A., George Romney, Martin Archer Shee A.R.A., Robert Smirke R.A. (and his son Robert), John Hoppner R.A., John Opie R.A., William Beckford, Walter Fawkes, Benjamin West P.R.A., and of course James Barry R.A. (expelled in 1799). For a detailed examination of the subject, see the present writer's forthcoming essay, 'Dissent in Somerset House: Opposition to the Political *Status-quo* within the Royal Academy 1794–1832'. Nor should it be forgotten that in 1799 Turner spent three weeks at Fonthill as the guest of William Beckford, the eccentric millionaire Jamaican sugar-planter, slave-owner, architectural fantasist and author of *Vathek*. Farington tells us that Beckford hated Pitt (*op. cit.*, Vol. III, p. 763, 4 February 1797). Naturally, Beckford's enmity was also compounded by his personal rejection by Pitt and others. This hatred is not surprising, for Beckford's father, a Lord Mayor and the MP for the City of London in the 1750s and '60s, had been an outspoken early champion of parliamentary reform. Not all of Turner's early patrons were pro-government men, and in Beckford, at least – as in Walter Fawkes later – he encountered a patron who would certainly have encouraged independent political thought. Moreover, there is also the possibility that as Turner had derived the topographical subject-matter of five of his eight 1800 R.A. exhibits from Beckford, so too the precise historical subject-matter of the Welsh castle pictures could have received some promp-

ting from that source as well, especially when one considers that the Claudian nature of *Caernarvon Castle* was heavily influenced by two important Claude paintings hanging at Fonthill which Turner seems to have looked at carefully during his stay there and which we shall examine below.

It is also worth noting that even by 1796 the man who would later be Turner's greatest friend amongst his patrons, Walter Fawkes of Farnley Hall, Yorkshire, held 'Republican principles', according to Farington (*ibid*, Vol. II, pp. 601–2, 10 July 1796).

45 Wilton, *op. cit.*, 1984, p. 28.

46 This contradiction leads Wilton to state (*loc. cit.*) that 'there can be no question of this image of oppression [i.e. *Dolbadern Castle*] being intended as an attack on contemporary governement policy'. However, there is just no way of knowing that for sure, and such a pronouncement totally ignores the degree of anti-government feeling that existed in the circles in which Turner moved.

47 In 1802 he quoted three lines of Biblical blank verse in connection with *The Tenth Plague of Egypt* at the R.A. but clearly this was simply to specify the exact nature of the plague, not to extend the meaning of the work in any way.

48 British Library, *Add, Ms.* 46151, N, p. 8. This lecture was possibly revised in 1812 and definitely so in 1818.

49 *Loc. cit.*, p. 8a.

50 British Library, *Add. Ms.* 46151, K (at end, unpaginated and interpolated leaf).

51 For example, Thomson himself collected paintings and prints, and owned works by or after Nicolas Poussin, Raphael, Carlo Maratti, Annibale Carracci and Domenichino.

CHAPTER TWO:
BETWEEN APPEARANCES

1 Ruskin, *The Harbours of England*, London, 1856, reprinted in *Works*, Vol. XIII, pp. 74–5. In addition to the two views of *Scarborough* discussed below (figs 43 and 44), the starfish can also be seen in the view of the town dating from about 1818, w. 529, and w. 751, dating from around 1825.

2 w. 559, and w. 560, both made for the 'Richmondshire' series in 1818; w. 791, dating from around 1825; and w. 808, dating from 1825–8, both of which were made for the 'England and Wales' series.

3 T.B. CXVII–Q; T.B. CXVIII–M; w. 430; w. 821.

4 For instance, see w. 477, *Portsmouth, Hampshire* of around 1824, w. 482, *Mount Edgecomb, Devonshire* of before 1818, w. 756, *Portsmouth, c.*1825, *Falmouth, c.*1825; w. 787, *Dartmouth Cove, with Sailor's Wedding, c.*1825; w. 794, *Saltash, Cornwall*, 1825; w. 813; *Dockyard, Devonport, Ships being paid off, c.*1825–9; w. 828, *Gosport, Entrance to Portsmouth Harbour, c.*1825–30; and w. 835, *Plymouth Cove, c.*1825–9. (In the above I have given Turner's first titles for the works and not the sometimes inauthentic titles subsequently attached to them.)

5 For instance, T.B. XXVII–X, *St. Mary's and the Radcliffe Camera from Oriel Lane, Oxford, c.*1795; w. 298 *A View of Worcester College, &c., c.*1803–4; w. 300, *View of Exeter College, All Saints Church &c. from the Turl, c.*1802–4; w. 853, *Christ Church, Oxford, c.*1830–3; and w. 887, *Merton College, Oxford, c.*1838.

6 For example, probably because he went to school in Margate for a short period around the age of nine or ten he was attracted to the place for the rest of his life, something that Ruskin found completely bewildering (see *Works* Vol. XIII, p. 60). Similarly, Turner's final abode was within a few hundred yards of the site of the White House, Chelsea, which was depicted by his great friend Thomas Girtin in a picture Turner knew well (see Shanes, *op. cit.*, 1981, pp. 9–10). This might also have been due to the strength of his associations.

7 R. 20, engraved by Rothwell. The drawing (w. 107) upon which it was based is untraced.

8 w. 829, reproduced as Plate 40 in Shanes, *op. cit.*, 1979.

9 See Ruskin on Turnerian 'litter' in Volume V of *Modern Painters* (*Works*, Vol. XII, pp. 375–80).

10 For instance, see the verses on Bridport he wrote on p. 102a of the 'Devonshire Coast No. 1' sketchbook (T.B. CXXIII) as a draft letterpress for the 'Southern Coast' series:

... the low sunk town
Whose trade has flourished from early time,
Remarkable for thread called Bridport twine.

(See also Shanes, *op. cit.*, 1981, p. 8).

11 Mrs Alfred Hunt, *Views in Richmondshire after Drawings by J. M. W. Turner, R.A. with descriptions by the Rev. Dr. Whitaker and notes by Mrs. Alfred Hunt*, London, 1891, p. 20.

12 *Lausanne* sketchbook, T.B. CCCXXXIV.

13 *Fribourg, Lausanne and Geneva* sketchbook, T.B. CCCXXXII–34.

14 *Lausanne* sketchbook, T.B. CCCXXXIV–10.

15 Andrew Wilton, *Turner and the Sublime*, London, Yale and Toronto, 1980–81, p. 186.

16 This was available to Turner on p. 302 of Volume XIII of Anderson's *A Complete Edition of the Poets of Great Britain*.

17 Ruskin, *Works*, Vol. IV, p. 261. On page 297 he also wrote of the 'transformations of the tree trunks into dragons' in this work.

The metaphor, and indeed the whole appearance of Turner's picture, was obviously not lost on John Martin when the latter came to paint his *Cadmus* of 1813 (Allen Memorial Art Gallery, Oberlin College, Oberlin, Ohio). Martin depicts Cadmus having slain the serpent beneath a split tree-trunk whose form exactly repeats that of the gaping jaw of the dead monster beneath it.

18 Hunt, *op. cit.*, 1891, p. 32.

19 For an authoritative discussion of the basis of this common and long-lasting belief, and the possible causes of the death of Harold Godwinson at the Battle of Hastings, see *The Complete Peerage*, Vol. XII, Part I, appendix L, pp. 44–7 and appendix K, part II, p. 44 where G. H. White analyses all the available evidence and existent conclusions. It is now impossible to determine the exact cause of Harold's death, mainly due to ambiguities in the imagery of the Bayeux Tapestry, the visual and only contemporary source of the story.

20 The rock is referred to in Exodus, XVII, 1–7 and Numbers, XX, 7–11. See also M. Omer, *Turner and the Bible*, Jerusalem, 1979, pp. 21–2. Omer also offers the useful observation that 'On the face of the rock [today] there are four or five fissures, one above the other, running along its breadth; and there is a channel worn between them by the running of waters . . . The rock is greatly venerated by the Bedouins who put grass into the fissures as an offering to the memory of Moses and as a fertility rite'.

21 Nelson had 27 ships at his disposal, his opponent Admiral Villeneuve some 33, although Nelson believed him to have more. There were precedents for Nelson's manoeuvre, however. As Nelson told Henry Addington (later Lord Sidmouth) before leaving England, 'Rodney [at the battle of the Saints in April 1782] broke the enemy's line in one place, I will break it in two', and he doubtless knew how Admiral Duncan had destroyed the Dutch fleet off Camperdown in October 1797 by cutting the enemy line into three.

22 Turner drew a key to the 1806 picture with a written description of the action on the reverse, on T.B. CXXI-K. A good number of maps showing the 'Nelson touch' at the Battle of Trafalgar were created soon after the engagement; for a typical example see the etching with letterpress text produced by John Fairburn and published on 30 November 1805, just a few weeks after the battle.

For this very reason Ruskin was incorrect in stating that in the drawing sailors are 'explaining the position of the Victory and the Redoubtable at Trafalgar by the help of models'. See M. Cormack, *J. M. W. Turner R.A.*, Cambridge, 1975, p. 49.

23 W. 721, *Venice, from Fusina* of 1821, where the twin forms seem to be created by *two* boats however; in W. 1172, *Naples*, dating from around 1827 and made as an illustration for Roger's *Italy*, but where the dual form is much less elongated and relates to the shapes of Mount Vesuvius and a lesser mountain to the left; in the oil-painting *Returning from the Ball (St. Martha)*, B.J. 422, discussed immediately below in the main text; and in an unexhibited watercolour sketch, *The approach to Venice: sunset*, T.B. CCCXVI –16.

24 This church is entirely fictitious, for although there was a church of St Martha in Venice, this was situated within the city itself, near the Giudecca, and not at the edge of a lagoon as depicted by Turner. It did not have twin towers either.

25 Turner would undoubtedly have known of such poetic imagery from 'Summer' in Thomson's *The Seasons*:

As from the face of Heaven the shattered
        clouds
Tumultuous rove, the interminable sky
Sublimer swells, and o'er the world expands
A purer azure.   [lines 1223–6]

As John Gage has demonstrated (*op. cit.*, 1969, pp. 145–7), Turner is very likely also to have been acquainted by 1838 with Shelley's *Queen Mab* where lines 31–5 run:

As Heaven, low resting on the wave, it spread
Its floors of flashing light,
Its vast and azure dome,
Its fertile golden islands
Floating on a silver sea;

### CHAPTER THREE: DECORUM

1 John Dryden in C. A. du Fresnoy, *The Art of Painting*, London, 1695, p. xxxvi. The passage was available to Turner in Reynolds, *Works*, 1809, Vol. III, p. 258.

2 de Piles, *op. cit.*, 1743, pp. 31–2.

3 *ibid*, p. 224.

4 *ibid*, p. 227.

5 For a perceptive study of this interest see Jerrold Ziff, 'Turner and Poussin', *The Burlington Magazine*, July 1963, pp. 315–321. When Turner visited Paris in 1802 he made written notes on some 15 paintings by Poussin in the Louvre, but his especially detailed analysis of Poussin's use of colour and his awareness of the way that Poussin relates colour to content makes it almost certain that he had read Félibien either well before then, or even read or re-read him when in Paris.

6 British Library, *Add. Ms.*, 46151, P, p. 15v.

7 Paris, Louvre, No. 709. See Anthony Blunt, *The Paintings of Nicolas Poussin, a critical catalogue*, London, 1966, No. 21, p. 18.

8 André Félibien, *Seven Conferences held in the King of France's cabinet of Paintings*, London, 1740, pp. 92–3, sixth conference, of Saturday 5 November 1667.

9 Paris, Louvre, No. 715, Blunt, *op. cit.*, 1966, No. 74.

10 Félibien, *op. cit.*, 1740, p. 129, seventh conference held on Saturday, 3 December 1667.

11 As Turner had not seen the painting since 1802 his highly-developed ideas regarding its colour must have been formed then. A comment written on the work at that time certainly proves this to be the case. On page 42 of the *Studies in the Louvre* sketchbook of 1802, Turner noted that 'the colour [of *The Deluge*] is sublime. It is natural – is what a creative mind must be imprest with in sympathy and horror'. Evidently Turner was struck by Poussin's ability to reconcile 'natural' with 'historical' (i.e. decorous) colouring.

12 See Gage, *op. cit.*, 1969, pp. 113–7 for a most valuable discussion of the subject.

13 Henry Sass, *A Journey to Rome and Naples performed in 1817*, London 1818, pp. 211–2. This book mentions Turner in its introduction and a copy of it was in his library. Turner would also undoubtedly have known of the 'bridge' from Oliver Goldsmith's *The Roman History* whose first edition of 1769 was also in his library.

14 This took place when the work was being engraved in 1842 by Edward Goodall (see W. G. Rawlinson, *The Engraved Work of J. M. W. Turner, R.A.* London, Volume II, 1913, pp. 336–7).

15 Walter Thornbury, *The Life of J. M. W. Turner R.A.*, 2nd Edition, London, 1877, p. 324. The picture by Jones (in watercolour) is now in the Brinsley Ford collection (see *Turner, 1775–1851*, London, 1974–5, p. 179, no. B40).

16 Ruskin, *Works*, Vol. XII, p. 159 where he states that the picture is 'Spoiled by Turner's endeavour to give funereal and un-natural blackness to the sails'. He also dismisses the work as 'valueless'.

17 Thornbury, *loc. cit.*

18 The report carried in *The Times* on 17 June 1841 (p. 5) specifically mentions that the yellow flag was hoisted at Gibraltar to warn off the *Oriental*.

19 British Library *Add. Ms.* 50118, folio 59 (see Gage, *op. cit.*, 1980, letter 329). The letter is undated but may have been written around 1818, for Turner included just such a mallard in a picture exhibited in that year, *Dort, or Dordtrecht, the Dort Packet-Boat from Rotterdam becalmed* (B.J. 137). It has been suggested that by using the term 'becalmed' in its title Turner could have been alluding to a painting of *Rotterdam* by Callcott commissioned in 1816 but which the artist

was having great difficulty in finishing and which he did not complete until 1819 (see David Blayney Brown, *Augustus Wall Callcott*, Tate Gallery exhibition catalogue, 1981, pp. 36–7). If this was the case, the mallard taking off in the painting might have been an additional allusion, and one reinforced by the mallard in his letter to Callcott. Perhaps it was a private joke between the two artists.

20 For a most convincing explanation of the underlying meaning of this work see John McCoubrey, 'War and Peace in 1842: Turner, Haydon and Wilkie', *Turner Studies*, Vol. 4, No. 2, Winter 1984, pp. 2–7.

21 Turner may here have been amplifying an allusive device he had already employed around 1832 in a watercolour of *Nottingham, Nottinghamshire* made for the 'England and Wales' series. See Eric Shanes, *op. cit.*, 1979, No. 59.

22 Ruskin, *Works*, Vol. XIII, p. 160.

23 *ibid*, Vol. VI, pp. 274–5.

24 *ibid*, Vol. VII, p. 191.

25 W. 497. The work was engraved by J. T. Willmore in 1854 (R. 673), the engraving being made 'exclusively for the Members of the Association for the Promotion of the Fine Arts in Scotland for the year 1854'. The last known owner was C. H. L. Wood in 1887.

26 Part II, lines 150–1. Turner must have made the watercolour of *Temple of Minerva Sunias, Cape Colonna* in connection with a literary source, for he had never been there and usually he only made pictures of such faraway scenes on commission, to illustrate literature of some kind.

27 Falconer's 'The Shipwreck' was available to Turner in volume X of Anderson's *Complete Poets*. It seems likely that Turner would initially have read the poem because of his interest in the sea and shipping. The poem includes thorough footnotes explaining nautical details, and it also works well as an explanation of human marine behaviour and the movement of ships at sea. Indeed, 'The Shipwreck' might well have proven a mine of nautical information for Turner the marine painter.

28 A good poetic example of this occurs on p. 9 of the *Greenwich* sketchbook of around 1808 (T.B. CII) where Turner wrote:

contentious as the warring clouds
at Winter's Eve the ariel powers crowd

29 *The Prose Works of Sir Walter Scott*, Vol. V, p. 102.

30 Scott (*ibid*, p. 91) tells us that 'The French . . . forces were gradually coming up during the evening' of the 17th. Turner's metaphor was evidently completely understood by the painter William Bell Scott (who was known to him – see Introduction, footnote 8 above), for in Bell Scott's picture *The Eve of the Deluge* of 1855 (with the Fine Art Society, London, in 1982) it is almost exactly repeated by a massive threatening cloud formation approaching from the right.

31 See A. G. H. Bachrach, 'The Field of Waterloo and beyond', *Turner Studies*, Vol. I, No. 2, 1981.

32 Scott also informs the reader (*loc. cit.*, p. 139) that 'Just as the English army had deployed in the line for the general charge [at the climax of the battle], the sun streamed out, as if to shed his setting glories upon the conquerors of that dreadful day'.

33 Quoted by Evelyn Joll in his entry for the work (No. 52) in his joint catalogue of Turner's oils (Butlin and Joll, *op. cit.*, 1984).

34 Turner wrote 'Our Situation at Calais Bar' across the bottom of a sketch of a small boat almost being overturned in a high sea on p. 70 of the *Calais Pier* sketchbook (T.B. LXXXI). This comment, and others like it, was added to the sketches at a later date, although most of the sketches in the book themselves seem to derive either from memory or imagination, or both.

35 *Calais Pier* sketchbook (T.B. LXXXI), pp. 58–9.

36 For a very full analysis of these manoeuvres, see A. G. H. Bachrach, 'Turner, Ruisdael and the Dutch', *Turner Studies*, Vol. 1, No. I, 1980, p. 22. Although the trawler is not specifically flying a French flag, the colours of yellow and white she is displaying are the colours of the Papacy and may thus embody an allusion to French Catholicism. No flag of this type is known to have been flown by any shipping in the North Sea at the time, although of course they could simply be the personal colours of the owner of the vessel. For a similar flag, and the problems it raises, see Eric Shanes, *op. cit.*, 1981, No. 67 and commentaries section, footnote 53.

37 Right through that autumn and winter the newspaper carried reports of French 'calumnies' against England. In exactly the same vein, an Opposition newspaper, *The Morning Chronicle*, almost every day reported fears of the recommencement of hostilities, suggesting (7 January 1803, p. 2) that their resumption was inevitable and that Napoleon planned to establish naval bases in the Netherlands (13 January 1803, p. 2). Matters finally reached a climax because of this very reason early in March 1803 (see below). Certainly there was little doubt within the Royal Academy of the possibility of the war with France beginning again. Joseph Farington mentions fears of the resumption of hostilities in his entries for 26 November 1802, 3 February, 9 March, 14 March, 15 March, 22 March, 4 May and 6 May 1803 (see Farington, *op. cit.*, 1979, Vols. V and VI).

38 Both *The Times* and *The Morning Chronicle* (to name but two newspapers) were thereafter filled with reports of the build-up of British military forces, parliamentary debates on the probability of war and the gradual depression of share prices until the war did finally break out again just over two months later.

39 Turner might well have known Hogarth's picture of 1748 (Tate Gallery, London) in its engraved form published in 1749. The print was accompanied by these notes:

> The first time anyone goes from hence to France by way of Calais he cannot avoid being struck with the Extreem different face things appear with at so little distance from Dover – a farcical pomp of war, parade of religion and Bustle with very little business – in short poverty, slavery and Insolence, with an affectation of politeness give you even here the first specimen of the whole country. Nor are the figures less opposed to Dover than the two shores. Fish women have faces of leather and soldiers ragged and lean.

Without perhaps sharing Hogarth's xenophobia, Turner does nonetheless amply present us with leathery fishwives and ragged, lean soldiery on the pier at the right.

40 *The Life and Writings of Henry Fuseli*, 2nd ed., ed. Knowles, London, 3 Vols., 1831, Vol. III, p. 149, aphorism 239.

41 For example, in 1796 James Northcote exhibited his series of ten paintings of the effects of 'Diligence and Dissipation' at the R.A. but requested that they should be displayed in sequence on the stairs or in the Council room. He also hired a man to recount the narrative to viewers. Unfortunately the cumulative dramatic effect of his series was somewhat compromised by having a picture by West placed right in the middle of it (see Farington, *op. cit.*, Vol. II, p. 504, 9 March 1796; p. 506, 10 March 1796; pp. 525–8, 18–23 March 1797).

42 The watercolours are *Heidelberg: Sunset*, w. 1376, Manchester City Art Gallery and *Heidelberg, with a rainbow*, w. 1377, Private Collection, UK. Turner's actual depiction of an historic Heidelberg occurs in the oil-painting *Heidelberg*, B.J. 440, Tate Gallery, London, which Martin Butlin has convincingly argued shows Heidelberg Castle before it was damaged in 1689. The work was engraved under the title *Heidelberg Castle in the olden Time*.

43 Turner undoubtedly knew of (and probably shared) Rogers' Whig sympathies, for he also produced a view of St Anne's Hill, the house of Charles James Fox, for the poem 'Human Life', as well as a tailpiece vignette of its garden for the poem by Rogers written in Westminster Abbey after Fox's funeral on 10 October 1806. The works are both in the Turner Bequest, Nos. CCLXXX–170 and 171 respectively).

44 Opie, *loc. cit.*, p. 62.

45 William James, *The Naval History of Great Britain*, London, 1826, Vol. IV, pp. 150–1.

46 See Gage, *op. cit.* 1980, letters 101 and 106.

47 See Edward Fraser, *Greenwich Royal Hospital and the Royal United Service Museum*, London, n.d., p. 158.

48 Géricault's masterpiece was exhibited at the Egyptian Hall, Piccadilly between 12 June and 30 December 1820. See Lee Johnson, 'The Raft of the Medusa in Great Britain', *Burlington Magazine* XCVI, August, 1954, and Lorenz Eitner, *Géricault's Raft of the Medusa*, London, 1972. Several Royal Academicians are known to have been present at the private viewing of the painting on 10 June and Turner could easily have been one of them, given his interest in marine-painting.

49 Lionel Cust, 'The Portraits of J. M. W. Turner', *Magazine of Art*, 1895, pp. 248–9. These observations were made by Sir John Gilbert (1817–97).

50 This was in Turner's library, unlike Horace's *Odes*, which has been suggested as 'the ultimate source' for Turner's painting by Andrew Wilton, *op. cit.*, 1980–1, p. 143.

51 Goldsmith, *op. cit.*, 1769, p. 247. The Romans behaved no better to the captives they held and, indeed, the widow of Regulus was so demanding in the horrors she exacted that even the Romans, with their strong stomachs, were shocked. As a result the punishments were soon stopped by the Senate.

52 Gage, *op. cit.*, 1969, p. 143.

53 This suggestion first seems to have emerged from Martin Butlin's catalogue entry for the work, *op. cit.*, 1977, No. 294.

54 Wilton, *op. cit.*, 1979, pp. 220–1. Turner had employed exactly this kind of location of the protagonist of a picture as a tiny distant figure in works such as *The Bellerophon, Plymouth Sound*, a watercolour (w. 1117) and engraving (R. 540) made for *Scott's Prose Works*, and *Fontainebleau* (watercolour w. 1115, engraving R. 538), also made to illustrate the same work. These drawings date from about 1833.

55 And not the Romans, as suggested by Andrew Wilton in his entry for the work in his catalogue *Turner and the Sublime*, p. 143. In a curious contradiction, Wilton effectively demonstrated in 1979 (*The Life and Work of J. M. W. Turner*, p. 221) that John Gage (*loc. cit.*) was wrong in stating that Regulus was absent from the scene because the engraving made after the work by Daniel Wilson under Turner's supervision in 1840 is entitled *Ancient Carthage – the Embarcation of Regulus* (R. 649) and it *does* show Regulus, whilst in 1980, in order to demonstrate an otherwise non-existent link with Horace as the source of Turner's subject, Wilton stated that the selfsame engraving does *not* show the city identified by the title, but Rome instead. As the engraving-title surely had Turner's sanction it must be Carthage we are looking at, something borne out by the allusions in the work.

CHAPTER FOUR:
LANDSCAPES OF MEANING

1 See Gerhardt B. Ladner, 'Vegetation symbolism and the concept of the Renaissance' in *De Artibus Opuscula XL, Essays in Honor of Erwin Panofsky*, ed. Millard Meiss, 2 Vols, New York, 1961, pp. 303–322.

2 British Library, *Add. Ms.*, 46161–H, p. 27. This dates from 1810 and was revised in 1818.

3 British Library, *Add. Ms.*, 46151–I, p. 11. This manuscript dates from 1810.

4 The part of the work that was engraved was reproduced in aquatint by Pietro Bonato (1765–1820). See *Immagini da Tiziano*, Gabinetto Nazionale della Stampe, Rome, Villa Farnesina alla Lungara, 1976–7.

5 See the *'Remarks' (Italy)* sketchbook (T.B. CXCIII, p. 4).

6 Erwin Panofsky, *Problems in Titian, Mostly Iconographic*, New York, 1969, p. 116. For a most lucid discussion of the notion of the 'paysage moralisé' (upon which I have drawn heavily) see Panofsky's *Studies in Iconology*, New York, 1962, p. 64.

7 Charles Hope, *Titian*, London, 1980, pp. 34–7.

8 *A Rising Gale*, now in the Toledo Museum of Art, Toledo, Ohio. The commission was passed from the Duke of Bridgewater to Turner by Lord Gower but Turner must have seen the van de Velde, for the central diagonal of his own work so strongly complements the diagonal of the picture which it was to hang alongside that it is impossible to believe that Turner could have created it simply by chance.

9 See William T. Whitley, *Art in England 1800–1820*, Cambridge, 1928, p. 176. In 1810 the Marquis extended the privilege to the members of the Associated Artists in Water Colours.

10 The work was known as *Allegory on Human Life* when it was in the Bridgewater Collection (see William Buchanan, *Memoirs of Painting*, London, 1824, Volume I, p. 114).

11 The author has drawn a good deal of this interpretation from Panofsky, *op. cit.*, 1969, pp. 95–6.

12 Turner could have seen this work as early as

1806 when it was brought to England by William Buchanan, or in 1813 at the Lord Kinnaird sale (see Whitley, *op. cit.*, 1928, p. 213), or when it was exhibited at the British Institution in 1816, or any time after 1826 when it was purchased by the National Gallery.

13 This is a direct quotation from *An Essay on Painting* by Count Francesco Algarotti, London, 1763, pp. 48–9.

14 This is an adapted quotation from *The Art of Painting* by Roger de Piles, London, 1716, Chapter XVIII, p. 33 ('Of Perspective') where de Piles states:

A Certain author has said, that Perspective and Painting are the same thing, because there is no Painting without Perspective.

15 Turner was evidently using this word to stand for those who indulge in hyperbole. In our day, of course, the term has assumed the role of a verb (i.e. 'to hype' something).

16 British Library, *Add. Ms.* 46151, T, p. 11. This manuscript has been identified by John Gage (*op. cit.*, 1969, p. 249, no. 169) as being the text of the second lecture of the 1818 series.

17 Here Turner evidently meant 'rules' in the sense of ruled lines, the sense he used it in connection with Poussin's *Landscape with a Roman Road* in the example given below. This we can determine from his use of the word '*machinery* of its rules', i.e. visual structure.

18 For example, he represented the Trinity by the traditional symbol of a triangle in the watercolour (w. 1274) and engraving (R. 616) of *Sinai's Thunder* made around 1835 to illustrate Thomas Campbell's poem 'The Pleasures of Hope' which was included in Campbell's *Poetical Works* published in 1837.

19 See the diagram of the hanging in Farington, *op. cit.*, Vol. V, p. 1775, where the work is listed as 'Raphaels Orleans Holy Family'.

20 Marcia Briggs Wallace, 'Turner's Circular, Octagonal and Square Paintings, 1840–1846', in *Arts* Magazine, April 1979, pp. 109–10.

21 The original painting is in the Hermitage, Leningrad, having gone to Catherine the Great in the collection of pictures formed by Sir Robert Walpole.

22 British Library, *Add. Ms.* 46151, P, p. 18.

23 *ibid*, p. 14v.

24 See Blunt, *op. cit.*, 1966, No. 178. Turner probably saw the work in 1802 or knew it through engravings by G. Audran or G. Chasteau.

25 Reynolds, *op. cit.*, p. 88.

26 National Gallery, London. Blunt, *op. cit.*, No. 144. The work only entered the National Gallery collection in 1831, so Turner must have seen it either at the British Institution in 1816 (No. 67) or when it came up for sale at Philips' in March 1819 and March 1821.

27 Turner discusses the work (British Library, *Add. Ms.* 46151, P, p. 15) wherein '. . . we look upon the dark, dark sky sparingly illumined *at the right-hand corner* by lightening' and with '. . . some antique buildings *on the left*' (my italics), whereas in the painting these pictorial elements are on the opposite sides of the work, something apparently not noticed by Ziff, *loc. cit.* who reproduces the painting (plate 19c) and thus unwittingly demonstrates the inconsistency. The print, published by John Boydell, was produced some seventeen years before the painting entered the Ashburnham collection in 1786. Turner could have seen the painting at Ashburnham House in London, rather than at Ashburnham Place in Sussex, the Ashburnham country residence which he visited in 1810, but it is evident from the above that he worked from a copy of the print when drawing up his lecture.

28 Dulwich Picture Gallery, London, to whom it was bequeathed by Sir Francis Bourgeois in 1811. Until 1807 it belonged to Noel Desenfans, in whose collection Turner saw it.

29 British Library, *Add. Ms.* 46151, P, p. 14v. This manuscript dates from 1810 and was revised around 1816.

30 Turner probably saw the work at the London home of the Duke of Bedford, to whom it belonged, rather than at Woburn, the duke's country seat. Andrew Wilton has kindly informed the author that he has not been able to find any record of the work hanging at Woburn during Turner's lifetime. Turner may also have partly based the layout of his *Jason* upon the vaguely similar configuration of M. A. Rooker's *Wookey Hole, near Wells, Somerset* (Victoria and Albert Museum, London) which was possibly exhibited

at the R.A. in 1800, although the trees in Rooker's work are not shattered in any way (see Patrick Conner, *Michael Angelo Rooker*, London, 1984, colour plate 11).

31  See Gerald Finley, '*Ars Longa, Vita Brevis*: The *Watteau Study* and *Lord Percy* by J. M. W. Turner,' in *Journal of the Warburg and Courtauld Institutes*, XLIV, 1981, p. 247, n. 28.

32  See Selby Whittingham, 'What You Will; or Some Notes on the Influence of Watteau in England' in *Turner Studies*, Vol. 5 No. I, Summer 1985, pp. 2–24 and *Turner Studies*, Vol. 5 No. 2, Winter 1985, pp. 28–48.

33  British Library, *Add. Ms.* 46151, C, p. 3, note in margin.

34  British Library, *Add. Ms.* 46151, K, p. 22*v*.

35  James Northcote, *The Life of Sir Joshua Reynolds*, London, 1813, p. 330. Northcote also discusses the portrait of Dr James Beattie which contains allegorical figures of the Angel of Truth beating down the Vices – one of which is personified by Voltaire (p. 188).

36  Opie, *op. cit.*, 1809, pp. 75–6.

37  R.A. 1785, Tate Gallery, London; Hermitage Museum, Leningrad; Proby or Cuthbertson Collection; Soane Museum; and coll. of Lady Burton (the version made as a present for Henry Hope).

38  Thornbury, *op. cit.*, 1877, p. 115.

39  For a perceptive study of that influence upon Turner, see Wilton, *op. cit.*, 1984, p. 10 ff. It can be observed especially strongly in works like the *Storm on Rocky Coast*, T.B. XXII-R, of *c.*1793 which is clearly dependent on paintings by de Loutherbourg such as his *smugglers landing in a storm* of 1791 (Victoria Art Gallery, Bath) and *The Shipwreck* of 1793 (Southampton Art Gallery).

40  Letter to F. H. Fawkes of 27 December 1847 (see Gage, *op. cit.* 1980, Letter 307, pp. 218–9).

41  David Solkin, Richard Wilson, *The Landscape of Reaction*, London 1982, p. 201.

42  'Summer', lines 1171–1219. For Turner's knowledge of Wilson's *Celadon and Amelia* and *Niobe*, see his letter to J. Robinson of 28 June 1822 in Gage, *op. cit.*, 1980, letter 97, pp. 86–7.

CHAPTER FIVE:
THE POWER OF IMITATION

1  Quoted by W. G. Rawlinson, *op. cit.*, 1906, p. li.n.

2  Michael Kitson, 'The Altieri Claudes and Virgil', *The Burlington Magazine*, CII, 1960, p. 317.

3  Marcel Roethlisberger, *Claude Lorrain, The Paintings*, 2 Vols, London, 1961, Vol. 1, pp. 24–5.

4  The *Liber Veritatis* numbers accord with the numbers of the first 195 paintings discussed by Roethlisberger in his catalogue. Thus the *Landscape with the temptation of St. Anthony* is also number 32 listed by him.

5  According to Roethlisberger, *op. cit.*, the original painting is 'Unknown', there being no literature pertaining to the work in existence. Beaumont's version is now in the National Gallery, London, to which institution it was given before 1828. The work is in a bad condition and is probably an eighteenth century copy.

6  W. G. Rawlinson, *op. cit.*, 1906, p. 100.

7  See the diagram of the gallery-hanging in Farington, *op. cit.*, Vol. V, p. 1775. That this picture is the Claude which hung next to the Turner 'Bridgewater Seapiece' may be deduced from the fact that the only two other Claudes owned by the Duke of Bridgewater (*LV* 161 and *LV* 171) are named as the 'Bouverie Claudes' (a reference to their provenance) and are thus identifiable.

8  Samuel Garth's translation of the section of Ovid's poem telling of the metamorphosis of the Apulian shepherd, available to Turner in Vol. XIV of Anderson's *Complete Poets*, p. 119. It was from this source that Turner derived the subject of his own painting *Apullia in Search of Appullus* (see below), something attested by the fact that it is Garth's translation alone which calls the Apulian shepherd 'Appulus'.

9  A very similar use of a pollard willow to echo human arm-waving can also be seen in Turner's oil-painting, *Vision of Medea*, exhibited at the R.A. in 1831, where such a tree in the distance amplifies the effect of Medea's wild gesturing and wind-blown clothing (see fig. 200, and front cover, *Turner Studies*, Vol. 2, No. I, Summer 1982).

10 It hardly seems likely that he elaborated his own very similar composition simply from memory, as suggested by Kathleen Nicholson in 'Turner's "Apullia in Search of Appullus" and the dialectics of landscape tradition', *The Burlington Magazine*, October 1980, p. 683, n. 22. Turner might also have seen the Claude in 1808 if it was the picture lent by Lord Egremont to the British Institution that year (see Gage, *op. cit.*, 1980, letter 50, n. 2).

11 As stated by Michael Kitson ('Turner and Claude', *Turner Studies*, Vol. 2 No. 2, Winter 1983, pp. 6–7).

12 Which lady is which has led to differences of opinion. Roethlisberger (*op. cit.*, 1961, p. 322) states that the woman between the two men is Rachel (over whom the two men 'bargain') with Leah on the right, and he is followed in this by H. Diane Russell (*Claude Lorrain*, New York and Washington, 1982, p. 171). Michael Kitson, on the other hand (*Claude Lorrain: Liber Veritatis*, London, 1978, p. 135), states that the woman on the right is Rachel and the woman on the left is Leah. This is surely correct, for if Jacob is going to have to wait another seven years before being able to marry Rachel, then it is fitting that she should be physically further away from him and divided from him by her father. The fact that Laban so emphatically points towards the leftmost woman – as if to say 'you *will* take this one as your wife' – accords with the story, and in any event the men are surely disputing, rather than bargaining. To the eyes of this writer at least, the woman on the right also looks somewhat younger and certainly more attractive than the woman on the left, but this is entirely subjective.

13 As can be seen, this emphasis is more pronounced in the engraving (as it is in the drawing after the painting) than it is in the painting itself, due to the greater area of shadow on the right in that work.

14 Farington, *op. cit.*, Vol. X, p. 3508, 6 July 1809. Farington was told this by Thomas Hearne.

15 *ibid*, Vol. II, p. 639, quoting from *The Oracle*.

16 *ibid*, Vol. XII, p. 4328, 8 April 1813.

17 *ibid*, Vol. XII, pp. 4223–4, 21 October 1812.

18 *ibid*, Vol. XI, p. 3945, 8 June 1811.

19 C. R. Leslie, *Memoirs of the life of John Constable*, London, 1951, p. 95.

20 Variant spellings of the name of 'the Apulian clown' can be observed between Turner's catalogue-title and that of the title he wrote on the picture itself. To avoid confusion I have adopted the catalogue spelling, although the picture spelling is undoubtedly more authentic.

21 For example, by Nicholson, *op. cit.*, p. 684, and William Chubb, 'Minerva Medica and the Tall Tree', *Turner Studies*, Vol. I, No. 2, 1981, pp. 30–31. Clearly they are barking up the wrong tree, for neither writer gives any explanation whatsoever as to why Apullia should be dancing upon hearing of the transformation of Appullus.

22 This identification is proven by the print that Turner made of *Apullia in Search of Appullus* for the *Liber Studiorum* but which was never published (Plate 72, etched by Turner, engraved by W. Say). There Turner omitted the grieving shepherd altogether, and made the dancing nymph point far more emphatically at the wild olive-tree whilst looking directly at Apullia, thus drawing the attention of Appullus's female counterpart to her loss with much greater forcefulness.

23 Farington, *op. cit.*, Vol. IV, p. 1219, 8 May 1799. Although Farington does not state which of the two works Turner was responding to, in the previous paragraph he refers to '. . . the Claude which has the Sacrifice in it', and he probably omitted to specify which work because he still implied that one. Farington also records Turner again being amongst the people viewing the Altieri Claudes at Beckford's house on the following day.

24 As Jerrold Ziff has pointed out ('Turner et les grands maîtres' in *J. M. W. Turner*, exhibition catalogue, Grand Palais, Paris, 1983, p. 26), Turner made a copy of the *Landscape with the Landing of Aeneas in Latium* on p. 122 of the *Studies for Pictures* sketchbook (T.B. LXIX), although there is nothing to support Ziff's hypothesis that the drawing was probably made on 8 May 1799. The drawing just records the landscape, without any figures whatsoever, but judging by the colour, the widening of the image to accord with his existing page-width and the slightly higher viewpoint of the landscape represented, it seems that Turner was making a free variation upon the

landscape, rather than 'a record of the basic compositional structure', as Ziff states (author's translation).

25 The earlier work was exhibited in the Old Master show held at the British Institution in 1816 (No. 28), the later work at the same venue in 1818 (No. 115). The pictures had been kept by the Altieri family in the bed-chamber on the upper floor of the Altieri palace in Rome, where they hung until 1798 or 1799.

26 Roethlisberger, *op. cit.*, 1961, p. 370.

27 According to Roethlisberger, Wollett made the engraving not from Claude's original painting but from an unknown copy, although it seems unlikely that Turner would have known this.

28 David Hill, *Turner in Yorkshire*, exhibition catalogue, York, 1980, p. 62. The work was one of three mountain views owned by Walter Fawkes and, as Hill argues, "This picture is the only one of Fawkes's Alpine scenes whose subject could easily be described as the source of the Arveiron. In the other two ex-Fawkes pictures which show the Mer de Glace [w. 365 where it is listed as being the work of this title and date, and w. 389] the actual source of the Arveiron is hardly an important feature of their composition. This is also the only view of the Mer de Glace which is taken from below it (both the other Fawkes pictures show the view from the Montanvert, looking *down* on the Mer de Glace), and it thus seems the best candidate for identification with the picture exhibited at the Academy in 1803 (396) as 'Glacier and Source of the Arveron, *going up* to the Mer de Glace'" [Hill's italics]. In addition, the drawing of the trees in w. 365, a work now in the Yale Center for British Art, New Haven, indicates that the watercolour clearly dates from much later than 1803, and probably from around 1809–1815.

29 *ibid.*

30 In the 'England and Wales' series watercolour of *Walton Bridge* (Private Collection, UK, w. 824, discussed and reproduced in Shanes, *op. cit.* 1979, No. 36) where lines initiated by straining pack-horses on the left lead up into the sky, and down a fisherman's rod and a line of reflections cast by a group of sheep. The divergence emphasises the strain of the horses very effectively.

31 *Recollections of J. M. W. Turner* by George Jones, published in Gage, *op. cit.*, 1980, p. 4. Jones composed these recollections between about 1857 and 1863.

32 Andrew Wilton, *op. cit.*, 1979, p. 57.

33 See Michael Kitson, *op. cit.*, 1983, pp. 5–6. Kitson sets out all the arguments as to which picture it was that Turner wept in front of but does not come to a definite conclusion. However, not too much store should be set by Jones's statement that Turner responded this way in front of one of Angerstein's Claudes 'when very young' (and thus before 1803), for Jones obviously obtained the story at second-hand, and in any case he was writing after Turner's death and in his own old age. The fact that *The Embarkation of the Queen of Sheba* was popularly called 'the Sea Port' in Turner's time (a description Turner observed in his own will) and the fact that Jones refers to '*the* Sea Port' by Claude (not *a* Sea Port) strongly suggests that it was this picture Turner had wept in front of. Above all, though, it is the very fact that Turner left what he considered to be his own masterpiece to hang alongside this Claude 'Sea Port' which more than anything seems to support such a belief. (Nor should it be forgotten that Turner was prone to weeping whenever moved throughout his adult life.)

34 Alaric Watts, 'Biographical Sketch of J. M. W. Turner', in Leitch Ritchie, *Liber Fluviorum*, London, 1853, p. XXIX.

35 This is from Christopher Pitt's translation of *The Aeneid* (lines 588–9), available to Turner in Volume XII of Anderson's *Complete Poets*.

36 J. C. Eustace, *A Classical Tour through Italy*, London 1813, Vol. II, p. 76.

37 This particular allusion was first explored by Ruskin in volume one of *Modern Painters* (see *Works*, Vol. III, p. 113).

38 Goldsmith, *op. cit.*, 1769, Vol. I, pp. 305–6.

39 At the end of the final volume of *Modern Painters*, published in 1860, Ruskin wrote of the crimson effect of Turner's sunset, whereas today that colouring is much subdued, tending towards orange rather than crimson. Evidently some of the deeper hues have faded in the interim.

40 British Library, *Add. Ms.* 46151, K, p. 22*v*. This manuscript first dates from 1810 but may have been revised in 1812. It was certainly added to in 1824.

41 'Macbeth' may have been *A scene in Macbeth* shown at the R.A. in 1777 (No. 127), *Lady Macbeth walking in her sleep* exhibited in 1784 (No. 66), *Macbeth, the cauldron sinking, the witches vanishing* of 1783 (No. 110), or – if this draft dates from 1812 or after – *Lady Macbeth seizing the daggers*, exhibited at the R.A. in that year (No. 39). 'Satan' could be *Satan starting from the touch of Ithuriel's lance*, exhibited at the R.A. in 1780 (No. 179). 'Achilles' could be *Thetis and Aurora, the mothers of Achilles and Memnon the Ethiopian, presented themselves before the throne of Jupiter, each to beg the life of her son, who were proceeding in single combat. Jupiter decided in favour of Achilles, and Memnon fell.* This work was displayed at the Academy in 1803 (No. 97). And the 'Bard' would be the work shown in 1800 (No. 48).

42 This could easily be achieved simply by adding another Claude to hang alongside *The Decline of the Carthaginian Empire*, thus achieving the correct balance, i.e. three Claudes to three Turners.

CHAPTER SIX: BEYOND APPEARANCES

1 John Britton, *The Beauties of England and Wales*, London, 1814, Vol. XV, p. 391. This exegesis follows a very standard interpretation of the two pictures (for example, see William Gilpin's almost identical explanation of the subjects of the works in his *Observations on the Western Parts of England relative chiefly to Picturesque Beauty*, London, 1798, p. 3, a book that Turner probably read).

2 The watercolour *Refectory of Kirkstall Abbey, Yorkshire*, (w. 234, Sir John Soane Museum, London) was engraved in Britton's *Architectural Antiquities of Great Britain* which appeared between 1805–26 (and not 1805–6 as stated incorrectly by Rawlinson, *op. cit.*, 1908, p. 40, who also gives the correct dates in his preliminary list of engravings). The engraving (R. 82) bears the date of publication 'May 1 : 1814'.

3 Rawlinson, *op. cit.*, 1908, p. 41. Rawlinson states that this work had recently been in the possession of a Mr Palser of King Street, Covent Garden, but it is now untraced, and is not listed in Wilton, *op. cit.*, 1979.

4 In the original painting, however, Claude showed this tree in full flower and not partially dead, as here. The broken tree to the right of the main tree is similarly undamaged in the painting. Only in the drawing did he develop this associative use of the form.

5 Roethlisberger, *op. cit.*, 1961, p. 390, entitles the work *Seacoast with Christ calling Andrew and Peter*. Nothing whatsoever is known of the painting upon which the *Liber Veritatis* image was based.

6 This was available to Turner in Volume XII of Anderson's *Complete Poets*, p. 2, lines 47–52.

7 This was available to Turner in the translation by Samuel Garth in Volume VII of Anderson's *Complete Poets*, p. 115.

8 Marcia Briggs Wallace has suggested (*loc. cit.*, 1979, p. 111) that the red sunset could also contain an allusion to the fact that Circe was daughter of the sun and that Turner probably 'visualised' her as such. However, if that were the case, the representation of the sun at any time of the day would have been dramatically just as apt.

9 Wallace (*Ibid*) also seems to suggest (and has been less equivocally followed in this by John Gage, *J. M. W. Turner*, Paris catalogue, 1983, p. 134) that Charybdis is the other of the two rocks on the horizon, whereas of course Charybdis was, and still is, a whirlpool in the Straits of Messina.

10 The works came up for sale at Christie's (Bonelli sale, 25 February 1804, lots 54 and 55). They were shown again at the British Institution in 1836 (Nos 115 and 119).

11 British Library, *Add. Ms.* 46151, BB, p. 27*v*. The main part of this manuscript dates from 1818, and revisions dating from 1827 are also appended.

12 Robert Southey, *Roderick, the last of the Goths*, London, 1814, Part III, lines 1–8.

13 For an even more subtle allusion by Turner to naval control in Portsmouth, see Shanes, *op. cit.*, 1981, No. 74.

14 However, it was not published in the same

part (VIII) of the *Liber Studiorum*, which appeared on 1 February 1812, but in the next part whose date of publication was 23 April 1812.

15 *Vision of Medea*, R.A. 1831 (see Cecilia Powell, 'Infuriate in the wreck of hope: Turner's "Vision of Medea"', *Turner Studies*, Vol. 2, No. 1, 1982, pp. 12–18) and *Undine giving the Ring to Massaniello, Fisherman of Naples*, R.A. 1846 (see Finley, Stuckey and Wallace, *op. cit.*, 1979). For Turner's theatre-going towards the end of his life see Thornbury, *op. cit.*, 1862, Vol. II, p. 234.

16 C. R. Leslie, *Handbook for Young Painters*, London, 1855, p. 270.

17 Curtis Price, 'Turner at the Pantheon Opera House, 1791–92', *Turner Studies*, Vol. 7 No. 2, Winter 1987, pp. 2–8.

18 See the *Fourth Eclogue*, in *Virgil: The Pastoral Poems*, transl. E. V. Rieu, London, 1967, pp. 53–7.

19 See Gage, *op. cit.*, 1980, letter 144, p. 122, where Turner wrote in November 1828 to Sir Thomas Lawrence from Rome that 'The Sistine Chapel Sybils and Prophets of the ceiling are as grand magnificent and overwhelming to contemplating as ever . . .'

20 John Gage (*op. cit.*, 1974, p. 74 and n. 42) has suggested that a group of three figures painted in oil on paper and now in the Turner Bequest (CCCLXIV–395) were originally figures representing the Fates and that they are the fragment referred to as having peeled off the original picture in a letter of 23 April 1878 to *The Times* by Vernon Heath. However, Heath relates Turner as saying that 'I determined . . . to paint *a* nude figure [italics mine] in the foreground [of *The Golden Bough*], and with this intention went one night to the Life School at the Royal Academy, and made a sketch in my notebook. Finding, next day, that it was the exact size I required my figure to be, I carefully, by its outline, cut it out of the book and fixed it on to the picture, intending, when I had time, to paint the figure in properly'. Gage does not explain this discrepancy between Turner's constant referral to *one* figure, and the fact that three figures appear in T.B. CCCLXIV –395. The latter fragment can therefore be discounted as having originally appeared in *The Golden Bough*.

21 This was first pointed out by Gage, *loc. cit.* and is surely correct.

22 F. E. Trimmer quoted in Thornbury, *op. cit.*, 1862, Vol. I, p. 164.

23 Anderson, *op. cit.*, Vol. XII, p. 570.

24 He was 84 years old when he died and seems to have been active right up to the end of his life.

25 Martin Butlin, letter to the author, 19 January 1984.

26 See Gerald Finley, *Landscapes of Memory, Turner as illustrator of Scott*, London, 1980, pp. 163–170, in connection with the picture of *Bemerside Tower*, and a passage in which Finley also convincingly elaborates the meaning of *Watteau Study by Fresnoy's Rules*.

27 Roethlisberger No. 222 (*op. cit.*, 1961, text volume, pp. 485–8).

28 British Library, *Add. Ms.* 46151, BB, p. 27*v*. where Turner states 'The chace of Claude must be classed as purely Italian'. As *Ascanius Shooting the Stag of Silvia* seems more Italianate than *the Coast of Libya with Aeneas hunting*, it is likely that Turner was referring to that picture. This part of Turner's manuscript appears to date from 1827, which suggests he may have seen the work at the 1826 Christie's sale.

29 See Eric Shanes, *op. cit.*, 1979, No. 84, p. 48.

30 Marcia Briggs Wallace (*op. cit.*, 1979, p. 111) claims that the beam is emanating from the child *to* the star.

31 Wallace has established this beyond doubt (*ibid*).

32 See Finley, *op. cit.* 1980, p. 122.

33 The final eight designs for Scott's *Poetical Works* were all made before 2 August 1832 (see Finley, *op. cit.*, 1980, p. 153). It had probably taken about a week for the pictures to arrive in Edinburgh from London, and Turner had most probably sent them as soon as they were completed.

34 Finley, *op. cit.* 1980, pp. 163–4. Finley illustrates one such plaque on p. 166.

35 *ibid.*, p. 164.

36 Michael Rosenthal, *British Landscape Painting*, Oxford, 1982, p. 112.

37 Because Claude very obviously based the

landscape in this painting upon the copy of the above-mentioned *Landscape with the finding of Moses* he had made in the *Liber Veritatis* (*LV* 47), he obviously could not be bothered to make drawing 88 the same as its painting, as this would have meant having two virtually identical drawings in the book. Instead, he varied the design of *Liber Veritatis* drawing No. 88 by omitting the bridge that appears in the distance of the painting, and by making various other small changes.

38 F. E. Trimmer, the son of the Rev. Henry Scott Trimmer. His memories of Turner were recorded by Thornbury. The identification in question is related in Thornbury, *op. cit.*, 1862, Vol. I, p. 171.

39 Cyrus Redding, 'The late Joseph Mallord William Turner', *The Gentleman's Magazine*, February 1853, p. 155.

40 Turner did exhibit two other works with similarly completely generalised titles, these being *What You Will!* of 1822 (B.J. 229), a Watteauesque landscape containing allusions to Shakespeare's *Twelfth Night* (for which *What you Will* is the subtitle), and the other being *The New Moon; or, 'I've lost My Boat, You shan't have Your Hoop'* of 1840 (fig. 57). Only in the latter title is there a mention of any action, and then it is both individualised and appears as a subtitle. As a result, the losing of the boat and denial of the hoop do not enjoy quite the same degree of importance in that title as does the word 'Crossing' in the title of this picture. A minor watercolour Turner displayed in his own gallery in 1809 that was known as *Cottage Steps, Children feeding Chickens* (W. 490) was re-exhibited at the R.A. in 1811 as *May: Chickens*, which completely removes any mention of the action being performed. Although Turner did exhibit many other pictures with generalised titles, these are always connected with their religious, poetic or historical content, works such as *Shade and Darkness – The Evening of the Deluge* of 1843, *Thomson's Aeolian Harp* of 1809 or the *War* and *Peace* pictures of 1842, but only in one of all of these is a generalised *action* described. This is *The Angel standing in the Sun* of 1846, but even here the title is particularised through association with a lengthy quotation from the Book of Revelation with which Turner accompanied the painting in the

R.A. catalogue, as well as a shorter quotation from a poem by Samuel Rogers that was also appended. Furthermore, even where the artist did exhibit landscapes that do not specify a location – works like *Sunny Morning* (B.J. 251, R.A. 1799) or *Frosty Morning* (B.J. 127, R.A. 1813), and *November: Flounder-fishing* (B.J. 18, R.A. 1811) – the titles do specify either times or conditions of the day or year. Similarly, although there are many seascapes which are not located in a particular place, this is obviously because unless one gives actual long or latitudinal bearings, out at sea there is often no way of specifying such locations. Even lonely beaches could present problems of identification. In any case, most such titles describe nautical circumstances such as *Ships bearing up for anchorage* (B.J. 18, R.A. 1802) or *The Shipwreck* (B.J. 54, R.A. 1805) and marine behaviour such as fishermen at sea (B.J. 1) and coming ashore (B.J. 3), or becalmed (B.J. 8), or endeavouring to put their fish on board (B.J. 14), or cleaning or selling fish (B.J. 69), or bargaining for them (B.J. 372). In this category of title can also be included *Keelmen heaving in Coals by Night*, B.J. 360.

41 Judging from the inscription at the bottom of the print stating 'se vend a Strasbourg chez l'Auteur'. Loutherbourg left Strasbourg with his whole family in 1755 when he was fifteen years old, in order to study with Carle van Loo in Paris.

42 That Thomson sold his *Crossing the Brook* at the R.A. dinner is stated by Whitley, *op. cit.*, 1928, p. 58. Farington (*op. cit.* Vol. VI, p. 2024) recorded on 4 May 1803 (i.e. 4 days after the dinner) that 'Thomson has sold his picture 'Crossing the Brook' to Sir John Leicester for 80 guineas. He had several offers for it.' Farington also records that he himself had 'laid the cards on the plates' for the Academy dinner along with Lawrence and Turner, which surely attests to Turner's attendance at the dinner. Thomson's picture was engraved by William Say and the print was published in January 1804.

43 In 1807 Leicester exchanged *The Shipwreck* for another painting by Turner, *Fall of the Rhine at Schaffhausen* (B.J. 61) but as the width of both paintings is almost the same (241.5 cm. for the former picture, 233.7 cm. for the latter) the Rhine picture probably hung in the same place

as *The Shipwreck*. For a view of the interior of the Hill Street gallery showing the Turner and the Thomson paintings in close proximity, see Selby Whittingham, 'A Most Liberal Patron: Sir John Fleming Leicester, Bart., 1st Baron de Tabley, 1762–1827' in *Turner Studies*, Vol. 6 No. 2, Winter 1987, pp. 24–36.

44 Private Collection. The work was engraved by Giuseppe Marchi.

45 see Farington, *op. cit.*, Vol. XII, pp. 4343–6, 8 May 1813.

46 In his valuable essay 'Turner in the West Country' (in *Projecting the Landscape*, ed. J. C. Eade, Australian National University, 1987, pp. 36–53), Sam Smiles identifies this structure as a tunnel mouth, and therefore the mouth of the Tavistock Canal Tunnel which was under construction when Turner painted *Crossing the Brook*. However, he is forced to concede that 'The tunnel is in fact downstream and on the other bank' (of the river Tamar). Smiles interprets the picture as an elaboration of the economics of the locale but does not offer any interpretation of the figures, even in socio-economic terms. Whilst Turner may well have employed architectural features of the Tavistock Canal Tunnel in the structure on the right, due to the absence of water it does not *appear* to be a tunnel mouth, but rather a grotto. The placing of a niche above the opening strengthens this identification.

47 Jack Lindsay, *J. M. W. Turner*, London, 1966, p. 152. The birthdates of Turner's two daughters by Sarah Danby are not known, but the recognition of them in this picture (and of one of them in *Frosty Morning*) by Trimmer suggests their age at this time.

48 For Turner's connection with Stourhead see Gage, *art. cit.*, 1974, pp. 59–87. For Turner's knowledge of Pope's grotto, see Gage, *op. cit*, 1980, p. 51, letter 43.

49 This reflection is omitted in the engraving (R. 656) by Robert Brandard published in 1842. The engraving carries the inscription 'Come along (my dog Banee) hold up Sister's bonnet'.

50 Letter of 16 May 1845 to Dawson Turner, published in Gage, *op. cit.*, 1980, letter 283. In the previous letter published by Gage (a letter to John James Ruskin of 15 May 1845) Turner states that 'I have been so unwell that I was

obliged to go away from Town to revival by a little change of fresh air'.

51 For instance, see Thornbury, *op. cit.*, 1862, Vol. II, pp. 53, 55.

52 For example, Turner definitely knew Richard Payne Knight's *An Account of the Remains of the worship of Priapus . . . [and] . . . A Discourse on the worship of Priapus, and its connexion with the Mystic Theology of the Antients* (London, 1786), and he may also well have read Tom Taylor the Platonist's translation of Aristotle's *History of Animals*, published in 1809, which contains a chapter on the menses.

53 For Ruskin's destruction of Turner's sketchbooks see John Walker, *Joseph Mallord William Turner*, New York, 1976, p. 14 and figs. 3 and 4. For extant Turner erotica see Peter Webb, *The Erotic Arts*, 2nd Edition, London, 1983, pp. 158–161, 357 and 358, as well as fig. 114.

### CHAPTER SEVEN: THE PATHS OF MUTABILITY

1 See Reynolds, *Discourses*, ed. Wark, 1975. Discourses IX, p. 171, and III, p. 44 respectively.

2 Preface by John Dryden in C. A. du Fresnoy, *The Art of Painting*, London, 1695, p. XXXIII. This was available to Turner in Reynolds's *Works*, ed. Malone, 1809, Vol. 3, p. 255.

3 C. A. du Fresnoy, *The Art of Painting*, translated by William Mason, York, 1783, p. 258, lines 65–78. This translation was also available in Reynolds' *Works* because of Reynolds's annotations to du Fresnoy (see above).

4 Reynolds, *op. cit.*, 1975, pp. 44–5.

5 Du Fresnoy, *op. cit.*, 1783, p. 300, Note III, verse 51 (available to Turner on p. 97 of Reynolds's *Works*, 1809). The poetic quotation is of lines 19–20. Turner's copy of this edition is no longer present in his library but has probably been sold some time since 1939 (information kindly supplied to the author by a member of the Turner family).

6 Reynolds, *op. cit.*, 1975, pp. 69–70.

7 de Piles, *op. cit.*, 1743, p. 224.

8 British Library, *Add. Ms.* 46151, P, p. 2*v*. Quite clearly the choice of the words 'select,

combine and concentrate' at the beginning of this quotation draws upon the passage by du Fresnoy (as translated by Mason) that is quoted above, where the poet states that the artist 'Selects, combines, improves, diversifies' (see footnote 3 above).

9 British Library, *Add. Ms.* 46151, AA, p. 3. The passage from Reynolds is as follows:

> . . . it became necessary to distinguish the greater truth, as it may be called, from the lesser truth; the larger and more liberal idea of nature from the more narrow and confined; that which addresses itself to the imagination, from that which is solely addressed to the eye. (Reynolds, *op. cit.*, 1975, p. 268)

For a good working definition of exactly what Turner may easily have understood by the word 'truth', we need look no further than to the definition given by Mark Akenside at the beginning of Part One of his poem 'The Pleasures of the Imagination' which was well known to Turner:

> Truth is here taken, not in a logical, but in a mixed and popular sense, or for what has been called the truth of things; denoting as well their natural and regular condition, as a proper estimate or judgment concerning them.

10 British Library, *Add. Ms.* 46151, C, p. 6.

11 For an excellent demonstration of this see Finley, *op. cit.*, 1980, pp. 108–11.

12 Wilton, *op. cit.*, 1984, p. 66, entry for *Llanberis Lake*, No. 88.

13 Yet Turner could use such discrepancy for positive purposes; for an example, where the artist introduced a girl dressed in French costume into a British scene almost certainly to allude to contemporary upheavals in France, see Shanes, *op. cit.*, 1979, No. 53, pp. 38–9, entry for *Northampton, Northamptonshire*.

14 British Library, *Add. Ms.* 46151, P, p. 18*v*.

15 For the remark concerning learning more from Watteau see Ruskin, *Works*, Vol. XXXV, p. 601. For an exhaustive analysis of the influence of Watteau upon Turner see Selby Whittingham, 'What You Will . . .', *Turner Studies*, Vol. 5 No. 1, pp. 2–24 and Vol. 5 No. 2, pp. 28–48, London, 1985.

16 Algarotti, *op. cit.*, 1764, p. 82.

17 Quoted from Cicero's *Orator ad Brutum*, II. 7 ff., available to Turner in Dryden's preface to du Fresnoy in Reynolds' *Works*, 1809, Vol. 3, pp. 302–3.

18 British Library, *Add. Ms.* 46151, G, p. 4*v*. This manuscript dates from either 1815 or 1816.

19 Reynolds, *op. cit.*, 1975, p. 124, Discourse VII.

20 British Library, *Add. Ms.* 46151, K, interpolated leaf at end.

21 British Library, *Add. Ms.* 46151, N, p. 23.

22 See, in particular, book ten of *The Republic* which propounds Plato's theory of art. It is clear that Reynolds had read this work (see Discourse XIII) but there is no evidence that Turner ever did so.

23 Annotation by Turner on p. 58 of his copy of Opie's *Lectures on Art*, London, 1809 (Turner family collection). This passage begins with Turner's most striking (and oft-quoted) statement of his outlook regarding visual enquiry:

> He that has that ruling enthusiasm which accompanies abilities cannot look superficially. Every glance is a glance for study.

The second of these sentences is clearly Turner's refinement upon the statement of Reynolds made in the second Discourse that 'Every object that presents itself [to a promising young painter] is to him a lesson' (Reynolds, *op. cit.*, 1975, p. 36). For discussion of the context of Turner's annotations see Venning, *art. cit.*, 1982, pp. 38–9.

24 British Library, *Add. Ms.* 46151, T, p. 11.

25 British Library, *Add. Ms.* 46151, S, p. 14. This manuscript dates from 1818 but like the other revised drafts carries over material from the earlier manuscripts. Thus citations of the two lines of poetry at the end also appear in lecture manuscripts drafted in 1810–11. See note 30 below.

26 *Paul Cézanne, Letters*, ed., J. Rewald, London, 1941, pp. 233–4, letter of 15 April 1904. For discussion of Cézanne's meaning in this passage see Theodor Reff, 'Cézanne and Poussin', *Journal of the Warburg and Courtauld Institutes*, XXIII, 1960, pp. 150–174.

27 In 1802 Turner exhibited a watercolour entitled *The Fall of the Clyde, Lanarkshire: Noon. – Vide Akenside's Hymn to the Naiads* at the R.A. (w. 343, Walker Art Gallery, Liverpool). Akenside's 'Hymn to the Naiads' appears after 'The Pleasures of the Imagination' in Volume IX of Anderson's *Complete Poets* so it is probable that Turner read the latter poem at around the same time, if not earlier.

28 He discusses memory in lines 348–55 of 'The Pleasures of Imagination':

> By these mysterious ties, the busy power
> Of memory her ideal train preserves
> Entire; or when they would elude her watch,
> Reclaims their fleeting footsteps from the
>                                        waste
> Of dark oblivion; thus collecting all
> The various forms of being to present,
> Before the curious aim of mimic art,
> Their largest choice;

To the word 'ties' in the first line of this quotation Akenside appended the footnote:

> The act of remembering seems almost wholly to depend on the association of ideas.

Turner paraphrased lines one to three of the above verse-quotation and then immediately cited the fourth to seventh lines in his first perspective lecture in connection with the associative power of colour and its ability to convey sentiment in Poussin's *Deluge* (see British Library *Add. Ms.* 46151, N, p. 22). Turner's knowledge of Akenside's statement that memory makes a vital intellectual contribution to the apprehension of the Ideal suggests that perhaps this passage of poetry also importantly motivated the artist to rely extensively upon memory for the formation of his works.

29 Book I, line 574.

30 In British Library *Add. Mss.* 46151, C, p. 16 (twice quoted); K, leaf added at end (twice quoted); M, pp. 25*v* and 31; and S, p. 14. Manuscript C dates from 1810–11; K from 1810–11, with revisions added in 1824; M from 1810; and S from 1818.

31 Lines 131–142.

32 British Library, *Add. Ms.* 46161, S, pp. 9*v*–10.

33 British Library, *Add. Ms.* 46161, S, pp. 14–15.

34 The fact that Turner wrote 'the person here alluded to was Mr Thomas Malton Jnr. who *during* the progress of his work of London and Westminster *mentioned* the difficulty he met with' (my italics), tells us that Malton had communicated his observation to Turner at the time rather than later. Turner's surprise supports this interpretation, for he would surely have known such things by a not much later date (see below).

35 British Library, *Add. Ms.* 46151, M, p. 25*v*–26. This manuscript dates from 1810.

36 Malton's work consisted of a hundred aquatints published in two volumes. The *North West View of Westminster Abbey*, published on 31 January 1793, was plate 7 in Volume I. The original watercolour from which the design derived is in the Museum of London. For details of Malton's scheme see Bernard Adams, *London Illustrated 1604–1851*, London, 1983, pp. 170–5, No. 72. Andrew Wilton has commented that 'The low viewpoint and plunging perspective of many architectural views by both Turner and Girtin seem to derive from Malton' (*Turner 1775–1851*, London, Royal Academy, 1974–5, pp. 22–3).

37 *Hastings* sketchbook, T.B. CXI, pp. 3a, 4, 4a, 5. I am indebted to Barry Venning for drawing my attention to this passage and for making his transcription of it available to me.

38 For example, see Farington, *op. cit.*, Vol. VI, p. 2307, 26 April 1804 for criticism of the *Boats Carrying out Anchors*: 'Opie said the water in Turner's Sea piece looked like a *Turnpike Road* over the Sea. Northcote said He should have supposed Turner had never seen the Sea'.

39 Peter Cunningham (in John Burnet, *Turner and his works*, London, 1852, p. 75) quoting Admiral Bowles upon seeing the picture when displayed at the British Institution in 1849.

40 Farington, *op. cit.*, Vol. X, p. 3509, 7 July 1809: '[Thomas] Hearne called [Turner's] Corwen Bridge "Vapour". His woolly undecided execution was remarked upon. Hearne repeated that his pictures have neither sublimity or dignity in them'.

41 These lines were paraphrased from Joseph Addison's translation of 'The Story of Aglauros, transformed into a Statue' which Turner

obtained from volume VII of Anderson's *Complete Poets*, p. 205.

42 Ruskin, *Works*, Vol. III, p. 587.

43 Turner told J. B. Pyne that he wished he could do without trees, although this may have been because he disliked the colour green. See W. J. Stillman, *Autobiography of a Journalist*, London, 2 Vols, 1901, Vol. I, pp. 141–2.

44 Ruskin, *Works*, Vol. III, p. 596.

Ruskin, *Works*, Vol. XXII, p. 490. He then adds that Turner 'meant it, as Zoroaster meant it; and was a Sun-worshipper of the old breed'. Elsewhere, in his *Ariadne Florentina* (*Works*, Vol. XXII. pp. 489–90), Ruskin also tells us that for Turner Apollo was genuinely God.

46 A note in the Cook and Wedderburn edition of Ruskin's *Works*, Vol. XII, p. 133, states that Ruskin's 'father sought out Turner's old housekeeper, Mrs Danby, and from her doubtless learnt the particulars of his last hours, which passed into all the biographies of the painter'. Although Mrs Danby was probably not present in Chelsea when Turner actually died, nonetheless she may have received the story from Turner's companion, Sophia Booth. Ruskin may alternatively have misunderstood or faultily remembered the account of Turner's death given to him by William Bartlett, Turner's Chelsea physician, that

> On the morning of his decease it was very dull and gloomy, but just before 9 a.m. the sun burst forth and shone directly on him with that brilliancy he loved to gaze on and transfer the likeness to his paintings. He died without a groan. (letter to Ruskin of 7 August 1857, quoted in Finberg, *op. cit.*, 1961, p. 437).

Another possibility is that Ruskin remembered the illustration by John Burnet showing the rays of the setting sun falling directly upon the window of Turner's house in Chelsea. This appeared opposite the account of Turner's demise on p. 30 of Burnet's *Turner and his Works* (London, 1852) and perhaps it fixed the idea of Turner's death at sunset in his mind.

47 Ruskin, *Works*, Vol. XXII, p. 512.

48 Ruskin, *Works*, Vol. XXVIII, p. 595n., letter to Frederick Harrison.

49 Ruskin, *Works*, Vol. XXXVI, p. 292, letter to Elizabeth Barrett Browning.

50 Andrew Wilton, 'Turner at Brunnen', *Turner Studies*, Vol. I No. 2, 1982, pp. 63–4.

51 Turner's last four pictures exhibited at the Royal Academy in May 1850 might have been worked on for some years previously, but it seems unlikely that he painted much after that. His general physical feebleness was widely commented upon at the time.

52 'Summer', lines 90–9.

53 *Liberty*, Part II, lines 222–233.

54 Mallet also added in a footnote to 'The Reward' (Anderson, Vol. IX, p. 711) that 'Apollo is the god of prophecy as well as of poetry'. Perhaps here lay a common source for Turner's identification of 'Poet and Prophet'?

55 Abraham Cowley (1618–1667), 'Hymn to Light' (in Vol. V of Anderson, p. 236); Thomas Parnell (1679–1717), 'Hymn for Morning' (Anderson VII, p. 58) and 'Hymn for Noon' (pp. 58–9); Elijah Fenton (1683–1730), 'An Ode to the Sun for the New Year 1707' (Anderson VII, p. 651–4); and Thomas Yalden (1669–1736), 'Hymn to the Morning in praise of light' (Anderson VII, p. 751–2). Turner is sure to have read Volume VII of Anderson's *Complete Poets*, for it was from this source that he gained Addison's translation of Ovid's 'Story of Aglauros, transformed into a Statue' from which he developed the painting *Mercury and Herse* of 1811 (see above) as well as the subjects of a number of other works.

56 Lomazzo, *op. cit.*, 1598, Book IV, Chap. 3, p. 139.

57 Page 41 of the *Perspective* sketchbook, T.B. CVIII, Clore Gallery for the Turner Collection, London. After the end of the passage already quoted Turner then goes on to state:

> [Third Primary Light to artificial light] the fire in the Broiling of St Lawrence by Titian where the angles [i.e. angels] have The Second Lights

Lomazzo himself cites this picture (Titian and workshop, *The Martyrdom of St. Lawrence*, Escorial, Spain) where 'Titianus expressed divine light about the gridiron whereupon S. Lawrence was broyled' (*loc. cit.*, p. 145).

58 For example, see lines 277–80 of 'The Pleasures of Imagination' where the poet addresses the beauty of the Divine Mind as

> thou, better sun!
> For ever beamest on the enchanted heart
> Love, and harmonious wonder, and delight
> Poetic. Brightest progeny of Heaven!

or see this passage:

> thus doth Beauty dwell
> There most conspicuous, even in outward
>                                        shape,
> Where dawns the high expression of a mind;
> By steps conducting our enraptured search
> To that eternal origin, whose power,
> Through all the unbounded symmetry of things,
> Like rays effulging from the parent sun,
> This endless mixture of her charms diffused.
> Mind, mind alone, (bear witness earth and
>      heaven!)
> The living fountains in itself contains
> Of beauteous and sublime (lines 471–83).

Akenside employs the term 'the Divine Mind' in the introduction to Part I of his poem, as well as within the poem itself.

59 Although Thornbury (*op. cit.*, 1877, p. 224) tells us that during his visits to the Rev. H. S. Trimmer at Heston, Turner 'always behaved with great decorum, and regularly attended church'.

60 Ruskin, *Works*, Vol. VII, pp. 441–2.

61 British Library, *Add. Ms.* 46151, N, p. 10*v*. The note appears to date from 1827.

62 Gage, *op. cit.*, 1969, p. 117.

63 *ibid*, p. 113.

64 Reynolds, *Works*, 1809, Vol. II, p. 382.

65 Opie, *op. cit.*, 1809, p. 136.

66 See Gage, *op. cit.*, 1969, n. 210, p. 252.

67 George Field, *Chromatics, or An Essay on the Analogy and Harmony of Colours*, London, 1817, pp. 56–7.

68 Thornbury, *op. cit.*, 1877, p. 227.

69 British Library, *Add. Ms.* 46151, H, p. 35: 'Light is therefore color, and shadow the privation of it by the removal of these rays of colour, or subduction of power'.

70 W. L. Leitch, 'The Early History of Turner's Yorkshire Drawings', *The Athenæum*, London, 1894, p. 327.

71 Although the work appears today to the edges of its square canvas, there is evidence that originally it was framed within that format as a circular picture. See Butlin and Joll, *op. cit.*, 1984, p. 244, No. 395.

72 Quoted in Katherine Sim, *David Roberts*, London, 1984, p. 214. She does not give the location of the letter.

73 *The Diaries of John Ruskin*, ed. Evans and Whitehouse, 3 volumes, Oxford, 1956–9, Vol. I, p. 273, entry for 29 April 1844.

74 See 'M. L.', *art. cit.*, reprinted in *Turner Studies*, Vol. 4 No. 1, Summer, 1984, p. 22.

75 *The Greater Oxford Dictionary* gives the following meaning as one of its four definitions of the word 'emulous': '3a. Greedy of praise or power'.

76 British Library *Add. Ms.* 46151, H, p. 35.

77 Minos being the presumed founder of Tyre, the inclusion of the city would therefore allude to the eventual outcome of the union of Europa and the bull. By being represented as decaying into ruins it would thus allude in a roundabout fashion to the brevity of civilisations.

78 The Rev. Stopford Brooke, *Notes on the Liber Studiorum of J. M. W. Turner, R.A.*, London, 1885, pp. 2–3.

79 From which, on p. 205, he obtained the story of Mercury and Herse painted around the same time.

80 Anderson, *loc. cit.*, Vol. VIII, p. 206.

CHAPTER EIGHT:
TURNER'S HUMAN LANDSCAPE

The Carraci quotation at the head of this chapter is derived from Denis Mahon, *Studies in Seicento Art and Theory*, London, 1947, pp. 261–2.

1 Ruskin, *Works*, Vol. XIII, p. 155–6.

2 See Adrian Stokes, 'The Art of Turner' in *Painting and the Inner World*, London 1963, pp. 49–85.

3 William Sandby, *The History of the Royal Academy*, London, 2 Vols, 1862, Vol. I, p. 316.

4 These are still in the possession of the Royal Academy, although they are by no means complete and have evidently been mutilated by autograph-hunters. For a list of Turner's attendances in the 'Life Academy', see A. J. Finberg, *Inventory of the Turner Bequest*, 2 Vols, London, 1909, Vol. I, p. 24. Finberg later amplified this list in his biography of the artist.

5 For example, see Farington, *op. cit.*, Vol. I, p. 281, 26 December 1794; Vol. II, p. 461, 31 December 1795; and Vol. III, p. 703, 27 November 1796.

6 As pointed out by Adele Holcomb (exhibition review, 'Turner and the Sublime', *Turner Studies*, Vol. 3, No. I, Summer 1983, p. 52), Turner's dedication of the mezzotint of this work to the 1st Baron Carysfort upon its publication in 1828 may have reflected the fact that the original painting upon which it was based might have been commissioned by Lord Carysfort (see Wilton, *op. cit.*, 1980, p. 139) and the inclusion of the black man could allude to Lord Carysfort's political commitment to the abolition of slavery.

7 A note in *The British Press* for 8 May 1804 stated that Turner had begun the work and planned to exhibit it the following year at the Academy. As the 1805 Exhibition would not have opened until the first Monday that next May, this intended long period of work may well reflect the fact that Turner was resorting to models to achieve complete accuracy in the portrayal of his figures.

8 See Farington, *op. cit.*, Vol. VIII, p. 3164, 12 December 1807:

> . . . Wilkie yesterday . . . told [Constable] that when He has made a sketch for a picture and settled His design, He then walks about looking for a person proper to be a model for completing each character in His picture, and He paints *everything from the life*. He said He sometimes walks about for *a week* before He can meet with the character of head etc. that will suit Him.

9 *ibid.*, Vol. VI, p. 2023, 3 May 1803.

10 For example, this was recognised in connection with Turner's first exhibited oil-painting, the *Fishermen at Sea* of 1796 when the author of the *Companion to the R.A. Exhibition* wrote that . . . 'the figures, by not being more distinct and determined, suit the obscure perception of the objects, dimly seen through the gloom of night, partially illumined'. (see Butlin and Joll, *op. cit.*, 1984, No. 1, p. 1).

11 Stokes, *op. cit.*, 1963, p. 69.

12 Turner was also Visitor in the R.A. painting schools in 1816, 1822, 1823, 1825, 1826, 1830, 1831, 1835, 1836, 1838, 1842 and 1843.

13 Michael Kitson, 'Turner and Claude', *Turner Studies*, Vol. 2 No. 2, winter 1983, pp. 9–10.

14 These are by no means the only works showing the influence of Van Dyck; for others see B.J. Nos. 445, 446 and 448.

15 Patrick Conner, *Michael Angelo Rooker, 1746–1801*, London, 1984. pp. 62 and 61. Elsewhere (p. 110) Conner also discusses Rooker's depictions of Oxford for the annual *Almanack* views, which Rooker supplied for twenty years after 1769, and draws attention once more to the 'deflationary role of Rooker's figures' in such views, 'where an undergraduates' punting party, or a road mending crew, or an unruly dog worrying some other creature, provides a foil to the reverently delineated architecture'. Turner definitely knew Rooker's Oxford pictures, for in fact the very first items in the Turner Bequest (T.B. I–A, W. 5, and another copy not inventoried by A. J. Finberg, *op. cit.*, 1909, Vol. I, p. 1) are copies of Rooker's *North-West View of Friar Bacon's study*, the design for the 1789 *Almanack* which was engraved by J. Basire; see Conner, *op. cit.*, p. 63, where Rooker's design is reproduced. In several of Turner's own designs for the Oxford *Almanacks*, the first of which he made in 1798, he frequently introduces exactly the same kind of 'deflationary' staffage.

16 For example, compare Rooker's watercolour of the *Interior of the Abbot's Kitchen, Glastonbury* (London, Tate Gallery, reproduced as Fig. 42, p. 83, in Conner, *op. cit.*) which displays a staffage of 'placid cows and a labourer sleeping in the hay', along with stacked wood and washing, with Turner's *Trancept of Ewenny Priory* (R.A. 1797, National Museum of Wales, Cardiff, w. 227, reproduced in Wilton, *op. cit.* 1979, p. 46, plate 28) with its pigs and chickens, harrow, wheelbarrow and other farm implements. For further discussion of these two works, and their reproduction together, see Eric Shanes, *J. M. W.*

*Turner: The Foundations of Genius*, The Taft Museum, Cincinnati, Ohio, 1986, pp. 25–6.

17 See Conner, *op. cit.*, 1984, p. 115.

18 Macklin's 'Gallery of Poets' was situated in Fleet Street. The first exhibition to have been held there took place in 1788, although engravings commissioned by Macklin had appeared in the previous year. Reynolds's painting was No. 1 in the 1790 exhibition, having been commissioned by Macklin to be copied for engraving as the Frontispiece to the first volume of his new edition of the New Testament, as well as on a larger scale for separate issue. (See Macklin's catalogue of the exhibition.) The ostensible model for Turner's painting was Titian's *Holy Family and a Shepherd*, sold with the W. Y. Ottley collection in London in January 1801 and now in the National Gallery, London. Sketches for the work also demonstrate the influence of Titian's *St. Peter Martyr* (T.B. LXXXI–62 and 63).

19 John Knowles, *The Life and Writings of Henry Fuseli*, 3 Vols, London, 1830, Vol. I, p. 364.

20 Farington, *op. cit.*, Vol. IV, p. 1541, 25 April 1801.

21 Wilton, *op. cit.*, 1979, p. 65.

22 For example, in several studies in T.B. XVIII, a collection of large drawings on blue and brown paper which probably date from around 1792. They are all of male subjects and several of them – notably C, F, G, H and K – are very adequate indeed, with a fine grasp of anatomy and an expressive modelling technique. Other good life-drawings exist in the *Academical* sketchbook, T.B. XLIII, dating from around 1798.

23 As suggested by Andrew Wilton (letter to the author of 5 December 1983), Fuseli may well have set the pose for this drawing.

24 There is a particularly striking correspondence between Turner's waving figures, with Hero and Leander standing below them, and the figures and their relationship in Fuseli's painting exhibited at the R.A. in 1820 (and related drawing) of *Ariadne, Theseus, and the Minotaur in the Labyrinth* (see Gert Schiff, *Johann Heinrich Füssli*, Zurich and Munich, 2 Vols, 1973; the painting, No. 1488, reproduced as plate 480, Coll. Richard Beyfus, Basel; the drawing, No. 1529, reproduced as plate 508, Coll. Mr and Mrs Paul Mellon, Upperville, Virginia).

25 Turner might well have been familiar with the similar pose of Fuseli's figure of *Silence* engraved as the Frontispiece of his *Lectures* published in 1801 and in the second (Knowles) edition published again in 1830 itself.

26 Ada Earland, *John Opie and his Circle*, London, 1911, p. 39.

27 *The Life and Writings of Henry Fuseli*, ed. J. Knowles, London, 1831, Vol. II, p. 314.

28 See Farington, *op. cit.*, Vol. II, 6 March 1796.

29 Catalogue of the sale of Holworthy's sister-in-law, Miss Hannah Wright, at Brookfield Hall, Hathersage, Derbyshire, 3rd day, 18 March 1868. Holworthy had died in 1841. Turner included the name of 'Holworthy Junr' as one of the subscribers to the print of *The Shipwreck* on p. 2 of the *Shipwreck (No. 1)* sketchbook, T.B. LXXXVII of around 1805.

The influence of Teniers the Younger upon Watteau has also been exhaustively analysed (see D. R. Edman, *The influence of David Teniers the Younger on the Watteau Circle*, Ph.D., Oberlin College, 1963). As Edman points out, Watteau was in reality a Flemish artist, being born in 1684 in Valenciennes which was one of the Flemish cities ceded to France after the Treaty of Nijmegen of 1678. He also reminds us that the title page of the *receuil Jullienne* identifies Watteau as 'Peintre flamand de l'Academie royale'. Jean de Jullienne was himself responsible for making at least two engravings directly from works by Teniers the Younger.

30 The painting came up for sale between 29–31 May 1794 at Greenwood's Auction Rooms (No. 40) and was bought by the Earl of Ashburnham. Subsequently it hung at Ashburnham Place until 1850. See J. Smith, *A Catalogue Raisonné of the Works of the most eminent Dutch, Flemish and French Painters*, London, 1831, Vol. 3, pp. 351–2, No. 347; J. Smith, *Supplement to the Catalogue*, London, 1842, Vol. 9, p. 436, No. 94; and Horst Vey, *Neuerwerbungen für die Gemäldegalerie 1972–1984*, Staatliche Kunsthalle, Karlsruhe, 1984, No. 2700. For Turner's 1810 view of Ashburnham Place (w. 433, where incorrectly titled and dated) see Eric Shanes, *op. cit.*, 1981, p. 18, No. 3 and plate 3.

31 Now untraced. John Smith, in his *Supplement to the Catalogue Raisonné of the Works of the Most*

*Eminent Dutch, Flemish and French Painters*, London, 1842, Vol. 9, p. 441 lists a painting (No. 104) of *A Village Kermess* which was 'Painted in a clear and silvery tone of colouring' that was probably this work.

32  British Library, *Add. Ms.* 46151, P, p. 18*v*.

33  See Michael Clarke and Nicholas Penny, *The Arrogant Connoisseur: Richard Payne Knight, 1751–1824*, Manchester, 1982, pp. 197–8. The 'Teniers' has recently been re-attributed to Gerard Thomas (sale, Christie's, 4 May 1979, No. 99). The Thomas is reproduced by Clarke and Penny.

34  Knight was to attack the meretricious taste of the Prince Regent in the *Edinburgh Review* in 1814 and to support Princess Caroline of Wales publicly (see Farington, *op. cit.*, Vol. XIII, p. 5404, 3 May 1814, when Payne Knight conducted the Princess around a soirée at the British Institution, although she was snubbed by virtually every other person present). Knight also sided with Fox against the Tories in the 1790s and was attacked at the time for his 'Jacobinism' (see Clarke and Penny, *op. cit.*, 1982, pp. 10–11 and 13).

35  This figure was arrived at by a study of the names and addresses of the various printsellers and publishers indexed by M. Dorothy George in her *Catalogue of Political and Personal Satires*, Vols V–VIII, London, 1935–47.

36  And Gillray was to associate closely with de Loutherbourg in 1793–4 (travelling through Flanders with him in 1793), so the French artist may have passed on an awareness of the virtues of Gillray's work to Turner in addition.

37  The poem appears in a verse-book still owned by a member of the Turner family. It is reprinted in full under the title of 'The Origin of Vermillion or the Loves of Painting and Music' in Jack Lindsay, *The Sunset Ship*, London, 1966, p. 121. The verse-book also contains lines on the demolition of Pope's Villa, and Thomson's Aeolian Harp, which suggests a date of around 1808–9 for it.

38  See the entry for the picture by John Gage in *J. M. W. Turner*, Paris exhibition catalogue, 1983, No. 15, p. 74.

39  See Shanes, *op. cit.*, 1979, pp. 38–9 and plate

53.  Hogarth's picture also had a demonstrable influence upon Gillray's print, *Middlesex Election, 1804* (see George, *op. cit.*, Vol. VIII, 1947, No. 10264) to which the *Northampton* equally demonstrates an affinity, especially in the placing of the public house on the right-hand side in the background. Turner may well have known Gillray's print, especially as Brentford, the county-town of Middlesex where the 1804 election took place, was a town he had known since childhood.

40  Henry Fielding, *Joseph Andrews*, Dublin, 1742, Vol. I, p. IX.

41  See Rüdiger Joppien, *Philippe Jacques de Loutherbourg, RA*, exhibition catalogue, London, 1973, n.p., introduction to section entitled 'Caricature and Humour', and catalogue Nos. 22 and 23.

42  The prints in the later set are in many cases re-workings of pictures already published in the earlier set (see Joppien, *op. cit.*, 1973, n.p., catalogue Nos. 29–31, 1–6). Turner would almost certainly have studied these series in preparation for his own scheme, the *Picturesque Views in England and Wales* of 1825–1838.

43  Coll. Mrs Margaret E. Crosfield (see Joppien, *op. cit.*, 1973, No. 30). In addition, de Loutherbourg also made a preparatory watercolour for the engraving of the work aquatinted in colour by J. C. Stadler and issued as Plate I in Loutherbourg's 'Picturesque Scenery of Great Britain', published in 1801. The work is in a private collection.

44  Sale, Christie's, 26–28 June and 1–2 July 1833. Turner bought four lots on 27 June (Nos. 94, 96, 97, 99) and five other lots bought at the sale by his own agent, Thomas Griffith, also found their way into the artist's possession and are now in the Turner Bequest.

45  T.B. CX, p. 1a.

46  British Library, *Add. Ms.* 46151, K, p. 14. It has not proven possible to identify the exact source of Turner's quotation from Rousseau. Similar phrases concerning the smallness of man can be found in Rousseau's *The Social Contract*, his *Essay on the Origins of Inequality* and his long didactic work on education, *Emilius and Sophia*, but the philosopher's moral conclusions are always very different from Turner's. It seems likely that Turner was paraphrasing Rousseau for his own purposes.

# *Index*

Many of the picture titles have been abbreviated. Page numbers in italics indicate illustrations.